MW01165695

“All-Electric” Narratives

"All-Electric" Narratives

Time-Saving Appliances and Domesticity in American Literature, 1945–2020

Rachele Dini

BLOOMSBURY ACADEMIC
NEW YORK • LONDON • OXFORD • NEW DELHI • SYDNEY

BLOOMSBURY ACADEMIC
Bloomsbury Publishing Inc
1385 Broadway, New York, NY 10018, USA
50 Bedford Square, London, WC1B 3DP, UK
29 Earlsfort Terrace, Dublin 2, Ireland

BLOOMSBURY, BLOOMSBURY ACADEMIC and the Diana logo are trademarks of Bloomsbury Publishing Plc

First published in the United States of America 2022

Cover design: Eleanor Rose
Cover image © Patty Carroll, "Cooking the Goose,"
from *Anonymous Women: Domestic Demise* (2016–2019)

Library of Congress Cataloging-in-Publication Data
Names: Dini, Rachele, author.
Title: "All-electric" narratives: time-saving appliances and domesticity in American literature, 1945-2020 / Rachele Dini.
Description: New York: Bloomsbury Academic, 2021. | Includes bibliographical references and index. | Identifiers: LCCN 2021016126 (print) | LCCN 2021016127 (ebook) | ISBN 9781501367359 (hardback) | ISBN 9781501367366 (epub) | ISBN 9781501367373 (pdf) | ISBN 9781501367380
Subjects: LCSH: Household appliances, Electric, in literature. | American literature–20th century–History and criticism. | American literature–21st century–History and criticism. | LCGFT: Literary criticism.
Classification: LCC PS228.H68 D56 2021 (print) | LCC PS228.H68 (ebook) | DDC 810.9/3564–dc23
LC record available at https://lccn.loc.gov/2021016126
LC ebook record available at https://lccn.loc.gov/2021016127

ISBN: HB: 978-1-5013-6735-9
ePDF: 978-1-5013-6737-3
eBook: 978-1-5013-6736-6

Typeset by Deanta Global Publishing Services, Chennai, India

To Ben(iamino), who makes every moment electric.

And to all the women everywhere, in hopes of a future
in which the whole world might feel like our home,
and our voices in all their variegations
—melodious murmurs! vociferous bellows! thrumming! pulsating! —
might be heard.
For we contain multitudes. And we cannot be contained.

CONTENTS

FIGURES

ACKNOWLEDGMENTS

This book would not have been possible without the help, encouragement, advice, and support of a great many people. I owe a debt of gratitude to Mark Ford, Una Mcllvenna, Laura Peters, Jane Kingsley-Smith, Shelley Trower, Nicola Humble, and Haaris Naqvi for seeing potential in this project from the outset; to Sheila Liming for offering feedback on more drafts of the manuscript than I can count; and to Rachel Moore for your eagle eyes and knowing the answer to my every editorial question. To Mark Turner: please accept, eleven years late, the MA essay on ice trays in Don DeLillo we discussed in March 2010. To Dora Tsimpouki, Susan Signe Morrison, Peter Boxall, and Maurizia Boscagli: thank you for your enthusiastic encouragement of my work, and to Chisomo Kalinga, a very special thank-you for your incisive, and generous, advice on writing on approaches to Black US literature. Thank you to Nicole King for introducing me to Paule Marshall, to Will Viney for enlivening me to Charlotte Perkins Gilman's writings on housework, and to Vicky Howard for your insights into the history of consumer debt. Thank you to Katie Stone for your advice on sci-fi criticism, and Rebecca Altman, Jane Carroll, Michael Collins, Daniel Fountain, Sorcha O'Brien, Stephen Shapiro, Susan Strasser, and Peter Ward for engaging with so *many* of my random questions on Twitter. Thank you as well to Rosie Cox for so many stimulating conversations about housework, mid-century design, and the overlap between geography and literary studies!

Thanks are due to Kathy Mezei, Chiara Briganti, Alice Bennett, Benjamin George, Giorgio Mariani, Tom Knowles, Stephen Shapiro, Alberto Fernandez-Carbajal, and Tim Atkins for generously reading my drafts; to Tim Atkins and Peter Jaeger for introducing me to *Zabriskie Point*; to Benjamin George, Arianna Dini, Karina Jakubowicz, Ian Kinane, David Fallon, Theo Savvas, and Nicola Chelotti for listening to me talk, *ad nauseum*, about all things appliance-related; to James George for discovering Patty Carroll's "Cooking the Goose"; to Benjamin George, Alison Waller, Dustin Frazier-Wood, and Ian Kinane for supporting me in my moments of self-doubt; and to Elizabeth Parker and Michelle Poland for encouraging my interest in the Gothic aspects of domestic mechanization. To Chiara Briganti, thank you, in order of importance, for shielding me as a baby from the loose wiring nella casa dei nonni, augmenting the lure of the microwave by refusing to buy one until 1992, and regaling me with stories about nonni's cucina americana and your adventures as a translator at General Electric Milan. To Paolo Dini, thank you in advance for reading beyond the first page (now this is in writing, you *have* to do it!). Thank you to Kim Gilchrist, Lucy Wishart, Angela S. Allan, and Alastair Hudson for your knowledge of appliances in music videos, album covers, and songs, which now populate my dreams and nightmares in equal measure. Thank you to Michael Collins for encouraging my obsession with postmillennial nostalgia—here's to *Feeling the Fifties,* which we absolutely will write.

I am also extremely grateful to the *many* antiquarians and sellers of vintage paraphernalia who helped me hunt down rare copies of appliance manuals and, in some cases, provided digital scans of articles or ads free of charge. Your help and enthusiasm were invaluable. Thank you especially to Jeff at Singularity Rare and Fine (Baldwinsville, NYC); Robert Mainardi and Trent Dunphy at The Magazine (San Francisco), Chentelle Nelson at stonelightcreations, and Eleanor Christine Mott at Lost in Time Vintage Ads, for supplying me with hundreds of little-known ads and pamphlets; Kellie Paulin at Between the Covers-Rare Books, Inc. (New Jersey), for securing one of the only remaining copies of *What Women Want in Their Kitchens of Tomorrow* (1944); Sophie at Pineapple Retro (UK), Irma Lee at Our Little Shoppe, John Boyd at curiositiques (https://www.ebay.com/str/curiositiques), and S. Davis-Barker at Bizingaar (https://www.ebay.co.uk/str/bizingaar), thanks to whom I obtained an original Sunbeam Model V14 (1962), Model 11 (1955–6), and Model 12 (1957–67) in turquoise and Model 12 in yellow, respectively; Glyn Fearby, provider of a hundred-odd *LIFE* magazines; the team at the Westinghouse Archives; and Robert Seger at Automatic Ephemera, whose cataloguing of hundreds—thousands?—of appliance manuals made my work much, much easier. I am indebted as well to Michigan State University for digitizing and making public the Alan and Shirley Brocker Silker Culinary Collection, thanks to which I was able to access hundreds of appliance cookbooks despite the Covid-19 lockdown, and to the creators of the Gallery of Graphic Design Online, whose digital archive of print ads spanning the twentieth century provided an invaluable resource at a time when traveling to the United States wasn't feasible. Thank you to Bill Stoltz and Linda Daniels at Wright State University, Lee Nisbet at Nasher Museum of Art, Eric Gignac at the Heinlein Trust, Michelle Nanney at Westinghouse, Nicole Burrell and Laurie Feigenbaum at *Popular Mechanics*, and (fellow Vonnegut fan!) Cean M Burgeson at Whirlpool for facilitating image permission requests, and to Larry and Suzanne Viner at the Advertising Archives for providing high-resolution images of hard-to-find ads. A *massive* thank-you to Cymene Howe, Joseph Campana, and Dominic Boyer for inviting me to take part in Rice University's Waste Histories & Futures seminar series, the honorarium of which funded my acquisitions of these materials. And an *extra* special thanks to Tony Hainault, aka Zia

Antonietta, for bringing me piles of appliance manuals from the United States: may you never, ever, ever, have to taste an actual dessert made by me and any of my Sunbeams.

Finally, and above all, thank you to Ben for reading so many, *many* drafts; for accompanying me on my hunts for old magazines and appliances; for letting me fill our cabinets with 1950s junk; for making me space-age-themed anniversary cards (LOMOUREX! Put a Rocketship Under YOUR Relationship!); for reassuring me I'm *not* like the woman in Laura Wade's *Home, I'm Darling* and yes, this *is* just for research . . . and for making wherever we are feel like home.

Introduction

Time-Saving Appliances and the American Century: A Case for the Significance of a Literary Trope

In January 2020, at a campaign rally in Milwaukee, Wisconsin, the forty-fifth US president, Donald Trump, reprised a promise made to his supporters throughout 2019:

> I'm approving new dishwashers that give you more water so you can Actually. Wash. And Rinse. Your dishes! Without having to do it TEN TIMES. Four. Five. Six. Seven. Eight. Nine. Ten. Anybody have a new dishwasher? I'm sorry for that. . . . It's worthless. . . . Remember the dishwasher? You'd press it, boom! There'd be like an explosion. Five minutes later you open it up, the steam pours out, the dishes—Now you press it 12 times. Women tell me—again. You get four drops of water. . . . And electric! Don't forget! The whole thing is worse! Because you're spending all that money on electric. So we're bringing back standards that are great.[1]

Trump's incoherent diatribe was a response to "Make Dishwashers Great Again," a petition launched in 2018 by the Competitive Enterprise Institute and FreedomWorks (an offshoot of the Koch Brothers' free-market-oriented think tank, State Policy Network) to roll back environmental regulations introduced by Jimmy Carter's administration in 1978.[2] But while the press focused on the nonsensical nature of claims that the appliance industry itself

---

[1] Andy Gregory, "President Vows to Make Appliances Great Again," *The Independent* (January 15, 2020).

[2] Energy Conservation Program: Energy Conservation Standards for Dishwashers, Notification of Petition for Rulemaking, 83 Fed. Reg. 17768 (proposed 21 March 2018); James Freeman, "The Dishwasher Rebellion," *Wall Street Journal* (June 27, 2018); Hiroko Tabuchi, "Inside Conservative Groups' Efforts to 'Make Dishwashers Great Again,'" *New York Times* (September 17, 2019).

refuted, and on the bizarreness of the description of the dishwasher that goes "boom," they overlooked the significance of the appliance itself as a focal point for nostalgia. This invocation of the once-functioning Great American Dishwasher echoed a rhetoric long used by manufacturers, advertisers, and government policy makers to promote domestic electrification and time-saving as embodying the quintessentially American ideals of life, liberty, and the pursuit of happiness. The reference to women desirous of more efficient domestic machines followed an equally long-standing tendency to frame domestic automation as liberating white middle-class women from both housework and unreliable Black servants. Trump's appeal to "remember the dishwasher" in this fascistic promise of a return to a previous imperial splendor was thus premised on the racialized, gendered, and classist narratives long used to promote the "all-electric" home and its gadgets. In this abstract past, men are men, and women know their place: at home, with the General Electric (GE) P-7 Automatic Self-Cleaning oven, Frigidaire Frost-Proof Refrigerator-Freezer, Sunbeam Mixmaster, Hamilton Beach DrinkMaster, Waring "Blendor", In-Sink-Erator garbage disposal unit, Westinghouse dishwasher, Electrolux vacuum cleaner, and so on. The statement "Make Dishwashers Great Again" is synecdochic for a return to prescribed gender roles, whiteness, and a mythical past that never existed outside of mid-century appliance advertisements, mid-century sitcoms, and retrospective treatments of the 1950s. That this rhetoric both resonated with Trump's base and was seized upon by journalists critical of his administration reveals the extent to which time-saving domestic appliances remain contested sites for the negotiation of competing ideas about citizenship, gender, labor, consumption, financial value, and moral rectitude.[3] Indeed, Trump's own political career owes a great deal to the "all-electric" home's mythos. The first celebrity president and the figure to which he is most frequently compared, Ronald Reagan, became an ardent supporter of big business while employed between 1954 and 1962 as GE brand ambassador, which involved extolling the benefits of electric power

[3] For examples of positive coverage of the "Make Dishwashers Great Again" campaign, see: Andrew Magloughin, "Secretary Perry Can Make Dishwashers Great Again," Freedomworks.org (April 4, 2018); Rebecca Garcia, "EPCA Reform to Make Dishwashers Great Again," *Loyola Consumer Law Review* 31.1 (January 14, 2019): 114–27; Tyler O'Neil, "Your Dishwasher Takes Too Long and It's the Government's Fault. Here's the Solution," *PJ Media* (July 3, 2019); Editorial Board, "Make Dishwashers That Clean Again: The Energy Department Wants to Give Consumers an Appliance Choice," *Wall Street Journal* (October 13, 2019); Tom Welsh, "The 'Make Dishwashers Great Again' Movement Isn't as Crazy as It Sounds," *Daily Telegraph* (February 2, 2020); For critical press coverage, see: Shawn Langlois, "How Come Trump Knows so Much about Dishwashers? 'Women Tell Me,' He Says," *Marketwatch* (December 19, 2019); Tamara Keith, "Trump vs. Toilets (and Showers, Dishwashers, and Lightbulbs)," *NPR* (December 27, 2019); Kenya Evelyn, "Trump Rails Against Refrigerators and Promises Cleaner Dishes," *The Guardian* (January 15, 2020); Dino Grandoni and Paulina Firozi, "The Energy 202: Trump Wants to Make Dishwashers Great Again. The Energy Department Has a New Rule for That," *The Washington Post* (January 17, 2020).

and free enterprise to industry leaders around the country, living in a GE "all-electric" home, and hosting the CBS show *General Electric Theater*.[4] To "remember the dishwasher" is thus to remember the prominence of time-saving appliances in American politics in the postwar era—from Reagan's promise to mid-century television viewers that "'From electricity comes progress in our daily living . . . in our daily work [and] in the defense of our nation; and at General Electric, progress is our most important product,'" to Richard Nixon's boast to Nikita Khruschev, during the "Kitchen Debate" at the American Exhibition in Moscow in 1959, that the "all-electric" kitchens provided under US capitalism "'ma[de] easier the life of our housewives'" better than socialism could ever hope.[5] It is also to be reminded of the extent to which the images of white women used to sell these objects invoked a nonexistent past to obscure the fact that the constructions of gender they promoted were unique to the postwar era. Finally, it is to be confronted with the racist principles on which the ideals of "all-electric" living were premised—namely, the historical reification of Black Americans as ancillary to the needs and requirements of white Americans.

This book examines the literary response to the politics of time-saving appliances and domestic electrification more broadly. It analyzes the depiction of electric refrigerators, vacuum cleaners, oven ranges, washing machines, dryers, dishwashers, toasters, blenders, standing and handheld mixers, garbage disposal units, grills, and microwave ovens across a range of literary genres and forms published between 1945, when the "all-electric" home came to be associated with the "good life," and the end of the 2010s, as contemporary writers consider the enduring material and spiritual effects of these objects into the twenty-first century. By examining the "all-electric" home in postwar US literature alongside its representation in print and television ads, I demonstrate how domestic electrification and the very concept of electricity as a resource fueled literary narratives in this period, providing both a new means to express notions of futurity, progress, and hope and to highlight the limits of technology and its potential, in fact, to exploit, oppress, and perpetuate nationalistic and imperialistic ideals. In attending to the myriad meanings of time-saving appliances in the work of writers as disparate as Jack Kerouac, Allen Ginsberg, Richard Brautigan, Bob Rosenthal, John Cheever, Richard Yates, Marge Piercy, James Baldwin,

---

[4] General Electric Theater was the third most popular show on US television by 1956, reaching 25 million viewers per week; Lou Cannon claimed that "More than anything, it is his GE experience that changed Reagan from an adversary of big business into one of its most ardent spokesmen" (qtd. in Garry Wills, *Reagan's America: Innocents at Home* (New York: Penguin, 1985), 315).

[5] Qtd. in William L. Bird, *"Better Living": Advertising, Media, and the New Vocabulary of Business Leadership, 1935–1955* (Evanston: Northwestern UP, 1999), 204; Sarah T. Phillips and Shane Hamilton, *The Kitchen Debate and Cold War Consumer Politics* (Boston, MA and New York: Bedford/St Martin's, 2014). See also Joy Parr, "Modern Kitchen, Good Home, Strong Nation," *Technology and Culture* 43.4 (October 2002): 657–67.

Ralph Ellison, Paule Marshall, Alice Childress, Toni Morrison, Alice Walker, Judith Merril, Ray Bradbury, Margaret St. Clair, Eleanor Arnason, Kit Reed, Philip K. Dick, Robert A. Heinlein, Ira Levin, Joanna Russ, Kurt Vonnegut, Don DeLillo, David Wojnarowicz, Joan Didion, A. M. Homes, Charles Johnson, Catherynne M. Valente, Lucy Ellmann, and Mattilda Bernstein Sycamore, I show how postwar and contemporary writers engaged with the cultural meanings of the "all-electric" home and its power to reinforce a particular vision of American identity both at home and abroad.

While scholars have acknowledged the significance of electricity in the work of a few specific writers and in literature published between the 1880s and 1950, the significance of *domestic* electrification in literature, and in the post-1945 literary landscape, remains unrecognized.[6] Domestic time-saving appliances provide a particularly fascinating subject due to their role in the social construction of home and family, and their imbrication with shifting understandings of hygiene, nutrition, work, temporality, scientific knowledge, and electricity itself. My chosen texts enlist these objects, and the rhetoric and imagery used by advertisers to promote them, to raise questions about gender norms and sexuality, racial exclusion, class inequality, labor exploitation, state and corporate power, the ramifications of mechanization and the potential replacement of humans by robots, the perils and possibilities of conformity, the limitations of patriotism, and the inevitable fallacy of utopian thinking, while often radically disrupting the literary forms in which they operated. Attention to the electrical gadgets in these texts allows for the texts themselves to be read in fundamentally different ways to how they have been conventionally read and reveals unexpected connections between authors with often very different politico-aesthetic agendas. In particular, such analysis reveals how the idea of currents, energies, and connectivity between individuals, communities, and nations influenced different literary forms, and was refashioned by writers intent on formulating alternative visions to the status quo.

The next section outlines my methodological approach and some of the central questions I seek to answer. Following this, I provide an overview, in five sections, of time-saving appliances' entanglement with the broader political, cultural, and social currents of the period 1840 to 1975, which I relate to notable appliance depictions from these same periods. The

---

[6] The exceptions to this are David Alworth's incisive chapter on the electric grid in Ralph Ellison's *Invisible Man* in *Site Reading* (Princeton, NJ: Princeton UP, 2015), 121–48; Marsha Bryant's excellent essays, "Plath, Domesticity, and the Art of Advertising," *College Literature* 29.3 (Summer 2002): 17–34 and "Ariel's Kitchen: Plath, *Ladies' Home Journal*, and the Domestic Surreal," in *The Unravelling Archive*, ed. Anita Plath Helle (Ann Arbor: U of Michigan Press, 2007), 206–35; Ginger Strand's *The Brothers Vonnegut* (Farrar, Strauss, Giroux, 2016); and Jennifer Liebermann's fascinating account of electricity in Mark Twain, Jack London, Charlotte Perkins Gilman, Ralph Ellison, and Lewis Mumford in *Power Lines: Electricity in American Life and Letters, 1882-1952* (Boston, MA: MIT Press, 2017).

summaries of my individual chapters are embedded within the last three sections of this introduction.

1. Why and How?

This project emerged from the research for my first book, *Consumerism, Waste, and Re-use in Twentieth-century Fiction: Legacies of the Avant-Garde* (Palgrave Macmillan, 2016). My investigations into Anglo-European and US experimental fiction's engagement with the temporal meanings ascribed to waste under capitalism led me to think about the representation of the relationship between filth and the machines developed over the last century for its more efficient removal, and the framing of these machines in both futuristic and nostalgic terms. *"All-Electric" Narratives* thus attends to how US writers have engaged with objects that bespeak the "new" (while paradoxically enabling the entrenchment of "old" ways), and that promise not only to accompany their owners in time, but to entirely transform the way that time is experienced. It is because of this abiding concern with appliances' capacity to "save" time, alter how time is spent, and conjure images of both an unknowable future and an irretrievable past that I refer to "*time*-saving appliances" rather than "*labor*-saving appliances." While both of these terms have been used throughout the history of domestic electrification, I argue that my chosen texts are more invested in unearthing the paradoxes inherent to appliance advertisers' claims of temporal transformation—their claims, that is, of appliances' capacity to "give back" time to their user, transport them into a technologically progressive future, or "return" them to some pastoral past.

To analyze these ideas, I bring together strands from literary object studies, design history, and the history of advertising, consumer culture and television, as well as domestic space studies and, to a lesser extent, energy studies. My approach is indebted in the first instance to scholars such as Douglas Mao, Bill Brown, Elaine Freedgood, Jane Bennett, Will Viney, Maurizia Boscagli, Steve Connor, and others who in the last twenty years or so have extended Marxist theoretical approaches to objects to acknowledge their entanglement with issues of consumption and disposal as much as production. Approaches such as "thing theory," which understands objects to be entangled in relations with people and places in ways that often defy their manufacturers' (or consumers') intentions and free them from their status as commodities, and queer phenomenology, which seeks to extricate objects from their roles within hetero-capitalism, enable us to understand the appliances in US literature as more than congelations of human labor.[7]

[7] Douglas Mao, *Solid Objects* (Princeton, NJ: Princeton UP, 1998); Bill Brown, *A Sense of Things* (U of Chicago Press, 2004); Elaine Freedgood, *The Ideas in Things: Fugitive Meaning*

Actor-Network Theory and New Materialism in turn allow us to unpack the meanings of time-saving appliances that have run amuck, producing effects greater than their manufacturers or owners could ever have envisaged.[8] In examining representations based on real-life products—and in some cases specific product *models*—I draw on the work of both design historians such as Ellen Lupton, Shelley Nickles, and Carroll Ganz, and feminist social historians such as Ruth Schwartz Cowan, Rachel P. Maines, Joy Parr, and Sarah Pink, who have demonstrated product design, manufacturing, and dissemination's imbrication in wider political discourses.[9]

Appliances are distinct from other objects, however, in their enmeshment with each other as dependents on a common energy source. The subject of electrification's cultural impact both materially and as a symbol of progress, social connectivity, and imperial strength has attracted renewed interest in the last decade. This is ascribable to both the approaching centenary of mass domestic electrification and the growing urgency of the climate emergency, which has rendered more exigent the search for more sustainable energy sources while making the last century's cultural understandings of resource extraction appear frankly quaint. David E. Nye's numerous social and corporate histories of electricity, Tim Raphael's *The President Electric: Ronald Reagan and the Politics of Performance* (2009), Paul Gilmore's *Aesthetic Materialism: Electricity and American Romanticism* (2009), Jennifer Lieberman's *Power Lines: Electricity in American Life and Letters, 1882–1952* (2017), Daniel L. Wuebben's *Power-Lined: Electricity, Landscape, and the American Mind* (2019), not to mention the various biographies of Thomas Edison, George Westinghouse, and Nikola Tesla published since 2000, demonstrate how electricity has functioned, throughout its history, as a site for competing political ideologies.[10] Meanwhile the work of feminist

---

in the Victorian Novel (U of Chicago Press, 2006); Jane Bennett, *Vibrant Matter* (Durham, NC: Duke UP, 2010); Will Viney, *Waste: A Philosophy of Things* (London: Bloomsbury, 2013); Maurizia Boscagli, *Stuff Theory* (London: Bloomsbury, 2014).

[8] Bennett, *Vibrant Matter*, vii–viii and 4–6; Boscagli, *Stuff Theory*, 3; Bruno Latour, *We Have Never Been Modern*, transl. Catherine Porter (Cambridge, MA: Harvard UP, 1993), 55.

[9] Ellen Lupton, *Mechanical Brides: Women and Machines from Home to Office* (Princeton, NJ: Princeton Architectural Press, 1993); Shelley Nickles, *Object Lessons: Household Appliance Design and the American Middle Class, 1920–1960* (PhD thesis, U of Virginia, 1999); Carroll Gantz, *The Vacuum Cleaner* (Jefferson, NC: McFarland, 2012) and *Refrigeration* (ibid., 2015); Ruth Schwartz Cowan, *More Work for Mother: The Ironies of Household Technology from the Open Hearth to the Microwave* (New York: Basic Books, 1983); and *A Social History of American Technology* (New York: Oxford UP, 1997); Joy Parr, *Domestic Goods: The Material, the Moral, and the Economic in the Post-war Years* (Toronto: U of Toronto Press, 1999); Sarah Pink, *Home Truths: Gender, Domestic Objects and Everyday Life* (Oxford: Berg, 2004).

[10] Tim Raphael, *The President Electric* (Ann Arbor, MI: U of Michigan Press, 2009); Paul Gilmore, *Aesthetic Materialism: Electricity and American Romanticism* (Stanford, CA: Stanford UP, 2009); Daniel L. Wuebben, *Power-Lined: Electricity, Landscape, and the American Mind* (Lincoln, NE: U of Nebraska Press, 2019). The most noteworthy of Nye's

historians such as Judith A. McGaw, Arwen Mohun, and Ruth Oldenziel has thrown into relief the imbrication of politicians' and manufacturers' conceptualization of electricity with a patriarchal capitalist imperialism premised on the framing of white women as housewives, the erasure of Black women, and the obscuration of class inequality.[11] Like these scholars, I am interested in the broader political and affective meanings of electricity—but I am *more* interested in how the latter intersect with the literary response to the last century's shifting understandings of home, gender, race, and class. How, I ask, do US writers after the Second World War repurpose politicians' and manufacturers' invocations of magic, scientificity, techno-utopian efficiency, and connectivity to imagine other forms of social organization and connection? How do they engage, toward the twentieth century's close, with the *iconicity* attributed to these objects—their perceived exemplification, that is, of a particular version of both national identity and the past? In what ways might domestic electrification still be mobilized to radical (aesthetic and political) aims? How have these possibilities been occluded by the more or less misogynistic and reactionary catastrophizing of a minority of heterosexual white male writers? And how have writers engaged with time-saving appliances' dual nature both as individual objects and as entities linked to other entities, and whose function is entirely dependent on the functionality of the power grid to which they are connected? Indeed, one of the supreme ironies of the time-saving appliance in American culture is its incorporation into both collectivist narratives premised on an image of the social body as a grid powered by the collective energies of its citizens and, equally, individualist narratives premised on the object's power to reflect back the values of its owner.

"All-Electric" Narratives also extends beyond the above-mentioned studies of literary objects and cultural studies of energy extraction in its focus on the relationship between real-life appliances and their mediated

books for our purposes are his "anti-biography" of Thomas Edison (Odense UP, 1983); *Image Worlds: Corporate Identities at General Electric, 1890–1930* (Cambridge, MA: MIT Press, 1985); *Electrifying America: Social Meanings of a New Technology* (Cambridge, MA: MIT Press, 1990); *Consuming Power: A Social History of American Energies* (Cambridge, MA: MIT Press, 1997); *When the Lights Went Out: A History of Blackouts in America* (Cambridge, MA: MIT Press, 2010); and *American Illuminations: Urban Lighting, 1800–1920* (Cambridge, MA: MIT Press, 2018).

[11] See Judith A. McGaw, "No Passive Victims, No Separate Spheres: A Feminist Perspective on Technology's History," in *In Context: History and the History of Technology: Essays in Honor of Melvin Kranzberg*, ed. Stephen H. Cutcliffe and Robert C. Post (Bethlehem PA: Lehigh UP, 1989), 172–91; Ruth Oldenziel, "Man the Maker, Woman the Consumer: The Consumption Junction Revisited," in *Feminism in Twentieth-Century Science, Technology, and Medicine*, ed. Angela N. H. Creager et al. (Chicago: Chicago UP, 2001), 128–48; Ruth Oldenziel, *Cold War Kitchen* (Boston: MIT Press, 2009); Arwen Mohun, *Steam Laundries: Gender, Work, and Technology in the United States and Great Britain, 1880–1940* (Baltimore: Johns Hopkins UP, 1999); Arwen Mohun and Roger Horowitz, ed., *His and Hers: Gender, Consumption and Technology* (Charlottesville: U of Virginia Press, 1998).

representations in literature, print and television advertising, magazine articles, and television sitcoms. To speak of the time-saving appliance in post-1945 US literature, I argue, is to speak of Edison, Electrolux, Frigidaire, GE, Westinghouse, Hoover, Hotpoint, In-Sink-Erator, International Harvester, Kelvinator, Norge, Whirlpool, Maytag, Speed Queen, Bendix, Sears Coldspot, Servel, Philco, KitchenAid, Hamilton Beach, Waring, Western Electric, and Sunbeam—not to mention the abstract notions of "modernity," "efficiency," "magic," "emancipation," "futurity," and "tradition" that over the course of the last century rendered them household names. To prove this argument, I examine my chosen texts alongside a wide range of print and television ads, magazine stories, and market research spanning the period 1930 to 1975, and I draw on those (primarily female) scholars who in the 1970s and 1980s established domestic labor as a valid field of academic enquiry, and those who since the 1990s have established the validity of studying consumerism, food cultures, and television, and recovered the history of Black Americans' role in the advertising industry, the history of consumer rights, and domestic work. Quite simply, this project would not exist were it not for Ann Oakley and Susan Strasser's groundbreaking anthropological and historical studies of housework, Elaine Tyler May's history of the Cold War home, Lynn Spigel and Anna McCarthy's histories of mid-century television, Sherrie A. Inness's and Laura Shapiro's histories of meal preparation, Grace Hale's history of segregation in the South, or Robert E. Weems' history of Black American purchasing power.[12] Nor would it exist without Amy Kaplan's equally groundbreaking analysis of the contemporaneous development of domestic discourse in the United States with the discourse of Manifest Destiny, wherein the domestic came to "not only lin[k] the familial household to the nation" but to imagine "the nation as a domestic space . . . in contrast to an external world perceived as alien and threatening."[13] I also draw on Ronald C. Tobey's revisionist history of domestic electrification, which counters the established account that "[e]lectrical modernization occurred

[12] Ann Oakley, *Housewife* (New York and Harmondsworth: Penguin, 1985 [1974]); Susan Strasser, *Never Done: A History of American Housework* (New York: Henry Holt, 2000 [1982]); Laura Shapiro, *Something from the Oven: Reinventing Dinner in 1950s America* (London: Penguin, 2004); Elaine Tyler May, *Homeward Bound: American Families in the Cold War Era* (New York: Basic Books, 1988); Lynn Spigel, *Make Room for TV: Television and the Family Ideal in Post-War America* (Chicago, IL: Chicago UP, 1992); Sherrie A. Inness, *Dinner Roles: American Women and Culinary Culture* (Iowa City, IA: U of Iowa Press, 2001), *Kitchen Culture in America: Popular Representations of Food, Gender, and Race* (Philadelphia, PA: U of Pennsylvania Press, 2001); Anna McCarthy, *The Citizen Machine: Governing by Television in 1950s America* (New York: The New Press, 2010); Grace Hale, *Making Whiteness: The Culture of Segregation in the South, 1890–1940* (New York: Vintage, 1999); Robert E. Weems, *De-Segregating the Dollar: African American Consumerism in the Twentieth Century* (New York: NYU Press, 1998).

[13] Amy Kaplan, "Manifest Domesticity," *American Literature* 70.3 (1998): 581–606. Citation on 582.

through private marketplace consumption" with a demonstration of the federal government's centrality in the 1930s and 40s in encouraging such consumption in the first place.[14]

The texts that appear in this study have been selected based on the striking nature of their depictions of time-saving appliances. The fact that remarkable examples of language's capacity to articulate the multifaceted nature of our dealings with objects happen to occur as often in texts that critics have dismissed as "pulp" as they do in ones deemed "canonical" is a further challenge, in my view, to the utility of distinguishing between "low" and "high" art. Likewise, while some of the representations I examine are well known, many of them are obscure, and in most cases the significance of their engagement with domestic electrification has been entirely overlooked. This neglect is attributable to literary critics' broader neglect, until very recently, of the domestic realm as a whole.[15] In the case of the male writers I have chosen, it is further attributable to the enduring tendency to read writing by men as solely concerned with the public realm, and indeed to link its value to its perceived elision of the minutiae of the domestic sphere in favor of the presumed complexity of the public sphere, be it global or parochial. The domestic time-saving appliances in my chosen texts challenge these assumptions.

2. From the "Electric Age" to the 1920s: Devilry, Engineering Genius, and Efficiency

The advent of time-saving appliances in the early twentieth century transformed not only the material conditions of domestic living arrangements and the nature of housework but the texture of domestic family life, and profoundly influenced Americans' sense of themselves as consumers of goods and inhabitants of specific family roles. The story of the time-saving appliance

---

[14] Ronald C. Tobey, *Technology as Freedom: The New Deal and the Electrical Modernization of the American Home* (Berkeley: U of California Press, 1996), 3. The "consumerism thesis" that Tobey challenges, whereby "an expanding, conservative capitalism, largely unrestrained by governmental regulation or unfocused by legislatively mandated social policy, deserves credit for domestic electrical modernization," and "private industry substantially accomplished domestic electrical modernization in the 1920s, before the New Deal, or created in the decade of the 1920s the pattern of its fulfilment in the economic boom after World War II" (3), is apparent in Harold L. Platt, *The Electric City: Energy and the Growth of the Chicago Area, 1880–1930* (Chicago: U of Chicago Press, 1991), 235–6, Cowan, 192; Lizabeth Cohen, *A Consumer's Republic: The Politics of Mass Consumption in Postwar America* (New York: Alfred A. Knopf, 2003), 123; and in the elision of the New Deal in Mark H. Rose's *Cities of Light and Heat: Domesticating Gas and Electricity in Urban America* (Penn State UP, 1995), 171–88 and Priscilla J. Brewer's *From Fireplace to Cookstove: Technology and the Domestic Ideal in America* (Syracuse UP, 2000), 241–60.

[15] For an incisive discussion of the field's recent growth, see Chiara Briganti and Kathy Mezei, "Introduction," in *The Domestic Space Reader* (U of Toronto Press, 2012), 3–15.

starts in the second half of the nineteenth century, which came to be known as the "Electric Age" due to the proliferation of electrical inventions it spawned. These included Samuel Morse's telegraph (1844); Alexander Graham Bell's telephone (1876); Thomas Edison's phonograph, incandescent light bulb, and electric distribution system (1877, 1879, and 1882); Mortimer Granville's electric vibrator (1880); Guglielmo Marconi's invention of wireless telegraphy (1896); and Reginald Fessenden's development of the wireless to carry voice as radio (1906).[16] In the late 1880s and 1890s, the benefits and perils of electricity were further sensationalized by the highly publicized competition between the Edison Electric Company (founded 1878, renamed General Electric in 1892) and the Westinghouse Electric and Manufacturing Company (founded 1886), over dominance of the electrical power industry (Coe, 169). In what came to be known as the "current wars," the two companies fought over whether Edison's direct current (DC) or the alternating current (AC) Nikola Tesla developed for Westinghouse was superior. When AC emerged as the winner, Edison sought to discredit it as unsafe for domestic use by persuading the state of New York to use it to power the recently invented electric chair (about which more later).[17]

Perhaps the most famous response to the "Electric Age" is Walt Whitman's paean to electricity, in "I Sing the Body Electric," first written in 1855 and revised in 1876 and 1881, in which the poet imagined American democracy itself as both a human body and a nation traversed by electric currents connecting selves to other selves.[18] Whitman's poem, which begins with the announcement "I sing the body electric, / The armies of those I love engirth me and I engirth them, / They will not let me off till I go with them, respond to them, / And discorrupt them, and charge them full with the charge of the soul," envisages a collectivism powered by solidarity and eros, both of which are rendered via images of anarchic "mad filaments" from which "ungovernable shoots" of energy play out and to which "the response [is]

[16] For a historical overview of the so-called electric age, see: David E. Nye, *Electrifying America: Social Meanings of a New Technology, 1880–1940* (Cambridge, MA: MIT Press, 1990); Gene Aldair, *Thomas Alda Edison: Inventing the Electric Age* (Oxford: Oxford UP, 1996); Jill Jonnes, *Empires of Light: Edison, Tesla, and the Race to Electrify the World* (New York: Random House, 2003); Lewis Coe, *The Telegraph* (Jefferson, NC: McFarland, 2003); Ernest Freeberg, *The Age of Edison* (New York: Penguin, 2013); and Frederik Nebeker, *Dawn of the Electronic Age: Electrical Technologies in the Shaping of the Modern World, 1914 to 1945* (Oxford: Wiley-Blackwell, 2009), which categorises not the period 1840 to 1900, but 1914 to 1945, as the "true" electric age.

[17] Notable examples include T.H. Metzger, *Blood and Volts: Edison, Tesla, and the Electric Chair* (New York: Autonomedia, 1996); Richard Moran, *Executioner's Current: Thomas Edison, George Westinghouse, and the Invention of the Electric Chair* (New York: Vintage Books, 2003); and Craig Brandon, *The Electric Chair: An Unnatural American History* (Jefferson, NC: McFarland, 2016).

[18] Walt Whitman, *Leaves of Grass, and Selected Prose* (New York: Holt, Rinehart, and Winston, 1949), 80–8.

likewise ungovernable" (1. i–iv; 5.vii). As Paul Gilmore notes, Whitman uses electricity "to describe the way that poetry, like sex, might become a vehicle, an act, of bodily connection shocking in its intensity and in its challenge to normative bodily boundaries" (148). Unsurprisingly, references both implicit and explicit to Whitman's electrical poetics surface in a number of texts discussed in this study.

The emergence of time-saving appliances in the first two decades of the twentieth century was buoyed by the controversy, fear, and enthusiasm generated by the events just discussed. But it was also driven by the simultaneous ascendance in the popular imagination of mechanical engineering, bacteriology, and the concept of scientific management, along with a shortage in professional cleaners that came to be known as the "servant problem" (a point to which I return). If the Chicago World's Fair of 1893 dazzled the public with scintillating displays of electric power and light, including an electric kitchen, the US public was equally in thrall to the more abstract figure of the engineer, who by the end of the nineteenth century had gained a quasi-mystical status thanks to inventions such as the skyscraper, steam engine, and locomotive (not to mention the lure of Thomas Edison himself).[19] The number of engineering graduates thus surged between 1870 and the early 1900s—as did the number of patents filed for new electrical devices after 1910 (Ganz, 42–3).

The popularization in the 1890s of germ theory, according to which diseases were spread by microbial bacteria, in turn transformed public understandings of hygiene and social attitudes to waste disposal, personal grooming, and housekeeping.[20] It also coincided with a new rhetoric of efficiency born from the growth of "scientific management"—the analysis of workflows to render factory production more time- and cost-efficient. Prior to industrialization, paid work and housework had all occurred in the home, and were shared between husband, wife, and children.[21] Following industrialization, housework was reframed as "women's work" as part of a broader effort to remove women from the factory floor.[22] A field known

[19] Gantz, 2012, 40–1; Todd Simmons, *Science and Technology in Nineteenth-century America* (Westport, CN: Greenwood Press, 2005), esp. 177–81.

[20] Sue Ellen Hoy, *Chasing Dirt: The American Pursuit of Cleanliness* (New York and Oxford: Oxford UP, 1996), 107; Nancy Tomes, "Spreading the Germ Theory: Sanitary Science and Home Economics, 1880-1930" in *Rethinking Home Economics: Women and the History of a Profession,* ed. Sarah Stage and Virginia B. Vincenti (Ithaca, NY: Cornell University Press, 1997), 34–54.

[21] For a more thorough account of the history of housework and its transformation following industrialization, see: Strasser, 2000 [1982]; Cowan, 1983, and Oakley, 1985 [1974].

[22] Early nineteenth-century employers hired women and children due to their willingness to work for lower wages than men. Early unions partnered with middle-class reformers who viewed factory work to be immoral to pass labor laws to protect working-class women and children from the "dangers" of the workplace. Irene Padavic and Barbara F. Reskin, "Gendered

variously as home economics, domestic economy, and domestic scientific management emerged to champion the value of domestic work alongside the importance of sanitation and efficiency. In the 1910s and 1920s, scientific management consultants such as Christine Fredrik and Lillian Gilbreth applied the ideas of F. W. Taylor's *The Principles of Scientific Management* (1911) to kitchen layouts and the scheduling of chores, using rhetoric that explicitly framed the kitchen as a factory.[23] By the 1940s, they were advising appliance manufacturers on how best to market their products. At the other end of the spectrum was the rational housekeeping movement, which in the 1920s moved beyond the question of household efficiency to champion electrification's potential to transform gender relations and, since a wired home and appliances were valuable assets, to protect families' economic security against the uncertainties of the labor market (Tobey, 50–2).

Schematically speaking, then, the Singer sewing machine (patented in 1889), GE ceiling fan (1892), Hotpoint electric iron (1903), GE electric iron (1905), GE toaster and electric teakettle (1907), Hotpoint electric toaster (1908), Hamilton Beach handheld mixer (1910), Westinghouse electric range (1917), Sunbeam Mixmaster standing mixer (1928), Waring "Blendor" (1937–8), and Hamilton Beach Milkshake DrinkMaster (1930) capitalized on the lure of engineering, "magical" electricity, and efficiency (Gantz 2012, 29; 34). Meanwhile the Thor and Whirlpool electric washing machines (1907 and 1911); Cecil Booth's electric vacuum cleaner and GE's "Invincible Electric Renovator" vacuum cleaner (1901 and 1908); the Hoover "Electric Suction Sweeper" (1909); the refrigerators by Dolmere (1913), Frigidaire (1918), Servel (1926), GE Monitor Top (1928), and Sears Coldspot (1928); and the June Day electric dryer (1938) benefited from growing awareness of hygiene, and the popularization of "scientific management."[24] Indeed, one can trace a direct line from the time-use studies that Gilbreth conducted in the 1920s to the marketing of appliances, over the next decades, as liberators of white women's time and energy.

But writers' engagements with time-saving appliances in later decades, and particularly the postwar era, trouble these schemas. These depictions unveil strange slippages between the dichotomies of "clean"/"dirty," "magical"/"mundane," "domestic"/"public," and "safe"/"dangerous." Some even link domestic gadgets with electric-shock therapy and the electric

---

Work in Time and Place," in *Women and Men at Work*, ed. Barbara Reskin and Irene Padavic (Thousand Oaks, CA: Pine Forge Press, 2002), 17–35.

[23] D. Graham provides an excellent analysis of Gilbreth's career in "Domesticating Efficiency: Lillian Gilbreth's Scientific Management of Homemakers, 1924–1930," *Signs* 23.3 (1999): 633–75. See also Janice Rutherford, *Selling Mrs. Consumer: Christine Fredrick and the Rise of Household Efficiency* (Athens, GA: U of Georgia Press, 2003).

[24] For a history of Domelre, see Gantz 2015, 177; Frigidaire: Gantz 2015, 97–100; Servel: Gantz 2015, 107; G.E.: Gantz 2015, 112–13; Sears Coldspot: Gantz 2015, 113.

chair, the latter of whose malfunctioning during the execution of Julius and Ethel Rosenberg in 1953 made international headlines.[25] In *The Bell Jar* (1963), which famously begins, "It was a queer, sultry summer, the summer they electrocuted the Rosenbergs, and I didn't know what I was doing in New York," Sylvia Plath connects state-sanctioned execution, the trauma of electric-shock therapy, and a stultifying postwar conformity exemplified by her narrator's visit to the show kitchen of the fictional *Ladies' Day* magazine.[26] Richard Yates, whose grandfather, the chaplain at Auburn State Prison in New York, witnessed the electric chair's first use in 1890, draws a similar connection in *Disturbing the Peace* (1976), which I examine in detail in Chapter 2.[27] Here, protagonist John Wilder's song to his lover, "'Benjamin Franklin discovered the spark / That Edison discovered would light up the dark / Marconi discovered the wireless telegraph / Across the ocean blue / But the greatest discovery / Was when . . . I discovered you,'" takes on a darker meaning after Wilder is sectioned in Bellevue and a nurse explains: "'You've heard of the electric chair. . . . Well, this here is an electric bed. All I have to do is press this button'" (*DTP*, 165; 238). The greatest discovery in this novel is not human connection or love but the electric currents used to domesticate unruly citizens.

In "I Sing the Body Electric," Ray Bradbury explores similar themes, portraying a postwar landscape in which electric gadgets are more reliable sources and subjects of affection than people.[28] Adapted in 1969 from his 1962 screenplay for *The Twilight Zone*, the story recounts a widower's attempt to placate his three children's grief at the loss of their mother by ordering them a made-to-measure "Electric Grandma" in the post. The customizable machine free of human fallibilities while capable of boundless, unconditional love arrives in a coffin-shaped box a few days later. The youngest daughter, Agatha, is skeptical of "Grandma," fearing she/it will one day abandon the family just as their mother did—until the day that "Grandma" jumps in front of traffic to save the child from being run over, and in so doing reveals herself to be incapable of dying. But this time-saving appliance does not just provide a solution to the problem of fallible, mortal, parents, or compensation for the time the children never got with their mother. She is an expedient means for this particular widower to outsource

[25] See Ilene Philipson, *Ethel Rosenberg: Beyond the Myths* (New Brunswick, NJ: Rutgers UP, 1993), 351–2.
[26] Sylvia Plath, *The Bell Jar* (New York: Faber and Faber, 2005 [1963]), 36–46.
[27] Blake Bailey, *A Tragic Honesty: The Life and Work of Richard Yates* (New York: Picador, 2003), 12. News of allegations of sexual misconduct against Bailey broke as this monograph was going into production. I wish to make clear that in citing Bailey's research into Yates's life, I am not dismissing or disbelieving these allegations.
[28] Ray Bradbury, "I Sing the Body Electric," *The Stories of Ray Bradbury* (London and New York: Alfred A. Knopf), 850–884. Henceforth, *TSORB*.

parenting, saving the time he would otherwise have had to expend on his children. Bradbury's bittersweet story parodies both Whitman's utopian rhetoric and the hyperbole surrounding electric goods in the postwar era to reveal a dearth of affective energy at the heart of the nuclear family. "Electric Grandma's" revelation, when the children grow up, that she will spend the rest of her days in a room "'where as many as thirty or forty of the Electric Women sit and rock and talk, each in her turn'" about the children they have raised, not only allegorizes the reduction of women to their role as caregivers, or machines for (grand)mothering. It conveys mechanization's inevitable reinforcement of female reification, which the utopian rhetoric of electrification in turn obscures (*TSORB*, 882).

The texts I examine similarly expose the mundane as horrific through references to time-saving appliances' long-standing entanglement with gender, race, and class inequality. An address to President Johnson published in the October 2, 1865, issue of *The Anti-Slavery Reporter* anticipated the potential to replace domestic slave labor with machines, while a study of electricity consumption in the 1920s described electricity as the "'willing slave'" of any "'household operation'" (qtd. in Nye, 247–8; 314). According to this logic, compliant electrical power could replace unruly Black labor power. Appliance ads in the 1920s and 1930s also capitalized on the so-called servant problem (no less since Josephine Garis Cochran, the inventor of the electric dishwasher (patented 1886), had claimed to be motivated by frustration at her servants' tendency to break her fine china![29]). But as Vanessa Hay has shown, the servant problem in the US was itself racialized, referring less to the shortage of servants generally (as it did in the industrialized European countries) than to the absence of *white* ones (115). Appliance ads reflected this racial dimension. Most notably, a 1934 ad by GE featured an illustration of a cross between Uncle Sam and Abraham Lincoln and the slogan: "Electricity is the modern Lincoln—General Electric is the modern emancipator—The Ten Best Home Servants banish slavery."[30] Appropriating the language of abolition, GE positioned the purchase of time-saving appliances as a feminist act that would save white women from both drudgery and the nuisance of Black help. In positioning the white housewife as a slave to her housework and GE appliances as the 10 *best* home servants, the ad simultaneously invoked and erased the material history of those who actually were slaves until recently, who now worked in menial jobs, and who, the ad suggested, could be replaced by a commodity as far better than its human antecedent (GE unfortunately denied permission to reproduce

[29] See Jessamyn Neuhaus, *Housewives and Housework in American Advertising* (New York and Basingstoke: Palgrave Macmillan, 2011), 149–150. Neuhaus notes that Cochran's claim obscured the fact that washing the dishes had "long been one of the few housework tasks often shared [between housewives and] other family members" (150).

[30] GE "You Shall Not Enslave Our Women!" *Woman's Home Companion* (July 1933): 58–9.

this ad, but it can be found online on a number of different sites devoted to early-twentieth-century print appliance advertisements).

Crucially, by equating fear or suspicion of time-saving appliances with a Blackness understood to be retrograde, ads that featured or invoked Black servants countered any uncertainty their white customers might harbor toward these objects. That is, they deployed Blackness to render untenable anything but the wholehearted embrace of domestic technology: because to be suspicious of that technology would not be "white."

This perception of time-saving appliances' inherent "whiteness" was paradoxically amplified by the efforts of reformers in Northern cities who sought, throughout the 1920s and 1930s, to counter negative perceptions of Black female migrants from the South by training them to use washing machines and vacuum cleaners, thereby transforming them into housekeepers worthy of employment, even as ownership of these objects remained out of reach.[31] Time-saving appliances' exclusivity, together with their subsequent role in the construction of American identity as white and middle class, forms an important strand of the texts I examine in Chapter 4, on time-saving appliances in postwar Black American fiction, as well as the appliance depictions in Marge Piercy (Chapter 3), Kurt Vonnegut (Chapter 6), and Charles Johnson and Lucy Ellmann (Chapter 7).

3. Emancipating Machines and Idle Housewives

Following the achievement in 1920 of women's suffrage and well into the 1930s, appliance manufacturers increasingly placed white women's liberation, and a rhetoric of progress and modernity, at the center of their promotional strategies, even as the price of the objects themselves made them inaccessible to working- and middle-class women.[32] The imagery and rhetoric of appliance ads and instruction manuals emphasized the distance between the housewife, who would merely direct her servants' work, and the gadget.[33] Crucially, while appliance manufacturers in the postwar era

[31] Vanessa Hay, *Unprotected Labor: Household Workers, Politics, and Middle-Class Reform in New York, 1870–1940* (Chapel Hill, NC: U of North Carolina Press, 2011), 153; Victoria W. Wolcott, *Remaking Respectability: African American Women in Interwar Detroit* (Chapel Hill, NC: U of North Carolina Press, 2001), 84.

[32] *Modern Ways for Modern Days* (Mansfield, OH: Westinghouse Electric Corporation, 1920); Frances Weedman, *Manual of Miracle Cookery* (Chicago, IL: Edison GE Appliance Co, 1935); *Meals Go Modern. . . Electrically* (New York: National Kitchen Modernizing Bureau Sponsored by Edison Electric Institute and National Electrical Manufacturers Association, 1937. Reprinted 1940). All sourced from Alan and Shirley Brocker Sliker Collection, Michigan State University Library (henceforth shortened to *ASBSC, MSUL)*.

[33] For examples of instruction manuals featuring this imagery, see: *The Kitchen of Her Dreams* (Chicago, IL: Edison GE Appliance Company, Inc. and Hotpoint, 1920); Herrick, *The Aristocrat of Refrigerators* (Waterloo, IA: Herrick Refrigerator Company, 1926); Jessie M.

would respond to the threat of white women entering the workplace by framing their products as allowing women more time to look after their husbands and children, time-saving appliances throughout the 1910s, 1920s, and even the Great Depression were posited as status symbols, facilitating both greater leisure and the hosting of dinner parties worthy of the aristocracy.[34] Such ads rarely featured children, while the women in them were often dressed to go out. GE's 1934 ads for its Monitor Top refrigerator (so called due to the exposed compressor's resemblance to the cylindrical turret of the Monitor Civil War gunship in another sign of the 1930s' nostalgia for antebellum and early postbellum America) removed the home altogether. In one, an illustration of men and women in eveningwear clustered around two GE refrigerators against a curtained backdrop suggested the unveiling of a much-anticipated artwork.[35] In another, titled "Style Sensation," the ad copy remarked, "Even in the movies you will note a General Electric Monitor Top refrigerator is almost invariably shown when the scene represents a modern kitchen" (Figure I.1).

Edith Wharton's description in *The House of Mirth* (1905) of "a world over-heated, over-upholstered, and over-fitted with mechanical appliances for the gratification of fantastic requirements" parodied these luxurious connotations, and suggested time-saving appliances' spiritually corrupting potential.[36] Sinclair Lewis's satire of small-town America, *Babbitt* (1922), echoed this critique, describing a community of wealthy women whose few children and homes equipped with "gas stoves, electric ranges and dish-washers and vacuum cleaners" leave them free to eat "chocolates, [go] to the motion-pictures . . . th[ink] timorously of the lovers who never appea[r], and accumulat[e] a splendid restlessness which they g[e]t rid of by nagging their husbands."[37] Lewis spliced the pastimes 1920s advertisers showed upper-class housewives doing with their newly freed time with the fears expressed by critics of such technologies, who wondered whether domestic mechanization would leave women altogether *too* free. In fact, the reality was very different: as Ruth Schwartz Cowan's now-canonical history of domestic technology has shown, the advent of time-saving appliances and modern cleaning products merely brought home tasks previously outsourced (laundry and ironing) and raised cleaning standards, ultimately increasing the amount of

---

DeBoth, *Frigidaire Frozen Delights* (Dayton, OH: Frigidaire Corp, 1927); *The "Silent Hostess" Treasure Book* (Cleveland, OH: GE, 1930); all *sourced from ASBSC, MSUL.*

[34] *The New Art of . . .* (Nela Park, Cleveland, OH: GE Kitchen Institute, 1934). *Reprinted 1935 and 1936. ASBSC, MSUL.*

[35] GE, "The Finest Refrigerators General Electric Ever Built!" *Fortune* (April 1934): N.P. Unfortunately, GE has denied permission to reproduce this ad, but it can be found online on a number of different websites devoted to vintage ads.

[36] For a more thorough account of the luxury status of appliances in this period, see Sherrie Inness, "Grace and Elegance: Electric Appliances," in *Dinner Roles*, 82–5.

[37] Sinclair Lewis, *Babbitt* (New York: Signet / New American Press, 1964 [1922]). Henceforth, *B.*

FIGURE I.1 GE. "They Created a New Style Sensation in Electric Refrigerators!" *The Saturday Evening Post* (1934): N.P. © Getty Images.

time spent on housework.[38] This portrayal, however, formed the template for postwar white male writers' depictions of vacant housewives either more enamored with their gadgets than their husbands, or incapable of keeping house despite owning the best cleaning machines (a point to which I return).

The time-consuming nature of supposedly time-saving technologies is foregrounded in Nick Carraway's observation, in the opening chapters of F. Scott Fitzgerald's *The Great Gatsby* (1925), of the day-to-day activities of the titular Gatsby. Carraway's depiction of "five crates of oranges and lemons" that arrive at Gatsby's house every Friday, only to "le[ave] his back door in a pyramid of pulpless [*sic*] halves" every Monday, frames the kitchen

[38] Cowan, 97–100. See also Strasser, *Never Done*; Rosie Cox, "House/Work: Home as a Space of Work and Consumption," *Geography Compass* 7.12 (2013): 821–31.

as a factory.[39] The description of "a machine in the kitchen which could extract the juice of two hundred oranges in half an hour if a little button was pressed two hundred times by a butler's thumb" parodies both the de-skilling of labor ushered in by the assembly line and the alienating effects of factory work, whereby the laborer becomes, as Marx put it, a mere "appendage of the machine."[40] Meanwhile the image of pulpless halves unceremoniously tossed in the garbage following the extraction of their juice literalizes the extraction of surplus value. Where Lewis equates the "all-electric" home with female indolence and the rigidity of upper-class norms in a critique that bears more than a trace of Thorstein Veblen's *Theory of the Leisure Class* (1899), Fitzgerald suggests how the time-saving appliance dehumanizes the servants who use it.[41]

4. From Luxury to Equality and Freedom "for All": The New Deal and the Second World War

While the earlier-discussed connotations of excess, greed, exploitation, and feminine indolence are apparent in many of the appliance depictions examined in this study, they are overshadowed by the associations these objects accrued from the mid-1930s on, as time-saving appliances entered the mass market and were enlisted in Franklin Delano Roosevelt's social democratic vision. Under the New Deal, both domestic electrification and appliance ownership were reframed as a democratic right, and as evidence of the state's commitment to elevating the quality of life of white Americans, through policies under the newly-formed Federal Housing Authority (FHA) that extended credit for appliance purchases, subsidized the electrical wiring of all new homes and the standardization of plugs and receptacles, and firmed up manufacturing regulations.[42] Thus by 1941, 52 percent of US households (63 percent of middle-class homes; 40 percent of working-class homes) had replaced the insulated cabinet known as the icebox, in which one placed a block or tray of ice that was replaced either daily or weekly, with an electric refrigerator.[43] As we shall see, these policies excluded Black Americans and Latinos, resulting in far lower household penetration of appliances (only 16 percent of Black Americans and 7 percent of Latinos owned a refrigerator in 1940).[44] This inequality was obscured by government-sponsored campaigns,

---

[39] F. Scott Fitzgerald, *The Great Gatsby* (New York: Penguin, 1985 [1925]), 41. Henceforth, *GG*.
[40] Karl Marx and Friedrich Engels, *The Communist Manifesto* (London: Penguin Classics, 2004 [1848]), 227.
[41] Thorstein Veblen, *Theory of the Leisure Class* (Oxford: Oxford UP, 2007 [1899]).
[42] Tobey, 2–3; 20.
[43] Cowan, 94, qtd. in Innes, *Dinner Roles*, 78; Jonathan Rees, *Refrigeration Nation* (Baltimore, MD: Johns Hopkins UP, 2013), 157.
[44] Tobey, 165–6.

which emphasized electrification's power to plane away class differences, using rhetoric that implied the subsidizing of domestic electrification would render "all-electric" living accessible to all. These were aided by appliance manufacturers' efforts, from the late 1930s onwards, to promote their products as benevolent purveyors of bounty for all at the same time as they designed the appliances themselves with white middle-class married mothers of young children in mind.[45] It is in this same period that the yellow tinge of the first refrigerators was replaced by DuPont's "sparkling white" "Dulux" refrigerator finish, and that the refrigerator itself came to be associated with whiteness. Shelley Nickles notes: "At a time when the middle class . . . feared slipping to working-class status, and when popular culture portrayed the working class, immigrants, and nonwhites as having lower standards of cleanliness," the purchase of a white refrigerator and "ability to keep the refrigerator white and devoid of dirt . . . suggested that women could maintain themselves and their family's standards through thrift and hygiene" (705). Such an association was based on "the conflation of non-white skin with dirt" codified in the eighteenth century to justify the expansion of slavery.[46] The anxieties identified by Nickles also explain the sudden appearance, in appliance ads of the 1930s, of Black servants portrayed as by turns fearful of being replaced by the appliance, or too uncivilized to understand it—a phenomenon I examine in detail in Chapters 4 and 6.

While appliance production ceased in 1941 as manufacturers contributed to the war effort and the US government encouraged citizens to invest their earnings in war bonds, a steady stream of ads invited Americans to look forward to an imminent postwar future, when they might spend their savings on a new generation of gadgets that embodied the nation's hard-won freedom.[47] Thus Sunbeam described its standing mixers as "Peacetime Makers," a slogan that positioned Sunbeam as the facilitator of the very peacetime that would enable its products to go back into production.[48] Westinghouse proclaimed that "A Bright Future is in the Cards" in an ad depicting a tarot reading whose cards featured images of time-saving appliances (Figure I.2). Hoover promised to reveal to Americans "the power of the American home in getting this war over *fast*" by teaching households how to salvage scrap, share foods, and make their vacuum cleaners last

45 Shelley Nickles, "'Preserving Women': Refrigerator Design as Social Process in the 1930s," *Technology and Culture* 43.4 (Oct. 2002): 693–727. Citation on 694. For a concise history of the icebox, see: Gantz, *Refrigeration*, 74–5; Rees, 119–39.

46 Carl A. Zimring, *Clean and White: A History of Environmental Racism in the United States* (New York: NYU Press, 2015), 137.

47 May, 160; Charles F. McGovern, "Fighting for the American Way: Consumption and Americanism, 1935–1945," in *Sold American: Consumption and Citizenship, 1890–1945* (Chapel Hill: U of North Carolina Press, 2006), 307–66.

48 ". . . and no other mixer has the Advantages of Sunbeam Automatic Mixmaster," *LIFE* (September 17, 1945): 19. See also May, 160 and Cohen, 122.

FIGURE I.2 Westinghouse. "A Bright Future Is in the Cards." *LIFE* (October 22, 1945): 28. ©Westinghouse. Reproduced with permission.

longer.[49] Meanwhile the *McCall's* "Kitchen of Tomorrow Contest" invited American women to submit 200-word essays stating their preference for a conventional kitchen equipped with conveniences available at the time or an open-plan kitchen featuring futuristic gadgets, and published the results for manufacturers to better refine their promotional messages.[50] Thanks to these campaigning efforts, by June 1944 time-saving appliances topped the list of the most desired consumer items, beginning with washing machines

[49] Hoover, "Meet a Home that Is Shortening the War," *LIFE* (October 11, 1943): 18.
[50] Mary Davis Gillies, *What Women Want in their Kitchens of Tomorrow* (New York: McCall Corporation, 1944), 8. Author's own. Courtesy of Between the Covers-Rare Books, Inc., New Jersey. For an in-depth discussion of the report's rhetoric and broader sociopolitical meanings, see Nancy Camilla Carlisle and Melinda Talbot Nasardinov, *America's Kitchens* (Historic New England, 2008), 157, and Laura Scott Holliday, "Kitchen Technologies: Promises and Alibis, 1944–1966," *Camera Obscura* 47–16.2 (2001): 78–131.

and followed by electric irons, refrigerators, stoves, toasters, radios, and vacuum cleaners (May, 160). And by 1950, 80 percent of US households owned a refrigerator (Cohen, 123).

Gertrude Stein's letters to Samuel M. Steward between 1939 and 1945, when she and her partner Alice B. Toklas were living in France, beautifully articulate the desire fueled by the wartime scarcity of what were still relatively new technologies.[51] Stein initially beseeched Steward not to send her and Toklas the Sunbeam Mixmaster Toklas coveted since "in this particular moment, everybody has time enough to mix by hand all the mixing that needs mixing" (*DS*, 145). Steward sent them the Mixmaster despite these protestations, and a few months later she exalted:

> The Mix master [*sic*] came Easter Sunday, and we have not had time to more than read the literature put it together and gloat, oh so beautiful is the Mix master, so beautiful and the literature [enclosed pamphlet] so beautiful . . . and everything so beautiful and now how much do I owe you Sammy dear because we are very happy to have it here, bless you Sammy, Madame Roux said *oui il est si gentil,* . . . Alice all smiles and murmurs in her dreams, Mix Master [*sic*] (*DS*, 147–8).

Stein's rhapsody to the appliance highlights its luxurious dimension in this period, its exoticism for European consumers for whom domestic gadgets would become commonplace only in the 1960s, and its particular poeticity for a writer enthralled by the meanings of everyday objects.[52] The allusion to "the literature so beautiful" underscores both the novelty of appliance pamphlets for a generation new to these technologies and the sheer artistry expressed in these print materials until the 1980s, by which point consumers' familiarity with them on the one hand and the explosion of specialist cookbooks on the other hand rendered redundant their curious mix of housekeeping pedagogy, recipe suggestions, and propaganda regarding the merits of electrification and the American way of life. Meanwhile, the description of Alice B. Toklas—who was a cookbook writer and chef—murmuring the Mixmaster's name at night imbues the appliance with an erotic charge that may or may not have been an intentional allusion to the

---

[51] *Dear Sammy: Letters from Gertrude Stein & Alice B. Toklas,* ed. Samuel M. Steward (Boston, MA: Houghton Mifflin, 1977), 144–55. Henceforth, *DS*. For another discussion of the Mixmaster and Toklas's cooking, see Laura Shapiro 2004, 115–16.

[52] Jackie Clarke, "Work, Consumption and Subjectivity in Postwar France: Moulinex and the Meanings of Domestic Appliances 1950s–70s," *Journal of Contemporary History* 47.4 (October 2012): 838–59.

Mixmaster's origins.[53] The "universal" (AC/DC) motor eventually used by Sunbeam was in fact originally created for the vibrator (the latter of which was invented in 1880 as a tool for medical doctors to render less onerous the masturbatory labor involved in "curing" women of their hysteria).[54] The two inventors' employers patented the motor in 1902 but repurposed it to develop the standing mixer, blender, and coffeemaker, which from 1910 they sold under the brand name Hamilton Beach (the inventors' surnames).[55] The frequency with which vibrators in the 1900s had been advertised as domestic appliances explains the logic of the motor's repurposing for use in cooking utensils, and encourages a reading of Stein's descriptions of the Mixmaster that acknowledges their erotic dimension—even if she knew nothing about the appliance's history (Juffer, 85). An erotic subtext is likewise apparent in Stein's next letter to Steward, in April 1940. Here, the proclamation, "Day and night Mix master [*sic*] is a delight . . . first we had to work it together but now Alice works it all alone and it saves her hours and effort," gestures to both conjugal sex and masturbation (*DS*, 149). The ensuing image of "how happy Mix master [*sic*] makes the home, we do not know whether [the pet dogs] Basket and Pépé know the difference but the rest of us do" suggests at once the post-coital satisfaction to which small children and pets remain oblivious, and the marital harmony that appliance advertisers promised their products could bring thanks to time- and labor-saving benefits that would restore wives' good humor (*DS*, 149). The exultation, "thanks again and again and again for Mix master [*sic*], three long cheers, neither war nor anything could stop it," conveys the endurance of the machine's own motor, capable of both outpacing and drowning out the war itself, and intimates the affinities between the persistent, repetitive percussion of the revolving Mixmaster and the slow build of female orgasm, whose *pleasure* "neither war nor anything could stop" (*DS*, 149). Indeed, the description reads as a parody of appliance advertising's foregrounding of heterosexual relations—no

[53] Such a reading chimes with analyses of Stein's writing by Jody Cardinal, who interprets Stein's 1927 poem, "Patriarchal Poetry," as an "elaborate display of the success of her sex life with Toklas" that "makes an implicit case for the stability—and indeed legitimacy—of their union" tied in part to associations of companionate marriage at the time with both national stability and whiteness. See Jody Cardinal, "'Come Too': 1920s Erotic Rights Discourse and Gertrude Stein's 'Patriarchal Poetry,'" in *Primary Stein: Returning to the Writing of Gertrude Stein*, ed. Janet Boyd and Sharon J. Kirsch (Lanham, MD: Rowman and Littlefield, 2014), 57–76. Citations on 66–7.

[54] Rachel P. Maines, *The Technology of Orgasm* (Baltimore: Johns Hopkins UP, 1999), 15 and 135.

[55] David John Cole, Eve Browning and Fred E. H. Schroeder, "Kitchen Appliances: Motorized," in *Encyclopedia of Modern Everyday Inventions* (Westport, CN: Greenwood Press, 2003), 169; E. J. Levy, "Of Vibrators," in *From Curlers to Chainsaws* (East Lansing, MI: Michigan State University, 2016), 70–7; Jane Juffer, "The Mainstreaming of Masturbation?" in *At Home with Pornography* (New York: NYU Press, 1998), 85–6.

less given Stein's claim that Toklas "can write a whole advertisement for Mix master [*sic*] she is so pleased" (*DS*, 149).

Stein's enthusiasm was not shared by all, however. For writers like Henry Miller and Alfred Hayes, time-saving appliances obscured a broader spiritual devastation engendered by the war itself. In "Reunion in Brooklyn" (1944), Miller recalled returning home in 1940, after nine years in Paris and a year in Corfu, to find his mother's new refrigerator in the kitchen, "ticking in a mechanically epileptic way."[56] He wondered: "Was everybody installing these new conveniences? . . . America has comforts; Europe has other things which make all those comforts seem quite unimportant" (*SATW*, 108). In Hayes's *The Girl on the Via Flaminia* (1949), a US soldier in wartime Rome justifies his payment of a young Italian woman to pose as his wife by contrasting this transaction with his fellow soldiers' preferred technique for seducing local women: a promise to "'marry them, put them on a ship, take them back to mamma's electric icebox!'"[57] Where Miller's text posits domestic mechanization as emblematic of the spiritually depleting effects of mass culture, the refrigerator in Hayes's novella is synecdochic of the United States' exploitation of poorer nations. Both authors link the time-saving appliance to the United States' use of consumer goods to deflect attention from mass death.

5. Paragons of the "Good Life": Time-Saving Appliances and Cold War Ideology

Echoes of both Miller and Hayes' critiques are apparent in the texts examined in this study, where they contribute to a portrait of a postwar America replete with time-saving paraphernalia and rhetoric, but little imagination for how those saved minutes and hours might be meaningfully filled, or the toll of such mechanisms on social relations. Such texts inevitably make reference to the ubiquity of time-saving appliances in the advertising of new homes built after the war, and an emergent Cold War rhetoric that linked consumerism to patriotism and the vanquishing of the communist threat.

Most homes built after the start of the Cold War in 1947 were concentrated in suburban developments as part of a strategy known as "dispersal" or "defense through decentralisation."[58] Government policy makers argued

---

[56] Henry Miller, "Reunion in Brooklyn," in *Sunday after the War* (1944), republished in *The Henry Miller Reader* (New York: New Directions, 1959), 95–133. Citation on 110. Henceforth, *SATW*.

[57] Alfred Hayes, *The Girl on the Via Flaminia* (London: Penguin, 2018 [1949]), 123.

[58] For a thorough account of decentralization, see Paul Boyer, *By the Bomb's Early Light: Atomic Thought and Culture at the Dawn of the Atomic Age* (Chapel Hill, NC: U of North

that depopulating the urban core would both minimize the number of casualties in the event of nuclear attack and dis-incentivize enemies from launching one. Meanwhile the G.I. Bill of Rights and the expansion of the FHA program enabled white veterans to take out loans to purchase their own homes, making it cheaper to buy than to rent (May, 161). The year 1947 also saw the publication of George F. Kennan's "The Sources of Soviet Conduct," which advocated a policy of containment of the Soviet threat, rather than direct overt warfare, and emphasized the importance of projecting an image of national cohesion to the rest of the world.[59] As Alan Nadel has argued, this ethos shaped the conservativism of the period 1947–60: "military deployment and industrial technology, televised hearings and filmed teleplays, the cult of domesticity and the fetishizing of domestic security, the arms race and atoms for peace" were all products of the perceived need to contain the communist threat.[60] Nationwide advertising campaigns by leading appliance manufacturers upheld containment ideals by fostering a pastoral image of the white middle-class family and the suburban "all-electric" home as symbols of the American way of life. It was in this period that the white middle-class housewife became a fixture in appliance ads and instruction pamphlets, replacing earlier illustrations of the white upper-class woman of the house and her servants. The "all-electric" home was now portrayed as a better alternative to employing domestic help via imagery that collapsed the distinction between upper-class white women and the middle- and working-class (Figure I.3). Catalogs such as GE's for "the small appliances most women want most" (1947) suggested the war had brought the benefits of the "all-electric" home to *all* Americans.[61] Thomas Hine calls this the period of "Populuxe"—an era characterized by the positioning of mass- produced goods as luxuries available to all via messaging that suggested the American Dream itself could be "turn[ed] out . . . on an assembly line." [62]

Appliance design and advertising rhetoric in the 1950s reflected these ideals, while invoking a range of other symbolically-charged new technologies. "Push-button" technology for example became a ubiquitous refrain in ads that indirectly referenced the newly ubiquitous shorthand for the instigation of a nuclear attack (Figure I.4).[63] Meanwhile appliance designers, who since the 1930s had looked to the aesthetics of automobiles for inspiration,

Carolina Press, 2005 [1983]), 136–8; 176; 327–8. For more on domestic furnishings, see Spigel 2001 and Karal Ann Marling, *As Seen on TV: The Visual Culture of Everyday Life in the 1950s* (Cambridge, MA: Harvard UP, 1994).

[59] George F. Kennan, "The Sources of Soviet Conduct," *Foreign Affairs* 4.25 (July 1947): 566–82. Citation on 582.

[60] Alan Nadel, *Containment Culture: American Narratives, Postmodernism, and the Atomic Age* (Durham, NC: Duke UP), 2.

[61] *The Small Appliances Most Women Want Most* (Bridgeport, CN: GE Company Appliance and Merchandise Department, 1947).

[62] Thomas Hine, *Populuxe* (New York: Alfred A. Knopf, 1984), 5.

[63] Hine, "Just Push the Button," in *Populuxe*, 123–38, esp. 133.

FIGURE I.3 A Happy Housewife Cooks on her New Pink Range. 1957. Screen print. (Photo by GraphicaArtis/Getty Images) © Getty Images.

created refrigerators and toasters whose curved edges resembled a car's sleek silhouette, and standing mixers whose front detail recalled a car headlight—a move all the more intuitive given that several of the major appliance brands (Philco, Frigidaire, Gibson, AirTemp, Kelvinator) were originally owned by car manufacturers (Ford, GM, Chrysler, Studebaker, American Motors Corp).[64] By the mid-1950s, the car industry's concept of annual styling had been incorporated into appliance ads that encouraged households to redecorate their kitchen in a new color every year (Archer, 78). For example, in 1955, KitchenAid launched versions of its Model K Standing Mixer (originally sold in 1937) in pink, yellow, green, chrome, and copper.[65] Refrigerator manufacturer Servel introduced multicolor door handles featuring a "gold, modified 'Cadillac V'" to appeal to working-class women who wanted "'white metal kitchens with Cadillac handles' on [the] appliances and

[64] Sarah Archer, *The Mid-Century Kitchen: America's Favorite Room from Workspace to Dreamspace* (New York: Countryman Press, 2019), 78.
[65] William Lidwell and Gerry Manacsa, *Deconstructing Product Design* (Beverly, MA: Rockport, 2009), 180.

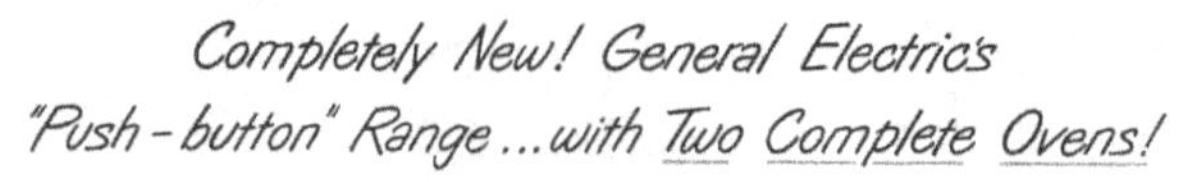

FIGURE I.4 GE. "Completely New! General Electric's 'Push-Button' Range. . ." Publication unknown. *Ca.* 1950. © Getty Images.

cabinets."[66] As Tobey notes, these efforts were partly motivated by market saturation: while sales of time-saving appliances surged in 1946, 1947, and 1948, and the outbreak of the Korean War in 1950 catalyzed a boom in appliance purchases from households scared of a similar interruption to consumer production as that which occurred during the Second World War, growth in sales after 1950 never reached the same height as the immediate postwar years (Tobey, 29). The ubiquity of time-saving appliances in ads, television, and literature of the period 1945–64 masked the fact that

[66] Eric Larrabee, "Rosebuds on the Silverware," *Industrial Design* 2 (February 1955): 62–3, qtd. in Qtd. in Shelley Nickles, "More Is Better: Mass Consumption, Gender, and Class Identity in Postwar America," *American Quarterly* 54.4 (December 2002): 581–622, citations on 592 and 593.

this period represented a long-term decline in sales growth, in keeping with the slowing of the postwar baby boom (29).

In turn, as David Snyder has argued, the rise of a mass culture for toy versions of time-saving appliances coterminously with that of appliances themselves trained children for gender-specific roles within the home while "diminishing adult work into the form of child's play."[67] Ads for Suzy Homemaker toy appliances for "busy little mother[s]" were virtually indistinguishable from ads for real appliances, while the Easy-Bake Oven, launched in 1963, and powered by two incandescent light bulbs, posited electricity's main benefit to be the baking of cakes "just like Mom's."[68] Where Westinghouse's toy appliances fostered brand loyalty long before the term entered common marketing parlance, its washing machine- and refrigerator-shaped piggy banks participated in shaping children's understanding of themselves as consumers of appliances purchased on credit.[69] A 1946 ad by the "170 Electric Light and Power Companies" that formed part of the Electric Industries Advertising Program rendered explicit this connection, while distancing electrification from New Deal-era collectivism (Figure I.5). The ad portrayed a child cheerfully placing coins in a (conventionally shaped) piggy bank, under the slogan, "Ah—A Capitalist!" The ad copy explained that when the boy's coins were deposited in an actual bank, some would end up invested in utility securities, giving him a "personal stake in the electric power industry," which "practically *every* American has." The ad's closing lines—"This is the American economic system. It's called capitalism. It's a good system. It helped make America great"—cemented the connection between electrical power, private industry, and the future of "opportunity for all little boys and girls with piggy banks."[70]

Willy Loman's diatribe against his malfunctioning refrigerator in Arthur Miller's *Death of a Salesman* (1949) is among the earliest and most famous critiques of such pastoral narratives. Loman's complaint, that "'The refrigerator consumes belts like a goddam maniac. They time those things . . . so when you finally paid for them, they're used up,'" anticipates the relationship between built-in obsolescence (the ensuring of a product's limited lifespan, so that it will have to be replaced with a new one), and

---

[67] David Snyder, "Playroom," in *Cold War Hothouses: Inventing Postwar Culture*, ed. Beatriz Colomina, Annemarie Brennan, and Jeannie Kim (Princeton, NJ: Princeton Architectural Press, 2003), 124–42, citation on 126.

[68] Sherrie A. Inness, "Cooking Lessons for Girls and Boys," in *Dinner Roles*, 51; Gary Cross, *Kids' Stuff: Toys and the Changing World of American Childhood* (Cambridge, MA: Harvard UP, 1997), 120; Todd Coopee, *Light Bulb Baking: A History of the Easy-Bake Oven* (Ottawa, ON: Sonderho Press, 2013).

[69] These banks have become something of a collector's item, retailing for between $20 and $50 on eBay.

[70] For an early critique of this campaign, see Harry Lewis Bird, "The Advertising of Intangibles," in *This Fascinating Advertising Business* (New York: Bobb-Merrill, 1947), 153–61.

FIGURE I.5 170 Electric Light and Power Companies. "Ah—a Capitalist!" *LIFE* (February 4, 1946): 103.

what Lisa Adkins calls "speculative time," or the "logic of speculation."[71] Where analysts of money and finance tend to tie surplus creation to labor power, Adkins argues that since the 1970s, "the critical site for the creation of surplus in present-day finance-led capitalism is not wage labor but the everyday payments that households make to ensure their existence": an appliance purchased on an installment plan does not so much liberate time as provide an incessant reminder of it.[72] Granted, Adkins's analyses are specific to financialization post-1970, which she defines as characterized by a shift from "a logic of the probable to a logic of the possible," wherein it is not assumed that the debt will be paid off (80–1; 90). But concern over the sustainability of an economy founded on consumer debt was already

[71] Arthur Miller, *Death of a Salesman* (London: Penguin, 2000 [1949]), 56–7.
[72] Lisa Adkins, *The Time of Money* (Stanford, CA: Stanford UP, 2018), 4.

high in the 1950s, as exemplified by *LIFE* magazine's 1955 story, "A Hard Look at Consumer Credit," which anxiously noted that nearly half of major household appliance purchases involved credit, and that household debt was outpacing income (qtd. in Cohen, 123–4). The "Populuxe" era, in other words, ran on credit. Miller's text gestures toward a similarly indeterminate future, in which the final instalment payment may or may not have been paid—and the item paid for may or may not already be in the dump, having long lost both its functionality and sheen.

The electric iron in Jewish American writer Tillie Olsen's short story, "I Stand Here Ironing" (1953–4), similarly exposes the scenes of domestic bliss presented in GE and Westinghouse ads as mirages—in this case, ones that obscure the "good life"'s inaccessibility to anyone "dark . . . and foreign-looking."[73] The story, which famously begins with the enigmatic line "I stand here ironing, and what you asked me moves tormented back and forth with the iron," recounts to an unspecified visitor the difficult circumstances of the narrator's nineteen-year-old daughter, Emily (*ISHI*, 9). While the foreboding tone of the opening pages sets up the reader to imagine Emily has died, the ending discloses a far more mundane tragedy. Emily is flunking out of school, worn down by years of discrimination by "a world where the prestige went to blondeness and curly hair and dimples" (a reference to child celebrity Shirley Temple), while her gift for stand-up comedy is destined to remain unfulfilled: as "a child of her age, of depression, of war, of fear," it is inevitable that "all that is in her will not bloom" (*ISHI*, 20). The iron stands for the socioeconomic circumstances that first deprived Emily of parental care and affection, as her mother left her to go work (it is implied, in other people's homes), while the act of ironing is framed as both the only space in which the narrator can smooth the creases of experience into a coherent narrative and fundamentally imprisoning. Indeed, Emily's quip, "'Whistler painted his mother in a rocker. I'd have to paint mine standing over an ironing board,'" positions the iron and board as physical barriers emblematic of the limiting of working-class women's opportunities in mid-century America (*ISHI*, 19). The narrator's closing assertion, that Emily is "more than this dress on the ironing board, helpless before the iron," paradoxically confirms the young woman's likely relegation to the position of a servant with less power than the electric gadget she wields (*ISHI*, 21).

That the "good life" that appliance ads framed as a universal right brought about by victory was in fact only available to white Americans is also expressed in the white enamel stove that taunts the speaker of Langston Hughes's poem, "Deferred," first published in *Montage of a Dream Deferred*

[73] Tillie Olsen, "I Stand Here Ironing" (1953–1954), in *Tell Me a Riddle* (New York: Dell Publishing, 1976 [1961]), 9–21. Henceforth, *ISHI*.

(1951).[74] The tempered hope of the poem's first lines, "Maybe now I can have that white enamel stove / I dreamed about when we first fell in love / eighteen years ago," slips back into despondency, as the speaker lists with economical precision the obstacles to the dream's fulfillment—"rooming and everything / then kids / cold-water flat and all that" (413. viii–x; xii–xiv). "Cold-water flats" were properties that until the early 1960s lacked a water heating apparatus, shower, or central heating. "Cold-water flat and all that" thus reads as a counter-slogan to "all-electric" living, "white picket fence," "two-car garage," and the many other expressions that in the first two decades after the war expressed the supposed accessibility of middle-class comforts to all. The stanza's second half, which describes the departure of the speaker's now-adult children and the speaker's imminent move to a different apartment, points to a bittersweet future. The joy of finally purchasing a white enamel stove is undermined by its belatedness—after all, postwar advertisers posited the "all-electric" home as a *starting* point for young families to raise their children, not something for their old age (413. xviii–xx). The speaker might thus justifiably follow the exclamation "Maybe I can buy that white enamel stove!" with the last lines of "Tell Me," an earlier poem in the same collection: "Why should it be *my* dream / deferred / overlong" (396. iii–v).

Beyond questions of accessibility, the myth of the "good life" relied on the comprehensibility of the electrical comforts it promised (hence the didactic tone of appliance manuals well into the 1960s, which took it upon themselves to explain the benefits of the "all-electric" kitchen, and to quantify the time saved by its different machines). The inscrutability of time-saving appliances for many first-generation immigrants is comically exposed in Maxine Hong Kingston's depiction of first-generation Chinese immigrants in *The Woman Warrior: A Girlhood Among Ghosts* (1975), a text credited with conveying the translations the immigrant self must perform "between the dominant tradition and her marginalized mode of meaning making and vice versa."[75] Kingston's time-saving appliances reveal the United States to be a machine that consumes young and able-bodied immigrants and transforms them into its own image (as exemplified by those working in the Chinese laundry industry that exploded between the 1870s and the 1930s),

[74] Langston Hughes, "Deferred," in *Montage of a Dream Deferred* (1951), in *The Collected Poems of Langston Hughes*, ed. Arnold Rampersad and David Roessel (New York: Vintage, 1995), 413–14. Henceforth, *D*.

[75] Maxine Hong Kingston, *The Woman Warrior* (New York: Vintage, 1977 [1975]). Henceforth, *WW*; Kristin L. Matthews, "Confronting Difference, Confronting Difficulty: Culture Wars, Canon Wars, and Maxine Hong Kingston's *The Woman Warrior* (U of Massachusetts Press, 2016), 132.

while spitting out the elderly and infirm.[76] The narrator's recently arrived elderly aunt's inability to comprehend, let alone assimilate into, US culture is conveyed via her misapprehension of both the washing machines in the family laundry business and the time-saving appliances in the family home. This is most vividly expressed in the aunt's efforts to decipher American life by narrating out loud to herself, in Chinese, her niece's operation of an electric eggbeater: "'Now she is taking a machine off the shelf. She attaches two metal spiders to it. She plugs in the cord. She cracks an egg against the rim . . . She presses a button, and the spiders spin the eggs'" (*WW*, 162). Her nieces and nephews must translate her words and activities into English to their spouses, who do not speak Chinese: "'Now she's saying . . . I'm attaching two metal spiders to it [and] the spiders are spinning with legs intertwined and beating the eggs electrically. . . . She's driving me nuts!' the children told each other in English" (*WW*, 164). The repetition of the image of metal spiders spinning eggs from these two very different perspectives humorously conveys the disconnect between first- and second-generation immigrants—not to mention the limits of language in the face of the new—while foreshadowing the aunt's descent into madness upon discovering her husband, who moved to the United States decades prior, has taken a second wife. The woman who hasn't the vocabulary to describe the mechanics of the domestic setting into which she has been thrust, let alone the capacity to understand the "all-electric" home's symbology in mid-century America, is no match for her husband's younger, assimilated Chinese immigrant wife, who performs American femininity as if it were second nature.

All of the postwar appliance depictions just discussed are also, and especially, critiques of the military-industrial complex and early Cold War propaganda, each of which narrowed the gap between the electric appurtenances of the home and the weapons of war. Many of the appliance manufacturers who contributed to the war effort continued supplying the US government with defense aircraft and missiles after the war's end—and they aggressively promoted their defense systems alongside their appliances in order to counteract Dwight Eisenhower's efforts to cut the government's military budget (Hine, 128). It is thus no coincidence, then, that the shape of some appliance models, such the Electrolux Model LXI and the 1955 model of the Sunbeam Mixmaster, actually resembled a missile, or that GE overtly advertised its experience producing "electrically-warm equipment for Army fliers" to promote its "improved" Automatic Blankets.[77] In 1961, in his Farewell Address to the Nation, Eisenhower warned the public of the "grave

[76] According to Renqui Yu, there were 7,000 to 8,000 Chinese laundry workers in New York City alone by 1930 (*To Save China, To Save Ourselves; The Chinese Hand Laundry Alliance of New York* (Philadelphia, PA: Temple UP, 1992), 8–9).

[77] Gantz, *The Vacuum Cleaner*, 127; Sunbeam Mixmaster Mixer, ca. 1955; USA; chrome-plated metal, molded glass, molded plastic; H x W x D: 32 x 25 x 34 cm (12 5/8 x 9 13/16 x 13 3/8

implications" of the "conjunction of an immense military establishment and a large arms industry" whose "total influence—economic, political, even spiritual—is felt in every city, every statehouse, every office of the federal government" and called for caution "against the acquisition of unwarranted influence, whether sought or unsought, by the military-industrial complex."[78] Echoes of this concern are apparent in the appliance depictions in Cheever (discussed in Chapter 2), Piercy (Chapter 3), postwar sci-fi (Chapter 5), Vonnegut and DeLillo (Chapter 6), and Wojnarowicz and Sycamore (Chapter 7).

Apart from these direct connections between the manufacturing of domestic goods and military weaponry, the Cold War era saw time-saving appliances enlisted in the promotion of American capitalism's superiority over communism. Indeed, the Nixon-Khruschev "Kitchen Debate" that took place in a GE "all-electric" kitchen at the American National Exhibition in Moscow in 1959 was but the most explicit of a decade-long effort to equate appliance ownership with American values. It also exemplifies what Greg Castillo has termed, after Joseph Nye, the "soft power" of mid-century design, which manufacturers cultivated via corporate-sponsored exhibitions, workshops, and other public events (Figure I.6).[79] Such an approach was typified by GE's marketing efforts between 1954 and 1966, which included the sponsorship from 1954 to 1962 of *General Electric Theater*, a television show on CBS hosted by then-actor Ronald Reagan. The show, which sought to promote "Total Electric" living as a way of life, exemplified what Lizabeth Cohen has described as the convergence of political and economic interests in the postwar era, whereby consumption was framed as a performance of patriotism, and the availability of goods a form of democracy.[80] Together with "You Live Better Electrically," a nationwide campaign GE, Westinghouse, and Edison cosponsored from 1958 to 1966 to offset the declining price of electricity by encouraging consumers to purchase more gadgets, *General Electric Theater* was also paradigmatic of what McCarthy has termed the values of the postwar "citizen machine," whereby the television network and corporate sponsor "instructed" the public in the social benefits of corporate science, consumerism, and free-market economics (Wuebben, 140; McCarthy, 8–9; 12). Crucially, these methods served as ideological weapons against the perceived threat of communism.

in.); Cooper Hewitt, Smithsonian Design Museum; 1993-150-1-a/h; GE, "How Wonderful . . . This Automatic Sleeping Comfort!" *LIFE* (September 2, 1946): 25.

[78] "President Dwight Eisenhower Farewell Address" in James Ledbetter, *Unwarranted Influence: Dwight D. Eisenhower and the Military Industrial Complex* (Ann Arbor, Michigan: Sheridan, 2011), 211–10; citation on 216.

[79] Greg Castillo, *Cold War on the Home Front* (Minneapolis, MN: U of Minnesota Press, 2010), vii–ix.

[80] Bird, 205; Lizabeth Cohen, *A Consumer's Republic*, 9.

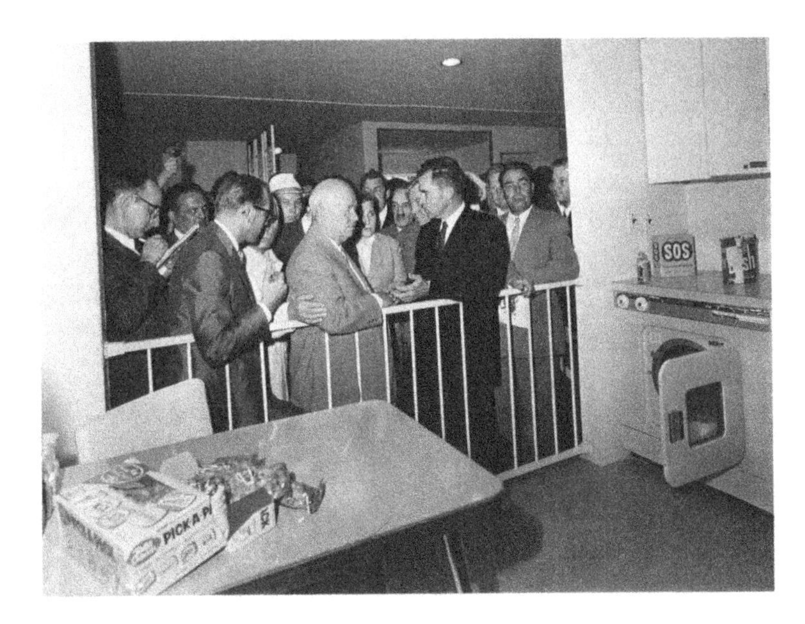

FIGURE I.6 "US Vice President Richard Nixon, Soviet Premier Nikita Khruschev Attending American Exhibition Resulting in 'Kitchen Debate.'" Moscow, USSR, 1959. (Photo by: Universal History Archive/Universal Images Group via Getty Images) © Getty Images.

To cook and clean with time-saving appliances was to demonstrate one's allegiance to the American way of life, and to participate in the fight against communist corruption—a message that Nixon's words during the Kitchen Debate merely rendered explicit. A 1953 ad by Westinghouse, for example, portrayed its new appliance range as "stars" in the "Westinghouse Freedom Fair"—a "show" attended by celebrities including Ronald Reagan, Betty Furness, and Edward G. Robinson. The slogan, "See these new appliances that will make Freedom Ring in your home," and the figures of celebrities fawning over refrigerators and washing machines, reinforced the connection between freedom from drudgery, the principles of American democracy, and corporate-sponsored status-climbing (Figure I.7).

This rhetoric is parodied in Raymond Carver's short story, "Popular Mechanics" (1978), whose title references the popular science magazine founded in 1902 to make science accessible to mainstream (primarily white male) audiences.[81] In Carver's story, a husband and wife in the midst of an acrimonious separation fight across the kitchen stove over who gets to keep

[81] Wayne Whittaker, "The Story of Popular Mechanics," *Popular Mechanics Golden Anniversary Issue* (January 1952): 127–32; 366–82. Citation on 382.

FIGURE I.7 Westinghouse. "Join America's Top Stars; Visit your Dealer's Big 1953 Westinghouse Freedom Fair!" *LIFE* (April 27, 1953): 155. ©Westinghouse. Reproduced with permission.

the baby, each pulling at the screaming infant's limbs—until, the ambiguous ending implies, the child is torn apart.[82] In this reimagining of the Judgment of Solomon, Carver turns the epicenter of the mid-century home into a site of violence, and the nuclear family into a producer of death. Where in the Judgment of Solomon the true mother is revealed when she relinquishes possession of the child rather than see him die, Carver's story suggests the extent to which parental love might be overridden by the animosity bred by heterosexual marriage in a culture of stultifying conformity. Reflecting the techno-utopianism of the Cold War media landscape, *Popular Mechanics* promised to render the world knowable, and as safe as one's kitchen. By contrast, Carver reveals the institution of marriage so celebrated by mid-century America to be the source of a violent, irascible instability that defies understanding. The child torn limb from limb over the kitchen stove suggests the limitations of the scientific method—and provides a counternarrative to the "story of the American way of life" that *Popular Mechanics* claimed to tell (Whittaker, 382). Meanwhile, the stove's apparent complicity in the

[82] Raymond Carver, "Popular Mechanics" (1978) in *What We Talk About When We Talk About Love* (London: Vintage, 2003 [1981]).

child's death serves to ridicule the decades-long positioning of appliances as "weapons" against communism.

Norman Mailer draws a similar comparison in *Why Are We in Vietnam?* (1967), where time-saving appliances are positioned as coconspirators in the "Electrox [*sic*] Edison world, all programmed out" that brought about the Vietnam War.[83] The novel's narrating protagonist introduces himself as the authority to "sell America its new handbook on how to live" in that world—thus positioning the American way of life itself as an appliance, its violent imperialist direction pre-programmed (*WAWIV*, 10). This portrayal echoed Mailer's quip in a 1961 interview that "Marx's proletariat has disappeared—they went when the refrigerator arrived," which described what he viewed to be consumer culture's supplanting of working-class solidarity with individualism.[84]

Arthur Miller, Raymond Carver, and Norman Mailer's appliance depictions also fit into a broader tradition strongly represented by the texts examined in the first two chapters of this study. Where Walt Whitman's homoerotic tribute to electricity in "I Sing the Body Electric" depicted electrification as a masculine source of untapped power, time-saving appliances in the postwar press, and in fiction by postwar white male writers, served as a lightning rod for anxieties about the emasculating effects of suburban living and corporate culture on white middle-class men. Some of these were comical, like *LIFE* magazine's comic strip-style story about "The New American Domesticated Male" (1954), which featured sketches of a new generation of white middle-class men who had married early, and whose alleged domestication was predicted to result in the further mechanization of the home, since "Cooking in an outmoded kitchen . . . riles the efficiency expert that every man imagines he is."[85] But the majority were entirely serious. Thus interventions such as Sloan Wilson's novel, *The Man in the Gray Flannel Suit* (1955), William M. Whyte's critique of corporate management, *The Organization Man* (1956), and Winston White's *Beyond Conformity* (1961), framed a consumer culture embodied in the "all-electric" home as a trap for the (white middle-class) American male who had "bec[ome] a yes-man to both wife and family" while, as Kenneth Paradis notes, eliding "that working-class males, people of color, and women had never had the luxury of a pretension to [the] self-reliance" these critics mourned.[86]

---

[83] Norman Mailer, *Why Are We in Vietnam?* (New York: Random House, 2017 [1967]), 10. Henceforth, *WAWIV*.

[84] Eve Auchincloss and Nancy Lynch, "An Interview with Norman Mailer," in *Conversations with Norman Mailer*, ed. J. Michael Lennon (Jackson, MI: UP of Mississippi, 1988), 39–51. Citation on 44.

[85] "The New Domesticated American Male," *LIFE* (January 4, 1954): 42–5. Citation on 44.

[86] Sloan Wilson, *The Man in the Gray Flannel Suit* (New York: Avalon, 1955); William M. Whyte, *The Organization Man* (New York: Simon and Schuster, 1956); Winston White, *Beyond*

The influence of this idea of postwar emasculation cannot be overstated—and it is palpable across mid-century popular culture, such as in the many scenes in early postwar television sitcoms in which husbands fall under, fail to fix, or struggle to afford to replace, the family refrigerator. Where Paul Gansky interprets these refrigerator slapsticks as allegories for mid-century white male anxieties about automation, I read them as allegorizing anxieties about female emancipation.[87] In *I Love Lucy* (1951–7), *Leave It to Beaver* (1957–63), *The Donna Reed Show* (1958–66), and *The Dick Van Dyke Show* (1961–6), Lucy Ricardo, Donna Reed, June Cleaver, and Laura Petrie's comparative dexterity with their time-saving appliances subtly suggests their husbands' obsolescence, while the refrigerator bearing the brunt of the "domesticated American male's" anger is more often than not a surrogate for his wife. The appliance depictions in postwar fiction by white male writers exacerbate these tensions, laying bare what the sitcom's slapstick humor deflected. Time-saving appliances in these texts serve to portray the institutions of both work and marriage as reifying men—a formula that is even apparent in *Death of a Salesman*, albeit in a more attenuated fashion.

These motifs are apparent in another story by Carver, "Preservation" (1983), in which a woman called Sandy returns from work one evening to find that everything in the freezer compartment has thawed. Her unemployed, unnamed husband briefly interrupts his reading of an article about a "peat bog man," discovered by archaeologists 2,000 years after his death, to diagnose the malfunction as resulting from a Freon leak. The story ends as Sandy attempts to cook all the food items from the freezer to prevent their spoiling, only to look up and see her husband standing in a pool of thawed ice that renders his feet eerily similar to the "shriveled" appendages of the "peat bog" man. Carver positions the unemployed, nameless husband as a malfunctioning, and indeed obsolete, appliance akin to the refrigerator he cannot afford to replace. Sandy's focus on his feet in the pool of refrigerator water both links him to the extinct man and accentuates his resemblance to the leaking refrigerator, providing a visual metaphor for his loss of power.

Similar themes are apparent in John Updike's novel, *Rabbit, Run* (1960). Here, "MagiPeel" appliance salesman Harry "Rabbit" Angstrom leaves his alcoholic wife Janice after she fails to understand the jokes he makes at her expense, which are "based on the 'image'" of the "modern housewife" that "the MagiPeel people tried to have their salesman sell to."[88] When Janice falls pregnant with their second child, Rabbit returns home and, upon discovering a renewed appreciation for both selling time-saving appliances

Conformity (Glencoe, IL: Free Press of Glencoe, 1961), 19; Kenneth Paradis, *Sex, Paranoia, and Modern Masculinity* (Albany: State U of New York Press, 2007), 198.

[87] Paul Gansky, "Refrigerator Design and Masculinity in Postwar Media, 1946–1960," *Studies in Popular Culture* 34.1 (Fall 2011): 67–85.

[88] John Updike, *Rabbit, Run* (New York: Penguin, 2006 [1960]), 12–13. Henceforth, *RR*.

and running the Electrolux, concludes his "instinctive taste for the small appliances of civilization" makes him ideally suited to his sales job (*RR*, 188). That perhaps Rabbit enjoys vacuuming because he doesn't have to do it every day, or that what he perceives to be his "gift for housekeeping" is a skill no better than his wife's, goes unmentioned (*RR*, 188). Like the "MagiPeel" and the suburban home Rabbit longs to escape, Updike's housewife is but a plot device in the story of the unsatisfied man, embodying postwar US culture's perceived limiting of white middle-class male potential.

6. Beyond White Male Ennui: Time-Saving Appliances, Gender, Race, and Class

One could write an entire book on the time-saving appliance's embodiment of the crisis of masculinity in the work of the male postwar writers just discussed—but this is not the book I wish to write. Thus, my first two chapters engage with white male writers whose work productively complicates the narrative of appliance-as-site-of-emasculation. Chapter 1 examines the depiction of refrigerators and domestic electrification in Jack Kerouac's writing between 1950 and the mid-1960s alongside a selection of appliance representations by his fellow Beats. I argue that the time-saving appliances in these texts embody three contradictory ideas: a conformist consumer culture that Kerouac conflates with the feminine, a desire for the very domesticity he claims to reject, and the starting point for a revolutionary aesthetic premised on a vocabulary of domestic electrification and domestic gadgetry divested of their associations with private interests, heteronormativity, or the military-industrial complex. Chapter 2 turns to the novels and short stories of John Cheever (a man who famously feared and mistrusted all electrical appliances), and Richard Yates (the son of an alcoholic regional sales representative for GE). Here I focus on the ways in which their realist narratives dismantle the idealized depictions of appliances in postwar radio, magazine ads, and television sitcoms, the majority of which were sponsored by the very same appliance brands that appeared in said sitcoms' storylines. The chapter also attends to Cheever and Yates's exposure of the violence underpinning the ideal of the "all-electric" home in the Cold War era, and the ramifications of allegorizing appliances as "weapons" in ideological warfare.

"All-Electric" Narratives' subsequent chapters attend to time-saving appliances' portrayal in writing by Black women and men and white women via an "interlocking" or "intersectional" lens—an approach that originated in the Combahee River Collective's call, in 1974, for "integrated analysis and practice" to "combat the manifold and simultaneous oppressions that all women of color face," and that gained wider recognition in the

late 1980s thanks to Kimberlé Crenshaw's work on the multidimensional discriminations faced by Black women within the legal system.[89] My discussions are likewise informed by bell hooks's now-canonical analysis of the historical exclusion of Black women from a white-dominated feminist tradition, *Ain't I a Woman? Black Women and Feminism* (1981).[90]

Chapter 3 examines time-saving appliances and the vocabulary of electricity in the early work (1969–89) of Jewish socialist feminist poet, novelist, and activist Marge Piercy, where they serve to interrogate gender and class violence and the co-option of American Jews by the capitalist project, and to imagine alternative modes of being. I read these depictions in relation to time-saving appliances' role in the work of second-wave feminist activists and novelists. For the narrator of Marilyn French's popular feminist classic, *The Women's Room* (1977), one might "sneer at" the 1950s' view of "the good life" as "made up . . . of frost-free refrigerators . . . and a clothes dryer," but "without them, and without the pill, there would be no woman's movement."[91] According to this perspective, which formed a central tenet of Betty Friedan's argument in *The Feminist Mystique* (1963), technologies that made housework less onerous (even as they increased standards of cleanliness) and that allowed women to decide how many children they had (and when) freed up time and energy to think about life beyond the home.[92] Panicked by feminism's potential to steal their customers, appliance manufacturers in the late 1960s launched ads that co-opted the movement's concerns, posing their products as remedies for women's frustrations, or positing themselves as protecting families from the tumultuous changes brought on by the counterculture as a whole, which threatened to shake the social foundations upon which their products' value was premised. Thus an ad for Frigidaire's appliance range in 1967 featured a housewife flexing a tattooed bicep and the provocation, "Is your wife getting muscles where she used to have curves?"[93] Requiring negligible physical effort to operate, Frigidaire appliances promised to redress what the brand suggested were Second-Wave Feminism's negative consequences.

---

[89] Combahee River Collective, "A Black Feminist Statement," in *The Second Wave: A Reader in Feminist Theory*, ed. Linda Nicholson (New York: Routledge), 63–70; Kimberlé Crenshaw, "Demarginalising the Intersection of Race and Sex," *University of Chicago Legal Forum* (1989), Iss. 1, Article 8, and "Mapping the Margins: Intersectionality, Identity Politics, and Violence against Women of Color," *Stanford Law Review* 43.6 (July 1991): 1241–99, citation on 1242.

[90] bell hooks, *Ain't I a Woman? Black Women and Feminism* (New York and London: Routledge, 2015), 146.

[91] Marilyn French, *The Women's Room* (London: Virago, 2004 [1977]), 75. Henceforth, *WR*.

[92] Betty Friedan, *The Feminine Mystique* (New York: Dell, 1974 [1963]).

[93] Frigidaire, "Is Your Wife Getting Muscles Where She Used to Have Curves?" *LIFE* (November 10, 1967): 3. Electrolux (which bought Frigidaire and Kelvinator in 1986) denied permission to reproduce this ad, but it can be found online via the *LIFE* magazine archive.

Piercy's depictions of time-saving appliances expose the fallacy of these messages and the "all-electric" home as an embodiment of gender and class oppression. Her sustained use of the vocabulary of electricity to imagine alternative forms of "power" to that derived from the monopolization of resources and inculcation of the masses to desire ever-more sophisticated gadgetry suggests the merits of reading her work as producing a *poetics* of electricity and of time-saving appliances specifically. In making these claims, I come close to interpreting Piercy's work as an example of what Donna Haraway, in "A Cyborg Manifesto" (1985), imagines as a "cyborg world" that while shaped by "the final imposition of a grid of control on the planet . . . in the name of defense," and "the final appropriation of women's bodies in a masculinist orgy of war," also allows "lived social and bodily realities in which people are not afraid of their joint kinship with animals and machines."[94] But, as I explain throughout this study, attending to the time-saving appliance in literature requires us to resist post-humanist discourse, and remain attentive to the material conditions and human stories that generated these objects in the first place.

Chapter 4 addresses the racial dimension of time-saving appliances in a selection of works by Black writers including Ralph Ellison, Toni Morrison, Alice Walker, James Baldwin, Alice Childress, and Paule Marshall, where domestic electrification and specific time-saving appliances are enlisted to interrogate the whiteness of the "good life" and to expose particular forms of racial and class violence. These include not only Black Americans' delayed access to time-saving appliances and appliance advertising rhetoric's long-standing reinforcement of the status of Black people as commodities, but the racist rhetoric and imagery used to promote appliances to Black consumers well into the 1960s. For example, Frigidaire's first ad to feature a Black model, which appeared in the June 1961 issue of *EBONY*, showed a (light-skinned) Black woman cleaning her "Pull 'n Clean Oven" juxtaposed with a call-out image of the same woman wearing a handkerchief-turban on her head and scrubbing a different oven's interior.[95] The ad thus posited the Frigidaire oven as the purveyor of freedom from both the drudgery of cleaning one's oven and a history of domestic servitude. A similar tone-deafness is apparent in "Today's Toasters Put their Best Face Forward," an ad Toastmaster ran exclusively in *EBONY* in 1962, and whose celebration of the brand's new toaster design featuring "Controls 'up front,' where they rightfully belong," gestured to the achievements of the 1955–6 Montgomery bus boycott

---

[94] Donna Haraway, "A Cyborg Manifesto: Science, Technology, and Socialist-Feminism in the Late Twentieth Century" (1985), in *Simians, Cyborgs, and Women* (New York: Routledge, 1991), 149–82.

[95] Frigidaire, "Only Frigidaire Offers the New 1961 Ranges with the PULL 'N CLEAN OVEN!" *EBONY* (February 1961): 24. The ad can be found online via the *EBONY* magazine archive, and on my website, https://www.racheledini.com.

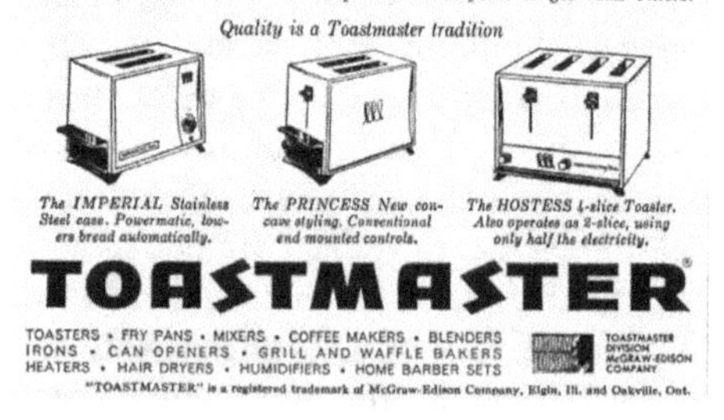

FIGURE I.8 Toastmaster. "Today's Toasters Put their Best Face Forward." *EBONY* (November 1962): 62.

(Figure I.8). The texts examined in Chapter 4 portray the attainment of appliances as both small consolation for centuries of oppression and symbols of Black Americans' long-standing reification. The racist ads I recover in this chapter and in Chapter 6, which have gone almost unremarked upon by advertising historians, also provide a fuller account of the history of time-saving appliances, and a corrective to its sanitized account in recent popular histories of advertising.[96] The reader will notice that only one of these ads is reproduced here: the manufacturers' denial of permissions perhaps explains these ads' absence from other illustrated histories of advertising, and also confirms, to my mind, the urgency of their recovery.

Chapter 5 examines speculative science fiction writers' engagement, between 1950 and the late 1970s, with what I call the "science fictionality" of time-saving appliances and domestic automation more broadly. The texts in this chapter represent a broader tendency in postwar sci-fi, wherein magical domestic gadgets parody postwar appliance manufacturers' and advertisers' own deployment of science fictional motifs to sell their products in futuristic terms. In many of these texts, appliances do not so much save time as facilitate time travel and housewives' escape from the home into other universes and temporal dimensions. In so doing, they reveal the preposterousness of appliance ads' promises of liberation. The minutiae of time saved by a machine is exposed as trivial in the face of the temporal possibilities opened up by science- fictional worlds. Authors examined in this chapter include Judith Merril, Ray Bradbury, Margaret St. Clair, James Tiptree Jr. (the pseudonym used by Alice Sheldon), Eleanor Arnason, Kit Reed, Philip K. Dick, Robert A. Heinlein, Ira Levin, and Joanna Russ. While acknowledging the differences in the ideological impetus behind these different texts' appliance depictions, I identify the points of connection between them, and, specifically, their authors' identification of the importance of domestic technology in any vision of the future where the concept of "home" still exists.

Chapter 6 moves from alternative-world scenarios to the realm of historiographic parody to examine the time-saving appliance's role in fiction that debunks official accounts of the United States' recent past, thus returning us to the events discussed in the first sections of this introduction. The chapter's first half focuses on Kurt Vonnegut's caricatures of time-saving appliances in his parodic accounts of slavery, the Second World War, and the New York World's Fair of 1964, in a selection of texts published between 1950 and 1990. These appliance depictions counter the rhetoric of GE's public relations arm (where Vonnegut himself worked as a copywriter from 1948 to 1950/51), repurposing the dialog, imagery, and comic devices of television (for which he himself wrote) to draw out the connections between the "all-electric" home and technology's more harrowing uses. The manufacturers' denial of permissions to reproduce the racist appliance

---

[96] The absence of any acknowledgment of the racialized history of time-saving appliances and the "all-electric" home more broadly is especially glaring in these otherwise excellent advertising and design histories: Sarah Archer's *The Mid-Century Kitchen*, and Carroll Ganțz's *Refrigeration* and *The Vacuum Cleaner*. Todd Coppee's *The Easy-Bake Oven* exemplifies the acritical quality of mainstream design histories whose structure and contents appear gauged to appeal to the nostalgic impulses of their readership.

ads that influenced Vonnegut's famous depiction of the "Robo-Magic Corporation of America's" mystifications of the past in *Breakfast of Champions* (1973) ironically confirms the fact that they warrant scrutiny. The second half of the chapter extends these ideas to examine the "all-electric" home in Don DeLillo's retrospective accounts of the 1950s, and in his explorations of neoliberal ideology, in his earliest short story, and a selection of texts published between 1971 and the end of the millennium.

The final chapter of *"All-Electric" Narratives* turns to the representation of time-saving appliances in a selection of turn-of-millennial and postmillennial US texts including A. M. Homes's *Music for Torching* (1999), Charles H. Johnson's "Dr. King's Refrigerator" (2005), Catherynne M. Valente's *The Refrigerator Monologues* (2017), Lucy Ellmann's *Ducks, Newburyport* (2019), and Mattilda Bernstein Sycamore's *The Freezer Door* (2020). These texts critique what I call the cult of the mid-century appliance that, I argue, has gained pace since the 1990s at the same time as appliance manufacturers have ventured into the futuristic realm of smart technology. The appliance depictions in these texts challenge the mythos of the "all-electric" home perpetuated by "retro" appliances and the postmillennial nostalgia apparent in the proliferation of mid-century period television dramas and films of the last thirty years. These texts also ironize the ways in which objects originally promoted as "time-saving" are, increasingly, celebrated as historical artifacts, collectables, icons, or portals into an idyllic past that bears no relation to the lived experience of people who actually lived through it.

* * *

In focusing on the relationship between certain of my chosen texts' appliance depictions and free-market ideology, I draw on the work of scholars whose accounts of corporations' influence on twentieth-century US culture, and of the relationship between corporate lobbying efforts, government policy, and cultural production, complicate sequential understandings of neoliberalism as following on from Keynesianism. In particular, I draw on Stephen Shapiro and Liam Kennedy's recent contention that "the cluster of macroeconomic ideas captured within the term Keynesianism" (including state regulation of businesses and high government spending in public services) "and the ones under the term neoliberalism" (namely, market deregulation, and privatization of public services) were "contemporaneous, and often interdependent" responses to the Great Depression, the rise of fascism in Europe, and the military aggression of Hirohito's Japan.[97] As well as highlighting the ways in which "American-led 'liberalism' after 1946 *depended* on the success of

[97] Liam Kennedy and Stephen Shapiro, "Introduction," in *Neoliberalism and Contemporary American Literature,* ed. Liam Kennedy and Stephen Shapiro (Hanover, NH: Dartmouth College Press, 2019), 6.

German neoliberalism, as the German abandonment of nationalist protections was the necessary feature on which the post-war American export economy depended," Kennedy and Shapiro note that "neoliberal influence was already key to shaping the [US] environment far before the 1970s" (8–10, emphasis in the original). This account chimes with those of Anna McCarthy, Roland Marchand, Michael L. Smith, William L. Bird, and Charles F. McGovern, whose work shows the prominent role of free-market rhetoric in both internal campaigns designed to foster employee loyalty and public campaigns in the periods 1920–9 and 1945–60, and on which I also draw heavily. It likewise helps to explain the presence of ideas and themes more usually associated with neoliberal ideology—the primacy of the market; individualism; speculative time-keeping—in those texts I examine published in the 1950s and 1960s.

The fact that so many of the writers I examine were related to, or friendly with, employees of the country's leading appliance manufacturers in turn reflects the high proportion of *Americans* employed by these companies between the end of the Second World War and the early 1970s, when manufacturing began moving overseas.[98] In other words, these authors are not selected, but, rather, representative—their direct connections to the manufacturers whose objects they describe bespeaks the ways in which appliance manufacturing, and the electrical utilities industry, knitted themselves into the lives of so many Americans in this period. Meanwhile, my chosen authors' more skeptical attitudes toward appliance manufacturers' promise of the "good life" is at least partly explained by these same brands' infamous record of strike-breaking and wage suppression.[99]

It remains for me to add a caveat. This study does not claim to be an exhaustive account of the time-saving appliance in US literature, or even in US literature after 1945—but, rather, to demonstrate the merits of studying this underexamined subject in the first place. As such, large gaps remain, and I am especially aware that overall, *"All-Electric" Narratives* gives greater space to the discussion of texts by white writers than writers of color, and by native-born Americans rather than immigrants (although it bears mentioning that Kerouac, Piercy, Marshall, and DeLillo were second-generation immigrants, and that this, as I suggest in the individual chapters, very much shapes their appliance depictions). Likewise, only one of the texts I examine depicts trans

[98] Between 1899 and 1950, the number of employees in the electrical machinery industry grew by 1,568 percent, from 48,491 to 765,613; the number of production workers grew by 1,309 percent, from 43,280 to 609,819. See Ronald W. Schatz, *The Electrical Workers: A History of Labor at General Electric and Westinghouse, 1923–1960* (Chicago: U of Illinois Press, 1987), 29.

[99] See in particular the Westinghouse strike of 1955–56: Schatz, 242, ff. 31; Ronald L. Filippelli and Mark D. McColloch, *Cold War in the Working Class: The Rise and Decline of the United Electrical Workers* (New York, NY: State U of New York Press, 1995), 161–6.

or non-binary characters.[100] This skew is not intended to reinforce particular notions of canonicity or literary value but rather reflects the overwhelmingly greater presence of time-saving appliances in literature by and about white cis-gendered people. As I note in the individual chapters, such predominance suggests, if not the "all-electric" home's greater hold on white demographics and cis-gendered people than minorities, then certainly its *equation* with whiteness and gender normativity. And, specifically, with a whiteness and gender normativity presented as classless and nondenominational but in fact bearing all the characteristics of middle-class WASP-ness. What's more, several of the texts I examine suggest that the "all-electric" home's symbolic charge as an embodiment of white middle-class respectability was most keenly felt by the white upper-working class (for whom appliance ownership signaled the attainment of a higher social status), and by the white middle class (for whom such objects symbolized the suffocating constraints of bourgeois life). As Catherine Jurca and others have shown, this impression was highly inaccurate, and contributed to the greater disenfranchisement of minorities.[101] Its influence, however, is palpable not only in the sheer proliferation of domestic gadgets in writing by and about white people published between the mid-1940s and the end of the twentieth century but in the ubiquity of these objects in retrospective accounts of mid-century white alienation, boredom, and entrapment across postmillennial fiction, television, and film—a point to which I return in Chapter 7.

My hope, then, is that *"All-Electric" Narratives* is but a first installment in literary appliance studies that will expand the critical discussion of the representation of time-saving appliances beyond the field of art history—the one area where what August Jordan Davis has termed the "woman-as-appliance" motif has been explored at great length—and that other scholars will take up where I have left off to examine how the "all-electric" home is enlisted to crystallize the specificities of immigrant or indigenous

[100] Apart from Mattilda Bernstein Sycamore's memoir, *The Freezer Door,* discussed in Chapter 6, the text that comes closest to engaging with trans identities is Joanna Russ's *The Female Man,* where in one of the dystopias, cis-gendered women have been replaced by narcissistic feminized men who embody the worst aspects of femininity under patriarchy. While some have argued that this portrayal is transphobic, Russ clarified in interviews that these characters were not trans women, but embodiments of coerced femininity, and apologized for any offense caused. See Jeanne Cortiel, *Demand My Writing: Joanna Russ, Feminism, Science Fiction* (Liverpool UP, 1999), 212–14; Amanda Boulter, "Unnatural Acts: American Feminism and Joanna Russ's *The Female Man,*" *Women: A Cultural Review* (June 19, 2008): 151–66; "The Legendary Joanna Russ, Interviewed by Samuel R. Delany," 2007; and Stephen B, "Joanna Russ 1937–2011," *Bad Reputation* (May 10, 2011), badreputation.org.uk/2011/05/10/joanna-russ-1937-2011.

[101] Catherine Jurca, *White Diaspora: The Suburb and the Twentieth-Century American Novel* (Princeton UP, 2001); Christopher Kocela, *Fetishism and Its Discontents in post-1960 American Fiction* (New York: Palgrave Macmillan, 2010); Erin Mercer, *Repression and Realism in Post-War American Literature* (New York: Palgrave Macmillan, 2011).

experience(s).[102] There is likewise ample scope to examine the representation of time-saving appliances in children's literature, where appliances often serve an explicitly pedagogic function in the shaping of the young citizen (one thinks of Robert McCloskey's *Homer Price* [1943], Thomas M. Disch's *The Brave Little Toaster* [1980], and Beverly Cleary's *Ramona* series [1955–99]), in the detective and thriller genres, where the freezer is so frequently a repository for corpses, and in popular fiction in mid-century print magazines, where appliances often serve a didactic function akin to that of the print manuals and print and television ads of the period.

I hope, too, that future scholarship will explore time-saving appliances' role in popular music. I am thinking, in particular, of John Cage's compositions for household appliances, *Water Walk* (1959) and *Variation VII* (1966), Frank Zappa's vacuum cleaner monster in *Chunga's Revenge* (1970), the "all-electric" home in Joni Mitchell's "The Last Time I Saw Richard" (1971), and the representation of the members of the Cure on the cover of *Three Imaginary Boys* (1979) as a a lamp, a refrigerator, and a Hoover vacuum cleaner.[103] I am also thinking of Freddie Mercury's vacuuming in drag in the music video to "I Want to Break Free" (1984), the resentful cartoon appliance delivery men in Dire Straits' "Money for Nothing" (1985), and the ode to the washing machine in Kate Bush's "Mrs. Bartolozzi" (2005).[104] And, of course, there is scope to examine appliance writing beyond the United States. One thinks of the children named after the free appliances

---

[102] August Jordan Davis, "Reading the Strange Case of Woman-as-Appliance: On Transfigurations, Cyborgs, Domestic Labour and the Megamachine," *Trans-figurations: Transnational Perspectives on Domestic Spaces* 29 (2015): 356–76.

[103] John Cage, "Water Walk," *Lascia o Raddoppia*, RAI 1, Milan (February 5, 1959); John Cage, *Variations VII*, New York (October 15, 1966). The cover of Frank Zappa's *Chunga's Revenge* (Bizarre/Reprise, 1970) features a vacuum-cleaner monster sucking up a wild landscape; a dangling microphone and the hint of a music studio console reveal that the entire landscape is being recorded. In "The Last Time I Saw Richard" (*Blue*, Reprise, 1971), Joni Michell conveys how the titular Richard sold out via the lines "Richard got married to a figure skater / And he bought her a dishwasher and a coffee percolator / And he drinks at home now most nights with the TV on / And all the house lights left up bright." The dilapidated lamp, vacuum cleaner, and refrigerator on the cover of *Three Imaginary Boys* (Fiction Records, 1979) were intended to represent Robert Smith, Michael Dempsey, and Lol Tolhurst.

[104] The music video of "I Want to Break Free" (dir. David Mallett, 1984) famously featured the members of Queen dressed as the female cast members of British soap opera *Coronation Street* doing housework. In Dire Straits' "Money For Nothing" (*Brothers in Arms*, Vertigo, 1985), the speakers complain that "We gotta install microwave ovens / Custom kitchen deliveries / We gotta move these refrigerators / We gotta move these colour TVs," while the "faggot" singers on the TV "get [their] money for nothing get [their] chicks for free." The accompanying music video (dir. Steve Barron, 1985) culminates with a computer animated head turning on the turntable of one of the microwave ovens, as part of a broader critique of the "manufactured" nature of 1980s pop music. In Kate Bush's "Mrs. Bartolozzi" (*Aerial*, EMI, 2005), the description of the titular housewife's rapturous attention to the laundry swirling in her washing machine conveys the loss of her grip on reality.

their births entitled their parents to receive from the government in Christine Rochefort's parody of postwar French pro-natalism, *Lés Petits Enfants du Siécle* (1961); George Perec's foregrounding of electric gadgetry in his scathing critique of French imperialism in *Things: A Story of the Sixties* (1965) and vignettes of apartment life that make up *Life: A User's Manual* (1978); the recurring piles of broken appliances in J. G. Ballard's short stories and novels (1963–2006); and Fay Weldon's depiction, in *The Life and Loves of a She Devil* (1983), of a housewife who blows up her house by turning on all of her appliances at once.[105] The time-saving appliances in these texts highlight not only issues of class and gender but the tensions between postwar reconstruction, Americanization, and consumer culture's obscuration of labor exploitation, as well as the European Left's resistance to these. There is likewise an entire book to be written about the electric grid in contemporary world literature, and in the fiction of specific nations such as Nigeria (notably, the unreliable power supply that has resulted in parts of the country having uneven access to electricity, and has turned ownership of a generator into a "marker of middle class status," is vividly rendered in Chimamanda Ngozi Adichie's fiction).[106] It is my hope that others will go on to consider the imbrication of literary appliances in both the critique and affirmation of postwar imperialist narratives in world literature.

In very different ways, my chosen texts undermine and repurpose both the myth of "all-electric" living upon which entire industries throughout the so-called American Century were built, and the attendant myths with which they were entwined. They reveal the users of time-saving appliances to encompass a much broader demographic than the white middle-class housewives foregrounded in appliance advertisements up until the mid-1970s, and to use these objects in ways distinctly different to how they were advertised. They also reveal the surprising ways in which specific appliance advertising slogans and images were appropriated and repurposed into powerful critiques of heteronormativity, patriarchy, white supremacy, and capitalist consumerism. Finally, and most importantly, these texts challenge the merits of "time-saving" itself. They ask us to consider alternative modes of being that we would do well to heed.

[105] Christiane Rochefort, *Les Pétits Enfants du Siécle* (Paris: Éditions Bernard Grasset, 1961); Georges Perec, *Things: A Story of the Sixties with A Man Asleep*, transl. David Bellos (London: Vintage, 2011 [1965 and 1967]), 38; Georges Perec, *Life: A User's Manual*, transl. David Bellos (London: Vintage, 2008 [1978]), 458; Fay Weldon, *The Life and Loves of a She Devil* (London: Sceptre, 1988 [1983]), 64–7.

[106] John Campbell, "Electricity Distribution is Holding Nigeria Back," *Council on Foreign Relations* (3 July 2018); Anthony Osae-Brown and Ruth Olurounbi, "Nigeria Runs on Generators and Nine Hours of Power a Day," *Bloomberg* (23 September 2019). I am grateful to Katie Cornelius for her insights into the politics of electricity in Nigeria, and its representation in Ngozi Adichie.

1

"Everything in the Icebox":[1]

Domestic Energies in Jack Kerouac and Beat Culture, 1950–76

In his contribution to "The Beat Mystique," a three-part feature published in the February 1958 edition of *Playboy*, Herbert Gold enlisted the mechanical features and simultaneously clinical and diseased environment of the refrigerator to decry what he viewed to be the Beat movement's warped inauthenticity. The Beats, he claimed, were like a "sick refrigerator, laboring with tremendous violence, noise and heat, and all for one purpose—to keep cool."[2] Like electrically generated cold, the Beats' "coolness" was not innate but engineered, and as the product of a "sick" appliance (a diseased mind), it was also potentially dangerous. A few decades later, Edward Abbey would riff on this same analogy, remarking (rather meanly) that "Jack Kerouac, like a sick refrigerator, worked too hard at keeping cool and died on his mama's lap from alcohol and infantilism."[3] These figurations of the Beat as a frenetic refrigerator are curious considering the extent to which the public perceived Kerouac and his peers to reject consumer culture and its attendant associations with the so-called American way of life.[4] As Paul O'Neil pithily described the movement in the November 30, 1959, issue of *LIFE*, "The Beats stand against virtually every aspect of American society: Mom, Dad,

---

[1] Jack Kerouac, *On the Road: The Original Scroll* (London: Penguin, 2007), 211.
[2] Herbert Gold, "What It Is, Whence It Came," in "The Beat Mystique," *Playboy* (February 1958): 20–1.
[3] Edward Abbey, *A Voice Crying in the Wilderness Notes from a Secret Journal* (New York: St Martin's Press, 1989)
[4] Mark Scarborough, "Red Scares," *Beat Culture: Lifestyles, Icons, and Impact*, ed. William Lawlor (Santa Barbara, CA: ABC CLIO, 2005), 295–6.

FIGURE 1.1 Fred W. McDarrah. "Allen Ginsberg, 1969." © Getty Images.

Politics, Marriage, . . . to say nothing of the Automatic Dishwasher . . . and the clean, or peace-provoking, H-Bomb."[5] And yet perhaps Gold and Abbey were onto something. Because for a writer whose entire aesthetic was predicated on resisting the early Cold War era's idealization of white middle-class domesticity—and whose best-known works were, as a direct consequence, set largely in the great outdoors—Kerouac had a surprising amount to say about electricity and the domestic gadgets it powers, as well as about the maternal associations of the refrigerator in particular. Indeed, as we shall see in this chapter, the electric refrigerator for Kerouac is explicitly linked with his own mother. Meanwhile, his fellow Beats enlisted time-saving appliances in stunts that reaffirmed the writers' status as critics and outsiders, from the "large upright vacuum cleaner" Lucien Carr stole from backstage at the Metropolitan Opera House, to Fred W. McDarrah's poster portrait of Allen Ginsberg in 1960 in front of the poet's refrigerator, on which were taped pictures of Edgar Allen Poe and Charles Baudelaire.[6] This portrait,

[5] Paul O'Neil, "The Only Rebellion Around," *LIFE* (November 30, 1959): 114–30. Citation on page 115.

[6] Barry Miles, *William Burroughs: A Life* (London: Weidenfeld & Nicholson, 2014), 102; Sean Wilentz, "Fred W. McDarrah's Bohemian Chronicle," in *Fred W. McDarrah: New York Scenes*, ed. Sean Wilentz (New York: Abrams, 2018), 16; 59; Beat lore is likewise replete with stories about Cassady and Kerouac's thefts of toasters and vacuum cleaners, and Cassady's stint selling pressure

which became a symbol of the counterculture in its own right, also embodied the movement's imbrication with the culture it purported to critique: the refrigerator against which Ginsberg stood was as much a subject as the poet and his muses, while the hanging of pictures of great literary figures on such a mundane surface had a flattening effect, elevating the status of the appliance while lowering that of the writers (Figure 1.1).

In this chapter, I propose that the tension between the figurations of "Beat *as* appliance" and "Beat as *anti*-appliance" provides a useful framework for understanding the complex role of domestic gadgets in Kerouac's writing and Beat culture more broadly. While making reference to important depictions of time-saving appliances in Ginsberg, William Burroughs, Richard Brautigan, and Bob Rosenthal, I focus on Kerouac due to the greater frequency with which time-saving appliances feature in his work, and because, in contrast to theirs, Kerouac's depictions complicate binary readings that might reduce these objects to critiques of consumerism in all of its forms. My focus on work by male writers is likewise intentional. The simultaneous absence of time-saving appliances in the work of female writers such as Diane Di Prima, Carolyn Cassady, Joanne Kyger, and Joyce Johnson and ubiquity of these objects in the work of male writers who never had to use them is in itself significant. In attending to the appliance depictions in these texts—an area entirely overlooked by Beat scholarship, which has tended to focus on the movement's relationship to the road, the outdoor built environment, and the natural world—I challenge readings of Kerouac as fundamentally rejecting the domestic sphere and the domesticating effects of consumer culture.[7] Close attention to the refrigerator and other time-saving appliances in his work reveals them to be sites of great tension, through which Kerouac elaborates at once his antipathy to an anesthetizing postwar conformity, his attunement to the poetic possibilities of electrification were it divested from its relation to the Cold War complex, and his sheepish delight in the material comforts provided by electrically powered cold storage. More broadly, examining texts few would assume to engage with domestic electrification, let alone in a positive way, provides a useful way into thinking about the extent of these technologies' presence in postwar US writing.

A number of recent studies situate the Beat aesthetic as a challenge to early Cold War conformity. For Penny Vlagopoulos, Kerouac and his fellow Beats' exploration of deviance was a reaction against the cultural homogeneity

cookers door-to-door. See Neal Cassady, *Collected Letters, 1944–1967* (London: Penguin, 2004), 209; Carolyn Cassady, *Jack Kerouac: A Biography* (New York: Penguin, 1990), 86.

[7] See, for example, Barbara Ehrenreich, *The Hearts of Men: American Dreams and the Flight from Commitment* (New York: Anchor Press, 1983), 52 and Victoria A. Elmwood, "The White Nomad and the New Masculine Family in Jack Kerouac's *On the Road*," *Western American Literature* 42.4 (Winter 2008): 335–61. Pierre-Antoine Pellerin usefully complicates this account in "Jack Kerouac's Ecopoetics in *The Dharma Bums* and *Desolation Angels:* Domesticity, Wilderness and Masculine Fantasies of Animality," *Transatlantica* 2 (2011).

advocated by George F. Kennan's policy of containment, according to which "'exhibitions of indecision, disunity, and internal disintegration within this country have an exhilarating effect on the whole Communist movement.'"[8] Ann Douglas likewise describes Kerouac's writing as an attempt to "declassify human experience, beginning with the male body, in an era that witnessed an unprecedented expansion of classified information" and "to make spontaneity and deliberate defenselessness supreme virtues" to challenge over-militarization (525–32). But attention to Kerouac's appliance depictions troubles these accounts. Without going so far as Manuel Luis Martinez, who argues that the Beat movement "share[d] similar ideological underpinnings with the conservative, puritanical culture" they claimed to oppose, I suggest that Kerouac's time-saving appliances challenge readings of his work as entirely antagonistic to consumer culture.[9] The first section of this chapter examines Kerouac's pastoral appliance depictions in *The Town and the City* (1950), his early poetry (1952–7), *Desolation Angels* (published in 1965, but most of which he wrote in 1955), *The Dharma Bums* (1958), and *On the Road* (1957). The second section examines Kerouac's gendered vilification of time-saving appliances and the "all-electric" home elsewhere in *Desolation Angels* and *The Dharma Bums* alongside their depiction in Burroughs and Rosenthal. The third section demonstrates how Kerouac's texts also reappropriate the time-saving appliance to create alternative currents of meaning, and an alternative domesticity, to those championed by Madison Avenue and Hollywood. Throughout, I contend that the time-saving appliance in Kerouac is an important site for the negotiation of tensions between early Cold War culture and its critics, whose examination troubles accounts of Beat writing as anti-consumerist, and anti-home. This negotiation involves a recognition of the beguiling attributes of time-saving appliances and their attendant comforts as much as their embodiment of the ideology of containment. The gendered dimension of the electric gadgets depicted in these texts is testament not only to the Beat movement's problematic attitude to women (and marginalization of women writers) but to the important role that time-saving appliances played in the articulation of specific postwar anxieties regarding the perceived domesticating, or neutering, effects of both corporate culture and suburban living.[10]

---

[8] Kennan, 582, qtd. in Penny Vlagopoulos, "Rewriting America: Kerouac's Nation of 'Underground Monsters'," in Kerouac. *On the Road: The Original Scroll*, 55.

[9] Manuel Luis Martinez, *Countering the Counterculture: Rereading Postwar American Dissent from Jack Kerouac to Tomás Rivera* (Madison, WI: U of Wisconsin Press, 2003), 24.

[10] See Ronna C. Johnson, "The Beats and Gender" and Jonah Raskin, "Beatniks, Hippies, Yippies, Feminists, and the Ongoing American Counterculture," in *The Cambridge Companion to the Beats* (Cambridge: Cambridge UP, 2013), 162–78 and 36–50; Michael Davidson, *Guys Like Us*, 76–98.

1. Time-Saving Appliances as Nostalgia-Makers: *The Town and the City* (1950), *Sketches* (1952–7), *The Dharma Bums* (1958), and *On the Road* (1957)

Kerouac's fascination with the refrigerator's connotations of home and plenitude, which bears the trace of the author's experience of the Great Depression and wartime rationing, becomes especially apparent when one examines these depictions alongside refrigerators ads from the period 1940–60.[11] Refrigerator ads in the 1930s emphasized cost-saving, but via depictions of a refrigerator paradoxically replete with food items that no family affected by the Depression would have been able to afford—as if, as well as using less electricity than previous models and helping preserve leftovers for longer, the appliance were capable of conjuring plenty out of nothing.[12] Refrigerator ads from 1941 to 1945 instead encouraged the consumer to invest in government bonds that would enable them to purchase an "all-electric" kitchen once the production of goods recommenced (May, 160). Finally, ads post-1945 showcased the housewife admiring a refrigerator whose exploding contents, and greater size (more than double that of prewar refrigerators) symbolized the end of rationing and the nation's hard-won prosperity.[13] The housewife in Kelvinator's ad for its 1950 range of "WonderWorkers" appeared to dance on the open door of her new oven while holding aloft a massive roast chicken as her husband and daughter waved in the background.[14] In Crosley's ads,

---

[11] Paul Maher, Jr. highlights the Depression's effects on Kerouac's hometown of Lowell, Indiana, in *Kerouac: The Definitive Biography* (New York: Taylor Trade Publishing, 2004), 40–1. For Jason Spangler, "Kerouac's work serves as memory bank and moral conscience for victims of Depression trauma" ("We're on a Road to Nowhere: Steinbeck, Kerouac, and the Legacy of the Great Depression," *Studies in the Novel* 40.3 (Fall 2008): 308–27, citation on 308).

[12] Westinghouse, "New Streamline Beauty! New Economy! New Convenience!" *Good Housekeeping* (June 1935): 193. See also: Frigidaire, "Inexpensively the Frigidaire Provides . . .," *Ladies' Home Journal* (April 1932): NP; Kelvinator, "When You Said 'I Have 4 Refrigerators' I Thought You Were Joking," *Good Housekeeping* (March 1935): NP. My reading departs from Sandy Isendstadt, who argues that the theme of plenty only emerged in ads after 1950 (see "Visions of Plenty: Refrigerators in America around 1950," *Journal of Design History* 11.4 (1998): 311–21). See also Susan Strasser's excellent analysis of the promotion of the refrigerator as facilitating the reuse of leftovers in *Waste and Want: A Social History of Trash* (New York: Metropolitan Books, 1999), 211.

[13] For examples of such rhetoric, see: Admiral, "There Are Others that Are New, but None so Truly Modern!," *LIFE* (March 13, 1950): 65; Kelvinator, "Take this Ad to your Kitchen... Compare What You've Got with an Amazing New Kelvinator!" *LIFE* (August 21, 1950): 1; Frigidaire, "Now—the Refrigerator Made for Once-a-week Shopping," *LIFE* (January 15, 1951): 47; Gibson, "Gibson Market Master: Space for an Extra Cart of Fresh Food," *LIFE* (November 7, 1955): 116.

[14] Kelvinator, "Kelvinator's New WonderWorkers for Your Kitchen!" *LIFE* (March 20, 1950): 57.

movie star and brand spokeswoman Margaret Lindsay posed in front of the 1953 Crosley Shelvador refrigerator and chest freezer, which heaved with meats and fresh vegetables. A heart frame, and the statement that "a care-free kitchen is the heart of your home," reinforced the connection between appliance, family, and affection (Figure 1.2).[15] In a Hotpoint ad from 1956, a little girl and her mother posed in front of an open "Big Bin" refrigerator whose pale pink hue recalled a toy for children, giving the impression that mother and child were merely "playing" house. And while the little girl was presumably decanting apples from her grocery basket *into* the fridge, the framing of the ad gave the impression that she was picking apples *from* it—as if the appliance itself were bearing fruit (Figure 1.3).

FIGURE 1.2 Crosley. "Crosley Shelvador Doubles your 'Front-Row' Space!" *LIFE* (March 2, 1953): 57. © Crosley. Reproduced with permission. Image courtesy of the Advertising Archives.

[15] Crosley, "A Care-free Kitchen Is the Heart of your Home so Set your Heart on a Crosley Shelvador," *LIFE* (March 2, 1953): 57.

FIGURE 1.3 Detail from "Only the New Hotpoint Big Bin Refrigerator Freezer Turns Itself *INSIDE OUT*." 1956. Image courtesy of the Advertising Archives.

This association of the time-saving appliance with both infinite food and infinite maternal love is apparent in the page-and-a-half description, in Kerouac's first novel, *The Town and the City* (1950), of the food items the protagonists' mother pulls from the refrigerator upon their return from war:

> Then they all went into the kitchen, and the mother, with a flushed and anxious expression on her face, wiping tears from her eyes, was at the refrigerator pulling out great quantities of food from her larder. "I've got some nice Maine sardines here," she said, "and here's some bacon, eggs, ham—and here's some hamburger steak nice and lean I got yesterday, and milk, and here's some lettuce and tomatoes. Do you want a nice salad? And some beef if you want it, some fruit salad, pineapples, peaches. And here, do you want some beans? . . . Here's some peanut butter, jam—" . . . And Rose was standing at her mother's side peering anxiously into the refrigerator. "And here's some nice cheese I just got at Wietelmann's," the mother went on, oblivious of everything in the world except that her sons had been starving to death away from home.

> "Oh, and if you want a snack before dinner, if you want a little lunch before dinner I can fry you some of this nice tenderloin steak—and I've got a few lamb chops left if you'd like that. Just say what you want. And here's some nice canned asparagus tips and ripe olives. Oh, and I've got plenty of Vermont maple syrup here. Do you want me to make you some pancakes?" . . . And as she said this, all the food was coming out of the refrigerator and being piled on the kitchen table.[16]

Written in a realist style modeled on that of Thomas Wolfe, and that predated the confessional mode for which Kerouac is better known, the text is saccharine, sentimental, and as detailed as an advertorial. The listing of food items calls to mind the strategy used by GE, in the early 1950s, to advertise their newer, larger, "space maker" refrigerator, and by Amana, in 1956, to advertise their "'Stor-Mor' Freezer Plus Refrigerator"

FIGURE 1.4 Amana. Detail from "New! Completely! See the New 'Stor-Mor' Freezer PLUS Refrigerator." 1956. Image courtesy of the Advertising Archives.

---

[16] Jack Kerouac, *The Town and the City* (London: Penguin, 2000 [1950]). Henceforth, *TC*.

(Figure 1.4). In both cases, an illustration of an enormous display of food communicated the seemingly infinite array of items that could fit into the bigger refrigerator model, while positioning the appliance as the bestower of that bounty.[17] The woman lovingly gazing out at the viewer alongside the heaving refrigerator cemented its status as a symbol of feminine affection. In its emulation of the rhetoric and imagery of such ads, Kerouac's nostalgic figuration of the refrigerator here demonstrates Catherine Jurca's contention, as summarized by Christopher Kocela, that "although male discontentment seems to express a longing for escape from the domestic sphere, in fact 'the alienation of men from the suburban home in the popular novel expresses the *desire for* domestic familiarity'" (Jurca 11, qtd. in Kocela 176).

Kerouac also enlisted appliances to nostalgic ends in "Rocky Mt. Aug. 7 '52" and "Aug. 5, '52"—two long "sketches," or spontaneous poems, he wrote between 1952 and 1957, that describe his sister Carolyn and her husband Paul's domestic life in Rocky Mt., North Carolina.[18] In the first of these poems, Kerouac describes Paul fixing the landlord's "deluxe" lawnmower under the watchful gaze of some farmers sitting on the porch of the store across the street:

> Intense interest is being shown in the lawncutter . . .
> Men are be-
> mused by machines. Americans,
> by new, efficient
> machines. (*BS*, 11: 31; 43–6)

So far, so playful: the image of a US masculinity enthralled to efficient machines places the lawncutter at a cool, critical distance, which the second poem maintains in its figuration of Carolyn among "some of / the incidental / appurtenances in / the life of a little / Carolina housewife / in 1952" (33: 28–34). There is likewise an ironic distance in Kerouac's figuration of red plastic-covered chairs, the "humanity" of whose "souls" has "no plastics to name it!" (*BS* 29: 23–30). But that distance soon collapses. The rest of the poem is in fact a sentimental vignette about Carolyn and her children, as exemplified by the account of Carolyn retrieving ice for their water:

[17] GE, "25% to 50% more Food Space . . .!" *LIFE* (October 16, 1950): 26. Unfortunately, GE denied permission to reproduce this image but it is available online via the *LIFE* magazine archives.

[18] Jack Kerouac, "Rocky Mt. August 7 '52" and "Aug. 5, '52," in *Book of Sketches 1952–1957* (London: Penguin, 2006), 8–24 and 28–44. Henceforth, *BS*.

In the kitchen, at
her refrigerator she
pours out ice

cube trays—
. . .
The little mother
gravely works on the
ice; above the sink,
with a crank, is an
ice cracker; she
jams in the ice cubes,
standing tip toe
reaches up & cranks
it down into a red
plastic container;
wiggling the little boys
wait & watch—The
kitchen is modern &
clean. (*BS*, 34: 3–19; 32–46;
35: 1–4)

FIGURE 1.5 Westinghouse. "It's Frost-Free." *LIFE* (May 22, 1950): 153. ©Westinghouse. Reproduced with permission.

The depiction of "the little mother," "wiggling" children, and gleaming kitchen turns the poem into the very thing the aforementioned irreverent reference to plastics as an identifier of humaneness might have originally appeared to critique. Indeed, the image of these little boys "standing tip toe" to watch their mother deftly use her implements resembles the myriad ads that by the end of the 1920s positioned the purchase of a refrigerator refrigerator as a demonstration of good parenting. The most notable of these was an ad GE ran in 1929, which depicted a little boy grabbing food out of the refrigerator under the slogan "The Food He Eats Is the Man He'll Be." Promising that "Nothing can give you greater assurance . . . than a General Electric Refrigerator," the ad posited the refrigerator as a guarantor of the next generation's health—and masculine vigor.[19] An ad Westinghouse ran in 1950 for "the world's first and only" frost-free refrigerator, which featured a mother pulling a cake out of the fridge for three children wearing birthday hats, portrayed the refrigerator as a purveyor of celebratory treats and a participant in child-rearing, its contents contributing to the children's growth, as symbolized by the birthday hats (Figure 1.5). Echoing this

[19] GE "The Food He Eats is the Man He'll Be," *Ladies' Home Journal* (Oct. 1929): N.P. Unfortunately, GE has denied permission to reproduce this ad, but it can be found online on a number of different websites devoted to vintage ads.

imagery, Kerouac's depiction of "The little mother" who "gravely works on the ice" to fill her son's drink against the backdrop of a kitchen that is "modern & clean" resembles a Madonna and Child for the electric age. Such a reading is made all the more compelling when one examines Kerouac's poem alongside "The Young Housewife" (1916), an early poem by William Carlos Williams, whose influence on the Beats is well documented.[20] Kerouac's depiction of the "little mother" reverberates not only with the echo of midcentury appliance advertising but with that of the "young housewife" who Williams's speaker glimpses while driving by in his car as she "comes to the curb / to call the ice-man" and "stands / shy, uncorseted, tucking in /stray ends of hair" (*TCPOWCW* 57, i; v-viii). This echo imbues Kerouac's "all-electric" poem with a further layer of nostalgia.

A similar sentimentality is evident in Kerouac's description, in *On the Road*, *The Dharma Bums*, and *Desolation Angels*, of road trips that culminate with returning home to eat "everything there is in the icebox" (*DA*, 178). In *The Dharma Bums*, Kerouac describes spying his mother through the kitchen window upon his return home:

> there she was at the white tiled sink in the kitchen, washing her dishes, with a rueful expression waiting for me (I was late), worried I'd never even make it. . . . And I thought of Japhy as I stood there in the cold yard looking at her: "Why is he so mad about white tiled sinks and 'kitchen machinery' as he calls it?"[21]

The passage discloses an abiding tension between Snyder, and more broadly the Beat sensibility's, rejection of mechanization's presumed role in eradicating individualism and domesticating nature, and his own, perhaps reluctant, appreciation of domestic modernization (*DB*, 72). Where Snyder inveighed in later interviews against appliances' alienating effects on children, who instead of learning responsibility by contributing to the dish washing now "stan[d] around with their dumb faces hanging out while the dishwasher is running," Kerouac's description of "kitchen machinery" in *The Dharma Bums* is almost loving.[22]

---

[20] William Carlos Williams, "The Young Housewife" (1916), in *The Collected Poems of William Carlos Williams Volume 1: 1909–1939*, ed. A. Walton Litz and Christopher MacGowan (New York: New Directions, 1991 [1986]), 57. Collection henceforth abbreviated as *TCPWCW*. For more on Williams's influence on the Beats, see Jonah Raskin, *American Scream: Allen Ginsberg's Howl and the Making of the Beat Generation* (Berkeley: U of California Press, 2004).

[21] Jack Kerouac, *The Dharma Bums* (London: Mayflower, 1969 [1958]), 97. Henceforth, *DB*.

[22] Denise Low and Robin Tawney, "An Interview with Gary Snyder" (1979), in *Conversations with Gary Snyder*, ed. David Stephen Calonne (UP of Mississippi, 2017), NP.

The refrigerator's associations with a male desire for home resurfaces in *Desolation Angels,* where Kerouac recounts a dream about an icebox:

> I do dream of the cold gray pool I'm swimming in. . . . it's raining in my dream head all right, I come out of the pool proudly and go fish in the icebox, Cody's "two sons" . . . see me poking for butter. . . . I . . . sit down and start eating raisin toast with butter and Evelyn comes home and sees me and I proudly boast how I've been swimming—It seems to me she eyes my toast begrudgingly but she says "'Couldn't you get something bettern that?'" (*DA*, 84)

Combined with the references to a "cold gray pool" and rain, the phrase "go fish in the icebox" that plays on the double meaning of "fish" as "get" and as "go fishing" creates a strange concatenation of meaning that connects allusions to amniotic fluid, fertility, the elements, and the domestic environment. There emerges an albeit tenuous and insufficient picture of home (as exemplified by the comment, "'Couldn't you get something bettern that?'") that situates the icebox at its center—a modern version of the hearth whose provision of butter and bread nevertheless draws the community close, and makes the dreamer feel secure.

Kerouac's interchangeable use of the words "icebox" and "refrigerator" in the earlier-quoted passages partly reflects the fluidity with which these words were used in the 1950s, when the events in *The Dharma Bums* and *Desolation Angels* took place (although the icebox in the passage just quoted might well be an *actual* icebox, it being a dream!). More specifically, while new owners of an electric refrigerator in the 1920s and 1930s would have used the term "refrigerator" to avoid confusion, John Rees's research suggests that as refrigerators supplanted their nonelectric predecessors, the term "icebox" enjoyed a resurgence that didn't peak until the 1970s.[23] But the use of this word also (and more importantly) reflects the legacy of William Carlos Williams, whose much-anthologized poem "This is just to say . . ." (1934) is arguably the most famous engagement with appliances in American literature (*TCPWCW* 372, ii–vi). In this poem, Williams's speaker begs forgiveness for having "eaten / the plums / that were in / the icebox," and which the note's recipient was saving for breakfast. With the exception of John Hines, scholars have tended to assume that this icebox is a refrigerator, and to read the object as connotative of the conveniences rendered possible

[23] According to Google Ngram, the use of the word "icebox" peaked in 1945 but remained in use well into the 1970s. While Ngram is not an infallible tool, it provides a useful estimate of the prevalence of specific words in print. See also Jonathan Rees's discussion of this etymology in "Ice Boxes vs. Refrigerators," *The Historical Society: A Blog Devoted to History for the Academy & Beyond* (December 12, 2013).

by electrical modernity.[24] This is despite the fact that, as I have mentioned, it was uncommon to refer to electric refrigerators as iceboxes in this period—and despite Williams's son's confirmation, in 1983, that the titular object was based on the family's "old icebox" situated in the rear entrance hall of a house that served, itself, as "a buttress against the advance of commercial progress into our neighborhood."[25] However, the proliferation of refrigerator advertising and aggressive promotion of domestic electrification in this period *does* make it tempting to read "This is just to say . . ." as conjuring the ghost of the icebox's future. No less, given the poem was published the same year as Franklin Delano Roosevelt's proclamation, that "'more and more are [electric refrigerators and oven ranges] considered necessities in our American life in every part of the country.'"[26] In this poem about prematurely consumed items that emulates a throwaway note, the use of the word "icebox" appears a calculated move intended to convey the speed of change at a time of intense modernization. It self-consciously gestures, that is, to the convulsive effects of industrial modernity on language, and the poet's own struggle to keep pace with them. [27]

But beyond the deployment of appliances in the cultivation of an aesthetic that bespeaks the new, or the use of the term "icebox" itself, the legacy of Williams's icebox in Kerouac is most notable in the gendered nature of this object. In Williams, the "note" clearly delineates the roles of man and woman in relation to the icebox. A female "steward" does the grocery shopping, fills the icebox, and plans the meals, while the male interloper, like a child, filches these items and upsets the carefully calibrated meal schedule and food budget

---

[24] While the assumption that the titular icebox is a refrigerator is apparent in a wealth of Williams scholarship, recent examples of this tendency include Ronald Schleifer and Richard Cureton's references to Williams's "refrigerator note" (Schleifer, *Modernism and Popular Music* (Cambridge: Cambridge UP, 2011), 62; Cureton, "Readings in Temporal Poetics: Four Poems by William Carlos Williams," *Style* 51.2 (2017): 187–206). Laleh Atashi reads the "cold" in the poem as communicating the displacement of natural pleasures (the sweetness of plums) by the machine-produced (electrically-generated cold) ("The Status of William Carlos Williams in American Modernism," *Messages, Sages, and Ages* 3.3 (2016): 54–63). John Hines' incisive gloss in *Voices in the Past: English Literature and Archaeology* (Cambridge: D.S. Brewer, 2004), 3, provides a refreshing counter to this tendency. I am grateful to Ian Copestake and Christopher MacGowan for their insights into whether Williams owned an electric refrigerator.

[25] William Eric Williams, "Life with Father," in *William Carlos Williams: Man and Poet*, ed. Carroll F. Terrell (Orono, Maine: National Poetry Foundation, 1983), 61–82, qtd. in Hines, 3; Tobey, 165. Williams himself confirmed that the poem started out as a note to his wife. See Neil Baldwin, *To All Gentleness: William Carlos Williams, the Doctor-Poet* (Atheneum, 1984), 127.

[26] Franklin Delano Roosevelt, "Extemporaneous Remarks at Tupelo, Mississippi," November 18, 1934, in *Roosevelt, Public Papers*, 3: 460–2, qtd. in Tobey, 96.

[27] My reading chimes with Tony Barnstone's contention of Williams's entire aesthetic as bound up with the "sacralization of novelty, technoscience and creativity." Intriguingly, Barnstone suggests that in its quest for endless, cyclical, renewal American modernism itself might be best allegorised as a washing machine ("William Carlos Williams and the Cult of the New," *William Carlos Williams Review* 36.2 (2019): 89–125).

(this, incidentally, is a point overlooked by scholars such as Charles Altieri, whose analysis of the note as expressing the speaker's "implicit faith in his wife's capacity to understand and accept his deed" erases the gender roles on which such understanding relies).[28] It is equally difficult to disassociate those moments of radical subversion of subject-object relations manifest in the consuming of "everything in the icebox" in Kerouac's texts from a specific kind of male privilege that leaves the housewife to clean up what is left behind, and refill the now-empty appliance. Indeed, Williams's depiction anticipates, and Kerouac's depiction recalls, a subgenre of early postwar ads in which the housewife is replaced by children, either alone or accompanied by a permissive father who participates in raiding the refrigerator for a midnight snack—as exemplified by International Harvester's 1949 ad promoting its refrigerator as a source of "Meals at All Hours!" (Figure 1.6). In these ads, the refrigerator is a vehicle for secret indulgence and rebellion against the stricture of scheduled mealtimes and sensible eating, the latter two of which are coded female.

The "icebox" marks Kerouac's homecoming twice more in *On the Road*, where it draws out the tension between the road and the domestic in complex, unintuitive ways. The first of these instances, described at the end of Book One, occurs upon his return from the West Coast in October 1947. Having not eaten for days, he arrives in Times Square disorientated and hallucinating with hunger:

> Where everybody? Where life? I had my home to go to, my place to lay my head down and recoup the losses I had suffered, and figure the gain that I knew was in there somewhere too. I had to panhandle a dime for the subway. . . . When I got home I ate everything in the icebox. My mother got up and looked at me. "Poor little John" she said in French "you're thin, you're thin. Where have you been all this time?" . . . My mother and I decided to buy a new refrigerator with the money I had sent her from California; it was to be the first one in the family. (*OTR*, 211)

The passage moves swiftly from a description of existential paralysis in the face of urban flux to one of domestic safety, as embodied in a worried, protective mother, and a full icebox where the tattered self, worn down from months of hitchhiking across America, can be replenished and made whole again. The purchase of this electric appliance contrasts sharply with the preceding pages' emphatic asceticism as Kerouac traveled "eight thousand miles around the American continent" (*OTR*, 206). It suggests a rejection of

[28] Charles Altieri, "Presence and Reference in a Literary Text: The Example of Williams' 'This Is Just to Say,'" *Critical Inquiry* 5.3 (Spring 1979): 489–510, citation on 501.

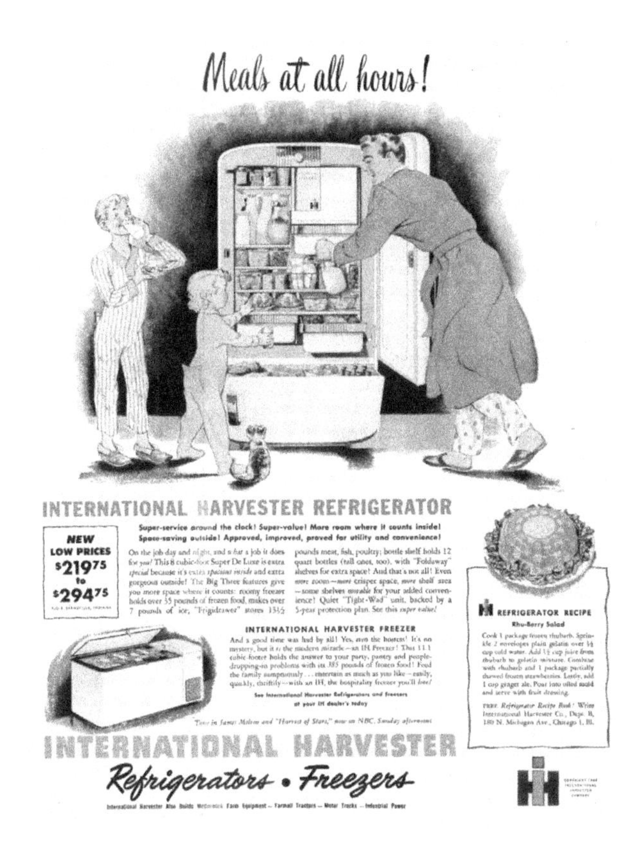

FIGURE 1.6 International Harvester. "Meals at All Hours!" *LIFE* (June 6, 1949): 84. © Whirlpool 2020. Reproduced with permission.

the road and a retreat into the modern comforts of the postwar home that elsewhere he so explicitly rejects.

The Kerouacs' refrigerator features again at the very end of Book Two, when on his return home from another road trip he stops in Detroit to visit his ex-wife. Upon failing to find her, Kerouac is overcome by longing and surmises:

> At the end of the American road is a man and a woman making love . . . all anybody wanted was some kind of penetration into the heart of things where, like in a womb, we could curl up and sleep the ecstatic sleep that Burroughs was experiencing with a good big mainline shot of M. and advertising executives were experiencing with twelve Scotch & Sodas in Stouffers before they made the drunkard's train to Westchester—but without hangovers. . . . I staggered back East in search of my stone, got home and ate everything in the icebox again,

> only now it was a refrigerator, fruit of my 1947 labors, and that in some measure was the progress of my life. (*OTR*, 278–9)

As with the icebox that punctuated the end of Book One, the refrigerator here is an electric cold storage equivalent to the hearth, or to the maternal bosom (particularly if one considers the resemblance of Kerouac's running home to eat its entire contents to the behavior of a child rushing home for food after a day playing outdoors). But following so soon after his failed attempt to see his ex-wife and satiate his sexual longings, it also reads as a substitute for women as a whole. Meanwhile the icebox's replacement with the refrigerator in the last sentence and the suggestion that this replacement "in some measure" marks "the progress of [his] life" both point to the specific nature of temporality under consumer capitalism, whereby progress is measured in the cycle of production and obsolescence. The grammatical structure of the sentence itself, which gives the impression of an animated appliance with its own agency springing from a kind of disembodied labor—labor effectively rid of its laborer—contributes to the passage's overarching portrait of postwar alienation. In particular, "the icebox again, only now it was a refrigerator," gives a sense of time itself having come undone, allowing objects to return but as different versions of themselves. The "icebox again, only now it was a refrigerator" is both an embodiment of this process and the disappointing endpoint of what we might term a "romantic, only now it was mundanely capitalist" postwar Odyssey, wherein Penelope has been replaced by a series of domestic machines connotative of home. The best this era actually offers, Kerouac suggests, is the expensive, hangover-free, inebriation of a Madison Avenue adman, or a refrigerator, more life-like than one's own depleted self, that will stand for that year's congealed labour-time (to paraphrase Marx).

2. Conformity Producers and Sex Machines: Jack Kerouac, William Burroughs, and Bob Rosenthal

Where the passages just examined reveal Kerouac's surprising sentimental attachment to time-saving appliances, those examined in this section highlight the centrality of time-saving domestic gadgets and mechanization more broadly to Kerouac's critique of Cold War conformity. In *The Dharma Bums*, Kerouac enlists time-saving appliances to portray suburbia as a mechanized space inhabited by automata who travel on wheels rather than on foot, and that uncritically consume whatever the television serves them. In the following passage, electricity figures as both an embodiment of the homogenizing, lobotomizing effects of containment culture and the means by which such effects are achieved:

> you'll see if you take a walk some night on a suburban street and pass house after house on both sides of the street . . . and inside the little blue square of the television, each living family riveting its attention on probably one show . . . dogs barking at you because you pass on human feet instead of on wheels . . . everybody in the world is soon going to be thinking the same way. . . . Only one thing I'll say for the people watching television, the millions and millions of the One Eye: they're not hurting anyone while they're sitting in front of that Eye. . . . I see [Gary Snyder/Japhy] in future years stalking along with full rucksack, in suburban streets, passing the blue television windows of homes, alone, his thoughts the only thoughts not electrified to the Master Switch. (*DB*, 77)

Kerouac portrays the suburban house as a container for atomized machine-citizens, components of a vast machine-nation that have been synchronized to blink, beep, and switch off at the same time. The best one can say for the human beings inside is that they are too anesthetized to do harm. Rather, they passively absorb the messages that the television conducts directly into their brains as if they were connected to it by wires. Of particular importance is the text's framing of bodies and minds as separate, distinct entities, at the same time as it collapses the distinction between human beings, machines, and divinity. Just as the sound of footsteps has been replaced by that of wheels, the suburban television viewer is merely an appliance plugged into a "Master Switch"—a powerful figuration of the perceived homogeneity of popular culture under Fordism. With its intimations of the divine, the expression "Master Switch" is also a sharp reminder of hierarchy—the power, as it were, can always be switched off at the source, reducing the suburbanite to a dysfunctional device. It also reminds the reader of the imbrication of domestic electrification with the political project that underlay the growth of the suburbs, already discussed in the Introduction to this study. The "Master Switch" simultaneously stands for the disproportionate authority granted to television talk show hosts and news readers in the medium's first decade; the conformity that results from everyone consuming the same content; and the reifying effect of the television appliance as an object, which is to say the extent to which watching the television reduces the viewer to an object while uncannily animating the appliance and the objects its shows advertise. The passage conveys a postwar landscape wherein television advertisements for new housing developments featuring the latest electric fittings, and television shows set in the suburbs and sponsored by appliance manufacturers, have created a population of suburban television viewers watching other suburbanites watching television and wielding gadgets. That depiction of reification works in conjunction with other moments in the novel in which specific gadgets are invoked to decry the fundamental wastefulness of consumerism—such as the complaint, by a traveling salesman with whom Kerouac hitches a ride, that "'Three hundred and sixty days out of the year we get bright sunshine here in El Paso and my wife just bought a clothes dryer!'" (*DB*, 114). Electrical goods and the electrification of the home, in these instances, are explicitly framed as tyrannical components of a push-button culture that reproduces conformity en masse. And, of course, the "Master Switch" recalls the most masterful switch of all—the one that would enable the detonation of another atomic bomb.

The parallels Kerouac draws between Americans and their time-saving appliances are in some ways analogous to William Burroughs's description of the United States in *The Wild Boys: A Book of the Dead* (1971), a novel about a youth movement run by gay men (the titular wild boys) intent on dismantling Western civilization.[29] In the following passage, an interpreter translates the mayor of Marrakech's welcome speech to the American CIA agents who have come to help suppress the gay uprising:

> "He say very glad Americans here. He say wild boys very bad cause much trouble. Police here not able do anything. . . . He say after dinner when ladies go he tell you things what wild boy do. He say time for big cleanup. He say Americans like vacuum cleaner." The interpreter bellows in imitation of a Hoover. (*WB*, 127–9)

The passage's humor derives partly from the absurdity of high officials imitating the sound of a domestic appliance, and partly from the implied double meaning of "Hoover": vacuum-cleaner brand and head of the FBI J. Edgar Hoover, who was notorious for his investigation of gay communities.[30] But it also derives from the strange slippage resulting from the absence of "are" and "a" in the statement "'Americans like vacuum cleaner,'" which turns an analogy about the power of US foreign intervention (which suctions away dissidence and creates power vacuums it then fills with leaders of its own choosing) into a statement about the American people's love of the *actual* vacuum cleaner. The image of America the Vacuum Cleaner, a nation supported by military men committed to cleansing the world of "'queers and dope freaks'" who threaten to sully Americanness, renders explicit both the heteronormative, nationalist, and capitalist imperialist tropes embedded in appliance advertising, and the deployment of appliances in the celebration of postwar containment culture (*WB*, 125). Going further than Kerouac, Burroughs indicates the tyrannical potential of the efficiency ethos. A nation whose international policies imitate a vacuum cleaner's suction is terrifyingly absurd—but no more so, Burroughs suggests, than the state propaganda that links time-saving appliances, the nuclear family, and traditional gender norms to the American way of life.

---

[29] William S. Burroughs, *The Wild Boys* (New York: Penguin, 2012 [1971]). Henceforth, *WB*.
[30] David K. Johnson, *The Lavender Scare* (Chicago: U of Chicago Press, 2006), 11.

While Burroughs's depiction of America the Vacuum Cleaner implicitly critiques the strict delineation of gender roles on which containment culture relied, the majority of Kerouac and his fellow Beats' anti-appliance depictions are in fact intensely misogynistic, conflating domestic gadgets with the women who wield them in order to posit consumer culture as both effeminate and feminizing. Most notably, in *Desolation Angels*, anxieties about consumer conformity are elaborated in the image of "supermarket doors [that] open automatically to ballooned bellies of pregnant shoppers" (*DA*, 118). The nation that like an assembly line mindlessly reproduces artifice is embodied in the figure of the pregnant shopper who purchases the assembly line's products, and whose movements and susceptibility to persuasion are as predictable as the supermarket's electrically powered doors. Fertile female shoppers likewise stand for the feminization of culture under consumerism in his later Beckettian meditation upon "the wheel of birth and dying turn[ing] on and on," which continues thanks to the fact that:

> men desire women and women scheme for men's babies—Something . . . which today makes us sick to think of it, whole supermarket electronic doors opening by themselves to admit pregnant women so they can buy food to feed death further. (*DA*, 297)

The electronic age has reduced the propagation of the human race to a cycle of shopping, eating, birthing of new generations of shoppers, and dying as predictable as the opening and shutting of automated doors. Consumerism is embodied in the women who simultaneously attract male desire, are powerless in the face of desirable goods, and will breed a new generation of consumers similarly powerless to those charms. The figuration of the untamed masculinity of the Beat poet injecting a stupefied female populace with the excitement and authenticity that consumer culture lacks is premised on the conflation of maleness with nature and the natural, and femininity with artifice.

Such feminization is in keeping with what Patricia Vettel-Becker identifies as the proliferation of images of women as mass-produced machines in mid-century US culture.[31] Rosalyn Baxandall and Elizabeth Ewan have likewise shown how efforts to demystify the suburbs "singled out" women "as the mainstay of suburban superficiality" and "blamed them for everything from juvenile delinquency to keeping up with the Joneses to producing a generation of morally inferior sons and Milquetoast husbands."[32] Eric Keenaghan argues further that the "sexualised masculinity" of Beat writing is inextricable from

[31] Patricia Vettel-Becker, "Clarence Holbrook Carter's *War Bride* and the Machine/Woman Fantasy," *Genders* 37 (2003): 1.

[32] Rosalyn Baxandell and Elizabeth Ewan, *Picture Windows: How the Suburbs Happened* (New York: Basic Books, 2000), 159.

the "gendered abuses of power" specific to the Cold War-era literary scene—particularly in its aggressive critique of "the straight and paternal family man, the suburban organization man," whose "compliance with Fordist socio-economic systems and interpellation as a consumer marked him as an effeminate subject lacking volition and innovative capability."[33] This conflation of the suburban housewife, her time-saving appliances, and the mechanized containment culture that produced both is most apparent in William Burroughs's portrayal, in *Naked Lunch* (1959), of the anxieties of the "AMERICAN HOUSEWIFE (opening a box of LUX)" who frets:

> Why don't it have an electric eye the box flip open when it see me and hand itself to the Automat Handy Man he should put it inna water already. . . . The Handy Man is outa control since Thursday, he been getting physical with me and I didn't put in his combination at all. . . and the Garbage Disposal Unit is snapping at me, and the nasty old Mixmaster keep trying to get up under my dress. . . . I got the most awful cold, and my intestines is all constipated. . . . I'm gonna put in the Handy Man's combination he should administer me a high colonic awready.[34]

Burroughs's housewife is a vapid machine as faulty as her malfunctioning gadgets, her constipation mirroring the blockage of the "Garbage Disposal Unit." The passage's humor derives from the housewife having been incapacitated by her push-button technology, so that she cannot countenance opening a detergent box manually and longs for a mechanical one to take its place—as if imagination, or indeed common sense, has been "programmed out" of her for the sake of efficiency. Meanwhile, the gadgets she does own are as handsy as the handy man, recalling—whether Burroughs knew this or not—the origins of the standing and handheld mixer, whose motor, as discussed in the Introduction, was first developed for electrical vibrators.[35] Lest the reader be in any doubt, to interviewer Daniel Odier's question regarding whether "'the constipated American housewife who is afraid her mixmaster [*sic*] will get under her skirts while she is waiting for the washing machine to finish its cycle'" suggested "'how [he felt] about women,'" Burroughs replied, "'I think they [women] were a basic mistake,' and the whole dualistic universe evolved from this error."[36]

---

[33] Eric Keenaghan, "Vulnerable Households: Cold War Containment and Robert Duncan's Queered Nation," *Journal of Modern Literature* 28.4, Poetry (Summer, 2005): 57–90. Citation on 67.

[34] William Burroughs, *Naked Lunch: The Restored Text*, ed. James Grauerholz and Barry Miles (London and New York: Harper Perennial, 2005 [1959]), 104. Henceforth, *NL*.

[35] *Encyclopedia of Modern Everyday Inventions*, 169; Maines, 15; 35.

[36] William S. Burroughs and Daniel Odier, *The Job: Interviews with William S. Burroughs* (London: Penguin, 2008 [1969]), 116.

Beat associate Bob Rosenthal, too, parodied the sexual dimension of appliance ads in *Cleaning Up New York* (1976), a short prose poem-qua-memoir about his stint as a house cleaner. The following scene is worth quoting at length:

> Hoover and I . . . start down the steps and because of a bad design in [my] boxers, my cock falls through the slit and rubs up and down the soft denim. After a few steps go by, I begin to lose my concentration. . . . I unzip my fly to see what's happening and a great erection grows out of it. Hoover is buzzing, humming next to me. I pull the rug attachment off and contemplate the bit on the hose. Now in my adventures, I can go all the way! I fuck the sucking vacuum. The suction is just strong enough to give realistic tension to the skin of my cock. It is nice. But it doesn't go anywhere, there is only one speed. I try altering the air valve on the side but it is boring. Fantasy might do, but I start to become too aware of Hoover and my best fantasy of an obliging vacuum cleaner doesn't do anything for either of us. So I pack it in. "We really came close!" I reflect while putting the rug attachment back on the Hoover.[37]

The exclamation "Now in my adventures, I can go all the way!" followed by the graphic statement "I fuck the sucking vacuum" deftly pokes fun at the sexually explicit appliance ads of the late 1960s and early 1970s. In 1967, Frigidaire promised husbands that "Your Frigidaire Dishwasher Turns You ON: You can get more wife and less housewife."[38] The time saved by this appliance would allow more time for sex—and turn back time, "returning" to them the wife they first married. In-Sink-Erator's 1969 campaign, "The Loved One" (Figure 1.7), portrayed the appliance itself as a purveyor of sexual pleasure, while Thermador's 1973 ad for "stacked" ovens compared these to the "stacked" (full-breasted) model standing in front of them (Figure 1.8). The ad copy's explanation that "the beauty photographed above, is a total cooking appliance strategically stacked and endowed with the most refined developments for culinary perfection" suggestively played on the interchangeability of the housewife and her gadget, reducing the former to a meal maker while elevating the latter to an object of erotic pleasure—a point emphasized by the description of the "Hot Food Server" that "keeps everything warm until you're ready for action." Meanwhile the phallic ad GE placed in *Playboy* in 1971, featuring an enormous frankfurter hotdog

---

[37] Bob Rosenthal, *Cleaning Up New York* (New York: The Little Bookroom, 2016 [1976]), 38.

[38] Frigidaire, "Your Frigididaire Dishwasher Turns You On," *LIFE* (December 1, 1967): 22. Frigidaire has denied permission to reproduce this ad, but it can be found online on various websites devoted to vintage ads, and on my website, https://www.racheledini.com.

FIGURE 1.7 In-Sink-Erator. "The Loved 1: IN-SINK-ERATOR." *LIFE* (June 13, 1969): 64. Copyright In-Sink-Erator. Reproduced with permission.

under the statement "Some frank talk about our Just-A-Minute oven," positioned the GE microwave oven as freeing up time for the male reader's many love affairs.[39] Perhaps unsurprisingly, however, no US advertisement

[39] GE "Some Frank Talk About Our Just-A-Minute Oven," *Playboy* (December 1971): 323.

FIGURE 1.8 Thermador. "STACKED for Convenience." *House and Home* (March 1973): 211.

for an appliance was quite as explicit as French brand Samy, which advertised its phallic vacuum cleaner with a photograph of a scantily clad housewife in the throes of ecstasy, the placement of the words "çe que toute femme désire" appearing to have been ejaculated from the appliance's tip.[40]

Rosenthal's subsequent matter-of-fact statements, which demystify the fantasy of utilizing the appliance as a sex toy and reveal it to be "nice" but "boring," explicitly counter the hyperbole of such ads and undermine the power of their erotic subtext by demonstrating its vacuity. To acknowledge the sexual dimension implicit in appliance ads will not result in a

[40] SAMY, "L'Aspirateur SAMY: Ce que toute Femme désire," *Vendre* (1958): N.P.

pornographic scene of appliance copulation but rather disclose that there is nothing sexually pleasurable about them. What is most compelling about Rosenthal's experience, in other words, is not that he has *tried* to fuck a vacuum cleaner but that he has *failed* to. The appliance has rendered him impotent, and thus failed to deliver on the promises implied by its advertisers for the last two and a half or more decades. This failure is highlighted, in the last sentence, in the shift from personifying the appliance ("Hoover") to referring to it as an object ("*the* Hoover"), which conveys both the fantastical nature of the advertising landscape's anthropomorphizing of domestic gadgets and the fantastical nature of sexual fantasies as a whole. The anticlimactic ending communicates a disillusion with the myth of the commodity akin to the thin trace of bewildered disgust that follows fantasy-induced arousal. Meanwhile the one-sidedness of the sexual encounter, wherein the only concern is Rosenthal's pleasure, unwittingly literalizes one of the most common criticisms of self-absorbed heterosexual men—that they treat women as things *to* fuck, rather than people with *whom* to fuck.

Kerouac's figuration of mindless, interchangeable, mechanized pregnant housewife shoppers participating in an endless process of consumption is very much in keeping with these depictions, and extends the critique of consumer conformity to the female sex as a whole. This imbues with a gendered dimension those moments in which he presents time-saving appliances as embodiments of that conformity.

3. "The Thing that Bound Us All Together in this World Was Invisible":[41] "All-Electric" Democracy

As well as challenging the constraining effects of mainstream culture and expressing a coterminous longing for "home," the texts just discussed invoke time-saving appliances to articulate an alternative vision of America. In particular, they reappropriate Walt Whitman's vision of electricity as a metaphor for collectivism, fraternity, and embodied democracy. As Harold Aspiz notes, the electrical imagery invoked in Whitman's poem, "I Sing the Body Electric" (1855; 1881), married both the science and the pseudoscience associated with electricity, which many at the time believed "could unlock the secrets of the universe and bridge the chasm between the material and spiritual worlds."[42] This electrical imagery also had a homoerotic subtext,

[41] *On the Road*, 308.

[42] Walt Whitman, "I Sing the Body Electric" (1855; 1881), in *Leaves of Grass, and Selected Prose* (New York: Holt, Rinehart, and Winston, 1949), 80–8; Harold Aspiz, "Sciences and Pseudosciences," in *A Companion to Walt Whitman*, ed. Donald D. Kummings (Oxford and New York: Wiley-Blackwell, 2009), 216–32. Citation on 229.

and in broader terms evidenced Whitman's faith in electricity's potential to bind individuals and societies together (Aspiz, 230). Where Keenaghan sees Kerouac and his fellow Beats' conflating of containment culture with an effeminate, "domesticated masculinity" as fundamentally incompatible with any "democratic principle of communalism" such as that espoused by Whitman, my contention is that that sense of communalism does in fact emerge, however contradictorily, at significant points in Kerouac's work (67). Crucially, it emerges in depictions of electricity in which the "aggressive masculinism" detected by Keenaghan falls away, resulting in subject-object relations that complicate what otherwise read as straightforwardly homocentric and misogynistic narratives.

In *On the Road*, Kerouac describes humanity itself as connected by a powerful, invisible energy:

> I told Neal that the thing that bound us all together in this world was invisible: and to prove it pointed to long lines of telephone poles that curved off out of sight over the bend of a hundred miles of salt. (*OTR*, 308)

This assertion echoes the vision of America Whitman articulated in a companion text to *Leaves of Grass* as "the thread-voice, more or less audible, of an aggregated, inseparable, unprecedented, vast, composite, electric *Democratic Nationality*," which Paul Gilmore reads as reflecting Whitman's understanding of poetry itself as "an electric medium . . . akin to the telegraphic lines criss-crossing the nation and girdling the world."[43] Echoing Whitman's fusion of techno-utopian nationalism, imperialism, and spiritualism, Kerouac compares the electricity coursing through telephone wires to the stuff that binds people together in order to advance a collectivist, spiritual, alternative to the atomized and atomizing rhetoric of electrical appliance advertising of the 1950s that decouples electrical currents and appliances from the meanings ascribed to them by the Cold War propaganda machine. Kerouac thus reclaims electricity as a metaphor for connectivity rather than private accumulation, and for an America consisting of interconnected currents (both literal and metaphorical), rather than isolated electrified households beholden to the "Master Switch" (*DB*, 77).

A similar effort to channel Whitman's democratic currents is apparent at the outset of one of the most oft-quoted passages in *The Dharma Bums*,

[43] "Preface, 1872, to 'As a Strong Bird on Pinions Free,'" in Walt Whitman, *Poetry and Prose*, ed. Justin Kaplan (New York: Library of America, 1996), 1000–5. Citation on 1005; Gilmore, 147. Gilmore further notes that just as the techno-utopian view of electricity linking humanity "in bonds of equality" ended in a vision of humanity that erased all but European norms, so Whitman's egalitarianism masks "the subsumption of racial and cultural difference to a heterogeneous, but finally unified, Americanism" (*Aesthetic Materialism*, 148; 152).

when Gary Snyder/Japhy quotes from "As I Sat Alone by Blue Ontario's Shores" to articulate his vision of revolution.[44] According to Japhy, the next generation of young people will abstain from participating in the Fordist economy as embodied in the purchase and disposal of time-saving appliances:

> *Cheer up slaves, and horrify foreign despots*, [Whitman] means that's the attitude for the Bard . . . see the whole thing is a world full of rucksack wanderers, Dharma Bums refusing to subscribe to the general demand that they consume production and therefore have to work for the privilege of consuming, all that crap they didn't really want anyway such as refrigerators, TV sets, . . . you finally always see a week later in the garbage anyway, all of them imprisoned in a system of work, produce, consume. . . . I see a vision of a great rucksack revolution thousands or even millions of young Americans . . . all of them Zen Lunatics who go about writing poems that happen to appear in their heads for no reason and also by being kind and also by strange unexpected acts keep giving visions of eternal freedom to everybody and to all living creatures. (*DB*, 72–3)

Whitman's postbellum paean to democracy, national unity, and geographical growth, which posited poets as uniquely positioned to "besto[w] on every object of quality its fit proportion . . . the equalizer of his age and land" (AISABBOS, 144; 146), is reimagined here for the postwar era.[45] The new struggle for democratic unity according to Japhy is embodied in the fight against the dehumanizing effects of Fordism, which "imprison[s]" citizens in their roles of worker-consumer, alienating them from their brethren and occluding the possibility of individual thought. Resistance to the socially corrosive effects of mindless consumption requires an uprising of young people who, in abstaining from participation in the cycle of production and consumption, might reconceive what Whitman termed "the great Idea, the idea of perfect and free individuals" and connect in a more meaningful way (AISABBOS, 158). Unplugging the refrigerator and leaving the suburban cul-de-sac opens up possibilities for metaphorically "plugging into" an alternative frequency.

---

[44] Walt Whitman, "As I Sat Alone by Blue Ontario's Shores" (1881), in Walt Whitman, *Poetry and Prose*, ed. Justin Kaplan (New York: Library of America, 1996), 468–83. Henceforth, "AISABBOS."

[45] For an incisive discussion of Whitman's revisions of the poem following the Civil War, see Thomas F. Haddox, "Whitman's End of History: 'As I Sat Alone by Blue Ontario's Shore,' Democratic Vistas, and the Postbellum Politics of Nostalgia," *Walt Whitman Quarterly* 22.1 (2004): 1–22.

The heroic attributes Kerouac ascribes to these "rucksack revolutionaries" who he imagines retrieving America's original purpose are paradoxically akin to those that Beat writer Richard Brautigan recalls ascribing to electricity itself, as a child, in "I Was Trying to Describe You to Someone" (1974).[46] In this 366-word pastiche of Shakespeare's "Sonnet 18" ("Shall I compare thee to a summer's day?"), Brautigan's speaker explains the difficulty of describing the woman he loves: "I couldn't say 'Well she looks just like Jane Fonda' . . . because you don't look like Jane Fonda at all" (60). Instead, he describes her as a "perfect 1930s New Deal morality kind of movie . . . about rural electrification" that he saw as a child in 1941 or 1942, about "farmers living in the country without electricity" and without "any appliances like toasters or washing machines" until they built a dam and "strung wire over fields and pastures":

> There was an incredible heroic dimension that came from the simple putting up of poles for the wires to travel along. They looked ancient and modern at the same time. Then the movie showed electricity like a young Greek god, coming to the farmer to take away forever the dark ways of his life. Suddenly, religiously, with the throwing of a switch, the farmer had electric lights to see by when he milked his cows. . . . The farmer's family got to listen to the radio and have a toaster and lots of bright lights to sew dresses and read the newspaper by. It was really a fantastic movie and excited me like listening to the Star Spangled Banner, or seeing photographs of President Roosevelt, or hearing him on the radio. . . . I wanted electricity to go everywhere in the world. I wanted all the farmers in the world to be able to listen to President Roosevelt on the radio. . . . And that's how you look to me. (60)

While Brautigan's story initially appears the antithesis of Kerouac's vision in its seemingly patriotic fervor, closer examination reveals the parallels between them. For the love expressed in Brautigan's text hinges on his recollection of electricity's utopian associations prior to their adulteration by an unbridled consumer capitalism and prior to the revelation of the fundamental shortcomings of the government claiming them. The story's power derives from the analogy it draws between adult love for a person and a childhood infatuation with an ideal conjured by a government propaganda campaign. The film he references is most likely *Power and the Land* (1940), commissioned by the Rural Electrification Administration (REA) and

[46] Richard Brautigan, "I Was Trying to Describe You to Someone," in *Revenge of the Lawn* (New York: Pan Books, 2014 [1974]), 60.

written by poet Stephen Vincent Benet.[47] The film portrayed electricity's transformative effects on the home of the Parkinsons, a farming family. As Daniel L. Wuebben notes, its depiction of power lines as "symbols of freedom, progress, and equality" recalled Walt Whitman's descriptions in "Passage to India" of "the seas inlaid with eloquent gentle wires" (Wuebben, 137–8; 18). By invoking this campaign, Brautigan conveys how the myths on which propaganda draws and the sensations it elicits embed themselves in memory, and influence later impressions, to the point of providing the language with which one makes sense of the world. More importantly, he conveys the child's mind's capacity to filter and refract propaganda, and in so doing counter its more nefarious effects. If from one perspective the effort to describe the speaker's beloved spectacularly fails, conveying less about her than about the nationalist and imperialist strains of 1930s and 1940s promotions of domestic electrification, from another perspective it succeeds in repurposing that nationalistic and imperialist rhetoric. The electric—and the campaign for an "all-electric" America—becomes a means to give voice not to the desire to "civilize" and "domesticate" the nation but rather to a body's desire to be with another body. And that desire is fueled by whole currents of energy: enough electricity to cross the entirety of the United States, if not the world, and to power the radios that once enabled Roosevelt's voice to be projected into living rooms across the nation. The rhetoric originally deployed to enlist an entire nation of citizens into a new mode of electrical living equated with US imperialism and the vanquishing of economic uncertainty is rerouted, so to speak, to instead spark connection between two selves. Both electricity as a resource and the values attached to it are reoriented.

The temporal setting of Brautigan's story endows it with added poignancy. For the memory of a small boy in love with the New Deal's vision of electricity is all the more naïve when viewed from the perspective of the early 1970s—a period characterized by energy shortages, blackouts, economic recession, and a new cynicism borne from the Vietnam War, the assassinations of John F. Kennedy, Martin Luther King, Jr., and Bobby Kennedy, the Pentagon Papers, and Watergate, not to mention the Civil Rights movement and Second-Wave Feminism. To resemble Roosevelt's vision of electrically powered toasters and washing machines is to resemble the myth before its demystification. The text thus posits the woman described as akin to the speaker's first love—a pre-Watergate, pre-Vietnam, pre-atomic bomb faith in raw resources and their capacity to enliven, enrich, and connect, and which these events, and revolt against the inequities that such faith papered over, have wholly debunked. Where *The Dharma Bums* channels the poetic currents of Whitman to envision an uncontained future,

[47] Joris Ivens, *Power and the Land* (Rural Electrification Administration, 1940). See also Wuebben, 135–7.

and identifies electrical wiring as a metaphor for human connectivity as opposed to a component of the Cold War apparatus, "I Was Trying to Describe You to Someone" conveys the power of domestic electrification as an ideology. Both gesture toward an alternative poetics by disentangling electrical modernization from its tyrannical associations—be these stated explicitly, as in *The Dharma Bums*, or implicit, as in Brautigan's story.

This Whitman-inflected effort to literally and figuratively reappropriate electricity is also evident in Kerouac's accounts of his and his fellow travelers' reliance, as they travel across the country, on "reefers," or refrigerated containers. The refrigerated railcar was invented in the 1880s to enable meat companies to transport meat carcasses, rather than live animals, thus lowering transport costs and, subsequently, the price of meat.[48] The nickname "reefer" comes from the "reefer points"—external electrical power points—required to charge them with enough electrical current to last a journey.[49] During the Great Depression, itinerant men looking for seasonal work rode these cars as a form of free transport, which is what Cassady teaches Kerouac to do in *On the Road* (*OTR*, 255).[50] In *The Dharma Bums*, Kerouac describes how "[w]ith the water dripping out of reefer refrigerators I gathered up palmfuls and splashed it in my face and washed and washed my teeth and combed my hair" before braving the "regular hell [that] is L.A." (*DB*, 86). The surreal quality of the passage derives from its subversion of the standard generic devices of the castaway narrative, wherein the survivor must domesticate natural resources. The wilderness here is not one of trees and brush but of refrigerated railcars barely visible beneath the smog of a sprawling city. The descriptions of drinking from refrigerated railcars provide a further way for Kerouac to align himself with a US tradition of living off the land that stretches back to the pioneers. But rather than domesticating nature, the Beat poet domesticates the electricity that has taken nature's place. The scene is all the more poignant when one considers the hypothesis advanced by some historians that the surge in refrigerator sales in the 1930s was driven by paranoia regarding the rise in itinerant men begging door to door, which cast suspicion on street vendors including ice delivery men (Tobey, 26). Where the refrigerator offered 1930s American homes a "defence" against "invasion" by the newly homeless, the refrigerated railcar in Kerouac's albeit idealized vision of elective transience offers an alternative domesticity, wherein the homeless circumvent the cloistered constraints of the indoors, and liberate domestic conveniences from the domestic space.

---

[48] Marc Levinson, *The Box: How the Shipping Container Made the World Smaller and the World Economy Bigger* (Princeton, NJ: Princeton UP, 2008), 15–16.

[49] John H. White, *The Great Yellow Fleet: A History of American Railroad Refrigerator Cars* (San Marino, CA: Golden West Books, 1986), 73–7.

[50] Kenneth L. Kusmer, *Down and Out, On the Road: The Homeless in American History* (Oxford and New York: Oxford UP, 2002), 312.

Elsewhere in *On the Road*, Kerouac enlists the refrigerator to break down the boundaries between "inside"/ "outside" and "domestic"/ "public" in a manner that also undermines heteronormative values. This is evident when Kerouac and Henri Cru break into a military barracks cafeteria and lunge toward the soda fountain:

> Here, realizing a dream of mine from infancy, I took the cover off the chocolate ice cream and stuck my hand in wrist-deep and hauled me up a skewer of ice cream and licked at it. Then we got ice cream boxes and stuffed them—poured chocolate syrup over and sometimes strawberries too—took wooden spoons—then walked around in the dispensary, the kitchens, opened iceboxes to see what we could take home in our pockets. (*OTR*, 172)

The scene transforms the efficiently run, Fordist cafeteria, with its spotless formica countertops, stainless steel hotplates, standardized portions, and industrial cold storage units calibrated for temperature-controlled safekeeping, into a space of sensual, messy, and erotically charged spillage. In this, it recalls what Christopher Schmidt has termed the "queer excess" apparent in twentieth-century poetics that generates waste and wastage at the level of form, while rendering visible the queer body.[51] Indeed, while Kerouac's anxieties about homosexuality are well documented, the sensual imagery he invokes in this passage as well as the presence of homosexual scenes in early drafts of the novel suggest the merits of reading the passage through a queer lens.[52] In particular, the men's night-time jaunt among the frozen delicacies of the cafeteria they are meant to be guarding against break-ins and deviant behavior reads as an extended allegory for queer desire, in which the misuse of appliances and sensual embrace of cold, sticky, ice cream serve as proxies for sex—an analysis that is made all the more compelling given cafeterias' function, in early- and mid-twentieth-century America, as cruising grounds.[53] More broadly, the nonnormative subject-object relations Kerouac depicts exemplify Scott Herring and Sarah Ahmed's understanding

---

[51] Christopher Schmidt, *The Poetics of Waste: Queer Excess in Stein, Ashbery, Schuyler, and Goldsmith* (New York: Palgrave Macmillan, 2014).

[52] My approach aligns itself with that of scholars following Roger Austin, who in his now-classical study, *Playing the Game: The Homosexual Novel in America* (New York: Boobs-Merrill, 1977), argued that Burroughs's framing in anti-capitalist terms of Times Square hustler Herbert Huncke's definition of "Beat," which Ginsberg, Burroughs, and Kerouac had appropriated, erased the movement's queer aspects (184–7). See also Dan Naplee's discussion of *On the Road*'s homoerotic elements: "On the Road: The Original Scroll, Or, We're Not Queer, We're Just Beats," *The Explicator* 69.2 (2011): 72–5.

[53] George Chauncey, "Lots of Friends at the YMCA: Rooming Houses, Cafeterias, and Other Gay Social Centers," in *The Gender and Consumer Culture Reader*, ed. Jennifer Scanlon (New York: New York UP, 2000), 49–70.

of queerness as encompassing not only sexual orientation but a whole host of forms of attitudes, behaviors, and modes of inhabiting the world that stand in opposition to an inherently heteronormative capitalist culture centered on and around the nuclear family and the reproduction of future-laborer-consumers.[54] From this perspective, the refrigerator that welcomes Kerouac's wandering hand reads as an expression of rebellion against the constraints of a containment culture in which the terms "homosexuality," "communism," and "degeneracy" were used interchangeably—as well as an allegory for a homosexual desire of which its author may not even have been aware.[55] This penetration recalls Ahmed's description of the ways in which queer inhabitancy involves "extending bodies into spaces that create new folds, or new contours of what we could call livable or inhabitable space" (11). In penetrating the ice cream, rendering it inedible (by the hygienic standards of the scientifically managed cafeteria) and introducing a foreign element into it—the hand—Kerouac indeed creates a new, if momentary, way of inhabiting the "space" of the cold storage unit.

The chaos just described also has an ironic political dimension. For in the passage following, Cru justifies the food theft by quipping, "'You know what President Truman said [...] we must cut down on the cost of living'" (*OTR*, 172)—a reference to Truman's much-publicized State of the Union Address of January 1946, where he called for Congress to fight inflation by extending the wartime freeze on the price of goods and services.[56] Cru then proceeds to make a series of purposefully inane statements vaguely reminiscent of political slogans, from "'Things are getting rough all around'" and "'We've just got to make it the best we can and that's all there is to it,'" to "'we're in this thing together'" (*OTR*, 173). The juxtaposition of references to national economic policy with sound bites akin to those used to promote such policies provides a textual equivalent to the desecration of the sanctity of the Fordist cafeteria just described. The epiphany that follows—"I suddenly began to realize that everybody in America is a natural born thief"—reads as a heavy-handed parody of both postwar economic policy and the patriotic slogans that defined wartime US culture (*OTR*, 174). This is all the more

[54] Scott Herring, *The Hoarders: Material Deviance in American Culture* (Chicago: U of Chicago Press, 2014); Sarah Ahmed, *Queer Phenomenology* (Durham, NC: Duke UP: 2006), esp. 9.

[55] Among the earliest and most well known of these arguments is John D'Emilio's "Capitalism and Gay Identity," in *Powers of Desire*, ed. Ann Snitow, Christine Stansell, and Sharon Thompson (New York: Monthly Review Press, 1983), 100–13, where D'Emilio argues: "th[e] elevation of the nuclear family to pre-eminence in the sphere of personal life" drives individuals under capitalism to "internalis[e] a heterosexist model of intimacy and personal relationships" (109). For an overview of the Lavender Scare's relation to containment propaganda, see May, 91–3 and David K. Johnson, 10–16.

[56] Harry Truman, "Message to the Congress on the State of the Union and on the Budget for 1947," Released January 21, 1946. Dated January 14, 1946. Public Papers, Henry Truman, 1945–1953.

evident in light of Kerouac's similarly sardonic description, in Book Two, of the experience of driving with Neil Cassady through the "great displays of war might" that "lin[e] Pennsylvania Avenue" on the inauguration day of Truman's second term (*OTR*, 236). In each instance, Americanness itself—as embodied in modern refrigeration, military pageantry, or the conflation of the two—is wrested of its imperialist meanings and made queer.

4. Conclusion

Both Kerouac's early writings and the novels for which he his best known betray a fascination with the refrigerator that bears the influence of Depression-era and early postwar era refrigerator advertising. Examining these depictions alongside advertisements from the period in which they were published throws into relief the indebtedness of Kerouac's aesthetic to the very same media landscape he claimed to oppose. Kerouac's time-saving appliances give credence to Martinez's suggestion that the Beats did not so much reject conformity as "ech[o], albeit dissonantly" the reactionary elements of 1950s America, and James Balwin's assertion that Beat writing was "the symptom of the same madness" as Eisenhower and Nixon's speeches.[57] But Kerouac's fetishization of the bountiful refrigerator exists in tension with his deployments, elsewhere, of domestic electrification to critique a Cold War containment culture figured as feminine and feminizing, and to reimagine US democracy as powered by connective forces akin to the electrical wires traversing the nation. Attention to those moments where Kerouac wrests the appliance of its early postwar associations without conflating it with a castrating femininity—those moments when, instead, he queers it—reveals a different, and more nuanced, dimension of his poetic vision. When examined through a queer lens, these reappropriations of the appliance read as radical challenges both to Cold War surveillance and conformity and to capitalist heteronormativity. We will find this effort to exhume electricity's late-nineteenth-century and Depression-era associations with democratic freedom, and reappropriate it to create an alternative idea of home, in the work of a number of other writers discussed in the chapters that follow.

[57] Martinez, 25; James Baldwin, "Notes for a Hypothetical Novel" (1960), *Nobody Knows My Name: More Notes of a Native Son* (London: Penguin, 1991 [1964]), 119–30. Henceforth, *NKMN*.

2

"The Lamentation of a Vacuum Cleaner":[1]

Appliance Disappointments in John Cheever and Richard Yates, 1947–81

Oh Mother, dear Mother, oh Mother,
Why is the sky so dark? . . .
It's nothing, my dear daughter,
This isn't the way the world ends,
The washing machine is on spinner,
And I'm waiting to entertain friends.
But Mother, dear Mother, please tell me,

Why does your Geiger counter tick? . . .
It's nothing, it's nothing, my darling,
It's really nothing at all,
My Geiger counter simply records
An increase in radioactive fall.[2]

An earlier version of this chapter was published as a standalone article in *Textual Practice* in August 2020. I am grateful to the editors for granting me permission to replicate this material.
[1] John Cheever, "The Enormous Radio" (1947), in *The Collected Stories of John Cheever* (London: Vintage, 2010 [1977]), 11–34. All short story titles from this collection are hereafter abbreviated *CSJC*.
[2] John Cheever, *The Wapshot Scandal* (London: Vintage, 2003 [1964]), 42. Henceforth, *WS*.

In her memoir *Home before Dark* (1984), Susan Cheever recalled visiting her father John Cheever at his home in Ossining New York shortly before his death.[3] Bedridden and in the final stages of cancer, Cheever could barely speak and Susan deduced, from his gestures, a request to unplug the electric heater by his bed, as he "never trusted electrical appliances. If a heater, toaster, or electric blanket was turned off without being unplugged, he was convinced it might still flash on mysteriously, with fiery and explosive consequences" (*HBD*, 213). But "from his face, [she] knew [she] had done the wrong thing"—and he sarcastically replied, "'How *clever* of you to think I want it unplugged'" (*HBD*, 213). Seven years later, Richard Yates's daughter Monica, who had moved into her father's house to monitor his increasingly frequent bipolar episodes, would awaken in the middle of the night to find her father "standing in her room wearing a raincoat, frantically pushing a vacuum cleaner and saying he couldn't work it—what could he do—?" (Bailey, 571). When Yates died in November 1992, the unfinished manuscript of his memoir, *Uncertain Times*, was found in the author's freezer (Bailey, 5). One finds, in these anecdotes of fathers manically vacuuming in the night, literary works stashed in freezers, and daughters causing disappointment for something as trivial as an electric plug, dynamics uncannily similar to the gadget-ridden domestic relations depicted in Cheever and Yates's fiction. This chapter examines a selection of appliance depictions in these writers' short stories and novels, which diverge from each other in important ways despite their shared effort to, in Kate Charlton-Jones's words, "dismember the American Dream."[4]

In Cheever's fiction, shiny new washing machines and handheld electric mixers malfunction with precisely those "fiery and explosive consequences" identified by the author's daughter. As in the (fictional) song that serves as this chapter's epigraph, such explosions are often linked to the explosive potential of the atomic bomb as part of a broader critique of the interrelation of the goods and arms races. Meanwhile Cheever's depiction of his immigrant characters' fascination with Americans' domestic gadgetry forms part of a broader comment on the nation's self-mythologization abroad. The jocose tone of these depictions allowed their critical dimension to go unnoticed during much of his lifetime, thus enabling him to maintain his carefully cultivated persona as a champion of the American way of life, and not a critic but a representative, as Joe Moran puts it, of a "collective national mood."[5] As Moran notes, the author cover story of Cheever published in the

[3] Susan Cheever, *Home Before Dark* (New York: Simon and Schuster, 1984), 213. Henceforth, *HBD*.

[4] Kate Charlton-Jones, *Dismembering the American Dream: The Life and Work of Richard Yates* (Tuscaloosa: U of Alabama Press, 2014).

[5] Joe Moran, "The Author as a Brand Name: American Literary Figures and the 'Time' Cover Story," *Journal of American Studies* 29.3 (December 1995): 349–63. Citation on 354.

March 27, 1964, issue of *Time*, like the magazine's subsequent coverage of his work, helped portray the author as a "New England squire" devoted to God and family, and to categorize his literary representations of homosexuality and alcoholism as "morality tales" rather than autobiographical accounts (353). The cheerful depictions of time-saving appliances in the journal entries Cheever chose to publish in *The New Yorker* throughout the 1960s and 1970s similarly tempered the more critical dimension of the appliance depictions in his fiction, which for a twenty-first-century reader stand out as very obvious challenges to Cold War America. As late as 1977, when Cheever's struggles with alcoholism and his stint in rehab had become public knowledge, such selectively picked entries presented a domestic context in which "Neither the vacuum cleaner nor the dishwasher will function, but the splendid thing about working happily is that it leaves me with very little energy for bitterness, anger, impatience, and long indictments," and in which lazy Sundays were punctuated by the happy sound of his wife "swear[ing] at the vacuum cleaner" (what the woman wielding the vacuum cleaner was thinking was not considered).[6]

In contrast to Cheever's ambivalently lustrous gadgets, appliances in Yates's more straightforwardly autobiographical fiction form part of an explicitly shabby backdrop from which they exert pressure in inevitably negative ways, participating in the obsessive repetition of the author's own unhappy childhood and adult struggles with financial precariousness, alcoholism, and psychiatric internment. The son of an alcoholic failed musician who worked as a regional sales representative for GE and a sculptress with unfulfilled aims to exhibit at the Whitney and live among New York's wealthiest (the two divorced when he was three), Yates focuses relentlessly on the lives of laborers, impoverished divorcées, and alcoholic organization men whose stories are seeded with anecdotes from his own life (Bailey, 13–14; 17). With the exception of the protagonists of his first novel, *Revolutionary Road* (1961), the characters in these texts live in squalid accommodation where, as the protagonist of *Young Hearts Crying* (1984) describes her "makeshift kitchen," "Nothing ha[s] ever worked."[7] The refrigerator meanwhile participates in the Sisyphean ritual of drink making, drunken self-aggrandizement, and morbid self-flagellation that always and inevitably ends where it began: in the cold embrace of the refrigerator doors. While it would be reductive to see the latter depictions solely in biographical terms, they are certainly consonant with Yates's own material circumstances in adulthood: the refrigerator in the tiny kitchen in the "bare, roach-infested" basement apartment he rented between 1959 and 1961 contained "nothing

[6] John Cheever, "From the Seventies and Early Eighties: Excerpts from a Diary," *The New Yorker* (August 4, 1991): 49.

[7] Richard Yates, *Young Hearts Crying* (London: Vintage, 2008), 117. Henceforth, *YHC*.

but bourbon and instant coffee" (Bailey, 196). Friends described the first of the two apartments on Beacon Street, where Yates lived between 1976 and the early 1980s, as "'fucking *grim*,'" singling out "[t]he refrigerator . . . stocked with three items: instant coffee, beer, and yogurt" (Bailey, 471). Of this and the second Beacon Street apartment, his friend Martin Napasteck recalls: "in each one [I] saw him open the refrigerator, which had long been uncleaned. Some beer, some bread, something left over. Less than a third of the space inside the refrigerator was occupied."[8] This frequent invocation of Yates's empty refrigerators as evidence of what his friend Mark Costello viewed as his eschewing of bourgeois values tells us a great deal about what this particular appliance symbolized for his generation, and provides a fascinating context for examining the texture of the grain against which Yates was writing (Bailey, 471).

While the tone of these two authors' appliance depictions may differ, the depictions themselves reflect a shared concern with the distance between reality and the fantasy world of television advertisements and sitcoms in the postwar era, as well as the authors' acknowledgment of these gadgets' status as veritable actors in the drama of a specifically white middle-class postwar domesticity. In particular, Cheever and Yate's time-saving appliances function as more than mere contributors to what Roland Barthes terms a text's "reality effect"—those objects in fiction that are superfluous at the level of plot but integral to the enhancement of the novel's realism.[9] Instead, these gadgets participate in subject-object relations that either explicitly or implicitly refer back to their mediated counterparts. Indeed, given the frequency with which the texts both make explicit references to television and radio and invert the tenets of the television sitcom through tragic plotlines, one might more accurately compare the time-saving appliances represented therein to the furnishings of a set on a TV sitcom gone awry. Where the brand-name appliances that populated the sets of *I Love Lucy* (1951–7), *Leave it to Beaver* (1957–63), *The Dick Van Dyke Show* (1961–6), *Ozzie and Harriet* (1952–66), and, later, *The Mary Tyler Moore Show* (1970–7) served as brand endorsements as well as elements in an extended and broad-ranging televisual demonstration of what Americans should aspire to own and be, Cheever and Yates's appliances serve as allegories for nuclear anxiety and a moral opprobrium that exposes the naiveté and spiritual corruption of believing in the gods of consumer goods.[10]

---

[8] Martin Napasteck, *Richard Yates Up Close* (Jefferson, NC: McFarland, 2012), 88.

[9] Roland Barthes, "The Reality Effect" (1967) in *The Rustle of Language*, transl. Richard Howard (Oxford: Blackwell, 1986), 141–8.

[10] For an overview of these particular brands' endorsements of American family sitcoms during the so-called Golden Age of television, see Jennifer Gillan, *Television and New Media: Must-Click TV* (London and New York: Taylor & Francis, 2010) and Lawrence R. Samuel, *Brought to You By: Postwar Television Advertising and the American Dream* (Austin, TX: U of Texas Press, 2001). Roland Marchand has further demonstrated the emphasis GM placed in its early

Where Barthes's notion of the reality effect is premised on objects that blend into the background of the narrative, lending credence without drawing attention to themselves, the time-saving appliances in Cheever and Yates call attention to the artifice and performativity of the "all-electric" home of which they are a part—a reading bolstered by both authors' time spent writing scripts for television (Cheever between 1945 and 1952, Yates throughout the 1980s).[11] The first section of this chapter contextualizes the two authors' appliance depictions within the history of early postwar television. The sections following provide in-depth readings of four texts by Cheever (sections 2–5), and four by Yates (sections 6–7).

1. Time-Saving Appliances and Early Postwar Television

Cheever and Yates's anti-televisual appliances stand out among a veritable panoply of sardonic references to television sitcoms and to print, radio, and television advertising in the two authors' works that create a sense of characters floundering among a network of multi-media messages that have no bearing on their own lived experience. In Cheever's *The Wapshot Scandal* (1964), teenage grocery delivery boy Emile is "disappointed," during his first airplane flight, "to find that [the airplane] was not so sleek as the planes in magazine advertisements and that the fuselage was dented and stained with smoke" (*WS*, 117). The description is imbued with all of the other disappointments that have preceded it, and in turn affects those following. Like a prism, it refracts the anticlimactic dissipation given off by mechanical objects throughout the rest of the text: each ensuing object of disappointment bears the stigma of both the event in which it participates and those that have come before. Yates's penultimate novel, *Young Hearts Crying* (1984), is likewise riddled with references to the protagonists' involvement with television scriptwriting to fund their more "serious" efforts to publish fiction (*YHC*, 195; 217). Metaphorically speaking, then, the energy on which time-saving appliances in Cheever and Yates run, and that they give out, is one of cumulative sadness that can be traced through the texts' multifarious engagements with domestic electrification and the broader rhetoric of Cold War consumerism of which the "all-electric" home was a part.

Scholars' neglect of the roles of domestic gadgetry and television in Cheever and Yates can be largely ascribed to the fact that the historical study

television ads on its ownership of Frigidaire (*Creating the Corporate Soul: The Rise of Public Relations and Corporate Imagery in American Big Business* (Berkeley, CA: U of California Press, 1998), 142–7).

[11] Lynne Waldeland and Warren G. French, *John Cheever* (New York: Twayne, 1979), 13; Bailey, 193; Naparsteck, 7.

of domestic technology, housework, and consumerism more broadly began just as Cheever in particular fell out of fashion (although it is interesting to note that the proliferation of gadgets in his work was explicitly remarked upon by Soviet reviewers, one of whom noted that "everyday life is not burdensome" for Cheever's heroes due to the "vacuum cleaners, washing machines, dishwashers, refrigerators which hold enough food for a week or more" at their disposal).[12] Yates, for his part, was overlooked by the academy until the early 2000s, as Blake Bailey's 2003 biography of the author, Jennifer Daly's 2017 edited collection, and Kate Charlton-Jones's 2014 book-length study discuss in detail.[13] However, the proliferation of studies of twentieth-century popular culture published since the 1990s, which has demonstrated the often complex commercial and ideological imperatives underpinning US radio and television networks' investment, opens up opportunities to revise our understanding of the period's fiction.[14]

Of particular note are Lizabeth Cohen's now-canonical account of the postwar era's framing of consumption as a form of civic duty, and Anna McCarthy's seminal study of 1950s and 1960s television's role in "creating favourable attitudes" to free-market principles far beyond what radio might have hoped to achieve.[15] Yates explicitly critiques this latter strategy via his depiction, in *Disturbing the Peace* (1976), of protagonist John Wilder's parents, who are evangelical supporters of the free market that enabled them to secure investment for their now-successful luxury chocolate brand.[16] Following a psychotic break that results in his psychiatric internment, this advertising salesman with aspirations to produce Hollywood movies ends up in a psychoanalyst's office, where he recounts: "'As long as I can remember, [the parents]'d be lecturing me about "Management" and "Free Enterprise" and "Venture Capital"'" (*DP*, 80). Wilder, whose very name suggests an ingrained opposition to "civilized" conformity, is unable to put his faith in either free enterprise or the promise of happiness advanced by television sitcoms. Upon his discharge from hospital, he stares across the dinner table

---

[12] Tatyana Litvinova, "John Cheever's *The Brigadier and the Golf Widow*," in *Soviet Criticism of American Literature in the Sixties: An Anthology*, ed. Carl R. Proffer (New York: Ardis, 1972), 24–6. Citation on 24. The exceptions to this neglect of Cheever are Christopher Kocela's excellent analysis in *Fetishism and Its Discontents*, 155–86, and Catherine Jurca's in *White Diaspora*, 133–59.

[13] Jennifer Daly, ed., *Richard Yates and the Flawed American Dream: Critical Essays* (Jefferson, NC: McFarland, 2017). News of allegations of sexual misconduct against Bailey broke as this monograph was going into production. I wish to make clear that in citing Bailey's research into Yates's life, I am not dismissing or disbelieving these allegations.

[14] See in particular: Gillan; Samuel; Marchand; Mary Beth Haralovich, "Sitcoms and Suburbs: Positioning the 1950s Homemaker," *Quarterly Review of Film and Video* 11.1 (May 1989); Spigel, *Make Room for TV* and *Private Screenings*; Gerard Jones, *Honey I'm Home: Selling the American Dream* (New York: Grove, 1992); Nina C. Leibman, *Living Room Lectures: The Fifties Family in Film and Television* (Austin, TX: U of Texas Press, 1995).

[15] Cohen, *A Consumer's Republic*, 9; McCarthy, *The Citizen Machine*.

[16] Richard Yates, *Disturbing the Peace* (London: Vintage, 2008 [1975]), 89. Henceforth, *DP*.

his wife and son, wondering: "How could any family as unhappy as this put on such a show every night, and how long could it last?" (*DP*, 144). In the novel's concluding pages Wilder falls headlong into a supermarket display of his parents' luxury chocolates in a literal refutation of the fruits of venture capital, then holes up in a dank apartment where he "eat[s] only scraps from the refrigerator" and drinks whiskey before being sectioned again (*DP*, 208–9; 216). Madness and confinement prove the only escape from a life of failed attempts to emulate the "plot of a television comedy" such as those his son enjoys describing at dinner (*DP*, 169). In recounting Wilder's rejection of venture capitalism's fruits, the television sitcom's formula for familial bliss, and the refrigerator as a source of bounteous meals, Yates critiques the narrative of corporate benevolence advanced by sitcoms in the first decades after the war. The reference to the—distinctly unbranded, anonymous—refrigerator populated only by scraps, which echoes the novel's earlier, pointedly ambiguous, description of Wilder going "to the place where the bourbon and the ice were kept" rather than to a sideboard, ice bucket, or refrigerator, counters the product placement efforts of appliance manufacturers that had become established in the two decades prior to the novel's publication (*DP*, 65; McCarthy, 44). Most notably, Hotpoint (at the time owned by GE) not only appeared in the commercial spots and opening credits for *The Ozzie and Harriet Show* (1952–66), which featured a seventeen-year-old Mary Tyler Moore as "Happy the Hotpoint Elf" dancing with a series of animated appliances."[17] The show writers also created storylines centered on Hotpoint appliances, while their formula of setting at least one scene per episode in the kitchen became the standard for the sitcom genre (Gillan, 189). Perhaps more importantly, *Ozzie and Harriet* helped foster what McCarthy terms an "alchemy of goodwill" (38)—a sense of the corporation's embeddedness in the lives of its consumers, be they the fictional characters on screen or the real people watching the show, as an inherently good thing (Gillan, 189). Yates's description of Wilder going wild in the supermarket and taking meager pickings from a refrigerator he more usually approaches for ice to top up his whiskey thrusts both corporate values in general and the appliance specifically into an unflattering light. The overtly clumsy description of "the place where the bourbon and the ice were kept" can moreover be seen as an effort to circumlocute the appliance: to *erase* the object that in a sitcom would be seen in every shot, and instead throw into relief the excessive alcohol consumption from which appliance manufacturers sought to distance their products (about which more later).[18]

Yates also engages with what Marsha Bryant identifies as the liveliness endowed to time-saving appliances in postwar advertising, which she notes,

[17] Gillan, 189, and McCarthy, 38.
[18] I am indebted to Dr. David Fallon for the coining of the expression "appliance circumlocution" to name the deflection I identify here.

quoting Roland Marchand's observations about early-twentieth-century US advertising, entailed a "'"re-personalization" of life' premised on 'a tacit recognition of an unvanquished public propensity toward animism—the belief that all objects are alive.'"[19] In *Revolutionary Road*, Yates subverts the trope of the helpful "all-electric" home via depictions of time-saving appliances that appear endowed with evil agency.[20] *Revolutionary Road* introduces Frank and April Wheelers's modern suburban home, from the very first pages, as a site of discord and its appliances as complicit in generating the kind of ugly pain that the sitcom seeks to deny. The Wheelers must "tens[e] their shoulders and set their jaws in attitudes of brute endurance" to withstand the "cheerful blaze of kitchen and carport lights," while the happy, helpful refrigerator of television here is but a prop against which an incensed April "paus[es] to steady herself" as she "sway[s] blindly through the kitchen," preparing herself for "the kind [of fight] that went on for days" (*RR*, 31; 32). In focusing on details such as the kitchen that, on the morning after the novel's opening fight, "gleam[s] to an industrial perfection of cleanliness," the electric stove with which Frank Wheeler "fumble[s]" while making coffee as a peace offering for his wife, and the lawnmower that April pushes in a manner that "seemed determined to prove, with a new, flat-footed emphasis, that a sensible middle-class housewife was all that she had ever wanted to be," Yates endows the "all-electric" home and its time-saving appliances with maleficent agency (*RR*, 42–4). They are coconspirators in the Wheelers's undoing, ensuring they never transcend their suburban surroundings or amount to anything but bad copies of the figures on the television that dominates their living room.

A similar shrinking of experience taking place underneath the veneer of abundance is apparent in Yates's references, in *Young Hearts Crying*, to a housewife's habit of "'ironing and watching television at the same time, morning, noon, and night'" and a father who explains the word "'dilemma'" to his young daughter with the example that "'maybe you want to go out and play . . . but there's a good show on television and you sort of feel like staying home and watching that instead. . . . You can use [the word] in a lot of ways'" (63; 112). In the Yates imaginary, the little girl who learns that words can be used "in a lot of ways," and that to be faced with a dilemma is to be faced with the embarrassment of two equally appealing choices, will inevitably grow into the housewife whose choice is to look either at her electric iron or at a television broadcasting images of electric irons. Yates builds on this latter image a few scenes later when the aforementioned housewife, Nancy Smith, "stand[s] at the ironing board" and tells the protagonist that her brother was blown up by a land mine

[19] Roland Marchand, *Advertising the American Dream: Making Way for Modernity 1920-1940* (U of California Press, 1985), 358, qtd. in Marsha Bryant, "Ariel's Kitchen," 229.
[20] Richard Yates, *Revolutionary Road* (London: Vintage, 2010 [1961]). Henceforth, *RR*.

in France just before the end of the Second World War (*YHC*, 128–31). The seemingly vacant housewife who consorts only with her time-saving appliances is revealed to be a woman long disillusioned by all that postwar America has to offer, and whose only true satisfaction is her son's handicap, since, as she concludes the story about her brother's death, "'Now they can never take him into the Army'" (*YHC*, 131). Her electrical gadgets are not cheerful companions. Rather, they are witnesses to suffering for which their alleviation of drudgery cannot compensate, and which their very existence has paradoxically created more time to endure.

Cheever and Yates's appliance depictions are also compelling in their reflection of what Tim Engles has termed the "white male nostalgia" unique to late-twentieth-century literature written by cisgender heterosexual white men and exemplified by Sloan Wilson's 1955 novel, *The Man in the Gray Flannel Suit*—to whose protagonist, incidentally, John Wilder in *Disturbing the Peace* is likened by another character.[21] While the original audiences, and even later critics, of texts such as Wilson's have tended to conflate author and cantankerous protagonist, Engles suggests these texts sought to expose the problematic nature of their characters' nostalgic longings and persecution complexes (Engles, 6). Although I am wary of entirely dismissing the often overtly misogynistic tone of Cheever and Yates's works, which it is, at times, difficult to see as anything but a reflection of the authors' own biases (and which might be why Engles does not include them in his study!), this approach does offer a way to engage critically with them. More to the point, Cheever and Yates's particular use of appliances to express the anxieties of middle-class men—or of female characters who read like the constructions of male writers—reveals much about the perception of time-saving appliances in this period by those who never had to use them, while also challenging assumptions about the reach of ads whose target audience was ostensibly female. It is moreover arguable that the *legacy* of the image of the all-American housewife and her gadgets owes as much to the refraction of her advertised image through the works of Cheever and Yates's generation of writers as it does to the ads themselves.

2. "All-Electric" Pandemonium: Inconvenient Noise in Cheever's "The Enormous Radio" (1947)

The time-saving appliances in Cheever's "The Enormous Radio" (1947) are projected not via a television but rather via television's precursor; the radio,

[21] Tim Engles, *White Male Nostalgia in Contemporary American Literature* (New York: Palgrave Macmillan, 2018).

which Ronald C. Tobey notes, "changed consumers' values . . . erod[ing] parochial and ethnic values by diffusing mass culture [and] intensifying mass consumerism" (160). Cheever's story playfully subverts these touted benefits by satirizing the advertising strategies used by appliance manufacturers of the late 1940s and those he would have observed while listening to the radio as a boy.

"The Enormous Radio" begins with Jim Westcott's purchase of a radio whose "mistaken sensitivity to discord" enables it to broadcast everything that takes place in the couple's building, effectively turning the neighbors' daily lives into radio plays performed for the sake of the listeners' entertainment, and, too, extensions of an electrically powered aural culture industry (*CSJC*, 11). Thus, Irene "discern[s] through the Mozart the ringing of telephone bells, the dialing of phones, the lamentation of a vacuum cleaner" and "elevator bells, electric razors, and Waring mixers, whose sounds had been picked up from the apartments that surrounded hers and transmitted through her loudspeaker" (*CSJC*, 51). The radio's sensitivity to the sounds of time-saving appliances and disagreements between different family members regarding unpaid bills, mounting debts, ennui, and sex renders the story an allegory for early postwar discord and their causal relationship to the era's reliance on consumer goods, and particularly *electrical* ones, bought on credit, that transformed the relationship between individuals and their domestic environment.

That the source of insight into these transformations is, itself, an appliance (albeit not a time-saving one) is no coincidence. Radio broadcasting, like television, was initially conceived to advertise consumer goods and increase domestic electricity use (Tobey, 156). Before it invested in the television show *General Electric Theater*, GE launched *GE Symphony Hour*, a radio show whose host's role was to "rhapsodiz[e]" to listeners about the "wizardry" of domestic electricity and particularly appliances.[22] Ingeniously, it is precisely because the interactions Irene hears are *not* family squabbles resolved by the purchase of a new coffee maker, but rather conflicts over bank overdrafts and articulations of deep existential angst, that she understands they aren't staged (*CSJC*, 54). Indeed, the sound of escalating family conflicts and relentlessly whirring appliances are correctives to the advertising jingles and testimonials traditionally found on the radio. They tell the true story of the time-saving appliance, or, more specifically, stor*ies*: a multiplicity of narratives, none of which points to either the supremacy of the manufacturer or consumerism, or to the appliance's effectiveness in rationalizing the messiness of everyday life.

Relatedly, the radio's broadcasting of disruptive appliance noises punctures the myth of modern technological efficiency and bourgeois respectability. For the radio wave "interference" also "interferes" with the

---

[22] Roland Marchand and Michael L. Smith, "Corporate Science on Display," in *Scientific Authority and Twentieth-century America*, ed. Ronald G. Walters (Baltimore, MD: Johns Hopkins UP, 1997), 162.

tranquillity of the Westcotts' home. Rather than helping the Westcotts save time, these appliances only offer sounds without use. And they mark the passage of time, but to *people who don't want to be told of it*. The day-long sound of the "whir of cooking appliances," followed by "the static" at sundown that indicates "the vacuum cleaners ha[ve] all been returned to their closets," merely reveals the neighbors' lives to be as mundane as the Westcotts' own, and the passage of days all too transient (*CSJC*, 51). The radio's appliance broadcasts thus counter both the efficiency ethos broadly and the instrumentalization of familial happiness in advertising specifically.

This counternarrative is also apparent in the story's parodic emulation of the discourse around social mobility of the immediate postwar era as expressed by the bulletins, promotional pamphlets, and other sponsored publications disseminated by GE, GM, and, indeed, Waring—the brand of blenders mentioned in the passage quoted earlier.[23] These publications, which were created by the companies' in-house public relations departments and largely aimed at fostering loyalty among company employees and prospective customers, relied on a rhetoric of unfettered growth grounded in statistical evidence gathered by a burgeoning consumer research industry.[24] The authoritative voice of the census bulletin, itself based on the presumed objectivity of numbers, is palpable in the story's opening lines—"Jim and Irene Westcott were the kind of people who seem to strike that satisfactory average of income, endeavor, and respectability that is reached by the statistical reports in college alumni bulletins"—while the tone of the focus group leader creeps in through details such as the couple's attendance at the theater "on an average of 10.3 times a year" (*CSJC*, 49). The language of the text mimics that of a consumer report, where the more minute the attention to detail ("You could not say that Jim Westcott looked younger than he was, but you could at least say of him that he seemed to feel younger"), the less one actually knows (*CSJC*, 49). The "stories" the Westcotts are exposed to via their magical radio erupt into this homogeneity, shocking their listeners with conflicts that no corporate-sponsored pamphlet can resolve, such as the woman who desperately tells her husband that "'you know, Charlie, I don't feel like myself anymore'" (*CSJC*, 54).

Where, like an electrically illiterate Adam and Eve, neither Irene nor Jim at the story's outset "understood the mechanics of radio—or of any of the appliances that surrounded them," by the story's conclusion they have been enlivened, if not to the gadget's literal mechanical functioning, then certainly to its imbrication in a consumer culture that requires participants to get into unprecedented levels of debt to maintain a tenuous semblance

---

[23] Howell John Harris, *The Right to Manage: Industrial Relations Policies of American Business in the 1940s* (Madison: U of Wisconsin Press, 1982), 187–92.

[24] McCarthy, 53; Andrew L. Yarrow, *Measuring America* (Amherst: U of Massachusetts Press, 2010), 96–7.

of allegiance to the ideal of "hard-won" prosperity (*CSJC*, 11). The radio acts as a proverbial apple whose taste, or in this case sound, ruptures the fragile Edenic bliss of the "all-electric" home by revealing the anxieties all but drowned out by the buzzing of its time-saving appliances.

3. "Il Frigidario": US Appliances and Immigrant Help in Cheever's "Clementina" (1964)

Cheever's "Clementina" is told from the (third-person) perspective of an Italian maid from the fictional Umbrian town of Nascosta (the Italian word for "hidden").[25] At age seventeen Clementina relocates to Rome to work for an American family before accompanying them back to the United States. The story is thought to have been partly inspired by Cheever and his wife's own maid in Rome, Iole Felici, who moved from Rome to work for the Cheevers in the mid-1950s.[26] Upon arriving in New York, Clementina is struck by the excess of the "all-electric" American home and by Americans' apparent substitution of religious faith and iconography with the gods of consumer goods. But her initial "suspicion" of conveniences such as the washing machine that "use[s] a fortune in soap" is soon overridden by marvel at its, and its fellow appliances,' capabilities:

> [F]irst she would put some dirty clothes in the washing machine and start that, and then she would put some dirty dishes in the other machine and start that, and then she would put a nice *saltimbocca alla romana* in the electric frying pan and start that, and then she would sit in the *salone* in front of the TV and listen to all the machines around her doing the work, and it delighted her and made her feel powerful. Then there was the *frigidario* in the kitchen, making ice and keeping the butter as hard as stone, and there was the deep freeze . . . and there was an electric egg beater, and a machine for squeezing the oranges, and a machine for breathing in the dust, and she would have them all going at once, and a machine for making the toast—all bright silver—where you put in the plain bread and turned your back and *allora*, there were two pieces of toast just the color you had asked for, and all done by the machine. (*CS*, 568)

The passage's utopian language conveys the cumulative effect of these machines: as in "The Enormous Radio," this is an entire network of mechanized objects. The closing statement, "All done by the machine," describes not just the toaster identified just prior but the "machine" that

---

[25] John Cheever, "Clementina" (1960), in *CSJC*, 561–79. Citation on 562.
[26] Scott Donaldson, *John Cheever: A Biography* (New York: Random House, 1988), 173–4.

the house has become through the introduction of these appliances, and the "machine" that is US modernity. The "and thens" that punctuate the passage contribute to a sense of cacophonous movement, an accretion of both time-saving appliances and sensations catalyzed *by* time-saving appliances—an assembly line of doing and feeling. The passage's sheer energy is amplified by the linguistic slippages, which indicate Clementina has not got the words to articulate the things she is witnessing and that she only partially understands. These are apparent not only in Clementina's reversion to Italian or the reference to the "machine for breathing in the dust" instead of "vacuum cleaner," but in her use of *frigidario* to refer to the refrigerator, rather than the actual Italian word, *frigorifero*, or "Frigidaire," the brand name that many Italians, like many Americans, used interchangeably with the official term until the late 1960s.[27] This latter slip is particularly interesting, as *frigidario* is not a synonym for *frigorifero* but the word for the room in Roman baths featuring cold water.[28] While one might assume that Cheever's use of this word is merely a misspelling of *frigorifero*, the story's narrative style, which very explicitly seeks to emulate the thoughts of an Italian person translated into English, suggests the slip is intentional. Just as the text's use of noun phrases and false friends contributes to the text's broader performance of linguistic foreignness, the reference to a *frigidario* conveys Clementina's unfamiliarity with this new technology of which she has never had occasion to speak, reflecting the fact that the assimilation of time-saving appliances in working-class Italian households only occurred in the late 1960s.[29]

From a more critical standpoint, one might argue that this ecstatic encounter with time-saving appliances perpetuates entrenched stereotypes about a "backward" Southern Europe, and reaffirms dubious histories of the "all-electric" home and particularly electrical refrigeration by US scholars, wherein these are understood as "gifts" a forward-looking America gave to a world waiting to be civilized by its modern inventions (indeed, the name of Clementina's village reads as a metaphor for an unindustrialized Italy from which the miracles of electricity have remained "nascosti," or hidden). One thinks here of Oscar Edward Anderson's *Refrigeration in America* (1953), which described refrigeration as "a triumph of Yankee enterprise" before expostulating that Americans had long "held a position of world leadership" in the "application of refrigeration to the problems of a great industrial and agricultural nation" (4–5). Or, indeed, more recent accounts such as Jonathan Rees's *Refrigeration Nation* (2015), which claimed that "[w]ith globalization, every country that can afford to pay can now eat like

[27] Janice Jorgensen, ed., *Encyclopedia of Consumer Brands, Volume 3: Durable Goods* (Detroit, MI: Gale/St James Press, 1994), 175.
[28] Treccani. http://www.treccani.it/vocabolario/ricerca/frigidario/. May 21, 2019.
[29] Donald S. Pitkin, *The House That Giacomo Built: History of an Italian Family, 1898–1978* (Cambridge: Cambridge UP, 1985), 152–4.

Americans do, consuming a diet of foods produced elsewhere and preserved by refrigeration on their journeys from all over the world," and Carroll Ganz's *Refrigeration: A History* (2015), which asserted that "the Russian people [at the end of the Cold War] were starved for the manufactured fruits of Western mass production, low costs, and high standard of living."[30] But the story's stance toward both modernity and America's role in it appears more skeptical when one takes into account Cheever's own aforementioned hatred of appliances, his well-documented veneration of Italian culture, and, crucially, the texture of Clementina's disdain, even at the story's end, for certain aspects of America, and her discovery that the countryside near her home has been ruined by "*la bomba atomica*" first invented by the United States (Donaldson, 200—230; *CSJC*, 571). Cheever might perhaps be faulted for portraying this peasant woman as a kind of noble savage—but the humor of his protagonist, who views at times with disgust this country where there is "ice water on the table, and what [i]s not cold [i]s flavorless and badly cooked," complicates this binary reading, too (*CSJC*, 566; 577). Clementina's horror at her employers' life of easy, convenience-equipped alienation, and the healthy skepticism she retains toward the technologies that have alleviated some of her work, makes this a story about more than simple immigrant assimilation.

4. Vanquished Aspirations: Vacuum Cleaners in Cheever's *The Wapshot Chronicle* (1957)

The figuration of time-saving appliances as embodiments of a Cold War containment culture premised on fear of difference and nuclear annihilation is apparent across Cheever's oeuvre, but is most evident in his first two novels, *The Wapshot Chronicle* (1957) and, its sequel, *The Wapshot Scandal* (1964). The first of these follows the life of brothers Moses and Coverly Wapshot, and takes place in their hometown of St Botolphs, which remains untouched by the cultural transformations of the twentieth century.[31] These scenes exploring the lives of the young men's eccentric great-aunt Honora and their aging parents contrast with the final third of the novel, in which Moses and Coverly encounter the Cold War machine that lies beyond St Botolphs. Moses moves to Washington to work in a job "so secret that it can't be discussed here," where he encounters the paranoid context of McCarthyism (*WC*, 130; 132). Coverly moves to New York, where he marries a woman named Betsey and trains to be a "Taper," learning code to "translat[e] physics experiments into the symbols—or tape—that could

[30] *Refrigeration in America* (Princeton: Princeton UP, 1953), 4–5; Rees, 187; Ganz 2015, 199.
[31] John Cheever, *The Wapshot Chronicle* (London: Vintage, 1998 [1957]). Henceforth, *WC*.

be fed into a computation machine" (*WC*, 153). He gets a job at a space rocket-launching station with an adjacent suburban complex that houses the organization's staff and their wives, where Betsey's ensuing depression is laid bare via a series of appliance-centered encounters.

The first of these occurs during her trip to the local shopping center for a replacement cord for her electric iron. Here she "cheerfully" asks a cashier where to get the appliance repaired, explaining in detail why she needs it and at what point in her errands she hopes to have the repair completed (*WC*, 228). She inflicts an even longer, if remarkably similar, monologue on the clerk at the hardware store next door:

> I'm a stranger here and when my ironing cord went yesterday while I was doing my husband's shirts I said to myself that I just didn't know where to take it and have it repaired but this morning I stopped it at the Grand Food Mart and that cashier, the nice one with the pretty, wavy hair and those dark eyes, told me that he recommended your store and so I came right over here. Now what I'd like to do is to come downtown and do my shopping tomorrow afternoon and pick up my iron on my way home because I have to get some shirts ironed for my husband by tomorrow night and I wondered if you could have it ready for me by then. It's a good iron and I gave a lot of money for it in New York where we've been living although my husband was out in the Pacific. . . . I don't understand why the cord on such an expensive iron should wear out in such a short time and I wondered if you could put on an extra-special cord for me because I get a great deal of use out of my iron. I do all my husband's shirts, you know, and he's high up in the Taping Department and has to wear a clean shirt every day and then I do my own personal things as well. (*WC*, 228)

Betsey's self-presentation as a woman who looks after her time-saving appliances with as much care as she looks after her husband and his shirts is symptomatic of her absorption of the images and rhetoric of the period's media. Mid-century television ads and promotional films for appliances presented life as a series of challenges that could be overcome with the right gadget. In *Young Man's Fancy* (Edison Electric Institute, 1952), teenager Judy's fears that her older brother Bob's college friend Alex is a "woman hater" are debunked when he expresses interest in her cooking—they fall in love as he explains to her the time-motion studies that render her mother's electric appliances so efficient.[32] In *Once Upon a Honeymoon* (Bell Systems, 1956), a group of angels intervenes in the life of newlyweds Mary and her songwriter husband Jeff, who have had to postpone their honeymoon

[32] Donald H. Brown, "Young Man's Fancy," Edison Electric Institute, 1952.

until Jeff completes a musical number called "The Wishing Song." As Mary wrestles with the malfunctioning appliances in her kitchen, inspiration strikes, and she sings a song about the kitchen she wishes they owned. The angels sprinkle down fairy dust, brand-new appliances magically appear—and the song is a hit, enabling them to go on their honeymoon.[33] And in *A Word to the Wives* (1955), a film short sponsored by *The Woman's Home Companion* and the American Gas Association to promote gas appliances as superior to electric, housewife Jane Peters escapes a life of drudgery by visiting her mother in Cleveland for the weekend and leaving her husband to fend for himself: two days of washing dishes and clothes by hand is enough to spur him to buy his wife a new house, complete with a dream kitchen equipped with Whirlpool appliances.[34] The daily appliance mishaps of the protagonists of mid-century sitcoms in turn endowed with much-needed levity anxieties about both the financial cost of these gadgets and the real damage that their malfunction could pose.[35] Such a template reinforced, too, the manageability and fulfilling nature of housework in the "all-electric" home—suggesting that electrification transformed the life of the housewife into a narrative punctuated by daily triumphs. Betsey's visit to the hardware store to buy a new cord follows this same formula, while revealing the fundamental loneliness that such ads obscured.

This loneliness becomes all the more apparent when one considers the passage immediately following. Betsey goes home, makes a sandwich with the peanut butter just purchased from the supermarket, decides she is pregnant despite her period being only seven days late, and envisions her house populated with small children to keep her company. She then lets in a door-to-door vacuum-cleaner salesman whom she subjects to her third monologue in two pages, explaining, this time, that while she currently can't afford a new one, "'I'm determined to buy a new vacuum cleaner sooner or later . . . I'm pregnant now and a young mother can't do all that housework without the proper equipment'" (*WC*, 229). The monologue self-consciously imitates the "before and after" structure of mid-century appliance ad

[33] Gower Champion, "Once upon a Honeymoon," Jerry Fairbanks Productions/Bell Systems, 1955.

[34] Norman Lloyd, "A Word to the Wives," TelAmerica, Inc, 1955.

[35] For example, S02E31 of *I Love Lucy* revolves around the faulty washing machine that Lucy and Ricky sell to Ethel and Fred, which spectacularly malfunctions before money changes hands. After a series of mishaps involving the machine, the episode ends with Ricky and Fred splitting the cost of both machine and the porch railing it fell through, as friendship wins over financial anxieties ("Never Do Business With Friends," June 29, 1953). In S03E26 of *The Lucy Show,* Lucy's demolition of her and Viv's refrigerator to prove that the mystery sound in a radio contest is that of a refrigerator breaking down plays on the lure of sponsored competitions, turning the relative confinement of the widowed housewife, her susceptibility to mediated messages, and the danger of a malfunctioning appliance into a source of comedy ("Lucy the Disc Jockey," 1965).

narratives—while her inclusion of her imaginary pregnancy and a future household populated with children evidences her willingness to delude herself that she is the universal first person of the mid-century advertising testimonial. It also reflects a broader tendency of mid-century appliance ads to reduce people to caricatures based on their roles (wife, office worker, mother) and to elevate products to the status of family members. Indeed, Betsey's desire for a vacuum cleaner to clean up after her imaginary children is of a piece with campaigns such as Westinghouse's offer, in 1953, to give a set of its newly launched "Laundry Twins" (a washing machine and dryer) to all parents of twins born on September 23, 1952—the date the "Laundry Twins" were "born" (Figure 2.1). An illustration of the "Laundry Twins" ensconced in two matching pink silk covered cots alongside ad copy that mimicked the rhetoric of a birth announcement, and the slogan, "Blessed Event," further conflated the appliance launch with the momentousness, and emotive charge, of a child's birth. Through Betsey's story, Cheever reveals how the mid-century "all-electric" imagination rendered people and commodities interchangeable via imagery and rhetoric that flattened the former and animated the latter.

FIGURE 2.1 Westinghouse. "Blessed Event! Westinghouse Proudly Announces the Arrival of the 1953 Twins." *LIFE* (September 8, 1952): 16–17. ©Westinghouse. Reproduced with permission.

5. Blown Fuses and Nuclear Blasts: Cheever's *The Wapshot Scandal* (1964)

Cheever extends these ideas in *The Wapshot Scandal* (1964), which leaves St. Botolphs behind entirely, following, instead, Coverly's work in nuclear research, Moses's decline into alcoholism, and great-aunt Honora's efforts to flee the country to escape prosecution from the Internal Revenue Service (IRS) for tax evasion. Time-saving appliances punctuate both the text's opening and closing scenes, which respectively take place on two Christmas Eves a year apart. In the first, Mr. Applegate, St. Botolphs's alcoholic rector, blesses the carollers in his living room and hallucinates that "he [can] hear their prayers: 'Lord God of Hosts, shall I sell the laying hens?' . . . 'Shall I buy a new icebox?'" (*WS*, 8). In the second, he drunkenly intones: "'Let us pray for all those killed . . . on the expressways [and] for all those wounded by rotary lawn mowers, chain saws, electric hedge clippers and other power tools'" (*WS*, 301). The novel thus begins with the (imagined) prayer for a new appliance and concludes with a prayer to not be destroyed by them, or by any of the other modern wonders of the postwar era capable of both improving Americans' quality of life and ending it altogether. Between these two moments, Cheever narrates a series of interconnected tragedies involving a long cast of more or less death-inducing gadgets indicative of their owners' redundancy. Thus Emile, the teenaged grocery boy with whom Moses's thirty-something wife, Melissa, has run away, laughs at her use of the old-fashioned word icebox instead of "Frigidaire":

> "that's a funny word, icebox. I never heard it before. . . . It's a funny thing to call a Frigidaire. But you speak differently, you know . . . you say lots of things are divine, but, you know, my mother, she wouldn't ever use that word, excepting when she was speaking of God." (*WS*, 120)

Beyond drawing attention to the difference in their ages, Emile's remarks underscore the speed with which the vocabulary of techno-modernity becomes outdated in line with the objects it identifies. They also inadvertently conjoin power-generated gadgets and godly power, highlighting the novel's preoccupation with the Bomb's, and techno-consumerism's, unleashing of energies whose capacity humankind has not even begun to fathom.

Such dark humor is characteristic of all of the appliance depictions in *The Wapshot Scandal*. The fact that most of the exploding domestic gadgets that feature in this novel are owned by households whose income derives from an organization capable of blowing up the earth as a whole endows these depictions with particular irony. These blown electrical fuses, broken washing machines, houses burned down by exploding furnaces, and lawn mowers that chew off their owners' legs function as a series of allegories for nuclear anxiety, the human toll of the nuclear arms race and space race (in which Coverly's organization is also involved), and a deep-rooted nostalgia for a time before both the Cold War and electrical cold storage. Indeed, while Cheever began working on the novel in early 1958, the fact that he wrote the bulk of it between 1959 and 1963 makes it tempting to read the text as a riposte to the Nixon-Khrushchev Kitchen Debate that took place at the American National Exhibition in Sokolniki Park, Moscow, in July 1959, already discussed in the Introduction to this study. Held in a model lemon yellow GE kitchen, the debate centered on the respective merits of capitalism and communism for women, in what amounted to a public relations stunt intended to distract from both the United States' inability to keep up with Soviet space and nuclear research and the prospect of global annihilation as the arms race heated up.[36] The appliance depictions in *The Wapshot Scandal* highlight the absurdity of early Cold War America's simultaneous veneration of time-saving gadgets and investment in nuclear weaponry that in annihilating the human race would render such time-saving redundant.

The shift in register from *The Wapshot Chronicle* to *The Wapshot Scandal* is signaled early in the latter text, with the description of Coverly Wapshot's move from working as a taper at the Remsen Rocket Launching site to public relations at the Talifer Missile Site, where he is in charge of weaving the site's space and weapons research into a broader narrative about the inviolable frontiers of the human spirit (*WS*, 34). But this narrative is undermined by the everyday reality of the neighboring suburban enclave's inhabitants, and especially those seemingly unconnected to the Cold War complex, such as housewife Gertrude Lockhart, whose malfunctioning appliances, described in detail over six pages, drive her to suicide (*WS*, 104–9). In this storyline, Cheever reveals the isolation that resulted from the social construction of mid-century time-saving appliances as rendering women self-sufficient, thus precluding any expectation of assistance from other family members, friends, or relatives. What the text refers to as "a house that had, in a sense, ceased to function" reflects a broader social malfunctioning, revealing a form of domestic reification, according to which the housewife is at the behest of her gadgets (*WS*, 104). Indeed, Cheever draws explicit parallels between the different breakages, the lack of available help, and Gertrude's own increasingly erratic behavior:

> She plugged [the electric heater] into an outlet in the kitchen and pulled the switch. All the lights in the house went out and she poured herself some more whisky and began to cry. She cried for her discomforts but

[36] See Phillips and Hamilton, *The Kitchen Debate*; Oldenziel, *Cold War Kitchen*; and Castillo, 160–9.

> she cried more bitterly for their ephemeralness . . . for a world that seemed to be without laws and prophets. . . . Some repairmen came and patched things up but when the children came home from school she was lying unconscious on the sofa. (*WS*, 107)

The description intentionally obfuscates the order of events and their causation—lights going out and the housewife drinking and crying appear to happen all at the same time, as if the pulling of the switch instigated all three. Likewise, her lying unconscious on the sofa after the fuse has been repaired, while purportedly the result of exhaustion and excessive alcohol consumption, reads, here, as one more power shortage or breakdown in a long series. The housewife has, herself, blown a metaphorical fuse.

The story of Gertrude Lockhart is of course partly tongue in cheek. Cheever is satirizing the mid-century obsession with household technologies and the nuclear anxiety that it obscured. And he is responding to Betty Friedan's diagnosis, in *The Feminine Mystique* (1963), of "the problem that has no name" with a series of problems that can, indeed, be named. But the text also playfully undermines the appliance narratives set out by manufacturers of the time. Cheever is being intentionally ludicrous when he describes malfunctioning appliances that drive a housewife to "thr[ow] her arms around the milkman" who rejects these advances and then, "in a blackmailing humor [,] stuff[s] the icebox" with items that she hasn't ordered, but will now have to pay for (*WS*, 108). But this narrative is no more ludicrous than the 1947 Frigidaire manual that personified an electric range as a "handsome and handy helper" who will "capture Mrs. Housewife's heart" and secure her "lasting affection"; the 1950 Westinghouse ad that personified an oven range and refrigerator as "the most exclusive couple in the world" (Figure 2.2); the 1953 Eureka ad in which a housewife proclaimed "'Pete is my husband—but my new Eureka Roto-Matic is my honey!'" (Figure 2.3); or the image of the housewife who is transported, in her dreams, to pirouette through Frigidaire's "Kitchen of Tomorrow" in GM's industrial film, *Design For Dreaming* (1956).[37] One might also read Gertrude's story as a counter-narrative to that advanced by an entire genre of wedding-themed appliance ads that emerged in the early 1940s, which promoted these objects as not only ideal engagement or wedding presents, but more covetable than marriage itself—and which implicitly conflated the "all-electric" home with an imminent postwar future. For example, Toastmaster's "The Hint that

[37] *The Wapshot Scandal*, 107–9; William Beaudine, "Design for Dreaming," MPO Productions/GM, 1956; *How to Stay in Love for Years...* (Dayton, OH: Frigidaire Division, GM Corporation, 1947), 3. Frigidaire has denied permission to reproduce this pamphlet, but images can be found online on various websites devoted to vintage ads, and on my website, https://www.racheledini.com.

FIGURE 2.2 Westinghouse. "The Most Exclusive Couple in the World!" *LIFE* (October 2, 1950): 71. ©Westinghouse. Reproduced with permission.

Came True" (1940) suggested the young woman in the ad had been waiting not for her boyfriend to propose to her, but for him to buy her a Toastmaster toaster.[38] The ads for Westinghouse's 1940 "Advise-A-Bride" contest invited contestants to write a letter to a bride, explaining the benefits of either an electric range or refrigerator, for the chance to win a free one of their own.[39] In Hotpoint's ad for its 1940 "all-electric" kitchen, "Bride's Wish Comes True!", a large illustration of a kitchen outshone the comparatively tiny call-out illustration of a groom peeking over a delighted bride's shoulder to admire the gadgets therein.[40] Where these ads positioned time-saving

[38] Toastmaster, "The Hint that Came True," *The Ladies' Home Journal* (July 1940): 125.
[39] Westinghouse, "Free! $23,000.00 in Electrical Prizes Westinghouse 'Advise-A-Bride' Contests," *LIFE* (April 22, 1940): 69.
[40] Hotpoint, "Bride's Wish Comes True!," *Better Homes and Gardens* (February 1940): n.p. Wedding and engagement themes comprised a crucial strand of appliance advertising over

FIGURE 2.3 "Pete Is my Husband—But my New Eureka Roto-Matic Is my Honey!" *McCall's* (1953): 94.

appliances as participants in a life-affirming rite of passage, Cheever reveals them to be disloyal disappointments whose failure to fulfil the housewife's dreams is rivaled only by that of her absent husband.

Elsewhere, Cheever relates time-saving appliances to the tentacular reach of US power abroad. While traveling by ship to Europe to escape the IRS man, Honora meets numerous US tourists whose technologies either possess them (a couple who chooses hotels based on whether they have washing machines capable of cleaning Orlon fabric) or destroy them (the repairman whose negligence resulted in a home blowing up its inhabitants). Together, these encounters provide an extended metaphor for the international reach of a military-industrial complex invested in the manufacture of domestic time-saving machinery and in weaponry whose effectiveness might well render moot the former's success. It is thus ironic that old Honora should blow an electrical fuse not once, but twice, on this journey, by plugging in a thirty-five-year-old curling iron that causes the generators powering the entire ship to malfunction. While the first time is a mistake that merely reveals her to be out of step with postwar culture, the second time is intentional, reflecting a protracted resentment of "appliances or other kinds of domestic machinery" that "seemed to her mysterious and at times capricious" and that "because she came at them hastily and in total ignorance . . . often broke, backfired or exploded in her face" (*WS*, 159). Plunging the vessel into darkness with her prewar appliance provides a metaphorical outlet for Honora's building rage as well as a momentary triumph over an inscrutable postwar techno-modernity.

6. Drinking and Horror Behind the Scenes: Blenders and Refrigerators in Yates's "Saying Goodbye to Sally" (1981) and "A Natural Girl" (1981)

Yates's appliance depictions are as a whole far darker than Cheever's, functioning as participants in a desolate dance of unhappy subject-object relations. In "Saying Goodbye to Sally," Yates invokes a blender to underscore the extent to which the household at the story's center revolves around drinking, and to foreshadow its inevitably unhappy ending. The maid who works for the titular Sally tells the narrator: "'See that blender? Empty, right? Well, twenty minutes ago that blender was full to the top with

---

the following four decades, which positioned toasters, blenders, coffee machines, and electric carving knives as ideal wedding gifts to accompany newlyweds into the future.

brandy Alexanders. And I mean I don't think that's very sensible, do you? [...] I like to see a little restraint.'"[41] While a key selling point of blenders in the 1950s and 1960s was, indeed, their suitability for mixing drinks, this use was underplayed in both the advertisements for such items placed in women's and general interest magazines (including in *The New Yorker*, where this story was initially published) and in the manuals and recipe pamphlets that accompanied them, lest the association with alcohol sully their image and scare away conservative customers. Thus, while Osterizer promoted its "Osterizer Liquifier-Blender Bar Mixer" as the appliance for "distinguished drinksmanship" to *Esquire* and *Playboy*'s male audience throughout the period 1966 to 1970, advertisements for items such as the "Drink Mixer" accessories (a cocktail and sieve) that GE launched in 1947 to accompany its standing mixer made no mention of alcohol at all.[42] The instructions and recipe pamphlet GE released that same year for its Portable Mixer likewise featured only one cocktail recipe at the very end of its beverages section.[43] Cocktail mixing was also conspicuously absent from the functions outlined for the blender in *Around the World Cookery with Electric Wares*, one of several brochures sent to households nationwide by the Edison Institute as part of "You Live Better Electrically," the campaign GE, Westinghouse, and Edison ran between 1958 and 1966 to increase domestic electricity use.[44] An exception to this rule was the book of recipes developed by home economist and *Chicago Tribune* cookery columnist Ruth Ellen Church for Osterizer, under the pen name Mary Meade. *Mary Meade's Magic Recipes for the Osterizer Original Liquefier Blender* (1952) featured an entire section on drinks, couched, however, in the language of good etiquette and prefaced with an explanation distinguishing between regular drinks and "'ladies drinks'—so called because they are pretty and delicious from the first sip," and clarifying the blender's unsuitability for making Manhattans and Martinis as "a blender would make them cloudy."[45] This inclusion is ascribable to the fact that the book did not come free with the appliance, but would have been sought out in bookstores, while the author's associations with

---

[41] Richard Yates, "Saying Goodbye to Sally" (1981), in *The Collected Stories of Richard Yates* (London: Vintage, 2008 [1996]), 200–18. Titles from this collection hereafter abbreviated *CSRY.*

[42] See, for example, Osterizer, "Press on to Exotic Drinksmanship," *Playboy* (June 1966): 68; "Secret of success in drinksmanship," *Esquire* (June 1967): 60; "yours for distinguished drinksmanship," *Playboy* (December 1970): 63.

[43] *Instructions and Recipes: General Electric Portable Mixer* (Bridgeport, CN: GE Company Appliance and Merchandise Department, 1947), 33. ASBSC, MSUL.

[44] "Get Maximum Use from Your Appliances," in *Around the World Cookery with Electric Housewares* (New York: Home Service Committee, Edison Electric Institute, 1958). ASBSC, MSUL. *For a discussion of "You Live Better Electrically,"* see Wuebben, 140.

[45] Ruth Ellen Church, "Drinks," in *Mary Meade's Magic Recipes for the Electric Osterizer* (Indianapolis and New York: Osterizer and Bobbs-Merrill Company, 1952), 104–36.

good taste would have helped to frame drinks-making as an extension of the excellent hosting she promoted in her column. By contrast—and despite what its title would suggest—*Easy-Do Parties Electrically* (1960), circulated at a municipal level by local water and power plants by the "You Live Better Electrically" campaign, featured only one cocktail recipe, providing instead a section on "Electric Blender Smoothies" such as milkshakes and juice and ginger ale-based drinks (Figure 2.4). The wrap-around cover illustration, of a heterosexual white couple preparing canapés in their open-plan kitchen while the guests dance in the living room beyond, was likewise a chaste affair, with no glass in sight, while the function of the blender perched on the counter was underscored by the chilled dessert dishes to which the host was adding maraschino cherries.

In this way, print advertising divested home entertainment of any elements that might be deemed deviant. Yates's depiction of the blender, then, plays on the distance between the image of the appliance used for brandy Alexanders

FIGURE 2.4 *Easy-Do Parties Electrically.* St Louis, MO: Milliken Publishing Company/You Live Better Electrically, 1960. Author's own.

that are unceremoniously consumed as soon as they are prepared in order to chase away a hangover, and those depictions of lovingly, carefully prepared milkshakes and soups that populated blender ads and pamphlets.

Where the blender in "Saying Goodbye to Sally" punctures the myth of the wholesome all-American family, the refrigerator in "A Natural Girl" undermines that of the stalwart masculine man.[46] "A Natural Girl" opens with the titular Susan telling her father, Edward, that she doesn't love him, that "'there's no more why to not loving than there is to loving. I think that most intelligent people understand that,'" and that she is marrying her (much older) history professor, David (*CSRY*, 201). After David has a nervous breakdown, Susan divorces him, repeating almost exactly the same words she first said to her father: this time, "'there's no more why to not loving than there is to loving. Isn't that something most intelligent people understand?'" (*CSRY*, 214). When she next visits her parents, her father avoids showing his emotional response to her return by fleeing to the kitchen to fix everyone a drink, where he takes shelter in the space between the open shelves and semi-open door of the refrigerator:

> He broke open a tray of ice cubes with more force and noise than necessary, hoping it might stifle his mounting rage, but it didn't. He had to turn away and press his forehead hard against the heel of one trembling hand . . . Girls. . . . Would their smiles of rejection always drop you into despair and their smiles of welcome lead only into new, worse, more terrible ways of breaking your heart? (217)

This instance in which repressed emotion is quickly followed by its explosive expression is an almost exact recapitulation of a prior episode, in Susan and David's house, when Susan:

> watched him [David] walk out of the room to the kitchen. She heard the soft slam of the big refrigerator door and the breaking open of an ice tray, and then came something unexpected and frightening: a burst of high, wild laughter that didn't sound like David at all. It went on and on, rising into falsetto and falling only part of the way down as he gasped for breath, and he was still in the grip of its convulsions when he came weakly back into the room with a very dark bourbon and water rocking and clinking in his hand. (211)

In both scenes, the refrigerator functions as a shelter for the "unmanly" expression of sorrow by men either about to be (in David's case) or who have already been (in Edward's case) hurt by a "cold" and unfeeling woman (Susan). Just as mixing a drink provides Yates's characters with something to do, and drinking itself provides a means of escape, the refrigerator itself, with its great, welcoming concavity in which one can bury one's head

[46] Richard Yates, "A Natural Girl" (1981), in *CSRY*, 200–18.

without eliciting concern, provides a momentary respite from a lifetime of repressed feeling. In both instances, the spot in front of the refrigerator is where these two men in the midst of their psychological breakdowns can allow themselves to be overcome by emotion, in an explicit subversion of normative male behavior that could just as easily be interpreted as catalyzed *by* the refrigerator as condoned by it. One might go so far as to argue that this appliance that is usually the domain of the woman of the house *infects* those who approach it with feminine feelings: that it elicits both David's "high, wild" laughter that "rises into falsetto" and Edward's abandonment to dramatic gestures at odds with his ordinarily stoic demeanor. Put differently, it is no coincidence that the unmanning of these two *paters familias* coincides with their self-relegation to the most marginal spot in the home: the journey into the arms of the refrigerator reflects an equivalent diminution in their authority. This repetition with difference both parallels and inverts the repetition of Susan's deadpan statement to both men—itself a subversion of the traditional dynamic of stalwart man and weeping woman overcome by affection. The pathos of both scenes derives from the obvious temporary nature of the respite found, and from the contrast between the clinical quality of this "haven" and the comfort sought—not to mention the contrast between the chilled contents and the man metaphorically melting in front of it. That a device for cold storage is the best the male characters can find to distract from the "coldness" of the women they love is an apt allegory for the crisis of masculinity that Yates so thoroughly explores in this and his other fiction.

7. Empty Refrigerators and the Stench of Recent Vacuuming: Yates's *Easter Parade* (1976) and "Oh Joseph, I'm So Tired" (1981)

In this last section, I examine a select few of Yates's later appliance depictions to suggest the merits of reading the works across his *oeuvre* as a whole as connected by the invisible currents of electrical modernization and its association with an American Dream that remains very much outside his characters' grasp. In keeping with the refrigerator depiction in "A Natural Girl" just discussed, we find in these texts an unexpected gender split, wherein time-saving appliances are a source of disgust for Yates's female characters, but tender nostalgia for his men.

In *The Easter Parade* (1976), two references to vacuum cleaning contribute to the novel's broader depiction of circumscribed, suffocating femininity. *The Easter Parade* narrates the story of sisters Emily and Sarah Grimes and their mother, a divorcée who aspires to wealth and fame but ends up dying of alcohol-related dementia in a home for the infirm. Neither of her daughters, as the novel's opening lines tell us, is destined to much better. Sarah develops a debilitating drinking problem in response to her husband's physical abuse, and whether it is a drunken fall or a particularly violent beating that causes her early death is left unclear. Meanwhile Emily has a series of failed relationships to horrible men and a faltering career as a journalist before ending up drunk and alone. The first reference to a vacuum cleaner occurs early in the novel, in a description of Emily's first visit, in the late 1940s, to her new husband Andrew's childhood home. Here she is received by her mother-in-law, a "blue-haired, wrinkled and powdered woman" who sits on a "chintz-covered sofa . . . in a room that smell[s] of recent vacuum cleaning [and] blink[s] at Emily repeatedly as if having to remind herself that Emily [i]s there" (*EP*, 70).

The smell of recent vacuum cleaning—which is to say, the smell of compacted dust particles and dirt mixed with exhaust—underscores the "airless," claustrophobic quality of this pristine interior (*EP*, 70). Everything here is clean, but nothing breathes. Dust, lint, and dead skin have been lifted from the floor, but the olfactory evidence of their presence endures, having nowhere to go. The smell of the vacuum cleaner is also paradoxically the only sign of time's passage (in the form of the removal of dirt, whose accrual signals temporality) and modernity (embodied in the appliance itself) in a room that has otherwise remained impervious to either. Indeed, this smell of mechanized dirt removal is the only counter to Emily's mother-in-law's belief that Andrew is still the same boy he was in the framed photograph to which she repeatedly refers during their visit (*EP*, 71). The lingering aroma of the absent vacuum cleaner renders palpable the anachronistic nature of the woman's longings for an irretrievable past, while imbuing the appliance itself with an aura of stasis that is all the more desolate in its distance from the depiction of vacuum cleaners in popular culture at the time. More broadly, this staleness throws into relief that of another framed image that looms large over the novel as a whole: the photograph of Sarah and her husband in the first days of their engagement, snapped during the New York City Easter Parade that gives the novel its title, and whose distillation of youth and happiness grows more unfamiliar as the novel advances its characters toward their tragic conclusions.

The second reference to a vacuum cleaner is central to *The Easter Parade*'s elucidation of the tyranny of Emily's lover Jack Flanders, a self-absorbed poet with whom she moves to Iowa City following her divorce from Andrew. Jack's statement that he likes writing in the living room, where he can look up and "'see you [m]oving in and out of the kitchen, hauling the vacuum cleaner, whatever the hell you're doing. Lets me know you're really here,'" conveys his obliviousness to both the material conditions and benefits of Emily's domestic labor, reducing it to a mere symbol of her devotion to him, and the vacuum cleaner to a prop in said devotion's performance (*EP*, 97). Jack's implicit if vague identification of the vacuum cleaner as a symbol of domestic bliss reveals him to be beholden to the mainstream culture he claims to critique and from which Emily has, throughout the novel, recoiled—and it finds its equivalent in his desperate desire to be the most popular creative writing teacher at the Iowa Writer's Workshop, even as he dismisses popularity as indicative of superficiality (*EP*, 86). Where Emily is so horrified by the resemblance of Iowa City's "sun-splashed residential streets [to] the illustrations in *The Saturday Evening Post*" as to ask, in dismay, "was this what America really did look like?," Jack's rapt absorption in her vacuuming suggests the ease with which the dissident male writer might in fact sell out (*EP*, 96).

I want to conclude this chapter with one of Yates's last short stories, "Oh Joseph, I'm So Tired" (1981), which returns to his 1930s childhood, and which, I suggest, provides a further key to understanding the skepticism toward time-saving appliances evident throughout the rest of his work.[47] The story takes place just after Franklin Delano Roosevelt's election in 1933, and is narrated by Billy, who at the time of the story's events is seven, but who is recalling them from some unidentified year in the future. Billy and his eleven-year-old sister Edith live with their mother, a sculptress and functioning alcoholic divorcée who votes Republican and "believe[s] in the aristocracy" (*CSRY*, 197). An electrical modernity just out of reach is gestured at through references to the children's father. A regional sales manager for GE's Mazda Lamps division, he gives the children "two fragile perforated sheets of what loo[k] like postage stamps, each stamp bearing the insignia of an electric lightbulb in vivid white against a yellow background, and the words 'More light'" (*CSRY*, 179). Bewildered as to the stamps' purpose, Billy uses them to decorate his bedroom, which, like the rest of the children's home is a far cry from the electric idylls promoted by GE on either their stamps or in their advertising more broadly. While Billy's mother owns a Majestic radio from which the three hear FDR's speech that "'the only thing we had to fear was fear itself,'" their roach infested kitchen [i]s barely big enough for a stove and sink that [a]re never clean, and for a brown wooden icebox with its dark, ever melting block of ice" (*CSRY*, 195; 178). The story's plot centers on Billy's mother's acceptance of a commission to sculpt the head of FDR in time for his inauguration. She ultimately fails, producing a piece that rather resembles a "bank for loose change" (*CSRY*, 195). The story ends with the children in bed, listening to the sound of their mother using her sculpting skills to "wor[k] the ice pick in the icebox" to "mak[e] herself another drink" (198).

The significance of the images of GE stamps advertising electric lighting through enlightenment rhetoric, FDR's voice coursing through the radio waves, and Billy's mother's final communion with the nonelectric icebox, becomes clear when one considers the symbolic meanings of electricity in the 1930s. As discussed in the Introduction to this study, the democratization of domestic electricity formed a crucial component of the New Deal and FDR's

[47] Richard Yates, "Oh Joseph, I'm So Tired" (1981), in *CSRY*, 177–99.

broader social welfare project (Tobey, 156). For the FDR administration, regulations that rendered electrification mandatory in all new homes and the subsidy of household purchases of time-saving appliances were integral to creating more work, boosting consumer spending, and improving the quality of life of white Americans across classes (Tobey, 197–206). Billy's father embodies this faith in the symbiotic relationship between electrical power and labor power: a member of the Democratic Party, he seeks to harness electricity as a force for equality by "establish[ing] Mazda Lamp distributorships in various parts of the city" to create more jobs (*CSRY*, 180). The story's tragic trajectory, however, gestures not to the hope FDR evinced among so much of the population, the economic improvements working-class families like Billy's would later experience, or, indeed, anything in the future-now-past other than the "long battle with alcohol" that his mother will "eventually lose" (*CSRY*, 178). This is *not* a story about modernization, progress, and upward mobility, nor is it about individual or collective success brought about by hard work. It is about people for whom big breaks don't come, for whom the advent of domestic electricity will not compensate for a lifetime of disappointment, and whose own fallibilities (in particular, Billy's mother's shrill anti-Semitism) render them difficult objects of sympathy. This worn-out hope is exemplified by the short story's very title, "Oh Joseph, I'm So Tired." This, according to Billy's mother's friend Sloane, another divorcée, was Mary's complaint to Joseph on the eve of Christ's birth (*CSRY*, 192). The dark, musty manger in Sloane's version of the nativity bears more than a passing resemblance to Billy's mother's dark apartment, while her account of Mary as a beleaguered pregnant woman, read alongside the story's references to Billy's mother and Sloane's own exhaustion, humanizes the story of the Christian birth while lending pathos to that of Yates's unhappy and financially struggling divorcées.

Yates's story about the early days of electric democratization—its "eve," so to speak—thus serves as an anti-advertisement for US progress, challenging the public service announcements and industry-subsidized newsreels released throughout the 1930s, and which, as discussed in Chapter 1 of this study, depicted a nation in the process of convulsive positive change. Both the story's trajectory and the future obliquely gestured at via its narrator's place in an unspecified period beyond the 1930s appear all the *more* tragic when one considers the depictions of time-saving appliances in the texts by Yates we have examined throughout this chapter, the majority of which were published before "Oh Joseph, I'm So Tired" but were set later (between the mid-1940s and 1960s). To read "Oh Joseph, I'm So Tired" on the back of these prior narratives about lonely housewives, divorcées, and bachelors fumbling with time-saving appliances whose embodiment of the postwar economic boom doesn't quite compensate for the other disappointments in their owners' lives is to *already know how the story ends*. The domestic modernization that Billy and his contemporaries will encounter in adulthood will bring with it neither epiphany nor enlightenment. To encounter the home with no electrical comforts in this text, whose closest approximation to electrical modernity is a picture of a light bulb plastered on a bedroom wall, is not to see the "before" in a narrative of transformation such as those exploited in appliance ads, but rather to see laid bare the shabby, unromantic everyday that such ads sought to cloak. This unfaltering ability to puncture the myths—of romance, familial conviviality, individual transformation, self-discovery—associated with domestic electrification and time-saving appliances, and to disclose the pain they obscure, is perhaps the single greatest distinguishing feature of Yates's appliance depictions.

If a redemptive strain can be found in the otherwise tragic conclusion to "Oh Joseph, I'm So Tired," it lies not in the suggestion of purchases of electrical appliances that will save Billy's mother time or affirm her social status, but rather in the reference to Billy and Edith's development of a sensibility, premised on the vocabulary of electric currents and connectivity, which allows them to see beyond their mother's alcoholic decline. This sensibility, originally crafted by Edith to quell her brother's night-time fears, entails imagining the hum of city life as a reassuring murmur comprised of all the noises produced by people going about living their lives, and whose sound is a reminder of the collective of which they are a part:

> [Y]ou see there are millions and millions of people in New York—more people than you can possibly imagine, ever—and most of them are doing something that makes sound. Maybe talking, or playing the radio, maybe closing doors, maybe putting their forks down on their plates . . . and because there are so many of them, all of those little sounds add up and come together in a kind of hum. But it's so faint—so very, very faint—that you can't hear it unless you listen very carefully for a long time. (*CSRY*, 189)

This placating pulse of a humanity whose anonymity endows it with a mechanized quality, like that of a whirring engine, is the antithesis to the oppressive intrusion of mechanical noise depicted in Cheever's "Enormous Radio," discussed at this chapter's outset. Where Cheever's story frames the cacophony of blenders, mixers, and telephones as oppressive and dehumanizing, in Yates's story the whirring sound of human life transformed into a mechanical drone is comforting in its defiance of one individual's comprehension. It is the sound of collective hope, and, I would argue not coincidentally, a sound whose description recalls the very New Deal-era rhetoric used to promote a nation connected by electrical currents. The ending in Yates's story mobilizes the rhetoric of electrical democratization and vocabulary of an electrically connected society, circumventing actual electrical appliances to posit a vision of collectivism rooted in imagination, compassion, and child-like hope.

8. Conclusion

In unearthing the cultural specificities of the objects depicted in the texts just discussed, I have sought to challenge the tendency among Cheever critics to either extrapolate from his texts a series of lessons about human nature, or view them as records of what one critic described as "changes in the American personality" over the course of the author's lifetime.[48] The fact that next to no scholarship on Cheever has been published in the last twenty years is arguably ascribable to the rigidity of these approaches. To dismiss Cheever as a paragon of white male privilege and middle-class ennui is to fall into the same trap as those members of the culture industry who in the 1960s and early 1970s appropriated him as a representative figure of the very myth of a "collective national mood" his writing sought to challenge. To dismiss Cheever on the basis of the image of him advanced in the *Time* magazine profile I mentioned earlier, and that early reviewers of his work helped perpetuate, is to miss a significant opportunity to engage with an author whose complicity with Cold War heteronormativity belied a fraught inability to accept his own homosexuality and whose seemingly playful descriptions of unruly appliances likewise belie a genuine anxiety about the ramifications of consumerism's unmet promises. Likewise, Yates's dour depictions of male chauvinists and misunderstood women surrounded by glowering appliances merit scrutiny as studied reworkings of actual historical objects whose invention radically altered the lives of Americans, and whose association with Cold War ideology remains among the most powerful examples of the politics of consumerism in the twentieth century.

[48] Robert G. Collins, "From Subject to Object and Back Again: Individual Identity in John Cheever's Fiction," *Twentieth Century Literature* 28.1 (Spring 1982): 1–13. Citation on 2.

3

"I'm a Toaster with a Cunt":[1]

Time-Saving Appliances and Errant Women in Marge Piercy's Early Fiction

In her autobiographical poem, "Breaking Out" (1984), Marge Piercy describes breaking the yardstick with which her mother and father beat her as her "first political act": "in destroying that stick that had measured my pain / the next day I was an adolescent, not a child."[2] The statement's defiance is heightened by an earlier description of the arrangement of the objects in the closet where the yardstick was stored, and the meaning they held for this eleven-year-old girl:

> A mangle stood there, for ironing
> what I never thought needed it . . .
>
> an upright vacuum with its stuffed
> sausage bag that deflated with a gusty
> sigh as if weary of housework as I,

N.B. Extracts of this chapter were first published in Rachele Dini, "The House Was a Garbage Dump: Waste, Mess, and Aesthetic Reclamation in 1960s and 70s 'Mad Housewife' Fiction," *Textual Practice* (August 2018). I am grateful to the editors for granting me permission to replicate this material.

[1] Marge Piercy, *Small Changes* (New York: Penguin, 1987 [1973]), 66. Henceforth, *SC*.

[2] Marge Piercy, "Breaking Out" (1984), in *My Mother's Body* (New York: Knopf, 1985), N.P, lines 37–8. Henceforth, *BO*.

who swore I would never dust or sweep
after I left home, who hated
to see my mother removing daily
the sludge the air lay down like a snail's track

so that when in school I read of Sisyphus
and his rock, it was her I
thought of, housewife scrubbing
on raw knees as the factory rained ash. (*BO*, 5–18)

Between the announcement of Piercy's political awakening and the description of her act of rebellion there lie nested a series of depictions of tawdry household implements framed in terms of the chores they help complete, but whose utility is either unclear, such as the ironing of items that don't require it, or temporary, as attested by the comparison of mopping to Sisyphus's toils. This latter comparison, on which the poem's concluding lines hinge, reflects the influence of Simone de Beauvoir, for whose work Piercy has often cited admiration, and who, in *The Second Sex* (1949), so famously noted, "Few tasks are more like the torture of Sisyphus than housework, with its endless repetition."[3] De Beauvoir's feminism rooted in resistance to female acculturation underlies the poem's closing lines: "This is not a tale of innocence lost but power / gained: I would not be Sisyphus, / there were things that I should learn to break" (*BO*, 39–41). More importantly, the closing lines stand out in their reaffirmation of a combative "I" whose capacity to make choices and act upon them invokes de Beauvoir's understanding of identity as forgeable over and beyond the material conditions of one's upbringing (including, in this case, the factory labor invoked in the reference to "factory ash"). Meanwhile the vacuum cleaner is identified not as an alleviator of effort but as one more participant in a lineage of subjects destined for a life of household drudgery. The female child's identification with the appliance's weariness—which she anticipates in her own future—results in a further sense of slippage between woman and thing. The vacuum cleaner that can feel exhaustion highlights the reduction of the housewife to a domestic tool with no agency beyond that to beat her daughter into a submission like her own. In these two stanzas, Piercy portrays a network of subject-object relations in which the time-saving appliances, actions they perform, objects on which such actions are performed, surfaces against which these actions take place, woman performing the actions, and child resisting becoming her are effectively inextricable from one another. The juxtaposition of the appliance with the yardstick with which the speaker is physically beaten

[3] Piercy notes de Beauvoir's influence in a number of interviews, including with Dawn Gifford in *Off Our Backs* 24.6 (June 1994): 14–15, 23 (14) and with Bonnnie Lyons in *Contemporary Literature* 48.3 (Fall 2007): 327–44 (336). Simone de Beauvoir, *The Second Sex*, transl. H. M. Parshley (New York: Alfred A. Knopf, 1997 [1949]), 470.

imbues both objects with a violent animism and reveals the violence that underlies metrics-based systems of maintaining order, be these social or physical. The effect is one of entanglement, and of events that once set in motion cannot be interrupted except through an aggression comparable to that which the custodians of the system have internalized, and which they in turn inflict on their subordinates. It is from this network that the defiant *I* at the end of the poem breaks out and forcefully envisions an alternative future for herself—one in which not time, but the self, is saved.

The appliance-human relations depicted in "Breaking Out" exemplify what I call Piercy's appliance poetics—an approach premised on the potential for electrical devices to furnish stories both of female oppression and female emancipation and creative freedom, and which can be traced across her entire oeuvre. More specifically, "Breaking Out" expresses Piercy's understanding of time-saving appliances as fetishized objects whose elevation to the status of miracle makers was, more often than not, premised on the reification of the women for whom they were intended, but also opened up possibilities for radical, and even violent, resistance. This chapter focuses on a selection of depictions of time-saving appliances in four of Piercy's early novels, *Going Down Fast* (1969), *Small Changes* (1973), *Woman on the Edge of Time* (1976), and *Braided Lives* (1982). I argue that these texts constitute the author's most sustained and compelling engagements with domestic electrification's capacity to expose and challenge gender inequality, suburban conformity, and normative whiteness. I situate them in relation to the second-wave feminist movement whose paradigm-shifting effects she herself has noted enabled their publication.[4] More broadly, however, I show how Piercy's fiction takes what we would now term an intersectional approach to the politics of time-saving appliances, insofar as her depictions of these are redolent with questions about class, race, Jewish identity, sexual expression, and the limits of techno-utopian thinking. Finally, I argue that Piercy's sustained use of the vocabulary of electricity to depict alternative forms of "power" to those derived from the monopolization of resources and inculcation of the masses to desire ever-more sophisticated gadgetry produces a poetics of electricity and of appliances specifically. In this poetics, the notions of electric energy and power are transformed into different articulations of collectivism, solidarity, erotic love, and creative potential to oppose capitalism, patriarchy, white supremacy, and environmental degradation, and to reveal their mutual imbrication.

---

[4] Bonnie Lyons and Marge Piercy, "An Interview with Marge Piercy," *Contemporary Literature* 48.3 (Fall, 2007): 327–44, citation on 336. In a 1998 interview Piercy similarly noted: "the first version of *Braided Lives* [1982] was written in the early 1960s. . . . A lot of stuff I wrote then just couldn't get published then because it was too feminist. . . . The way I first got published was by using the male viewpoint in my fiction." John Rodden and Marge Piercy, "A Harsh Day's Light: An Interview with Marge Piercy," *The Kenyon Review New Series* 20.2 (Spring 1998): 132–43, citation on 140.

Piercy's depictions of these objects are inextricable from the author's own lived experience. In her 2002 memoir, *Sleeping With Cats*, this daughter of a woman devoted to housework, and an electrical appliance repairman for Westinghouse with whom the only way to have conversation was to "ask him about some process, [such as] how electricity was generated," recounts a life seemingly shaped by appliances, including the mangle and vacuum cleaner that inspired "Breaking Out."[5] An early boyfriend is remembered for the fact that in his parents' house in Paris "there was no refrigerator but there was a maid" (*SWC*, 108), while her account of the time following their short-lived marriage opens with a description of moving to "a rooming house overrun with mice . . . even in the refrigerator" (*SWC*, 119). Domestic electricity likewise demarcates the stages of her relationship with her second husband, Robert, a lover of gadgets who objected to the vibrations of electric refrigerators, who on one Thanksgiving accidentally severed his finger with an electric carving knife, and with whom she graduated from an apartment with communal washing machines on the roof (!) to a home with its own washing machine and dryer (*SWC*, 176; 253; 135). Such anecdotes are an important reminder of the novelty of these objects for Piercy's generation, and of the ambivalent fascination with which they were held even by their feminist critics.

In what follows, I begin with an outline of pivotal moments in Second-Wave Feminism relevant to the history of time-saving appliances and their cultural reception. Section 2 examines a selection of appliance depictions in the work of notable second-wave feminist writers. Like the woman in Piercy's *Small Changes* (1973) who exposes her husband's expression of love as an abstract desire for "'a toaster with a cunt,'" these texts juxtapose female body parts and time-saving appliances to render explicit the reduction of American women in postwar popular culture to little more than fuckable gadgets (*SC*, 66). The rest of the chapter examines the form(s) that Piercy's appliance poetics take in a select few scenes from each of the individual novels just mentioned.

1. Time-Saving Appliances and Second-Wave Feminism

Unsurprisingly for someone writing in late 1940s France (where appliance ownership was limited to the upper classes) Simone de Beauvoir makes only one mention of an appliance in *The Second Sex*, noting, in passing, the function of the refrigerator as a status symbol (474; Clarke, 838–59). By contrast, Betty Friedan's *The Feminine Mystique*, whose publication in 1963 helped launch the Women's Liberation Movement in the United States, is veritably littered with references to the mechanized home. This proliferation of references is

[5] Marge Piercy, *Sleeping with Cats* (New York: HarperCollins, 2002), 36. Henceforth *SWC*.

partly due to the book's later publication and its author's US nationality (appliance ownership in France did not become ubiquitous until the 1960s[6]). But it is mainly attributable to their centrality to Friedan's argument: that the anxieties of her generation of white, educated, middle-class housewives stemmed precisely from the fact that the relative comforts brought about by time-saving appliances failed to address the deeper dissatisfactions inherent to a life confined to the home. Implicit in Friedan's account of the "millions" of women frustrated from years of forced "smiling as they ran the new electric waxer over the spotless kitchen floor" was that appliances didn't eliminate the basic repetitiveness and monotony characteristic of preindustrial housework (Friedan, 14). They merely shortened the time in which such tasks were done and alleviated the effort involved, opening up mental space, and time, for women to contemplate what else they might be doing. What's more, while appliances eased labor and reduced the time spent on some chores, they didn't make housework any less repetitive—and in any event, the appliance and commercial cleaning products industry soon filled these new pockets of liberated time by habituating their customers to round-the-clock cleaning.[7] A cornerstone of Friedan's polemic was thus her revelation of the story behind the "pretty pictures" with which her generation had been bombarded (Friedan, 18). She dedicated an entire chapter to a consumer survey on women's attitudes to time-saving appliances, commissioned in 1945 by the publisher of "a leading women's magazine," for companies that would have to replace war contracts with sales of consumer goods (Friedan, 200). The 4,500 educated middle-class married female respondents were divided into three categories: women devoted to housework but suspicious of new devices, "Career Women" who hated housework, and, finally, "Balanced Homemakers" (qtd. in Friedan, 201). The latter were the ideal demographic: women with no career aspirations to work outside the home, but hungry for modern conveniences that would help them feeling "'personal achievement'" for saving time: "As one young housewife said: 'It's nice to be modern—it's like running a factory in which you have all the latest machinery'" (qtd. in Friedan, 201). Friedan's book by contrast attested to what might happen if the "Balanced Homemaker" received intellectual stimuli that seduced her away from her frost-free fridge.

A wealth of scholarship over the last four decades has complicated Friedan's account of the unhappy mid-century housewife, beginning with Angela Davis's critique of its role in eliding the oppression of Black, working-class, and immigrant women, and bell hooks's critique of it as

---

[6] Clarke, 238–59.

[7] Rosie Cox notes that increasing the frequency of cleaning was central to the advertising strategy of commercial cleaning products from the 1930s onwards, both in the UK and the US ("Dishing the Dirt: Dirt in the Home," in *Dirt: The Filthy Reality of Everyday Life*, ed. Rosie Cox et al. (London: Profile Books, 2011), 37–74).

"narcissis[tic], insensitive[e], sentimenta[l, and self-indulgen[t]."[8] For Jane Elliott, in stating that "'desperate problems' on the material level foreclosed the problem that has no name," Friedan revealed popular feminism's focus on the white middle-class housewife to be *intentional*, a product of the assumption that "the defining mode of female oppression . . . only existed when women's material needs were met."[9] By contrast, Daniel Horowicz argues that Friedan's feminism was inextricable from her early efforts as a journalist for the official publication of the United Electrical, Radio, and Machine Workers of America union (UE) between 1946 and 1952, where she took a radical stance on rights for female and Black workers at GE and Westinghouse (a stance she would later disown).[10] He quotes from her pamphlet, *UE Fights for Women Workers* (1952), in which Friedan highlighted the irony of female workers' rights being eroded by companies whose main customers were women: electrical manufacturers, she noted, mythologized "'the American woman—in her gleaming G.E. kitchen, at her Westinghouse laundromat [...] Nothing [...] is too good for her'"—unless she was one of their employees.[11] For our purposes however the extent of Friedan's obscuration of nonwhite middle-class women is less important than her text's landmark status in the history of *appliance* literature as among the very first books for a popular audience to accuse the imagery used in appliance ads of causing women psychological harm (the first excerpts of her book were published in *McCall's* and *Ladies' Home Journal*).

Time-saving appliances would go on to feature in the work of later feminists as well, where they were explicitly enlisted to critique the relationship between patriarchy and capitalism. In *Sexual Politics* (1970), Kate Millett described women's relationship to the refrigerator as akin to that of colonial subjects who produce and use objects but are denied access to their means of production:

> [T]he refrigerator is a machine all women use, some assemble it in factories, and a very few with scientific education understand its principles of operation . . . in the absence of males, women's distance from technology today is sufficiently great that it is doubtful that

[8] Angela Davis, "The Approaching Obsolescence of Housework: A Working-Class Perspective," in *Women, Race and Class* (New York: Vintage, 1983 [1981]), 128–39; bell hooks, *Feminist Theory: From Margin to Center* (Boston: Pluto Press, 1984), 2–3. See also Stephanie Coontz, *A Strange Stirring: The Feminine Mystique and American Women at the Dawn of the 1960s* (New York: Perseus, 2011). Kirsten Swinth provides a useful account of Friedan's later disavowal of Second-Wave Feminism, in *Feminism's Forgotten Fight: The Unfinished Struggle for Work and Family* (Cambridge, MA: Harvard UP, 2018), 236–40.

[9] Jane Elliott, *Popular Feminist Fiction as American Allegory* (New York: Palgrave, 2008), 82.

[10] Daniel Horowicz, *Betty Friedan and the Making of the Feminine Mystique* (Amherst, MA: U of Massachusetts Press, 1998), 121.

[11] Betty Goldstein, *UE Fights for Women Workers* (United Electrical, Radio and Machine Workers of America, 1952), qtd. in Horowicz, 138.

> they could replace or repair such machines on any significant scale . . . a large factor in their subordinate position is the fairly systematic ignorance patriarchy imposes upon women.[12]

Echoes of Millett's critique of the passivity expected of female consumers toward time-saving appliances reverberate throughout Piercy's depictions of women endeavoring to learn how new technologies work, and to participate in their development—as do echoes of Beverly Jones's claim, in "The Dynamics of Marriage and Motherhood," an essay published in the radical feminist anthology edited by feminist poet and activist Robin Morgan, *Sisterhood Is Powerful* (1970), that "the most automated appliance in a household is the mother."[13] The influence of Germaine Greer's contention, in *The Female Eunuch*, published the same year as Millett's book and Jones's essay, that "it would be a serious blow to the industries involved if women shared, say, one washing machine between three families, and did not regard the possession of the latest model as the necessary index of prestige and success," is likewise evident in Piercy's visions of female communal living and shared labor in *Small Changes* and *Woman on the Edge of Time*.[14]

Piercy's work also implicitly engages with the ideas of white feminist activists in the US, UK, and Italy involved in the "Wages for Housework" movement. These activists expressed skepticism about the argument made by some economists at the time—and which endures to this day—that appliances' emergence was an integral component in enabling women to enter the workforce. This narrative, they argued, obscured the fact that women continued to be disproportionately responsible for domestic labor even as growing numbers were employed in full-time paid work.[15] They called for housewives to be paid by the state, noting that their invisible labor both enabled male workers to do their jobs outside of the home and ensured

---

[12] Kate Millett, *Sexual Politics* (New York: Columbia UP, 2016 [1970]), 41.

[13] Beverly Jones, "The Dynamics of Marriage and Motherhood," *Sisterhood Is Powerful*, ed. Robin Morgan (New York: Random House, 1970), 46–61. Citation on 56.

[14] Germaine Greer, *The Female Eunuch* (London: Fourth Estate, 2006 [1970]), 364.

[15] This argument was reiterated as recently as 2005 in Jeremy Greenwood, Ananth Seshadri, and Mehmet Yorukoglu's widely cited article, "Engines of Liberation," published in *The Quarterly Journal of Economics* 72.1 (January 2005): 109–33. The authors used a simulation based on the principles that "(1) female labour-force participation increases over time; (2) housework declines over time; (3) the diffusion of new appliances through the economy is gradual with the rich adopting first" to demonstrate a causal relationship between points (2) and (1). (The same argument made international headlines in 2009, after the Vatican's official newspaper, *Osservatore Romano*, published an article titled "The Washing Machine and the Emancipation of Women: Put in the Powder, Close the Lid and Relax," which sought to undermine the revolutionary effects of the contraceptive pill by arguing the greater emancipatory value of the washing machine. See Miranda Bryant, "The Washing Machine 'Liberates Women,'" *The Independent* (March 8, 2009). It reared its head again in March 2021 in a *Bloomberg* article published in honor of Women's History Month (Virginia Postrel, "How Job-Killing Technologies Liberated Women," *Bloomberg* (March 14, 2021).

the health and well-being of the next generation of workers—children. In *Women and the Subversion of Community* (1973), two of the movement's founders, Selma James and Mariarosa dalla Costa, remarked wryly that full domestic automation would "never happen," however, as it was incompatible with "the maintenance of the nuclear family": "to really automate [domestic work], capital would have to destroy the family as we know it."[16]

Most importantly, the texts by Piercy discussed in this chapter stand out as exceptions to what bell hooks describes, in *Ain't I a Woman? Black Women and Feminism* (1981), as the inherent "racism and classism of white women's liberationists," which "was most apparent when they discussed work as the liberating force for women," where "it was always the middle class 'housewife' who was depicted as the victim of sexist oppression and not the poor Black and non-Black women who are most exploited by American economics" (146). Set primarily in working-class communities and contending with the challenges faced by Jewish, Latino, Italian American, and Black American women, several of whom are, or are married to, employees of electrical manufacturing plants, Piercy's texts present time-saving appliances as both distillations of postwar consumer capitalism's unfulfilled promises and, crucially, embodiments of congealed labor, recalling Friedan's early critiques of appliance manufacturers' treatment of their female labor force and Kate Millett's efforts to demystify the refrigerator's "magic." In focusing on the stories of those physically involved in the production and repair of objects that consumer capitalism has been so quick to turn into abstractions, Piercy obliges the reader to contend with the material conditions from which these symbols of American exceptionalism and techno-utopian futurity emerged. In this way, her appliance depictions expose different forms of co-option, and act as a corrective to the white-washed narratives of some of her feminist contemporaries, which I discuss in the next section.

2. "I Was Just an Appliance":[17] Time-Saving Domestic Gadgets in Sue Kaufman, Joyce Rebeta-Burditt, Emily Arnold McCully, and Marilyn French

It is well established that *The Feminine Mystique* catalyzed a national conversation around the plight of suburban housewives, engendering what

[16] Selma James and dalla Mariarosa Costa, *The Power of Women and the Subversion of the Community* (Bristol: Pétroleuse Press, 1973), 21.

[17] French, *WR*, 410. I am indebted to Rebecca Bardsley-Ball for pointing out this line in French's novel.

Imelda Whelehan terms the genre of "mad housewife" popular fiction.[18] But that the (longed for, malfunctioning, reproachful) gadget might be a defining narrative trope of both the "mad housewife" novel and of popular media accounts of the desperate housewife has gone unnoticed. A brief review of some of the more compelling instances of this trope in the work of feminist writers, such as Marilyn French, Joyce Rebeta-Burditt, and Sue Kaufman, provides a useful context in which to situate Piercy's own work and to identify what makes her appliance depictions so distinctive.

Time-saving appliances play an instrumental role in the ending of Sue Kaufman's *Diary of a Mad Housewife* (1967).[19] The titular housewife, Tina Balser, who has been having an extramarital affair, is about to go buy a pregnancy test when an elevator in her building catches fire. After the fire is extinguished, she and the other housewives on her floor are invited by Carrie, a wealthy actress and owner of an exclusive "Ladies' Gymnasium," to enjoy coffee from Carrie's "'wizard' coffee-maker that could make twenty cups . . . in six minutes" (*DMH*, 255). While they sit in Carrie's "huge, glorious buttercup-yellow kitchen gleaming with brass and copper pots, and fitted out with every new electrical appliance on the market" (*DMH*, 256), Tina "bec[omes] aware of the physical sensations [she is] having and what they mea[n]":

> I'd been so absorbed I'd forgotten all the things that not having them had meant; I had completely forgotten that morning's important errand. Refusing to get excited—it could be just a false alarm—I finished my coffee and strudel and reluctantly rose to go. I'd been having a marvelous time. I . . . said goodbye to all the ladies in rollers and slacks and Brunch Coats, and after . . . promising I'd come ride the exercycles at [Carrie's] gymnasium, walked back up the two flights to our apartment and confirmed the good news. (*DMH*, 256)

Having begun menstruating, Tina will not have to resort to the illegal abortion she had planned to have if the pregnancy test came back positive. But more importantly, the building's malfunctioning technology, Connie's pristine "all-electric" kitchen, references to the women's gymnasium furnished with electric exercycles, and the "ladies in rollers and slacks and Brunch Coats," all conspire to return Tina to a place of acquiescence and acceptance—indeed, delight—at a life she has spent the entire novel longing to escape.

---

[18] In *The Feminist Bestseller* (New York: Palgrave Macmillan, 2005), Imelda Whelehan identifies this genre dominated by white, middle-class, and predominantly heterosexual writers as concerned with the "intense pressure to perform . . . femininity" according to the dictates of popular media, and the boredom and humiliation inherent in performing everyday chores in the service of others (63–4).

[19] Sue Kaufman, *Diary of a Mad Housewife* (Harmondsworth: Penguin, 1971 [1967]). Henceforth, *DMH*.

Drinking "the best coffee [she has] ever had" from the "Wizard" coffeemaker and sitting in a "buttercup-yellow" kitchen that recalls the famous yellow GE kitchen in which the Nixon-Khrushchev Debate took place in 1959 is enough to reacclimatize Tina to the status quo. The housewife maddened by lack of intellectual stimulation and a marriage empty of affection is strangely lulled by the threat of death-by-elevator and the seduction of a gleaming "all-electric" domestic modernity, and by the prospect of relinquishing herself to the mechanical authority of the exercycle, whose molding of thighs and buttocks renders it akin to an appliance for disciplining and preparing the body for the consumption of a male gaze. This is important, for the circumlocutory manner in which Tina describes her period and its physical effects without ever explicitly naming them accentuates the passage's broader elision of both body and autonomous self. In their place are a series of objects and responses to various miraculous technological functions. Just as Carrie's "all-electric" kitchen distracted Tina from her pregnancy fears, the vision of a future visit to Carrie's similarly appliance-bedecked gym edges out both any explicit mention of the menstrual blood that requires Tina to go home, and, more importantly, any consideration of the anxieties and frustrations about her life that preceded the pregnancy scare. Instead, the passage foregrounds desire for a glimmering and awe-inspiring array of gadgets and their capacity to enhance—even illuminate—female experience in a manner akin to that presented in countless ads for modern fitted kitchens. The time Tina has spent writing in her diary—the time of the novel itself—has been merely a momentary diversion from the prescribed trajectory. From now on, the novel implies, she will spend the time saved by her existing appliances (and those she plans to purchase) on more sensible pursuits than novel reading, daydreaming, and infidelity.

Time-saving appliances have far more harrowing connotations in Joyce Rebeta-Burditt's *The Cracker Factory* (1977), perhaps in keeping with the heightened cynicism of the post-Pentagon Papers, Watergate, and Vietnam era (although it is worth noting that Kaufman's novel is replete with references to nuclear fallout).[20] In the novel's opening pages, narrator Cassie Barrett describes her son grabbing her arm as she pours a steaming pot of food into the garbage disposal in the sink before the family has even eaten (*TCF*, 8). Her husband's response, "'Tell Alexander [her psychiatrist] I want my money back,'" confirms the housewife's fear that her value is measured against her output (*TCF*, 8). In using the language of product guarantees, he conflates her with the appliances she uses. The broken housewife who disposes of the meal she has prepared before she has even served it amounts to a malfunctioning machine to be sent back to the supplier to be serviced—which is indeed what happens as Cassie checks herself into a rehabilitation

[20] Joyce Rebeta-Burditt, *The Cracker Factory* (Deadwood, OR: Wyatt-MacKenzie, 2010 [1977]), 8. Henceforth, *TCF*.

clinic and begins a twelve-step program to get sober. In this way, the novel adheres to a narrative formula in which the housewife gets help, is cured of her affliction, and at the novel's end goes back to being a good housewife, newly grateful for the life from which she once escaped through drink. Such a formula merely reaffirms the notion of the housewife as a living appliance to be kept healthy so that she can better perform her housework—and whose use of time to do anything else is cause for suspicion.

A similar circumscription of domestic dissatisfaction is evident in a subgenre of appliance advertisements of the late 1960s and early 1970s, which often appropriated the language of the Women's Liberation Movement to posit civil or psychological unrest as resolvable via the introduction of an appliance that "fixed" the malfunctioning housewife, and resolved marital conflict. Thus a 1969 ad by Hamilton positioned its washing machine and dryer combo as a better wedding gift than a toaster, electric carving knife, or blender in its capacity to prevent newlyweds' arguments over housework.[21] A 1971 ad by the consortium of Electric Light and Power Companies posited the washing machine as the solution to the frustrated housewife's rage.[22] Also in 1971, Roper urged its customers to "make your vote for women's lib really count – vote for Roper gas or electric!" in an ad featuring women holding protest signs expressing opposition to "pot watching," "oven scrubbing," and "menu monotony" (Figure 3.1). An ad for GE's 1969 range of dishwashers appropriated the rhetoric of the "Wages for Housework" movement in its quantification of women's labor—with the crucial difference that the tagline, "For $179.95, You Can Keep Your Mother Out of Scrapes," was aimed at those who stood to lose most from the movement's success.[23] The tagline softened what amounted to a boast about this time-saving appliance's capacity to deter rebellion, referring to both the scraping of dirty dishes and to the more violent "scrapes" into which many involved in the Women's Liberation Movement and associated anti-war protests were getting themselves. The framing of the housewife as "mom" rather than "wife," while a frequent tactic used in ads of the period to foreground so-called family values and to position housework as an expression of love (Neuhaus, 48; 109), served in this instance to soften what might otherwise be read as an ad for keeping one's woman in check—just as the focus on familial happiness in the resolution of *The Cracker Factory* obscures the fact that Cassie is effectively right back where she started from. One could complicate this reading however and argue that

[21] Hamilton, "How a New Hamilton Washer and Dryer Can Get a Marriage Off on the Right Foot," *LIFE* (September 19, 1969): 81.
[22] Electric Light and Power Companies, "Try Telling the Lady She'll Have to Start Washing by Hand," *LIFE* (June 11, 1971): 2.
[23] GE "For $179.95, You Can Keep Your Mother Out of Scrapes," *LIFE* (April 18, 1969): 17. Unfortunately, GE has denied permission to reproduce this ad, but it can be found online via the *LIFE* magazine archives.

FIGURE 3.1 Roper. "Roper Votes for Women's Lib!" *House and Garden* (December 1971): 46. © Whirlpool Corporation. Reproduced with permission.

second-wave feminist fiction was not engaging with this new generation of ads infused with feminist (or, as in the case of the GE ad, anti-feminist) rhetoric, so much as rejecting appliances' *long-standing* positioning as emancipatory—as exemplified by Westinghouse's 1950 campaign for its frost-free refrigerator, in which the latter was posited as freeing a housewife dressed in a black-and-white striped convict's outfit from the "prison" of servitude (Figure 3.2).

The appliance depictions in *The Cracker Factory* echo those in the first chapter of Piercy's second novel, *Small Changes* (1973). Published at the height of the Women's Liberation Movement and set in the late 1960s, *Small Changes* most closely fits the template of the "mad housewife" genre both in its narrative arc and in its deployment of time-saving appliances. In particular, the world of domestic gadgets in the novel's first chapter

FIGURE 3.2 Westinghouse. "At Last! I'm Free. . . Thanks to my New Westinghouse Refrigerator." *LIFE* (October 30, 1950): 83. ©Westinghouse. Reproduced with permission.

highlights the distance its female protagonists travel both ideologically and geographically over the following 400 pages, as they join various countercultural movements and seek to escape the constraints of patriarchal capitalism. In the opening scene, protagonist Beth's mother circumvents her daughter's anxieties about getting married by reassuring her that she can exchange one of the two blenders she received as wedding gifts for an electric carving knife—eerily affirming the rhetoric of wedding-themed appliance ads discussed in Chapter 2 (*SC*, 15). Time-saving appliances in turn haunt Beth's articulation of her husband's frustration with her failures as a housewife: "She was something that was not working as it was supposed to. He was still trying to fix it. Soon he would lose his patience. Then would he return it or break it?" (*SC*, 32). This image of herself as a broken implement—and an *it* rather than a *she*—leads to a meandering daydream as Beth chews on leftover meatloaf. Here, she likens herself to a box turtle she brought home, as a child, from one of the company picnics held by her father's employer, GE, but let loose after witnessing its frantic efforts to escape:

> A trapped animal eating a dead animal . . . Who then was the ally? . . . Only the Turtle Flag she was flying secretly. That private morale-building was all very well. Turtles laid eggs in the mud and walked away, but she was going to be stuck. . . . She was a lousy cook, he was right. . . . She would rather be cooked for than cook, which made her an unsatisfactory wife right there. She must not forget that again, if she was lucky enough to get out of here. Remember the cold meat loaf. From the refrigerator she got the ketchup and doused it liberally. . . . Meat, a dead animal that had been alive. . . . Could she persuade him that her period was starting tonight? Dipping a finger in the ketchup, she carefully worked her finger into herself, smearing ketchup on her genitals, on her panties. (*SC*, 33–4)

In this stream-of-consciousness narrative that ventures far beyond the scope of either French or Rebeta-Burditt's appliance depictions, Piercy connects appliance manufacturer, corporate-sponsored entertainment, marital institution, individual time-saving appliance, processed food, meat, female flesh, and the taming of wildlife. The tentacular reach of the corporation is evident in the description of "private morale-building," which ironically gestures back to the morale-building motives behind the GE company picnic where young Beth found the turtle. Likewise, the refrigerator stands out as one more participant in a network of subject-object relations shaped by corporate and state power. Indeed, what renders this imagery terrifying is that it goes beyond conveying the entrapment of the housewife in her suburban "all-electric" home to convey the entrapment of *everything* within the web of an "all-electric" capitalist modernity. The GE picnic that builds the morale of company employees and indoctrinates their children into associating leisure with the corporation also affects the surrounding wildlife—just as the advertisements for the time-saving appliances manufactured by the company are premised largely on their capacity to better preserve and cook meat in particular. Meanwhile, the image of the trapped turtle imbues the scene of the housewife examining her limited (life and culinary) options with greater urgency—as does the image of the housewife herself as a trapped animal akin to the refrigerated animal meat she is eating. The refrigerator thus emerges as a keeper of trapped and killed animals—a mausoleum for the preservation of carcasses of once-life. Finally, the image of a refrigerated processed food ordinarily used as a condiment for cold meats being re-purposed to deflect attention away from the "meat" of the housewife's genitalia vividly conveys the extent to which she has learned to view her body as an item for male consumption. Piercy presents the appliance as at once a time-saver, corpse preserver, participant in the deflection of the male member, and extension of corporate power.

The tropes just described are reiterated in Emily Arnold McCully's short story, "Is Your Vacuum Cleaner Working?" (1976), in which an unnamed depressed housewife's preparations to commit suicide are interrupted by an elderly appliance repair-and-salesman and his young apprentice.[24] While the repairman persuades her to speak to her husband about replacing her vacuum cleaner, the apprentice persuades her to invite him over later that evening. The story ends with the two having clumsy sex on the living room couch, while she considers whether making her husband Eggs Benedict the next morning instead of cereal will be enough to assuage her guilt. McCully's deployment of the motifs of time-saving appliance, appliance repair-and-salesman, and depressed housewife is notable in its frankly unoriginal recapitulation of both the concerns of earlier "mad housewife" novels and the narrative perpetuated in the media stories that followed the publication of *The Feminine Mystique*. This sensationalist narrative recast feminists as selfish women whose quest for self-actualization posed a direct threat to the American way of life—a bit like the mother in the GE ad who risks getting into "scrapes." The most flagrant example of the trope was the cover story of the March 17, 1972, issue of *LIFE* magazine, "Dropout Wife: A Striking Current Phenomenon," which argued that "women libbers" were failing their families and letting down American society (34–44). McCully's story is interesting precisely for its formulaic, and fundamentally unimaginative, reiteration of many of the commonplaces of both this media narrative, and the "mad housewife" novel—from the narrator's financial worries and nostalgia for lost youth, to her frustration with children, husband, and a house that is never up to the standard of women's magazines. By adhering to this generic formula, McCully's story serves as a meta-commentary on the "generic" nature of both the housewife's life and of the "mad housewife" genre. In explicitly parodying a series of clichés about time-saving appliances and their purveyors, McCully's protagonist comments on the place of the housewife herself in society—including the extent to which her electrical accoutrements have become part of a broader industry parasitically feeding off of her misery without doing anything to alleviate it.

Where Kaufman and Rebeta-Burditt's appliance depictions maintain the status quo, and McCully's reads as a parody of the "mad housewife" genre and media response to the Women's Liberation Movement, Marilyn French's *The Women's Room* (1977) enlists time-saving appliances to articulate the value of women's narratives over and above those of their male counterparts. Here, protagonist Mira, who got married and had children in the early 1950s, uses the example of the "filthy refrigerator" that the housewife will inevitably find herself cleaning, despite any aspiration she

---

[24] Emily Arnold McCully, "How's Your Vacuum Cleaner Working?" *The Massachusetts Review* 17.1 (Spring, 1976): 23–43.

might have to loftier intellectual endeavors, to highlight the ways in which the lives of her generation of women were shaped by and rooted in mundane domestic concerns. Her fellow (female) PhD students proceed to tease her for being "'[s]tuck forever through history with the stinking refrigerator!'" (*WR*, 250). When one suggests she write a paper on "'The Image of the Refrigerator in the Twentieth-century Novel'" or "'The Frost-Free Syndrome in "Fire and Ice"'" (referring to Robert Frost's poem by the same title), Mira replies that "'It has to be a filthy refrigerator, one that needs to be cleaned, not just defrosted'" (*WR*, 250). In specifying these details, Mira reveals a side to the refrigerator obscured in mid-century ads, where, as the titular protagonist of Sheila Ballantyne's *Norma Jean the Termite Queen* (1975) puts it, "some vague woman go[es] after dust balls with her Electrolux . . . [and] ha[s] orgasms in the laundry room while inhaling the whiteness of her wash."[25] When Mira's friends thank her "'for always remembering the stinking, filthy refrigerator!'" they are recognizing the object's value as both a cultural artifact and an allegory for gender inequality. The dirt of the home is also the stuff of women's history—something that academics would do well to remember. In the next sections, we see how Piercy's early fiction builds, expands on, and complicates these tropes.

3. "A Baby, a Husband, and an Electric Carving Knife": *Going Down Fast* (1969)

Piercy's understanding of time-saving appliances' allegorical potential is evident in her very first novel, *Going Down Fast* (1969), which traces the interrelated stories of a group of Chicagoans affected by an unnamed university's plans to buy up and raze a primarily Black working-class neighborhood to build luxury apartments. The novel follows the lives of Anna Levinowitz, a white adjunct sociology lecturer displaced by the renewal plans, and her peers: her wealthy, white, pro-gentrification, ex-husband Asher; her white, working-class, anti-gentrification ex-lover Rowley; Rowley's Black middle-class landlord Harlan; their white middle-class friend Leon; and Caroline, a white actress engaged to a wealthy white businessman who plans to purchase her one of the luxury blocks. Throughout, Piercy enlists time-saving appliances as allegories for gender, race, and class inequality. The fire originating from an electric broiler that nearly burns down Rowley's apartment in the first-third of the novel, for example, foreshadows the arson that burns down the neighborhood elementary school at the novel's end (*GDF*, 68). But the fates of those involved in these two fires are very different.

[25] Sheila Ballantyne, *Norma Jean the Termite Queen* (New York: Penguin, 1983 [1975]), 4. Henceforth, *NJTTQ*.

Caroline, who starts the first fire while attempting to cook Rowley a steak, survives unscathed, and goes on to entertain a stream-of-consciousness fantasy about the "closed-circuit TV as a security precaution. All-electric wall kitchen. Central air-conditioning" that will grace her future apartment (*GDF*, 236). Meanwhile Rowley's friend Vera, a Black schoolteacher, dies in the arson fire foreshadowed by the broiler incident, a *mere page* after having ridiculed Caroline for aspiring to "A baby, a husband, and an electric carving knife; what more could she ask?" (*GDF*, 270). In juxtaposing Vera's pity for Caroline's unimaginative aspirations with the Black woman's violent death, Piercy slyly remarks upon the focus of both feminist activists and the media on the plight of white middle-class women above the material, and in some cases life-or-death, concerns of Black women.

Going Down Fast also enlists time-saving appliances to reveal the contradictions both inherent to and obscured by the rhetorical flourishes of urban renewal. Most notably, in describing his sense of unwitting complicity with the city council's plans to displace Black Chicagoans, Harlan terms himself a "human garbage disposal" (*GDF*, 96). The expression denotes his status both as a disposer of "human garbage"—people deemed less valuable—and as a *human version* of the appliance fitted in kitchen sinks to grind up and dispose of garbage directly into the sewer system, and whose promotion in the 1960s relied on a rhetoric that equated the disappearance of waste with the maintenance of upstanding morals and good taste. Most notably, In-Sink-Erator claimed that "The fashion houses of Paris know no smarter styling" than that of its Gold Comet Garbage Disposer. An illustration of a fashion model being fitted with a gold couture dress, and the offer of a "lovely embossed Florentine change purse" for visiting one's plumber for a quote, aligned the garbage disposal unit with luxury and good taste (Figure 3.3). The power of Harlan's quip derives from both the history of this particular appliance, and his identification of developers' dehumanizing categorization of people from low-income households as "garbage" to be removed, lest "its" unseemly sight scares away potential investors.

The subtext of Harlan's quip becomes clearer a page later, when he invokes another appliance with powerful class connotations: "'[J]oining the middle-class is like ordering one of those pink light-up phones from the telephone company [...] Because you never stop paying, you pay every month of your life, and it would be cheap at one tenth the price'" (*GDF*, 98). The "pink light-up phone" is a reference to the Princess Telephone launched in 1959 by Bell, distributed by AT&T, and promoted as a bedroom extension to encourage households to install a private line and rent a second phone.[26] The light-up rotary to facilitate use in the dark, and its small size and light weight, which were intended to make it easier to rest on one's

---

[26] John Murphy, *The Telephone* (New York: Chelsea House/Infobase Publishers, 2009), 63; Lupton, 63.

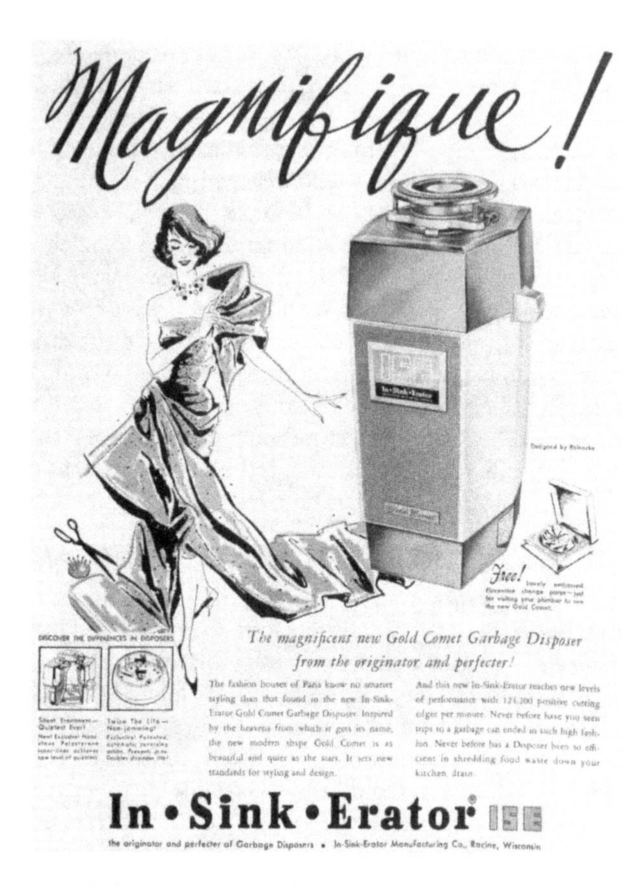

FIGURE 3.3 In-Sink-Erator. "Magnifique!" *The Saturday Evening Post* (May 4, 1960): 98. Courtesy of In-Sink-Erator.

chest while lying in bed, imbued the Princess with an erotic charge, while the name, pastel range of colors (pink, yellow, baby blue, pale green), and curvaceous shape targeted young women specifically. The phone's femininity was underscored by the slogan, "It's little, it's lovely, it lights!" and tiny pastel-colored plastic phone-shaped charms that salesmen handed out to prospective customers to incentivize purchase (Lupton 1993, 35–6 and 2014, 23). The Princess Telephone quickly became notorious however for what the director of the American Telephone Consumers' Council, in a lawsuit against the New York Telephone Company, termed "forever charges": a Princess extension phone would cost the customer $258 over ten years when New York dealers sold it for $35 cash.[27] While Harlan's

[27] Federal Communications Commission, *Activities of Regulatory and Enforcement Agencies . . .* (Washington: US Government Printing Office, 1966).

remarks are a direct reference to this lawsuit and the multiple others that followed, they are also a comment on the unattainability of the middle-class respectability that the Princess Telephone promised for anyone who wasn't already middle class, and which commentators in the 1960s were quick to notice. A 1968 article in the *Archives of General Psychiatry*, for example, singled out middle-class medical students' response to the presence of the Princess Telephone in low-income patients' homes as emblematic of a punitive response to poverty, according to which "the poor were not really so bad off, [and] had brought about their own misfortunes through stupidity and perverse unwillingness to be provident."[28] A similar sentiment was highlighted in an exposé in *The Ladies' Home Journal* in 1962 of the treatment of working-class Black unwed mothers, in which a male benefits officer was described as viewing with contempt the "pink princess telephone on an end table" in the home of a young mother he was visiting.[29] Harlan's statement "You never stop paying, you pay every month of your life" refers to both the financial cost of performing middle-classness and the judgment this is likely to incur: the middle class will *make you pay* for aspiring to join it. And while the metaphors of the garbage disposal unit and the Princess Telephone might at first appear to sit on opposite ends of the ideological spectrum (despite In-Sink-Erator's efforts, the disposal unit never became a fashion must-have!), Piercy's text shows the hidden connections between them. The city council employee who functions as a garbage disposal unit for a system hell-bent on eliminating those deemed unprofitable, unseemly, and likely to sully the (figurative and literal) landscape acts in concert with the status object whose possession by low-income households plunges them into debt while serving as fodder to justify their contemptuous treatment. That Harlan alights upon a product for women to denounce class inequality can be read as either a conflation of middle-class values with femininity that reflects the internalization of a male-centric countercultural rhetoric that Piercy later acknowledged characterized her first novels, or as a comment on the greater toll of aspiration on low-income women.[30]

The ways in which time-saving appliances both shape and reflect gender relations is most thoroughly explored however through Anna and Rowley's trajectories following their break-up. Rowley's lover's incredulous reply, "'*Icebox?*,'" when he requests she make him a sandwich from "'[a]nything out of the icebox,'" suggests a symbiotic relationship between the use of this archaic word and the archaic expectation being expressed (*GDF*, 77). A

---

[28] Arthur W. McMahon and Miles F. Shore, "Some Psychological Reactions to Working with the Poor," *Arch Gen Psychiatry* 18.5 (May 1968): 562–8.

[29] Margaret Parton, "Sometimes Life Just Happens," *The Ladies' Home Journal* 79 (October 1962): 28–33. Citation on 32.

[30] Marge Piercy, *Parti-Colored Blocks for a Quilt* (Ann Arbor: U of Michigan Press, 2001 [1982]), 205.

man who still uses the word "icebox" is bound to expect women to wait on him . . . and a man who expects women to wait on him is bound to still use that word. Piercy exposes the myopia inherent in this conflation of women and appliances when she narrates, first from his perspective, and then from Anna's, an encounter between him, Anna, and her vacuum cleaner:

> Her face was flushed with exertion and looking around he saw a vacuum cleaner plugged in. . . . She looked younger, leaner, yet domestic: the vacuum, the splash of cleaner on her pantleg. . . . Quickly her eyes covered the room, measured her progress and allotted herself a break. . . . She presided where she sat now ankles crossed and head pensive on hand, eyes cleaning the rest of the room. (*GDF*, 211)

> She had just started cleaning when someone knocked. . . . She opened the door and there stood Rowley. Perhaps she was too startled to feel anything. . . . He plunked into a chair and looked glum. . . . His eyes made her restless. She kept turning to the vacuum cleaner in the corner to look away from him. (*GDF*, 225)

Where Rowley absorbs the sight of Anna and her vacuum cleaner, Anna merely *watches herself being watched*. Likewise, where Rowley musingly interprets the vacuum cleaner's relationship to Anna as an implement of empowerment, situating her in a narrative of his own devising based on an amalgamation of images from television and print advertising, it transpires that Anna is resorting to the appliance to escape his gaze. In doing so, she sacrifices a broader field of vision: averting her eyes and focusing on the vacuum cleaner necessitates shutting out everything else. This imbalance between Rowley's visual engulfing of woman and appliance and Anna's deployment of the appliance to avoid locking eyes with him recalls John Berger's description of the gendered construction of sight: "[w]omen watch themselves being looked at [which] determines not only most relations between men and women but also the relation of women to themselves."[31] The vacuum cleaner both complicates and strengthens this account: where in the first version of the scene the appliance is an extension of the feminine mystique Rowley has ascribed to her, in the second version it is exposed as a tool of evasion that simultaneously reinforces his normative perception of her femininity. The disparity between these two perspectives, and the shifting function of the time-saving appliance in the two versions, stands out all the more in light of the fact that this is the only scene in the novel Piercy chooses to narrate twice.

But attention to the time-saving appliance in the closing scenes of the novel, in which Rowley and Anna reconcile when he finds her squatting in

[31] John Berger, *Ways of Seeing* (New York: Penguin, 2008 [1972]), 47.

what remains of her apartment, enables a more nuanced analysis of what otherwise very much reads as an ending in which issues of class supplant gender. The first of these scenes is especially pertinent insofar as it serves as an inverse to Rowley's perception of Anna vacuuming:

> Woman. Anna. Wrapped in an old black winter coat, three sweaters and a scarf, she squatted behind a hibachi from which smoke curled. . . . Her hands were bare and she warmed them at the small flame. Over her the ceiling was smudged. She was bundled into shapelessness. (*GDF*, 302)

"Bundled into shapelessness" and tending not an electric appliance but a hibachi grill—a charcoal stove more generally used for camping or outdoor barbecues—Anna in this closing scene of the novel is the antithesis of the curvaceous mid-century housewife surrounded by her modern implements who Rowley perceived in their previous encounter. The fact that the hibachi grill was at its most popular in the 1950s, a decade prior to the novel's setting, renders the grill itself a kind of relic of fickle food fads.[32] What's more, Anna has turned her apartment into the antithesis of what the contractor for the university's expansion plan envisions for the buildings that will replace it: developments whose "housing package would include . . . barbecue pit, swimming pool, carpeting, furniture, appliances and even car" (*GDF*, 246). As the two disrobe and have sex in front of the smoldering hibachi grill, Piercy suggests—perhaps overly optimistically—that they free themselves of both Rowley's preconceptions and the tyranny of the surrounding culture.

4. Desiring Machines, Electrical Currents, and the Meat of Fleshy Women: *Woman on the Edge of Time* (1976)

The time-saving appliances in Piercy's most famous novel provide a means to interrogate US technocracy more broadly, and to connect the "all-electric" home to patriarchal capitalism, the erasure of immigrant and working-class people, and the psychiatric-industrial complex.[33] In this classic work of feminist speculative fiction set between a psychiatric institution in the late 1960s and two futures—a socialist, gender-free utopia where built-in

[32] Merril D. Smith, *History of American Cooking* (Santa Barbara, CA: ABC-CLIO, 2013), 77.

[33] Lisa Cosgrove and Robert Whitaker in *Psychiatry Under the Influence* (New York: Palgrave Macmillan, 2015) trace the increase in the pharmaceutical industry's financial influence on the APA to the development of *DSM-III* in the 1970s (198). See also Eric M. Greene, "The Mental Health Industrial Complex: A Study in Three Cases," *Journal of Humanistic Psychology* (February 15, 2019).

obsolescence has been replaced by a sharing economy, and a mechanized hyper-capitalism where women are little more than reproductive machines—Piercy places electric-shock therapy, electrically based mind-control experiments, and time-saving domestic gadgets on a continuum. The feature they share is the reduction of women to laboring subjects divested of agency, desire, or resistance, and whose time is never their own. The psychiatric institution is framed as the place women are turned into automata and taught to comply with a system that sees them first and foremost as producers of children and custodians of the home, be it as mothers and housewives whose free labor will assist in the smooth functioning of the capitalist apparatus, or as house cleaners from minority backgrounds acculturated to be grateful to the white households that have deigned to employ them despite their time in psychiatric care. In framing the psychiatric institution as a mirror image of the suburban home—a partner in domestication and disempowerment—the novel is also able to explore different forms of female reification and their interconnection with one another. Piercy shows that the housewife popping tranquilizers in her "all-electric" kitchen and the underpaid cleaner in her employ merely inhabit a stage prior to the lobotomized women wired to electrical nodes. Indeed, the place of working-class and migrant women is made clear in Connie's translation of her welfare officer's plans for her once she is discharged: she will join "a training program that sound[s] like someone's bright idea for producing real cheap domestic labor without importing women from Haiti," and eventually "clea[n] some white woman's kitchen" (*WOTEOT*, 35).

The imbrication of psychiatry, patriarchy, and institutionalized racism and classism—which is also to say, the mutual constitution of the psychiatric-industrial complex and the military-industrial complex of which time-saving appliances are a part—is rendered explicit in the novel's depiction of the dystopian future that Connie has been enlisted to help avert. In that future, "useless" people have been eliminated, while those women lucky enough to be middle- or upper-middle-class have been "cosmetically fixed for sex use," their "inessential" organs removed to create "pure, functional, reliable" beings that "embody the ideal" of womanhood: "[N]ever deflected, never distracted," and never "disloyal" to the multi-national corporation that owns them (*WOTEOT*, 298; 299). Connie and her fellow psychiatric patients ultimately avert this nightmarish future via the commitment of violent acts involving time-saving domestic appliances—a form of reappropriation that turns these gadgets into tools of radical resistance. Liberated from the act of saving time cutting meat or fueling busy doctors, the electric carving knife and coffee maker become participants in revolutionary acts that alter the course of time itself. Time-saving appliances effectively prevent the processes being trialed in the psychiatric institution at the novel's center from reaching their natural conclusion: the reduction of women to human appliances designed to uphold patriarchal capitalism.

Piercy's text was arguably influenced by the startling images of time-saving appliances in Ken Kesey's *One Flew Over the Cuckoo's Nest* (1962).[34] In one of these, the narrator, Big Chief, states that the ward walls are "polished cleaned as a refrigerator door, and the black face and hands [of the nurses] seem to float against it like a ghost" (*OFOTCN*, 27–8). The grammatical choice at the end of the sentence to refer to "it" rather than "them" has the effect of conflating the walls with the refrigerator door to which they have been compared. The refrigerator analogy's significance is revealed in the next sentence, as Big Chief describes the symbiotic relationship between Nurse Ratched and these nurses, who "tun[e] in closer and closer with [her] frequency" via "a high-voltage wavelength of hate," thanks to which they anticipate "before she even thinks it" the command to disconnect an electric-shock patient's wiring (*OFOTCN*, 28). Electric circuitry (both actual and metaphorical) and a hospital ward whose walls are akin to a pristine refrigerator door coalesce to convey an automated hatred of, and desire to expunge, otherness. Kesey's psychiatric institution runs on two currents: the electric wiring of shock-therapy machines, and racial oppression that reduces Black laborers to automated tools and objects of fear—a theme that recurs throughout the text in its myriad references to medical implements and fixtures that resemble "frosted refrigerator coils" and "vacuum cleaners" (*OFOTCN*, 130; 29).

But while implicitly indebted to Kesey's novel, Piercy's novel stands out in its focus on the psychiatric institution's role in reprogramming women specifically to be either compliant wives or servants. This is most explicitly shown in a description of the electric-shock patients on her ward:

> they would send voltage smashing through your brain and knock your body into convulsions. After that they'd give you oxygen and let you come back to life, somebody's life, jumbled, weak, dribbling saliva—come back from your scorched taste of death with parts of your memory forever burned out. A little brain damage to jolt you into behaving right. Sometimes it worked. Sometimes a woman forgot . . . what she had been worrying about. Sometimes a woman was finally more scared of being burned in the head again, and she went home to her family and did the dishes and cleaned the house. Then maybe in a while she would remember and rebel and then she'd be back for more barbecue of the brain. (*WOTEOT*, 81)

Electric shock "fixes" the malfunctioning housewife by erasing the memory of her anxieties and rendering acquiescence to her household duties a

[34] Ken Kesey, *One Flew over the Cuckoo's Nest* (City: Publisher, Year [1962]). Henceforth, *OFOTCN*.

more attractive prospect than having her brain "barbecued"—a graphic description that highlights the barbarity of the psychiatric procedure by linking it to the "wholesome" family foodstuffs, meal occasions, and cooking implements to which she is expected to adhere (and which the procedure will enable her to take up once more). Meanwhile the description of shock therapy as returning the housewife to "somebody's life" rather than her own highlights the relationship between psychiatric procedures and the generic conformity so crucial to Cold War containment culture, and so threatened by the feminist movement. Electric shock deindividualizes the housewife, eradicating any memory of "the problem that has no name" that might lead her to venture beyond the home.

It is likewise no coincidence that the other female patients in the psychiatric institution incorporate appliances into their paranoid fantasies: for example, the aptly named Sybil believes the doctors remove the rings from her fingers before her shock therapy due to their "'poten[cy]'" and "'bombard'" the rings "'with rays . . . in a microwave oven . . . to destroy the power in them'": when they give them back to her after treatment, she claims, "'it takes me weeks to restore their strength'" (*WOTEOT*, 84). This image of electric-shock treatment as a microwave oven that saps the patient of her combativeness plays on the radiation scares around the first microwave ovens.[35] But it also reflects the conflicting social meanings ascribed to this gadget, whose associations with a new generation of working housewives with less time to cook dinner from scratch at once rendered it a symbol of female liberation and an obfuscator of the enduring inequality in men and women's household responsibilities.[36] The image of electric-shock treatment as a microwave oven that saps the patient of her combativeness thus extends the novel's figuration of the "all-electric" kitchen as sapping the power of the women who work in it. This understanding of domestic and psychiatric technology as involved in the same oppressive project is emphasized in Connie's accounts of the psychiatric experiments in which she is about to be enlisted, and which involve connecting patients' brains to electrodes. Her dismissal of these experiments as "a crazy fantasy—like Sybil's microwave ovens that burned out magic" and of the doctors who champion them as "sound[ing] like a repairman from the telephone company calling in to

---

[35] See Cynthia Cockburn and Susan Ormrod, *Gender and Technology in the Making* (London: Sage, 1993), 32–5, and Andrew F. Smith, *Eating History* (New York: Columbia UP, 2009), 206–7.

[36] See R.S. Oropesa, "Female Labor Force Participation and Time-Saving Household Technology: A Case Study of the Microwave from 1978 to 1989," *Journal of Consumer Research* 19.4 (March 1993): 567–79. Articles about the place and function of the microwave oven were stand-out features in the magazine *Working Mother* from its inception in 1978, as exemplified by titles such as "The Right Place: Where to Put Your Microwave Oven" and "Microwave Mastery: Tasteful Presents," both of which appeared in the December 1987 issue (144–5; 137–49).

report on a job" reaffirms the relationship between the electric circuitry of the "all-electric" home and a psychiatric institution that reduces human beings themselves to little more than appliances (*WOTEOT*, 193; 202).

Piercy makes these links explicit in the novel's opening pages, where the imagery of domestic electrification underscores Connie's loss of agency as she is first assaulted against the kitchen stove and then placed in a psychiatric hospital straitjacket in a process she likens to "[f]olding a sheet warm from the machine in the laundry room" and as being "trussed like a holiday bird for the oven" (*WOTEOT*, 18). Piercy enlists appliance imagery again to describe Connie's somnambulant wanderings through a white suburban enclave following her (temporary) escape from the psychiatric institute:

> Slowly the street swung around her . . . A street not made for people. Little houses. In each a TV, a telephone or two, one or two cars outside, toaster, washing machine, drier, hair drier, electric shaver, electric blanket, . . . a spray iron, an electric coffeepot. Surely in each an appliance on legs batted to and fro with two or three or four children, running the vacuum cleaner while the TV blared out game shows. (*WOTEOT*, 254)

The phrase "little houses" is a reference to Malvina Reynolds's song, "Little Boxes" (1962), which Piercy references obliquely in *Going Down Fast* and explicitly in her 1982 novel, *Braided Lives* (about which more later), and whose refrain is "and they all look just the same."[37] Piercy amplifies Reynolds's critique of suburban conformity by adding the housewife *herself* to the list of the gadgets that likely furnish suburban homes and that signal their embodiment of consumer culture's vacuity. The allusion to "an appliance on legs" presents us with an image of a housewife-automaton that implicitly recalls the patient-automaton propped, post-electric-shock therapy, in front of the common room television described just a few pages prior. To escape the electrified asylum, the text suggests, is to merely plunge into another kind of electrically-charged madhouse—a point Connie later renders explicit in her comparison of the open-plan design of her brother Luis and his wife Adele's suburban house to "a big hospital ward" (*WOTEOT*, 350). The alienating effects of such faith in gadgetry is highlighted a few sentences later in the description of Connie "passing an appliance store" and seeing "a salesman . . . opening and closing the door of a stand-up freezer, his mouth going nonstop" (*WOTEOT*, 255). The absence of any mention of the person to whom the salesperson is purportedly speaking conveys the perpetual motion of a consumer culture that appears to operate regardless of the presence of buyers. Connie perceives this erasure once more when

[37] Malvina Reynolds, "Little Boxes" (1962), Track#3 on *Malvina Reynolds Sings the Truth*, Columbia, 1967; qtd. in *GDF*, 90–1; *BL*, 381–2.

she works as a cleaner for Luis and Adele. Thus she notes of herself, Adele, and her niece clearing up after dinner: "We are not three women. . . . We are ups and downs and heavy tranks [tranquilizers] meeting in the 'all-electric' kitchen and bouncing off each other's opaque sides like shiny pill colliding" (*WOTEOT*, 358). The image of women-as-pills dancing in a gadget-laden kitchen illustrates Connie's sense of her and her generation's reification under patriarchal capitalism.

Luis and Adele's "all-electric" home is also host, however, to two of the four instances of explicit resistance that occur in the novel's final sections, each of which involves a time-saving appliance. The first of these describes Connie's bewilderment at the "refrigerator in the kitchen, huge and golden brown," whose "golden space crammed with food . . . ke[eps] drawing her sleepy gaze":

> She imagined herself rising slowly from her chair and with her Thorazine shuffle . . . stumbling into the kitchen to the refrigerator, sitting down on the floor, and pulling out one item at a time until she had eaten everything in the whole golden box. It all called to her in wonderful soprano siren voices. . . . Each time she opened the door to that paradise of golden possibilities, she felt buffeted by choice. . . . She went back and forth from the dinette to the refrigerator, carrying each time one new treasure. (*WOTEOT*, 351)

Brightly colored food items inside a golden-brown appliance and blue and white cheese that resembles Adele's "blue and white electric percolator" conspire to create a heady vision of sensual excess (spanning multiple pages) that is starkly at odds with the utilitarianism of the psychiatric hospital's machines (*WOTEOT*, 354). Meanwhile Connie's movements between dinette and refrigerator, which involve not housework but consumption for consumption's sake, contrast with the efficiency anticipated in the time-motion studies of domestic economists. The refrigerator whose contents appear infinite, and the consumption of whose contents "slow[s] down" her "time sense," counters the interminability of modern domestic work, instead extending the time of food in order for the woman to use up time eating it (*WOTEOT*, 354–5). Notably, this scene recapitulates a similar intimation of radicalism that occurred in the novel's very first pages, before Connie was dragged to the psychiatric hospital and sedated. In this earlier scene, Connie does a mental tally of all her brother's ex-wives before turning to the task of preparing dinner. Finding pinto beans in the refrigerator, she "yearn[s] for meat":

> How she would like to sink her teeth in a pork chop. Her mouth watered in faint hope. She turned on the little black-and-white TV she was always hauling back and forth from bedroom to kitchen. . . . The set was company, a human—or almost human—voice. . . . Below in the street evening hummed to the rhythm of high and low drums, a rising

> tide of dealing and hustling, the push of the young and not so young to score, to get laid. At a simmer, the slow bubbles rising through the thick air, sex and traffic quickened El Barrio. . . . That electricity in the streets brushed static from her. She longed to be moving toward someone . . . she wanted to be touched and held. (*WOTEOT*, 47–8)

The passage juxtaposes the electrically powered refrigerator and the meat it does not contain with the desires of the flesh and a collective sexual energy allegorized as an electric current, while the surreal description "At a simmer, the slow bubbles rising through the thick air, sex and traffic quickened El Barrio" suggests that the neighborhood itself is being cooked on Connie's stove. Situated after the descriptions of her brother's discarded wives, the passage presents the time-saving appliance as part of a network of unmet longings, objectified women, and animated objects. We might in fact read this passage through the lens of Deleuze and Guattari, for whom desire does not signify lack, but rather a productive force ("desiring-production").[38] In *Anti-Oedipus*, they describe this productive desire as a "desiring-machine" (which might be either produced by individual people or systems of meaning), which produces a flow of desire that connects the "desiring-machine" to other "desiring-machines" as well as to a larger system or network of "desiring-machines." Individual desiring machines are connected to each other, and to the social body, and none can exist outside of the social body. In Piercy's text, this productive force is expressed in Connie's hungry identification with the urban landscape and visualization of herself as part of a swarming multitude producing its own erotic impulses. As well as highlighting the constraining effects of a patriarchal system that makes women's freedom contingent upon their ability to hold onto a man, the passage explicitly draws attention to the bodily cravings of those traditionally viewed only as bodies to *be* craved. In so doing, it reclaims flesh as the starting point for an agency grounded in desire. It is significant in fact that Piercy shifts from a description of hunger for animal meat to a longing to be part of the movement of human meat on the street below. Even more significant is her representation of a woman refuting literality (the electricity that powers refrigerators) in favor of the metaphorical ("electrical" sexual energy). The line, "That electricity in the streets brushed static from her" conveys Connie's desire as a hunger for both that which the refrigerator cannot provide (since it contains no meat, and since the electricity on which it runs is mundanely literal) and for currents of energy and fleshy bodies that one must leave the home to find (*WOTEOT*, 48).

---

[38] Gilles Deleuze and Felix Guattarí, *Anti-Oedipus*, transl. Robert Hurley, Mark Seem and Helen R. Lane (Minneapolis: U of Minnesota Press, 1983), 4–10.

The freedom gestured at in these two refrigerator depictions pales in comparison however to the violent radicalism of the two appliances deployed in the novel's final pages. In the first instance, a patient called Skip commits suicide in his parents' kitchen, slitting his throat with their electric carving knife—an act that Connie sarcastically describes as proof he has been cured "of fumbling, of indecision" (*WOTEOT*, 286). If the electric-shock therapy to which Skip was subjected was designed to reduce him to a near-inanimate state that would render him "easier" to deal with, his suicide by electric carving knife shows the endpoint of such a logic. Even easier to deal with than a barbecued brain is a sliced and diced corpse ready to be served on a proverbial plate. Skip's act of self-destruction parodies the systems that reduced him to despair in the first place and serves as a sly, intertextual riposte or Fuck You to the "steel machine" with "purse sectioned lips, like a vacuum-cleaner hose" that in *One Flew Over the Cuckoo's Nest* is tasked with "spurt[ing] a clot of chewed-up ham" onto the plates of the toothless lobotomized patients known as "the Vegetables" (*OFOTCN*, 29). Contrary to the quasi-animate machine that in Kesey's text sustains humans in a vegetative state from which they cannot escape, the appliance in this passage of Piercy's text is an implement of resistance.

But the appliance's radical potential is best illustrated in *Woman on the Edge of Time*'s violent and absurd conclusion, when Connie puts poison in the doctors' "fancy automatic coffee machine," thereby killing them before their next surgery, and impeding the development of brain-altering technologies on which the dystopian future she momentarily glimpsed was predicated (*WOTEOT*, 341; 374). While this act seals her own fate, as the discovery of her crime will result in her permanent internment, the novel implies this is a worthwhile self-sacrifice. While Skip's suicide by electric knife provides individual escape, Connie's use of the electric coffee machine to murder the doctors provides collective salvation, rendering possible the realization of the utopian future she has visited intermittently throughout the novel. It allows, that is, for the possibility of the development of a future society entirely free of oppressive technology—a society that prizes attributes other than time-saving and efficiency.

5. "We Have Our Most Intense Scenes in Kitchens": *Braided Lives* (1982) and Capitalism's Co-option of American Jews

Set in Detroit between the early 1950s and the late 1960s, *Braided Lives* enlists time-saving appliances to illustrate narrator Jill's development as a woman and as a class-conscious Jewish feminist living in the United States' industrial heartlands. While Jill claims that "We have our most intense scenes in kitchens," it is the electric objects in or absent from those kitchens, and the metaphors and allegories that they suggest, that from the novel's very first pages enable Jill to narrate the tensions between her Jewish, working-class, and female identities and the most fraught moments of her life. In particular, class and gender anxieties come to the fore in the description of appliances' function in Jill's family as proxies for wealth, which Piercy frames as illustrative of the co-option of American Jews into the capitalist project.

As a number of scholars have shown, Jews' assimilation into mainstream US culture was a process of attaining "whiteness."[39] Where country clubs, sororities, and particular neighborhoods initially banned both Jewish and Black people, these strictures were loosened for Jews who accrued capital, who demonstrated their capacity to perform white middle-classness by participating in mass consumption, and who in the postwar era purchased suburban "all-electric" homes.[40] This process however was gradual, and uneven—as Piercy herself remarked in a 2019 interview, when it came to working-class families, "'Jews and blacks were lumped together'" well into the 1950s.[41] Like Piercy's Welsh father and Jewish mother, Jill's parents too aspire to a whiteness beyond reach, which they pursue by "bedeck[ing]" their house "with flounces and gadgets" bought on credit (*BL*, 110). The family's "hatbox kitchen is surprisingly modern, bristling with electric frypans and electric can openers with a huge slab of refrigerator lording it over the wobbly old table," and though "the refrigerator and the TV [are] still not paid for," her father continues to compulsively purchase more devices (*BL*, 29; 17). The image of Jill's mother's devotion to a "vacuum sweeper" whose "grinding" noise follows her around the house, and to telling "interminable stor[ies] about what went wrong with the washing machine," conveys the claustrophobia of working-class Jewish female experience, wherein the pursuit of cleanliness that will make one's home look WASP involves relinquishing life beyond its walls (*BL*, 30; 63). Jill's parents' status-seeking

[39] See Karen Brodkin, *How Jews Became White Folks and What That Says About Race in America* (New Brunswick, NJ: Rutgers UP, 1998), 46–9; George Lipsitz, *The Possessive Investment in Whiteness* (Philadelphia, PA: 1998), 154–5; Catherine Jurca, *White Diaspora*, 38; 213, ff. 28; Eric R. Goldstein, *The Price of Whiteness: Jews, Race, and American Identity* (Princeton, NJ: UP, 2006).

[40] See Andrew Heinze, *Adapting to Abundance: Jewish Immigrants, Mass Consumption, and the Search for American Identity* (New York: Columbia UP, 1990), 22; 134. While Heinze's argument that electrical appliances "transformed" the home between 1919 and 1929 rather overstates the extent of household penetration of appliances in this period, his point regarding the significance of these objects to the cultural imagination, and to cementing an image of American prosperity to which immigrants would be particularly susceptible, is apt.

[41] See John Rodden, "A Harsh Day's Light: An Interview with Marge Piercy," *The Kenyon Review*, New Series 20.2 (Spring 1998): 132–43, citation on 132; Amy Schwartz, "At Home with Marge Piercy," *Moment Magazine* (June 3, 2019).

through appliances is juxtaposed with the utter indifference to gadgets of Jill's first husband Mike's wealthy WASP parents, who instead employ a Black maid in a kitchen "stuffed with 20-year-old appliances [Jill's] mother would pity," while their "refrigerator is empty" (*BL*, 144). The antiquated appliances do not denote impoverishment, but a patrician prosperity premised on self-restraint. The empty refrigerator intimates that this family has no *need* to imitate the images of mechanized domesticity propagated in mid-century advertisements. Their social status is already assured.

Piercy's articulation of domestic electrification's function in the co-option of Jews by US capitalism cannot but recall Philip Roth's famous account of Jewish assimilation in *Goodbye, Columbus* (1959), in which working-class Neil Klugman falls in love with the recently assimilated middle-class Brenda Patimkin.[42] That the Patimkins, who eat dinner "in the steady coolness of air by Westinghouse," are *on their way* to whiteness is highlighted in Neil's account of the "tall old refrigerator" he finds in their basement alongside "innumerable electrical appliances" (*GC*, 16; 60; 30). He notes:

> This same refrigerator had once stood in the kitchen of an apartment . . . probably in the same neighborhood where I had lived all my life. . . . After Pearl Harbor the refrigerator had made the move up to Short Hills; Patimkin Kitchen and Bathroom Sinks had gone to war . . . I opened the door of the old refrigerator; it was not empty. No longer did it hold butter, eggs, herring in cream sauce, ginger ale, tuna fish salad . . . rather it was heaped with fruit, shelves swelled with it. . . . There were . . . cherries flowing out of boxes and staining everything scarlet . . . and on the top shelf, half of a huge watermelon, a thin sheet of wax paper clinging to its bare red face like a wet lip. (*GC*, 30–1)

While Judith Oster reads Roth's refrigerator as embodying Neil's seduction by the Patimkins' luxury and Mr. Patimkin's pride at having come so far, I interpret it as an electrical equivalent to a picture in an attic, whose contents may be ripe and juicy but exude danger.[43] The substitution of the refrigerator's traditional Jewish foods with sensual fruits allegorizes the lure of whiteness as well as implicitly suggesting it is a temptation to be resisted—a point underscored, later, in the "kinship" Neil feels toward the Black maid who spits cherry pits directly into the garbage disposal unit as she cooks and cleans, taking advantage of their bountiful fruit without letting herself be seduced by it (*GC*, 55). Meanwhile, both this substitution of Jewish foods and the move of the refrigerator itself down to the basement function as

[42] Philip Roth, *Goodbye Columbus* (New York: Bantam, 1982 [1959]), 1–98.
[43] Judith Oster, *Crossing Cultures: Creating Identity in Chinese and Jewish American Literature* (U of Missouri Press, 2003), 134.

symbols of Mr. Patimkin's repression of his Jewish working-class identity. The distinction Neil makes between the refrigerator's rapid trajectory and his own more modest one both contributes to the passage's articulation of human reification at the behest of capital and foreshadows Brenda's eventual rejection of him: like the refrigerator from Newark, the unassimilated Jew is *not suitable for display*. More importantly, the refrigerator's place in the basement suggests Mr. Patimkin's shame not only regarding the refrigerator's "ancient" appearance but at his delight in its bountiful contents. Just as the empty refrigerator in Mike's mother's house in *Braided Lives* displays an abstemiousness that is coded white, the refrigerator in *Goodbye, Columbus* is hidden in the basement in order to conceal the excess within it, which if visible would betray Mr. Patimkin's working-class vulnerability to the lure of luxury. And just as the absence of new appliances in Mike's house reflects their quasi-aristocratic standing, the description of the sheer number of shiny appliances in the Patimkins' home underscores the artificiality of their class performance—as exemplified by Neil's quip to Brenda that if she tried to plant the cherry pits from the fruit refrigerator, "'they'd grow refrigerators and Westinghouse Preferred,'" not fruit (*GC*, 38).

Piercy's racial coding of appliances goes beyond Roth's, however. The absence of the latest appliances in Mike's mother's kitchen in *Braided Lives* conveys a deliberate abstention from participation in a mass culture understood to be not only ungainly and tasteless, but at odds with antebellum values. This is exemplified in Mike's dehumanizing description of the family's maid as "'fifty, coal black, and big as a house'" (*BL*, 144). The depiction simultaneously plays on the Mammy stereotype—the desexualized, happy slave—and reinforces the notion of the Black "help" as human appliances, implicitly referencing appliances' initial promotion, in their first decades of existence, as mechanical slaves.[44] This old-fashioned kitchen whose trusty Black servant of thirty years is a much more reliable "device" than any new-fangled washing machine or refrigerator stands in contrast to Jill's family's kitchen. Here, in the scene immediately following her visit to Mike's mother's home, Jill must raise her voice for her mother to hear her over the "whir of an electric mixer" that suggests "Mrs. McCallen next door must be baking a cake" (*BL*, 149). The depiction is in keeping with Shelley Nickles's identification of the difference between the kitchen's social meaning for wealthy Americans who rarely ventured there and for working-class families, for whom it was "'one of the most important parts of their existence.'"[45] Far from embodying a futuristic techno-modernity, the noise of the mixer that intrudes upon this intimate domestic scene reminds

[44] Nye, *Electrifying America*, 247–8.

[45] "'Preserving Women,'" 702. See also Nickles's discussion, in "More Is Better," of the significance of appliances as status symbols for working-class women in the 1950s.

Jill of her place in the all-too-shabby present—and that the many gadgets that furnish her family's home have *not* made them middle class. Via these back-to-back scenes, Piercy upends the image of the "all-electric" kitchen as a symbol of postwar prosperity, revealing instead its centrality to postwar working-class Jews' pursuit of whiteness, and postwar wealthy WASPs' contemptuous self-definition in opposition to *arrivistes* on the make.

Like *Woman on the Edge of Time*, however, *Braided Lives* intimates how the electrical implements used to circumscribe women within the home might also be used as tools of subversion. Where an electric iron at one point prevents Jill's mother's self-expression and communication with the outside world—as conveyed in Jill's father's explanation, "'Your mother burned her hand ironing, which is why she hasn't written'"—this same appliance serves as a tool for resistance for Jill (*BL*, 133). When her boyfriend sexually assaults her while she is home alone ironing her father's shirts, terror "twitche[s her] violently as a bad shock" before she brandishes the hot iron at him—a response that is recounted twice more over the course of the novel, and the violence of which is amplified more with each repetition (*BL*, 31–2; 162; 255). The statements, "if he didn't rape me on the kitchen floor, it was only because I took a hot iron to him," and "If I were truly that passive . . . Freddie would have had me on the kitchen floor at age fourteen while the iron burned through my father's shirts above," each raise the stakes of Jill's resistance—the victim of electric-like "shock" now wields electric force of her own (*BL*, 162; 255).

Piercy amplifies and subverts the class and race distinctions just discussed in the last section of the novel. Here, Jill's cousin Donna describes her new apartment in the suburbs, where "'[e]verything's electric [...] You don't even have garbage, like ordinary people. There's a machine in the kitchen that eats it. And a dishwasher. Even Peter's mother doesn't have that—just a Negro maid'" (*BL*, 382). In contrast to Jill, for whom the inextricable link between time-saving appliances, her parents' middle-class aspirations, and her mother's subjugation makes them a source of shame, Donna luxuriates in her "all-electric" home, pointedly distinguishing it from her mother-in-law's, whose reliance (like that of Mike's mother) on a Black servant marks it out as retrograde. At the same time however she also expresses longing for a different kind of electricity: "'that kind of electricity [that is] necessarily a phenomenon of not knowing the person yet [s]o that you can invent marvellous fantasy figures to inhabit that momentarily charged body'" (*BL*, 382). To the sterility of this "all-electric" home whose saving grace is that it (sometimes) does away with the exploitation of Black people (although her dehumanising description of her mother-in-law's maid suggests that the emancipation of Blacks is not foremost on her mind), Donna counters a daydream of sexual electricity, building on a vocabulary of sexual currents in search of an outlet that Piercy has enlisted throughout the novel (*BL*, 158; 250; 302). In this way, Piercy reiterates the longings expressed in her earlier fiction, while tempering the critiques therein with a recognition of domestic electrification's benefits that reflects the novel's publication date nearly two decades after theWomen's Liberation Movement began.

6. Conclusion

The texts just discussed are but a mere sample from an oeuvre replete with time-saving appliances and electrical imagery. In their incisive identification of time-saving appliances' role in propagating a particular kind of femininity coded as white, in co-opting American Jews into the United States' capitalist project via access to white suburbia, and in normalizing—indeed, domesticating!—electric-shock therapy and normativity more broadly, Piercy's works stand out as milestones of both second-wave feminist fiction and countercultural postwar writing. Piercy identifies the exploitative, oppressive dimension of time-saving appliances not in order to condemn electricity outright but to suggest the many other ends to which it might be more productively used. If the electric power on which time-saving appliances run and the rhetoric of electrical "magic" and modernity weaponized by appliance advertisers are frequently revealed, in Piercy's work, to exist in inverse proportion to the social disempowerment of the women who wield them, Piercy's appliance poetics redirect the metaphorical currents of this rhetoric and use the vocabulary of electricity to instead envision more egalitarian and emotionally meaningful ways of being. Piercy's appliance poetics suggest that for true gender and class equality to occur, not only must wealth and resources be redistributed and social roles reimagined: the colonialist, patriarchal language long used to depict resources such as electricity as symbols of empire must be interrogated and replaced.

4

"I've Never Been Able to Get Another Girl as Efficient or as Reliable":[1]

Time-Saving Appliances in Black American Fiction, 1952–2003

In her autobiographical short story, "To Da-duh, in Memoriam" (1983), Paule Marshall recalls visiting her native Barbados in 1937, when she was eight, and telling her grandmother all about the "refrigerators, radios, gas stoves, elevators, trolley cars, wringer washing machines . . . toasters, [and] electric lights" in the United States: "'flip this little switch on the wall and all the lights in the house go on. Just like that. Like magic. It's like turning on the sun at night.'"[2] To "Da-duh's" playful question whether "'the white people have all these things too or it's only the people looking like us?'" her granddaughter replies: "'What d'ya mean [...] The white people have even better'" (*ROS*, 103). In *My Garden (Book)* (1999), Jamaica Kincaid in turn identifies her first experience of electrification, while a child in Antigua, as the source of her distrust of both winter and the United States. Upon putting her hand in the "freezer part" of a friend's refrigerator:

Heartfelt thanks to Chisomo Kalinga for her invaluable advice on this chapter.

[1] Paule Marshall, *Brown Girl, Brownstones* (Eastford, CT: Martino Fine Books, 2014 [1959]), 288. Henceforth, *BGB*.

[2] Paule Marshall, "To Da-duh, in Memoriam," in *Reena and Other Stories* (Feminist Press at CUNY, 1983), 103. Henceforth, *ROS*.

> I became convinced . . . (and remain so even now) that cold air is unnatural and manmade and associated with prosperity (for refrigerators were common in the prosperous North) and more real and special than the warm air that was so ordinary to me; and then I became suspicious of it, because it seemed to me that it was also associated with the dark, with the cold comes the dark, in the dark things grow pale and die.[3]

Where Marshall's text sardonically highlights the racial dimension of appliance ownership, Kincaid's text is almost mournful. Within what J. Brooks Bouson has termed Kincaid's sustained exploration of the relationship between gardening, colonial conquest, and her own identity, the manufactured cold of the refrigerator serves as an extended metaphor for the "cold" culture of an industrialized, prosperous, inauthentic, and violently imperialist North.[4] While providing very different visions of domestic electrification, both Marshall and Kincaid's texts stand out in their explicit association of time-saving appliances with whiteness, and help to explain why these objects appear far less frequently in writing by Black writers and immigrant writers of color than in that of white writers.

This chapter explores the racial dimension of domestic appliances in a selection of novels by Black writers published between 1957 and the late 1990s—a topic that has been almost entirely overlooked by literary critics.[5] Section 1 contextualizes, within the history of appliance ownership and advertising, James Baldwin's scathing critique of 1960s advertising in *Just Above My Head* (1979), and the more nuanced depictions of appliance ownership in Ralph Ellison's posthumously published unfinished novel, *Three Days Before the Shooting* (2010) and Toni Morrison's *The Bluest Eye* (1970), *Tar Baby* (1981), *Paradise* (1997), and *Love* (2003). Section 2 analyzes a selection of appliance depictions that portray domestic electrification as a grotesque embodiment of structural racism broadly and the exploitation of Black Americans specifically. The texts I examine here include, once more, Toni Morrison's *Paradise* and James Baldwin's *Just Above My Head*, as well as Ralph Ellison's *Invisible Man* (1952) and Alice Walker's *The Third Life of Grange Copeland* (1970).

[3] Jamaica Kincaid, "The Garden in Winter," in *My Garden (Book)* (New York: Farrar, Strauss, Giroux, 1999), 63.

[4] J. Brooks Bouson, *Jamaica Kincaid* (New York: SUNY Press, 2006), 185.

[5] The exceptions to this silence are Justine Baille's brief reading, in *Toni Morrison and Literary Tradition* (London: Bloomsbury, 2013), of the limits of time-saving appliances in Toni Morrison's *Home*, where she argues that peace for the protagonists "lies in nascent creativity and work without alienation, not in the purchase of a Philco refrigerator" (202), and David Alworth's chapter in *Site Reading* on the radical impetus of the narrator's theft of electricity in *Invisible Man* (121–48).

Sections 3 and 4 each zoom in on one novel—Alice Childress's *Like One of the Family: Conversations from a Domestic's Life* (1956) and Paule Marshall's *Brown Girl, Brownstones* (1959) respectively. I devote greater space to Childress and Marshall not only because of the striking significance of times-saving appliances to their respective narratives but due to these authors' underrepresentation in literary studies compared to those discussed in sections 1–3. In particular, while Dorothy Hamer Denniston's publication in 1995 of the first book-length study of Marshall's fiction led to renewed interest in the author's work, and Mary Helen Washington's groundbreaking research into Childress's political activism has recovered the radical leftist strains across her plays and fiction, both Marshall and Childress remain underdiscussed compared to Ellison, Baldwin, and Morrison.[6]

Certain of the passages I quote refer to Black people as "negroes," "coloreds," "n*gra," or "n*****." I have replaced the "i" in the penultimate of these with an asterisk (as, elsewhere in this study, I never spell out "n*****"), in order to distinguish between terms that at the time of the texts' publication were descriptive (albeit still problematic due to their original conception by white people to refer to slaves) and those that were explicitly understood to be pejorative slurs.[7] These replacements are also intended to acknowledge the fraught history of "n*gra" and "n*****" and their enduring power to pithily dehumanize people of color—a point I return to in Chapter 6, in my discussion of the expression "N***** work" in Vonnegut's *Breakfast of Champions.*

---

[6] Dorothy Hamer Denniston, *The Fiction of Paule Marshall* (U of Tennessee Press, 1995); Mary Helen Washington, "Alice Childress, Lorraine Hansberry, and Claudia Jones: Black Women Write the Popular Front," in *Left of the Color Line: Race, Radicalism, and Twentieth-Century Literature of the United States*, ed. Bill V. Mullen and James Smethurst (U of North Carolina Press, 2003), 183–204; Mary Helen Washington, "Alice Childress: Black, Red, and Feminist," in *The Other Blacklist: The African American Literary and Cultural Left of the 1950s* (Columbia UP, 2014), 123–64; Dayo Gore, *Radicalism at the Crossroads: African American Women Activists in the Cold War* (New York: New York UP, 2011); Erik McDuffie, *Sojourning for Freedom: Black Women, American Communism, and the Making of Black Left Feminism* (Durham, NC: Duke UP). See also Kate Baldwin, "Cold War, Hot Kitchen: Alice Childress, Natalya Barnskaya, and the Speakin' Place of Cold War Womanhood," in *Globalizing American Studies*, ed. Brian Edwards and Dilip Parameshwar Gaonkar (Chicago, IL: U of Chicago Press, 2010), 135–54.

[7] Randall Kennedy's *Nigger: The Strange Career of a Troublesome Word* (New York: Pantheon, 2001) provides the most exhaustive account of this word's trajectory from its origins ("negar," 1619). While the exact period it became pejorative is unknown, it was "a familiar and influential insult" by the 1830s (4–5). In *The N Word: Who Can Say It, Who Shouldn't, and Why* (New York: Houghton Mifflin, 2007), Jabari Asim notes that "n*gra" was merely the result of white Southerners' attempt to pronounce "negro" (127, asterisks my own).

1. The Racialized History of Time-Saving Appliances

The tendency among manufacturers and reformers, which lasted well into the 1940s, to portray time-saving appliances either as replacements for "unreliable" Black servants, or as objects white women would have to teach them to use, forms the subtext of Toni Morrison's accounts of her after-school job in the early 1940s as a maid to a white woman (Nye, 247–8; Hay, 115; Wolcott, 82). Where, in an interview in 1994, Morrison quipped that the job "'wasn't uninteresting. You got to work these gadgets that I never had at home: vacuum cleaners,'" her 2017 essay, "The Work You Do, the Person You Are," laid bare the tensions inherent in domestic work, and which the advent of domestic technology heightened in its expansion of the distance between a technologically savvy white hegemonic culture and a Black working class perceived as regressive:

> All I had to do for the two dollars was clean Her house for a few hours after school. It was a beautiful house, too, with . . . a white enamel stove, a washing machine and a dryer—things that were common in Her neighborhood, absent in mine . . . I knew how to scrub floors on my knees and how to wash clothes in our zinc tub, but I had never seen a Hoover vacuum cleaner or an iron that wasn't heated by fire.[8]

Morrison reveals time-saving appliances to be coconspirators in the social construction of a domestic space replete with technologies available only to white people. Meanwhile her focus on relations between a woman servant of color and white female employer complicates the straightforward narrative of many white first- and second-wave feminists, whose focus on patriarchy's oppression of white housewives overlooked the role that white women themselves played in maintaining racial hierarchies—and, indeed, the ways in which dehumanizing Black servants provided a means for white women to assert at home the authority they were denied in public. As Saidiya Hartman describes in her (archive-based) speculative history of early-twentieth-century Black American women, "wage labor, servitude, improper guardianship, failed maternity, chance coupling, serial marriages, and widowhood marked the difference" between the lived experiences of Black and white women.[9]

---

[8] Claudia Dreifus, "Chloe Wofford Talks About Toni Morrison," *New York Times* (September 11, 1994), 73; Toni Morrison, "The Work You Do, the Person You Are," *The New Yorker* (June 5 and 12, 2017).

[9] Saidiya Hartman, *Wayward Lives, Beautiful Experiments* (New York: W.W. Norton, 2019), 184.

Morrison's first novel, *The Bluest Eye* (1970), which is set in Depression-era Ohio, subtly hints at this racialized history.[10] Morrison's nine-year-old narrator, Claudia, describes the fascination and horror she feels at her white doll, whose "sweet and plaintive cry 'Mama'" sounds, to her, "like the bleat of a dying lamb, or, more precisely, our icebox door opening its rusty hinges in July" (*TBE*, 19). Claudia's rage against the doll, like her loathing of the child actress Shirley Temple, transforms quickly into rage against *all* white girls, whose cries if pinched, she reflects, "would not be the sound of an icebox door, but a fascinating cry of pain" (*TBE*, 19). Like Jamaica Kincaid in the text quoted at the outset of this chapter, Claudia enlists the icebox to convey the alienating artifice that underpins the white beauty ideal which her friends embrace, and which the adults in her life impose on her through the gift of white dolls. The description of the rusty hinge, and of an icebox rather than a refrigerator, conjures an image of an old, perhaps second-hand, device far removed from the gleaming electrically powered items that featured in 1930s ads and films—and far removed from the sheen of the white woman's kitchen in which Claudia's mother works. What's more, these references amplify the frightening, hauntological, quality of the doll, revealing its proximity to not only death and the loss of innocence (allegorized in the cry of the dying lamb) but a mechanistic quality implicitly linked to whiteness. In this way, Morrison makes a direct connection between child socialization into white supremacy, and participation in the apparatus of an American techno-modernity premised on white supremacist ideals.

As attested by Morrison's autobiographical account of encountering her first vacuum cleaner as a servant, appliance ownership remained segregated throughout the 1930s and 1940s, even as these objects entered the mass market through New Deal polices that enabled white working-class households to purchase them on credit (Tobey, 70; 165). The New Deal's programs tied domestic modernization to home ownership, which was rare for minorities, as segregation suppressed the amount of housing available for them to purchase (Tobey, 167). The Federal Housing Authority's identification of racial change in a neighborhood as eroding property values also rendered inaccessible government subsidies for the wiring of new homes, as builders could only obtain insurance if they demonstrated the property's value would not decline during the period of the mortgage (Tobey, 167). Black Americans in Southern states were likewise excluded from the Electric Home and Farm Authority's (EHFA) efforts to educate rural households about electricity's benefits, and Black Americans as a whole were likely excluded from the fairs, demonstrations, and other forms of pageantry the EHFA put on in the

[10] Toni Morrison, *The Bluest Eye* (London: Vintage, 1994 [1970]). Henceforth, *TBE*.

1930s to show off the "magic" of domestic electrification.[11] While figures from the period 1940 to 1945 indicate that electricity consumption rose in minority households due to the increased incomes of minority soldiers and of immigrant workers from the South who took higher-paying jobs in the new armament factories, and as second-hand appliances became more available, appliance ownership in minority households did not become commonplace until after the defeat of housing segregation in 1948 (Tobey, 167; 194–5).

This political dimension of appliance ownership—as both hard-won right and status symbol—is discussed in Chapter 5 of Book I of Ralph Ellison's *Three Days Before the Shooting. . .*, an over 1,000-page novel still unfinished when Ellison died in 1994, and which he spent the previous forty years writing.[12] Here, an economics expert and a group of reporters—all white men—discuss a Black man who set his Cadillac on fire as an act of public protest (*TDBTS*, 49). One of the reporters, McGowan, warns the others that "'a n*gra who'd burn a Cadillac would do just about anything,'" before expostulating that "'everything the n*gra does is political'":

> "If a n*gra buys a woman a washing machine—watch him, he's dangerous! And if he gets her a clothes dryer and a dishwasher—put that n*gra under the jail, he's trying to undercut our American way of life. . . . there are few things in this world as political as a black N*gra woman owning her own washing machine! Now don't laugh. You Yankees must remember that the Industrial Revolution was *revolutionary,* because if y'all don't know it, the n*gra does, and he never stops scheming to make it more so." (*TDBTS*, 53–5, asterisks my own)

McGowan reveals the machines of the home to be just as politically charged as the Cadillac, which a story in the September 1949 issue of *EBONY* argued was "an instrument of aggression" that symbolized "for many a Negro that he is as good as any white man."[13] More specifically, McGowan enlists the washing machine as an emblem of white supremacy contingent upon its exclusivity. Curtailing Black Americans' freedom, according to McGowan, requires curtailing their access to "higher" things—from literature and new media to the machines that, his reference to the Industrial Revolution implies, led to the end of slavery. More importantly, it involves preventing them from *sullying* the world of white people—a claim premised on the

[11] Michelle Mock, "The Electric Home and Farm Authority, 'Model T Appliances,' and the Modernization of the Home Kitchen in the South," *The Journal of Southern History* 80.1 (February 2014): 73–108. See esp. 99, ff. 96.

[12] Ralph Ellison, *Three Days Before the Shooting . . .*, ed. John Callahan and Adam Bradley (New York: The Modern Library, 2010). Henceforth, *TDBTS*.

[13] John S. Johnson, "Why Negroes Buy Cadillacs," *EBONY* (September 1949), 34.

conflation of blackness and dirt, whereby a Black person with access to a washing machine also has access to cleanliness and purity that US culture codifies as white. Indeed, this was the subtext of the rhetoric used by washing machine and laundry detergent brands in their emphasis on the achievement of "whiter than white whites" (which referred to white linens, but in a culture that values whites above people of color was charged with racial undertones), not to mention the rhetoric around "sparkling white" appliances more broadly.[14]

As well as having delayed access to time-saving appliances, Black Americans were largely ignored by appliance advertisers until the 1960s—thirty years after Black business owners began lobbying for advertisers to target Black consumers, and fifteen years after agencies began heeding these calls. Grace Hale notes that Black people's historical reification in advertising rendered them on par with consumer goods: "Advertising, both by picturing subservient blacks with products and celebrating whites as sovereign consumers implicitly and explicitly figured the national consumer as white" and as someone "who could command the service of both blacks and consumer products" (167). Jason Chambers adds that "if one looks at advertisements as documentaries, then the world for much of the twentieth century was one in which whites enjoyed the fruits of consumption and blacks, if visible at all, contentedly served them from the margins."[15] While the National Negro Business League and Colored Merchants' Association's plan for an annual survey, beginning in 1931, of the purchasing habits of Black housewives across the United States failed due to financial pressures associated with the Great Depression, interest in Black consumers among advertisers and manufacturers gained momentum in the 1940s.[16] Meanwhile the increase in Black appliance ownership, together with the rise in Black incomes, and the first valuation, in 1942, of the Black consumer market, contributed to the trade press's, researchers', and agencies' growing interest in the untapped potential of what was then known as the "Negro market" (Chambers, 73). Advertising-space buyers meanwhile argued the need to hire Black marketing "specialists," the latter of whom, by the early 1950s, were enjoining agencies targeting Black consumers to use Black models, and to "avoi[d] copy that implied that Blacks' buying motivations simply mirrored those of whites" (50; 73; 86). These efforts were complemented by those of John H. Johnson, the founder of magazines including *EBONY*

[14] For insight into the racist roots of laundry detergent advertising, see Ann McClintock, "Soft-Soaping Empire: Commodity Racism and Imperial Advertising," in *Travellers' Tales*, ed. George Robertson, Melinda Mash, Lisa Tickner, Jon Bird, Barry Curtis, and Tim Putnam (London and New York: Routledge, 1994), 128–52. For the equation of white appliances with whiteness, see Shelley Nickles, "Preserving Women," esp. 699 and 705.

[15] Jason Chambers, *Madison Avenue and The Color Line* (U of Pennsylvania Press, 2008), 5.

[16] Robert E. Weems, *De-Segregating the Dollar* (NYU Press, 1998), 19–20.

(1945), whose company sponsored several industry publications and films espousing the benefits of treating Black Americans as a market in their own right (Weems 53, 74, 128; Chambers, 41–9).

Hall Montana, the Black narrator of James Baldwin's *Just Above My Head* (1979), provides a scathing critique of these developments. A former account manager for a white advertising firm who has just joined the marketing team of a Black magazine, Hall states that he "could never, at bottom, take advertising seriously," for:

> [t]he sense of life which advertising imbued [the public] made reality, or the truth of life, unbearable [and] above all, unreal: they preferred the gaudy image . . . The music of the commercial simply reiterates the incredible glories of this great land, and one learns, through advertising, that it is, therefore, absolutely forbidden to the American people to be gloomy, private, tense, possessed; to stink, even a little, at any time. (*JAMH*, 464–5)

This is not a diatribe against any particular product category, or, indeed, against capitalism per se. Rather, Hall's problem is with an industry complicit in cementing an artificial idea of America and in divesting everyday life of complexity. The ascendance of the language, rhetorical devises, and formal structures of the television commercial has cast sadness and uncertainty as inconveniences to be removed like a bad odor. These ideas are exemplified in Hall's depiction of love, in the very next sentence, as requiring the "Good Housekeeping Seal of Approval" (*JAMH*, 465). This seal was first developed in 1900 by home economists at *Good Housekeeping* magazine's product-testing site, the Good Housekeeping Institute, as a quality assurance guarantee for food and, after 1910, appliances.[17] In 1939 the Federal Trade Commission accused the Institute of receiving payments from the very manufacturers whose products it was testing, and of misleading readers of *Good Housekeeping*, who might assume the Seal of Approval applied to all the products advertised in the magazine (McGovern, 321). Given the nationwide media coverage the case received, it is safe to hypothesize Baldwin was aware of the Seal of Approval's (temporary) fall from grace, and that Hall's quip is an explicit comment on the flattening of experience under consumer capitalism, whereby the "quality" of human relations and a washing machine are judged by the same corrupt "metrics." But even if Baldwin were unaware of the allegations, his statement reads as a warning about the potential for the criteria governing the purchase of a refrigerator or vacuum cleaner to insinuate themselves into the most intimate parts of our existence, altering those very relations—love and sex—that the advertising

[17] Tracy Deutsche, *Building a Housewife's Paradise: Gender, Politics, and American Grocery Stores in the Twentieth Century* (Chapel Hill: U of North Carolina Press, 2010), 263, fn. 9.

industry has so long touted as to render them meaningless. Indeed, one might add to his list of grievances the racialized construction of the "all-electric" kitchen for which the objects tested in the Good Housekeeping Institute's test kitchens were designed.[18]

Hall next challenges the claim that advertisers' targeting of Black consumers constitutes progress: "our breakthroughs seemed to occur only on those levels where we were most easily expendable and most easily manipulated" (*JAMH*, 466). Historical studies of Black Americans' expenditure in the postwar era confirm Hall's suspicion, exposing racism's influence on Black consumer habits in the 1950s, particularly among the middle class: according to one study published in 1961, racism had had the unexpected benefit of spurring Black Americans to "'spend more disposable income on clothing, TV, appliances than whites'" as a form of status seeking.[19] But Hall's statement is also interesting insofar as it exaggerates the extent to which the advertising landscape, in the period when this passage takes place, had in fact changed. A comparative analysis of appliance advertisements in popular magazines of the postwar era reveals such ads only began appearing in *EBONY* in 1960, nearly a decade after agencies began discussing the so-called Negro market. They also featured in *EBONY* far less frequently than in *LIFE*, *LOOK*, or *House Beautiful* and *Good Housekeeping* (the latter two of which were aimed at white middle-class women). Kelvinator, Montgomery Ward, Thermador, Electrolux, Thor, Crosley, Domey, Aerodyne, Apex, Bendix, Universal Coffeematic, and International Harvester, whose ads proliferated in *LIFE*, *LOOK*, and *The Saturday Evening Post* throughout the 1940s, 1950s, and 1960s, never advertised their appliances in *EBONY* at all. Indeed, the ads International Harvester placed in *EBONY* in 1968 to promote its efforts to diversify its workforce were in keeping with brands' longstanding tendency to view Black Americans as labourers in the production of goods for white consumers, rather than consumers in their own right.[20] Admiral placed four ads for its televisions and stereos between 1966 and 1968, but none for its refrigerators. Of the six ads Westinghouse placed between 1966 and 1988, only two were

[18] For more on the racial dimension of the Cold War-era kitchen, see Kate Baldwin, *The Racial Imaginary of the Cold War Kitchen* (Lebanon, NH: Dartmouth College Press, 2016).

[19] qtd. in Susannah Walker, "Black Dollar Power: Assessing African American Consumerism since 1945," in *African American Urban History since World War II*, ed. Kenneth L. Kusmer and Joe W. Trotter (Chicago: U of Chicago Press, 2009), 376–403. Citation on 384. See also Andrew Wiese, "'The House I Live In': Race, Class, and African-American Suburban Dreams in the Postwar United States," in ibid., 160–80; Carl H. Nightingale, *On the Edge: A History of Poor Black Children and Their American Dreams* (New York: Basic Books, 1993); and Mary Pattillo-McCoy, *Black Picket Fences: Privilege and Peril Among the Black Middle Class* (Chicago: University of Chicago Press, 1999) esp. 147–8.

[20] International Harvester, "Why Not Connect Where the Opportunities Are Just About Infinite?" *EBONY* (March 1968): 20.

for their appliances. And Philco only placed one appliance ad, for the Philco "Instant Cold" Refrigerator, focusing instead, like International Harvester, on promoting its efforts to diversify its workforce.[21] Hotpoint and Proctor-Silex each placed a total of two ads, the former in 1960 and the latter in 1972 and 1973, while Norge placed three ads between 1959 and 1965.[22] Of the thirteen appliance manufacturers that *did* place ads in *EBONY*, only seven (Maytag, Frigidaire, Toastmaster, Speed Queen, GE, Sears Coldspot, and Sunbeam) used Black models, and most did so only sporadically. Several of these ads contained a racial, and racist, subtext, challenging the findings of scholars such as Jessamyn Neuhaus, who argues that "racial stereotypes essentially disappeared from housework advertising by the last decades of the twentieth century."[23] And as scholars have shown, until the late 1960s, Black women models who did feature in ads (for any industry) had light complexions, straight hair, and Eurocentric features.[24] The "breakthrough" that Baldwin critiques, in other words, had not really happened.

Such obscuration may not have mattered to Baldwin, whose point, in both *Just Above My Head* and his essays, was that access to messages manipulating Black people to spend their money merely represented a further form of subjugation. But together with the delay in granting Black Americans access to the objects themselves, the delay in representing Black people in appliance ads goes some way to explaining one of the main differences between certain appliance depictions by Black writers in the postwar period (albeit not Baldwin's) and the majority of appliance depictions by postwar white writers. Where the latter focus almost entirely on the mechanizing and dehumanizing effects of time-saving domestic technology, a significant strand of writing by Black women frames these objects as either entirely liberating, or as liberating in ways that obscure more insidious forms of

[21] Westinghouse Atomic Power Divisions, "Westinghouse is NOW," *EBONY* (August 1968): 162 and "Westinghouse Is GO," *EBONY* (October 1968): 38; Westinghouse, "If Our Hand Wash Agitator Can Wash This Pucci Scarf, It Can Wash Your Linens," *EBONY* (April 1973): 27; Westinghouse, "Spending Big Money on Clothes, That's Not Pearl's Idea of a Thrill," *EBONY* (April 1977): 21; Westinghouse Electric Corporation Careers, "I Want to Shape the Future," *EBONY* (June 1988): 151; Philco, "1,386 Salads from Now You'll Still Be Glad You Bought a Philco 'Instant Cold' Refrigerator," *EBONY* (May 1964): 153; "LET ME TELL YOU About Our Career Opportunities," *EBONY* (March 1968): 128.

[22] Hotpoint, "The Biggest Refrigerator News in Years!" *EBONY* (June 1960): 127 and *EBONY* (July 1960): 25 (Despite the seemingly progressive tone of the copy, the model in the ad was a white woman); "Frozen Passion: Let Proctor-Silex freeze . . ." *EBONY* (May 1972): 34; Norge, "Only Norge Dispensomat Washer pre-loads as many as 4 Different Laundry Wonder Products," *EBONY* (November 1959): 25; "Norge Extras Give You the 15 lb. Washer That Keeps This Promise," *EBONY* (April 1965): 22; "Norge Designs Refrigerators for the Woman Who Wants Everything," *EBONY* (July 1965): 18.

[23] Jessamyn Neuhaus, *Housewives and Housework in American Advertising* (New York: Palgrave Macmillan, 2011), 51–2.

[24] Sharon McGee, "Advertising and Marketing," in *Encyclopedia of African American Business: A-J*, ed. Jessie Carney Smith (Santa Barbara, CA: Greenwood Press, 2006), 11–15; citation on 12.

racial discrimination and inequality. Most notable among these are Toni Morrison's appliance depictions in *Tar Baby* (1981)—about which more later—and her late novels, *Paradise* (1997) and *Love* (2003).

Tracing the founding and eventual self-destruction of an all-Black utopia between 1949 and 1976, *Paradise* both confirms and complicates historical accounts of appliance ownership, Black domestic labor, and social mobility.[25] The novel takes place in and around the all-Black town of Ruby, established in 1949 by the founding fathers of another all-Black community, Haven. When the founders establish Ruby to renew their commitment to stamping out racism, they take with them the iron oven they first built for the women of Haven, and display it to commemorate the town's origins. Divisions soon emerge, however, between Ruby's nine racially "pure" dark-skinned families, its lighter-skinned mixed-race families, and those women whose resistance to traditional gender roles the town views as corrupting. The eventual mass murder of these women in their shared kitchen enables Ruby's leaders to ignore the true source of conflict: prejudice against the lighter-skinned inhabitants and the younger generation's involvement in the Civil Rights movement convulsing the rest of the nation. Throughout *Paradise*, Morrison enlists time-saving appliances to first describe, and then dismantle, the characters' visions of the ideal home and community. The iron oven itself casts a long shadow over the narrative, a reminder of the hardship that preceded both domestic mechanization and the development of this community free of white people.

One passage in particular stands out for our purposes. Here, the text recounts the "sudden" appearance in Ruby, in 1963, of gardening as a hobby and status symbol following the advent of free time:

> The women who were in their twenties when Ruby was founded, in 1950, watched for thirteen years an increase in bounty. . . . In every Ruby household appliances pumped, hummed, sucked, purred, whispered and flowed. And there was time: fifteen minutes when no firewood needed tending in a kitchen stove; one whole hour when no sheets or overalls needed slapping or scrubbing on a washboard; . . . two hours because food lasted and therefore could be picked or purchased in greater quantity. Their husbands and sons, tickled to death and no less proud than their women, translated a five-time markup, a price per pound, bale or live weight, into Kelvinators as well as John Deere; into Philco as well as Body by Fisher. (*P*, 89)

Gardening emerges as a product of the time liberated by domestic machines, a pursuit driven by "no good reason except there was time in which to do it"

[25] Toni Morrison, *Paradise* (London: Vintage, 1999 [1997]). Henceforth, *P*.

(*P*, 89–90). Ruby's time-saving appliances are charged symbols of a belated access to a mass market made accessible to the white population thirty years earlier, and of emancipation from domestic drudgery and access to technological modernization come late. These objects alert us to the temporal dimension of *female* Black experience, echoing feminist historian Evelyn Brooks Higginbotham's assertion that "in societies where racial demarcation is endemic to their sociocultural fabric and heritage . . . gender identity is inextricably linked to and even determined by racial identity. We are talking about the racialization of gender and class."[26] This is an aspect that, as we shall see, Baldwin's and Ellison's appliance depictions entirely elide.

Morrison's depiction of time-saving appliances' liberating aspects also contradicts the findings of those historical studies of domestic labor published in the 1970s and 1980s (discussed in Chapter 3), which argued that appliances increased the time housewives spent working by obliging them to take on work they would have outsourced to laundries outside the home, or allocated to hire help—a contradiction attributable to such studies' focus on *white* households.[27] It shares more, instead, with Angela Davis's revisionist account, "The Approaching Obsolescence of Housework: A Working Class Perspective" (1981), in which Davis argued that Second-Wave Feminism's focus on the white middle-class housewife erased the experiences of slave women, newly "free" women who were obliged by economic necessity to seek paid employment after the Civil War's end, and white immigrant women who worked in factories, focusing on the plight of middle-class white women who wished to join the workforce to become self-actualized at the expense of those already obliged to participate in it.[28] The movement's focus on the humiliation of unpaid housework and the call for housewives' "wages," she argued, obscured the humiliation that professional cleaners endured due to the indignity with which broader society viewed their work (136). Nothing short of a "radical transformation" of housework into communal work incorporated into the industrial economy and supplemented by state-funded labor-saving appliances more sophisticated than those currently available would correct this inequality (128). While on the surface Davis's argument is a disavowal of the image of leisure brought about by the time-saving machines that Morrison's text

[26] Evelyn Brooks Higginbotham, "African-American Women's History and the Metalanguage of Race," *Signs* 17.2 (Winter 1992): 253–4. Citation on 254. Echoing Higginbotham, Rose M. Brewer highlights the ease with which "internal issues of gender and class are subsumed to a unitarian position of African-Americans" wherein "class is hidden or misspecified and gender is rendered invisible" ("Theorizing Race, Class, and Gender: The New Scholarship of Black Feminist Intellectuals and Black Women's Labor," *Race, Gender & Class* 6.2 (1999): 29–47, citation on 34).

[27] See Cowan, *More Work for Mother*; Oakley, *Housewife*; and Strasser, *Never Done*.

[28] Angela Davis, "The Approaching Obsolescence of Housework: A Working-Class Perspective," in *Women, Race and Class* (New York: Vintage, 1983 [1981]), 128–39.

instead appears to endorse, the two depictions share a common trait: the effort to glean, from historical accounts of racial oppression, modes of imagining the shape of a liberation to come. Thus, the passage in Morrison's text describes an alternative 1950s in which white people are absent, and Kelvinator and Philco appliances represent both belated access to the "good life" and an intimation of the "good life's" *limits*. Indeed, the text implies that the paradisiacal elements of the "all-electric" homes to which these women now have access will not be sufficient to prevent the inevitable catastrophe foreshadowed in the opening pages and gestured at throughout the novel. A different solution is needed. This utopian image of appliances liberating time that later culminates in a series of statements that suggest the characters' eventual undoing allows the text to gesture to the racism that the postwar boom experienced by Ruby's inhabitants has repressed but has not eradicated, and which will ultimately catalyze the community's destruction. Meanwhile the emphasis on the circumscribed uses of these women's time—housework, gardening—foreshadows the novel's later preoccupation with what happens when women choose to allocate their time to *other* pursuits.

A similarly nuanced depiction of time-saving appliances emerges in *Love* (2003), where Morrison describes the main character, Vida's, recognition, while ironing her work uniform, that "her paycheck had helped fill her house with the sounds of gently helpful bells: time up in the microwave oven, the washing cycle, the spin dryer. . . . Lights glowed when coffee brewed, toast toasted, and the iron was hot."[29] In contrast to the by turns reproachful, ominously portentous, and overtly hostile domestic technologies described in the texts by Cheever, Yates, and Marge Piercy we have thus far discussed, the technologies Morrison describes here are *kindly*. They complement human endeavor rather than replacing it. The result of hard graft, their purchase provides vital help to their overworked owner. Read against Morrison's remarks about her own ambivalent relationship to these objects so inaccessible to Black Americans in the 1930s and 1940s, the passage just quoted thus reads as an expression of appreciation for goods whose availability is not to be taken for granted. What's more, Vida's other main feeling in this passage—"frustrat[ion]" at the "male idiot . . . who believed a three-ounce iron was better than a heavy one. Lighter, yes, but it didn't iron anything that needed it, just things you could unwrinkle with your own warm hands" (*L*, 35)—highlights a point often obscured in literary critiques of time-saving appliances and particularly those by male writers. Very simply, there is the thing for which the object stands, and then there is the actual *function* of the object. Vida's abiding concern in this passage is not what the electric iron might symbolize in the fraught history of US race relations, but whether it will allow her to press her uniform efficiently

[29] Toni Morrison, *Love* (London: Vintage, 2004 [2003]), 35. Henceforth, *L*.

before she has to go to work, and why it is that the engineering of products like this is entrusted to men who know nothing about the tasks they are intended to facilitate. This is not to say, however, that Morrison negates time-saving appliances' more violent potential—as we shall see in the next section, which examines the politico-aesthetic function of an array of horrific and monstrous appliance depictions in a selection of texts by Morrison and her Black American antecedents.

2. Monstrous Machines: Appliance Interventions in Toni Morrison, Ralph Ellison, James Baldwin, and Alice Walker

In *Paradise*, discussed earlier, the tension between the utopian possibilities of building an all-Black community and the inescapability of internalized racism (even in the absence of any white people) is embodied in the novel's depiction of the attempted murder, by one of the characters, of her mixed-race daughter with a 1950s GE electric iron:

> She tried to remember . . . what had been said that had her running up the stairs with a 1950s GE electric iron called Royal Ease clutched in her fingers to slam against her daughter's head. She, the gentlest of souls, missed killing her own daughter by inches. . . . Trying to understand how she could have picked up that pressing iron, Pat realized that ever since Billie Delia was an infant, she thought of her as a liability somehow. (*P*, 203)

The GE electric iron here is not associated with time-saving, efficiency, or postwar plenty, but rather with a horrific act that goes against the laws of nature (that mothers love and protect their children) while revealing an entrenched racism (as Pat's fear of Billie Delia stems from the latter's mixed-race heritage, which threatens the purity of the dark Black race of the town's original founders). The iron thus embodies racial loathing and its violent repercussions, but its identification as a *GE* iron rather than a generic iron calls attention to the racial dimension of the consumer culture from which the object stemmed. The horror of the attempted murder is heightened by its involvement of a branded appliance redolent, particularly for Black Americans of the immediate postwar period, with a hard-won slick modernity, and in its resemblance to a kind of obverse-ad in which the branded object is aligned with the opposite of the brand's values. Finally, the violent usage of this domestic object—an object associated with housekeeping and *home*—underscores the novel's preoccupation with internalized racism, which is to say, the ways in which racism embeds itself in the interior of individual and collective psyche, shaping (and harming) social relations within the family unit itself. The near-murder of a child by her mother with a time-saving domestic appliance otherwise emblematic of convenience, feminine liberation within the home, and domesticity, foreshadows the eventual destruction of this community by the descendants and relatives of its original founders, which takes place in the home of a group of women the community has ostracized for being "unfeminine." The 1950s GE electric iron is almost Gothic in its intimation of a pullulating violence that, when it comes, will come from within.

This account echoes Morrison's foregrounding of time-saving appliances in *Tar Baby* (1981), where they highlight the self-delusion of the white millionaire protagonists, Valerian and Margaret Street.[30] Most notably, Valerian deludes himself that the Black washer woman he employs does the washing by hand in the washhouse, bent over "a scrub board rubbing pillow slips with a bar of orange Octagon soap," even though he "kn[ows] perfectly well that a washer and dryer [a]re installed there" (*TB*, 140). This willful self-deception forms part of his efforts to recreate the memory of the day of his father's death, when the Black washer woman employed by his parents, who was the first person with whom he shared the news, enlisted his help with the laundry to take his mind off his grief (*TB*, 140). While Valerian's mother fired the washer woman for making the boy do menial work, Valerian cherishes the memory of her care. To go back in time to this pastoral moment, however, requires pretending his current washer woman has no recourse to time-saving gadgets. In this context, both electrical modernization and the material conditions of the Black servant class are an *inconvenience*. The white colonialist must ignore both in order to keep intact his antebellum fantasy—an act of obscuration that renders the washer woman little more than an appendage not only of the machine (to paraphrase Marx) but of her white employer's imagination.

But the violent dimension of time-saving appliances also arises in texts published decades before *Paradise* and *Tar Baby*. The narrator of Ralph Ellison's *Invisible Man* (1952) leaves the funeral of a Black radical and wanders, in the city heat, through a crowd that he describes as "boiling figures seen through steaming glass from inside a washing machine" while white armed police officers look on.[31] The image of people being boiled clean recalls the violence of a white hegemonic culture intent on ridding itself of the impurity of dissenting elements (*IM*, 460). It also calls to mind the Black radical just killed, while reminding the reader of the shared vocabulary of domestic technology, bacteriology, and scientific racism, all three of which relied upon the careful cultivation of fear of the sullying

---

[30] Toni Morrison, *Tar Baby* (London: Vintage, 2004 [1981]). Henceforth, *TB*.
[31] Ralph Ellison, *Invisible Man* (New York: Penguin, 2001 [1952]), 460. Henceforth, *IM*.

effects of dirt and those *deemed* dirty, filthy, or lesser.[32] The narrator's vision of a washing machine window through which the police can watch the populace being cleansed of resistance provides a harrowing insight into what a fully mechanized white supremacist police state might look like. By contrast, as David Alworth has shown, the survival of Ellison's narrator ultimately hinges on his capacity to steal electricity from the city to power his underground home—a tactic that allows him to take back "power" while remaining connected, however obliquely, to others.[33]

Ellison's novel was the inspiration for the Black American painter Kerry James Marshall's *Portrait of the Artist as his Former Self* (1980), a black-and-white portrait that played on the aesthetic of minstrelsy, and *Portrait of the Artist & a Vacuum* (1981), in which a large bright yellow vacuum cleaner dominates the foreground of a bare room on whose wall Marshall's 1980 painting hangs (Figure 4.1). In a 2017 interview, Marshall clarified that the first painting was inspired by Ellison's exploration of "the condition of simultaneously being present and absent in the world, but not as a phenomenal condition."[34] In the second painting, the relationship of large bright appliance to the shrunken caricature of a Black man draws attention, at once, to the invisibility of Black domestic workers and obscuration of domestic labor, the historical elision of Black artists from public life, and the confinement of people of color to categories and stereotypes defined by a white hegemonic culture. The difference between the size and visibility of the vacuum cleaner compared to the portrait gestures to twentieth-century avant-garde and neo-avant-garde art's preoccupation with challenging the separation of art and everyday life and division of "high" and "low" culture, but it reveals that subversive tradition to be premised on white privilege by calling attention to the invisibility of Black art in a culture that only "sees" Black Americans as unskilled labor. Finally, the painting calls attention to the place of the artist and the Black American by not disclosing *who* the room and vacuum cleaner portrayed belong to, and by capitalizing on the double meaning of "vacuum"—appliance, and empty space waiting to be filled. While Marshall states that the vacuum-cleaner portrait was inspired by the novel as a whole rather than specifying the washing machine scene, the enlisting of a domestic

---

[32] John Ettling cites Southern newspapers' coverage of hookworm, which claimed that "damage that has been done to the white people of the South by the diseases brought by this alien race" (qtd. in *The Germ of Laziness* (Cambridge: Harvard UP, 1981), 173). Andrea Patterson notes microbiology's use in the American South to promote scientific racism and Black people as disease carriers ("Germs and Jim Crow: The Impact of Microbiology on Public Health Policies in Progressive Era American South," *Journal of History of Biology* 3.42 [Fall 2009]: 529–59. Citations on 537; 538).

[33] Alworth, *Site Reading*, 148.

[34] Chris Dercon, "Kerry James Marshall and the Invisible Man," *032c* (May 9, 2017).

FIGURE 4.1 Kerry James Marshall. *Portrait of the Artist & a Vacuum*. 1981. Acrylic on paper. 62.5 × 52 3/8 × 2 inches. Collection of the Nasher Museum of Art at Duke University, Durham, North Carolina. © Kerry James Marshall. Image courtesy of the Nasher Museum of Art at Duke University.

appliance in this exploration of elision, obscuration, and erasure is telling, and arguably stems from a shared understanding of the deeply racialized symbolic charge of time-saving appliances in US culture and in the history of US race relations.

The vacuum cleaner has a far more horrific meaning in James Baldwin's *Tell Me How Long the Train's Been Gone* (1968), where Baldwin describes his characters approaching the subway and "reach[ing] the brightly lit kiosk, which came up out of the sidewalk like some unbelievably malevolent awning or the suction apparatus of a monstrous vacuum cleaner."[35] The appliance emerging from the ground and sucking the city's inhabitants into its belly is the antithesis of the miracle of modernity celebrated in appliance advertisements, suggesting instead the veritable annihilation of citizens by an urban machine that sucks them in only to spit them out. A similar sentiment can be found in Baldwin's speech, "Notes for a Hypothetical Novel," which he first delivered at a symposium sponsored by *Esquire* in October 1960, and subsequently published in *Nobody Knows My Name: More Notes of a Native Son* (1964). Here, Baldwin identified the refrigerator as emblematic of the mutual imbrication of technological progress, consumer culture, and nationalist myth-making. In a nation in which scientific advances are geared toward economic growth, empire-building, and the elevation of one race over another rather than the material and spiritual advancement of all, the writer's task is to expose these myths for what they are. Asserting that "this country is yet to be discovered in any real sense," Baldwin argued:

> There is . . . a myth about America to which we are clinging which has nothing to do with the lives we lead. . . . Without having anything whatever against Cadillacs, refrigerators or all the paraphernalia of American life, I yet suspect that there is something much more important and much more real which produces the Cadillac, refrigerator, atom bomb, and what produces it, after all, is something which we don't seem to want to look at, and that is the person. (*NKMN*, 128)

The refrigerator and Cadillac's juxtaposition with the atom bomb reminds the reader of the "good life's" reliance on the interrelation of the ideals of leisure, and leisured domesticity, with a powerful war complex. The veneration of "Cadillacs, refrigerators or all the paraphernalia of American life" (including the atom bomb) obscures the human beings that made them, and the ethical dimension of their participation in such production. If, as Baldwin goes on to say, "[a] country is only as good [and] as strong as the people who make it up and the country turns into what the people want it to become," then what does that suggest about a country made up of appliance and bomb makers? (*NKMN*, 128).

Baldwin also enlists refrigerators at various points in *Just Above My Head* (1979), whose critique of advertising we have already examined.[36] The novel's most notable refrigerator depiction appears in a flashback to 1949: "Brother Miller opened the refrigerator—refrigerators were still fairly rare in Harlem then—and took out a bottle and began opening it" (*JAMH*,

---

[35] James Baldwin, *Tell Me How Long the Train's Been Gone* (New York: Penguin, 2018 [1968]), PAG.E. Henceforth, *TMHLTTBG*.

[36] James Baldwin, *Just Above My Head* (New York: Penguin, 1994 [1979]). Henceforth, *JAMH*.

118). The depiction and interruption are noteworthy, for they occur in the midst of a fraught series of disclosures. Brother Miller's wife (and Hall's friend Julia's mother), Amy, has been bedridden since having a miscarriage. The passage intimates more tragedies are in store. These are revealed to be Amy's death, Brother Miller's subsequent raping of his daughter, his coercing of her to work as a child preacher, and her pregnancy with his baby. The passage's juxtaposition of a remark about the rarity of refrigerator ownership in Harlem in 1949 with the unveiling of a woman's miscarriage and the foreshadowing of the incest whose effects reverberate across the novel does more than shock. It links a series of—dramatically different—manifestations of racial inequality: access to goods and technology, and father-daughter incest, which, as Lynn Orilla Scott argues, in this novel allows for an "investigat[ion of] the problems of African American identity formation within a racist society" and the ways in which economic, emotional, and sexual exploitation are turned inward.[37] The lack of access to electric refrigeration that pales in comparison to the horrific manifestations of racial inequality in the subsequent passages amplifies their horror.

The refrigerator that punctuates the period just preceding Hall's brother Arthur's death serves a similar function. After asserting that "I find myself before many things I do not want to face," and acknowledging that "what is coming is always, already on the road and cannot be avoided," Hall succeeds in nevertheless delaying narrating the death by describing his, Julia, and Julia's brother's daily life at the time:

> Julia and I were not yet living together—that was to come, so much was to come—but we spent a lot of time together. [Julia's brother] Jimmy had keys to both our doors, and pranced in and out—mainly, as it seemed to me then, in and out of our Frigidaires. All I really remember of Jimmy, then, is sneakers, beer, sandwiches, and ice cream. (378–9)

The description of food items and the sneakers that Jimmy wears as he traipses "in and out of" the couple's Frigidaires both delays and amplifies the tragedy to come. The qualifier "that was to come, so much was to come" reverberates with the novel's myriad earlier references to the deferred dreams—to misquote Langston Hughes's poem—of the protagonists and the broader Black community for which they are synecdochic. In their focus on a mundane domesticity explicitly characterized by objects associated with a postwar bounty that remained inaccessible to Black Americans until

---

[37] Lynn Orilla Scott, "Revising the Incest Story: Toni Morrison's *The Bluest Eye* and James Baldwin's *Just above My Head*," in *James Baldwin and Toni Morrison*, ed. Lovalerie King and L. Orilla Scott (New York: Palgrave Macmillan, 2006), 94.

the 1950s, and which Arthur's death forecloses, the two scenes debunk the narrative of continuous progress expounded by John H. Johnson's generation of businessmen.

Similar skepticism is apparent in the emasculation felt by the titular protagonist of Alice Walker's *The Third Life of Grange Copeland* (1970), when confronted by the indoor plumbing and electrification for which his wife Mem's new job has paid, and which allow him to live "like a white man."[38] Grange resists the "feeling of doing better-ness" elicited by "the refrigerator, another example of Mem's earning power, [which] although not new by some years, had nothing to do with melted ice or spoiled food" (*TTLOGC*, 103). Instead, he "secretly savor[s] thoughts of how his wife w[ill] come down when he place[s] her once more in a shack" (*TTLOGC*, 103). Walker highlights what postwar advertisements obscured, and their white creators most likely didn't know: the refrigerator's potential to symbolize emasculation in Black households in which the wife earned more than her husband.[39] The double negative "not new" and "nothing to do with melted ice" begrudgingly acknowledges the object's functional benefits, while simultaneously refuting its usual associations with plenitude. Such refutation is similarly apparent in the novel's later solicitation of the image of a refrigerator to depict Grange's granddaughter Ruth's confused reaction to the first white people she sees. After noticing "they were not exactly white, not like a refrigerator, but rather a combination of gray and yellow and pink," she asks Grange whether "'anybody ever tr[ied] to find out if they's real *people*'" (*TTLOGC*, 181, emphasis in the original). In contrast to Grange, who has known racism since he was conscious but has had to habituate himself to the electric lights and refrigeration of white people, for Ruth the *refrigerator* is an everyday object to be taken for granted, while *white people* are a novelty. Walker thus creates a space to imagine—if only momentarily—a future in which domestic technology is both ubiquitous and divorced of its connotations of whiteness, while whiteness is unknown.

The next two sections extend this discussion of the horrific connotations of time-saving appliances by examining the representation of these objects as they relate to consumer culture, mechanization (both in the home and the workplace), and labor exploitation in two novels by Black writers published in the late 1950s.

---

[38] Alice Walker, *The Third Life of Grange Copeland* (New York: Phoenix/Orion, 2004 [1970]), 102. Henceforth, *TTLOGC*.

[39] Laura Katz Olson notes that due to the suppression of Black men's wages (around half of white men's) in the 1960s, they "rarely earned a family wage"; by 1970, "nearly 25% of African-American women headed up their own households" ("Whatever Happened to June Cleaver? The Fifties Mom Turns Eighty," *Race, Gender and Class* 10.1 (2003): 129–43, citation on 136).

3. "[L]ike Lookin' in Your Icebox and Seein' Nothin' But Your Own Reflection!":[40] Alice Childress's *Like One of the Family: Conversations from a Domestic's Life* (1956)

Like One of the Family consists of a series of sixty-two individually titled vignettes comprising of a one-sided conversation between a domestic worker called Marge and her neighbor, Mildred, whose responses are only gestured at via ellipses that sometimes interrupt Mildred's speech, and to which her next words respond. These monologues were originally published in serial form in Paul Robeson's socialist newspaper, *Freedom*, and as Mary Helen Washington argues, should thus be read "as texts produced in the midst of Cold War tensions, in a left-wing newspaper, dramatically transformed by their dialogic relationship to the other stories and writers in the paper" (142). Racial inequality and the exploitation of domestic workers form the subtext of most of Childress's vignettes, while the Civil Rights movement becomes a focal point in the second half of the novel, thus rendering palpable that these conversations are taking place against a rapidly shifting cultural landscape. While the first vignettes establish Mildred's assertiveness in the face of her employers' patronizing attitudes, the novel soon blasts apart the myths of advertising and consumer culture more broadly, before engaging, in the last vignettes, with the North-South divide, the absence of Black Americans in official histories of the United States, and the turning point that the Civil Rights movement poses.

Since most of these vignettes take place in Mildred's kitchen, and since the anecdotes she tells are generally about encounters she has while she is doing paid domestic work, time-saving appliances are ever-present, giving texture to her narrative. But more than realist devices, the appliances in this text propel the plot forward, and remind the reader of the work that ordinarily circumscribes Mildred's movements and confines her to other (white) women's homes—as exemplified perhaps by her quip that regaling the little boy of one of her employers with fables regarding the origins of music "was a good way to get out of an afternoon's ironin'" (*LOOTF*, 8). More specifically, Mildred enlists time-saving appliances to blur the distinction between "skilled" and "unskilled" labor, to puncture the logic on which the oppression of Black Americans is premised, to express skepticism about the consumerist paradigm to which the culture she inhabits expects her to be in thrall, and, finally, to challenge human reification by foregrounding social relations at the expense of commodities.

[40] Alice Childress, *Like One of the Family: Conversations From a Domestic's Life* (Boston: Beacon Press, 2017 [1956]), 89. Henceforth, *LOOTF*.

The first and last of these functions is most evident in "Hands," where Mildred reminds Marge that "everyone who works is a servant" and that:

> you can take any article and trace it back like that and you'll see the power and beauty of laboring hands. This tablecloth began in some cotton fields tended in the burning sun. . . . Find the story, Marge, behind . . . your stove, the electric light, books, cigarettes, boxes, the floor we're standin' on, this brick building, the concrete sidewalks, the aeroplanes overhead, automobiles, the miles of pipe running under the ground. . . . Why, you could just go on through all the rest of time singin' the praises of hands. (*LOOTF*, 60)

Mildred is not looking to idealize manual labor and the fraught history of particular forms of labor (such as cotton picking, which prior to 1865 was done by slaves). Rather, she is framing all of these forms of work as servitude in order to further her argument: that domestic workers should have unions like factory workers. Her rhetoric echoes the words of radical left activist Claudia Jones's famous essay, "An End to the Neglect of the Problems of the Negro Woman!" (1949), with which, as Washington notes, Childress was almost certainly familiar, and which likely influenced her construction of Mildred.[41] In this essay, Jones cited the Commissioner of the State Labour Department's recent "admi[ssion] that Negro women are not voluntarily giving up jobs, but rather are being systematically pushed out of industry" and into domestic work—a trend accompanied by "an ideological campaign to make domestic work palatable" (54). Jones singled out the "[d]aily newspaper advertisements" which "base their arguments on the claim that most domestic workers who apply for jobs through USES [The United States Employment Service] 'prefer this type of work to work in industry,' are propagandising the 'virtues' of domestic work, especially of 'sleep-in positions'" (54). Crucially, however, Childress never has Mildred mention Jones outright. And by portraying Mildred as unaware that there already exists a union for her and her peers (the Domestic Workers Union that Jones discusses in her essay), Childress positions Mildred not as a militant activist, but, rather, as a laborer working out ideas about inequality and exploitation at a remove, and based on her own experience—a tactic that allows for a subtle seeding of critique rather than outright dogma.

This is particularly apparent in the passage just cited, where Mildred *seemingly* unwittingly integrates time-saving appliances into a network of

[41] Washington, 143; Claudia Jones, "An End to the Neglect of the Problems of the Negro Woman!" *Political Affairs* 28 (1949): 51–67. See also Teresa Amott and Julie Matthaei, *Race, Gender, and Work: A Multicultural Economic History of Women in the US* (Boston: South End Press, 1996), esp. 324–31.

subject-object relations and their histories that implicitly references Marxist understandings of commodities as "congelations" of human labor. In enjoining Marge to "find the story" behind the stove, electric light, linoleum floor, and canned goods on the shelf, Mildred challenges both industrial capitalism's obscuration of human labor and the categorization of domestic work as less valuable than manual labor. In so doing, she complicates her earlier point, in the novel's titular vignette, regarding the hypocrisy of her employers' description of her as "like one of the family" (*LOOTF*, 2–3). Where in this scene she argued, "'I know that if I dropped dead or had a stroke, you would get somebody to replace me,'" echoing Jones's contention that "the very economic relationship of Negro women to white women, which perpetuates 'madam-maid' relationships, feeds chauvinist attitudes," Mildred's monologue in "Hands" demonstrates the *indispensability* of so-called "unskilled" labor—especially when it is invisible (*LOOTF*, 2–3; Jones, 66–67).

This latter claim reflects Mildred's broader preoccupation, throughout the novel, with revealing the hidden connections between people that capitalism divides along class and race lines. Most notably, in "If Heaven Is What We Want," Mildred imagines herself demanding to be put in "'the section of Heaven that's all mixed with different kinds of folks'" but free of "'Jim Crow houses and schools and all manner of ugly things like that,'" so as to "'meet ship-buildin' people, dancin' people, lawyers and doctors and vacuum cleaner salesmen, and subway motormen and poets'" (*LOOTF*, 188). Heaven is not, in Mildred's view, a place of ease or exclusivity, but rather a place where workers around the world unite to produce objects and ideas whose value is not monetary but tied to their connective capacity. In both Mildred's description of the "story behind your stove" and her vision of a paradise comprising vacuum cleaner salesmen and poets, the manufacture and circulation of goods are stripped of their associations with exploitation and transformed into facilitators of equitable social relations in a manner reminiscent of the connective poetics of Whitman, Kerouac, and Piercy discussed in earlier chapters. To Willie Loman's indictment in *Death of a Salesman* of the refrigerator's tyrannical participation in saddling the white middle class with debt, Mildred offers a surreal utopian vision in which fair wages, and the eradication of structural inequalities, effectively neutralize the time-saving appliance's potential nefarious meanings. In this vision, a vacuum-cleaner sale merely facilitates human connection, while time itself, in the absence of either installment payments, exploitative labor practices, or the need for housework, is presented as gloriously infinite, and full of possibility.

The second function of time-saving appliances in Childress's text is to highlight the role of the semantics of dirt and cleanliness in upholding racial hierarchies. Thus, in "In the Laundry Room," Mildred recounts meeting a white domestic worker in the laundry room of her employer's building as they both load laundry into the washing machines (*LOOTF*,

105). When Mildred brushes against the dirty clothes the white woman has placed on a bench, "She gives me a kinda sickly grin and snatched her clothes away quick" (*LOOTF*, 105). In response, Mildred draws the woman's attention to their shared struggles as domestic workers whose employers "'cram eight hours of work into five and call it *part time*'" (*LOOTF*, 106, emphasis in the original). She also highlights the affinities between the woman's repulsion at Mildred touching her dirty clothes and their respective employers' treatment of them both as unclean, before concluding: "'when you got to plunge your hands in all them dirty clothes in order to put them in the machine . . . how come you can't see that it's a whole lot safer . . . to put your hand in mine and be friends?'" (*LOOTF*, 106). Functioning as a catalyst for dialog between the white and Black working class, the washing machine also embodies the paradoxes and contradictions of hierarchies premised on socially constructed notions of cleanliness. In setting this encounter against the backdrop of machines that just decades prior were marketed as slave- or servant-replacements, Childress highlights both the urgent need of solidarity between workers broadly and the violent history of domestic work specifically.

The third function of time-saving appliances in Childress's text is to at once embody the pace of political change in the postwar era, where innovations in domestic technology serve as physical manifestations of a larger social shift toward racial equality, and, at the same time, to highlight the enduring chasm between white middle-class people's lives and that of the Black working class. "I Could Run a School Too" opens with Mildred expostulating: "I tell you, this is a wonderful age to live in! No, dear, I'm not talkin' about washin' machines and such although I must say I'm glad somebody sat down and thought that up, too" (*LOOTF*, 107). At first glance, this reference to washing machines appears merely a catalyst for the vignette's focus: Mildred's friend's daughter's enrolling in acting school, Mildred's own expertise in identifying the narrative formulae around which modern films are structured, and, by extension, her own potential to run an acting school herself. But the resurfacing of the washing machine's invention in the later vignette, "Discontent," should give us pause. Here, Mildred enlists the machine to convey the political power of dissatisfaction:

> [P]ublic schools were not started by parents who were content with private ones. Why, whoever invented a washing machine must have figured that an awful lot of women were discontented with washin' boards . . . and when it comes to you remarkin' the fact that everybody ain't dissatisfied, all I can say is there was a whole gang of folks who didn't think Social Security or Unemployment Insurance was necessary, *but try to take it away from them now that they've got it, and you'll hear a different tone*! (*LOOTF*, 172, emphasis in the original)

The invention of the washing machine is not just a "wonderful" development as Mildred's first description suggested, but rather a manifestation of the causal relationship between exploitation and sociopolitical change. In equating the washing machine's invention with the transformation of education—itself a fraught topic, as it relates to Mildred's comments in other vignettes regarding *Brown v. Board of Education*, racist attacks on school children, and the prohibitive cost of university tuition for racial minorities—Mildred imbues it with political meaning. That the example of the washing machine is followed by that of social security and unemployment benefits, whose elimination would be cause for revolution, renders that meaning all the more charged—no less given the novel's recurring concern with the conditions of domestic workers. The passage thus frames the washing machine as *not* just a nice convenience to have (or, as in Cheever, Yates, and Kerouac, a symbol of white men's emasculation by a culture hell-bent on taming them). Rather, Mildred posits it as a vital tool whose disappearance might on the one hand rupture or upend what the novel as a whole has shown to be a delicate balance between white employers and Black domestic workers, and on the other hand contribute to the latter's oppression (its facilitation of domestic labor essentially justifying wage suppression).

This ambivalent charge is perhaps the most significant aspect of Childress's appliance depictions and is evident at numerous points elsewhere in the novel where time-saving appliances alternate between underscoring and subverting the distance between Mildred and her employers. Thus, on one occasion Mildred comments that all her anxiety-ridden employer "need[s] to cure her is one good-sized real trouble. You know, like lookin' in your icebox and seein' nothin' but your own reflection!" (*LOOTF*, 89). The empty icebox, which is anathema to the rhetoric of efficiency and plenty inherent to mid-century refrigerator advertisements—which centered on the container's capacity to store several weeks' worth of groceries, thereby cutting down on trips to the store—stands here for the distance between the problems faced by white middle-class people and those faced by the Black working class (Isendstadt, 311–21). By contrast, that distance is subverted in "I Liked Working at That Place," where Mildred describes an exchange with her employer Mrs. L. a few minutes before she was to leave work for the day. Here, Mrs. L. wonders aloud whether she should wear a dress instead of the suit Mildred has just ironed for her:

> the whole time we was talkin' I had one eye on the ironin' board which was still warm from me pressin' that suit and the one thought uppermost in my mind was how I could keep from ironin' that old long, ruffly organdie dress. . . . Now I must admit, Marge, that it did need the touch of a[n] iron here and there, but time was passin', the temperature was risin' and I was a mite on the tired side. "Well," she

> says, "I think it needs to be ironed." And with that she plugs the iron in the wall again, so I reached over to take the dress from her, but she holds on to it real tight and says, "I will iron it." "That's all right, Miss L.," I said, "it's awful hot today, I'll do it." Marge, she looked at me kind of funny and then said somethin' real nice. "I don't feel the heat any more than you do, and if it's hot for me, it's hot for you too." And then she went on and ironed that dress. (*LOOTF*, 67)

In the passage's first sentences, the electric iron amplifies the perceived tension between Mrs. L. and Mildred, setting up Marge and the reader, like Mildred herself when the event was taking place, to assume Mildred will be forced to extend her workday. Recalling the narrator's supplication of the reader, in Tillie Olsen's "I Stand Here Ironing" (discussed in the Introduction to this study), to stop her daughter being flattened by her future "like this dress on the ironing board, helpless before the iron," the iron at the beginning of Childress's passage gestures toward the inevitability of Mildred's reification (*ISHI*, 21). In both instances, the object appears to have more power than the women who wield it. But Mrs. L.'s unexpected refusal to relinquish the iron and her insistence on doing the ironing herself momentarily disrupts Mildred, Marge, and the reader's expectations of how the "story" of employer and domestic worker goes, and the narrative formula premised on the predictability of these relations. Where both the story's opening sentence, "I must admit I'm not wild about housework, but on the other hand I must also say that I'm good at it," and the electric iron hovering in the background of Mildred's exchange with Mrs. L., appeared to foreshadow humiliation (or at the very least Mildred's exploitation), Mrs. L.'s retention of the electric iron enables the narrative to perform a *détournement* (*LOOTF*, 67). The iron turns out to be a red herring, its perceived menace neutralized in a manner that anticipates Mildred's later vision of vacuum-cleaner salesmen and lawyers cavorting in the Kingdom of Heaven. While it would be a mistake to overemphasize the significance of this subversion of subject-object relations (after all, Mildred's respite from ironing is only a temporary one, and there is a long tradition, too, of idealizing white female employers who treat their Black servants humanely as "white saviors"), the vignette and the appliance's role within it are instructive, demonstrating both Childress's appreciation for nuance and the function of literary appliances themselves in the performance of such nuance.

I want to conclude this section with an analysis of two final vignettes in which Mildred critiques the financial and temporal expense that the purchase of consumer goods, performance of domesticity, and pursuit of self-improvement advocated by mid-century television and print media entail. Mildred's statements in these vignettes challenge the universality of the housewife figure that, as we saw in Chapters 1, 2, and 3, was central to mid-century popular depictions of time-saving appliances in advertising, the television sitcom, and women's magazines. In "All the Things We Are," Mildred tells Marge about a magazine ad that promises to help women "make themselves over." After listing all of the consumer goods she would have to purchase to make over her body, wardrobe, and mind, Mildred realizes:

> You see there! . . . . I'm forgettin' the most important thing of all . . . Yes, time! I should have one hour a day just to loll aroun' in my scented tub while I think pretty thoughts. I need time to shop carefully and make sure that I'm buyin' only the things that suit my very own personality. I need time to plan well-balanced meals, I need time to . . . make myself into the ideal American woman and. . . What? Girl, I had no idea it was getting' so late! And here I have to make early time in the morning and be over on the East Side at eight o'clock sharp! . . . Pour the coffee, Marge! I guess I'll have to put up with bein' myself for a long while to come. But I can't help wonderin' about the women who go through that routine all the time. . . I mean. . . when it's all over, what have you got? . . . You're right. Like the song says: "Another day older and deeper in debt!" (*LOOTF*, 63–5)

Mildred's monologue shifts from an enumeration of all the consumer goods a woman must accrue to make herself over, to all of the *time* that using these objects takes up. In so doing, the monologue also shifts from a meditation on the price of objects (such as the automobile) that were formerly deemed luxuries and that are now deemed necessities, to a meditation on the luxury of leisure time, and an indirect comment on the treatment of the self as an object—indeed, an appliance!—to be optimized not to do more paid work but for its own sake. Mildred's abrupt interruption mid-monologue confronts the reader with the contrast between a rhetoric of self-improvement that capitalizes on the white middle-class housewife's access to infinite expanses of time (and a patriarchal culture's desire to keep her at home) and the reality of the working-class woman who spends her days cleaning the former's home, and her evenings looking at things she might buy and use had she the time to do either. While mid-century advertising posited appliances as freeing up the time of a universal white woman who stood for all women in order that they might spend more time either looking after their husbands and children or improving themselves, "All the Things We Are" highlights the extent to which appliances were used by domestic servants whose time was filled up looking after multiple homes (including their own). The title highlights the tensions inherent to a culture that on the one hand sees people as the sum total of their possessions and on the other hand allocates the resources and time to consume those possessions unevenly.

In calling attention to the ludicrousness of such advice, Mildred is echoing her and Marge's conclusions, at the end of an earlier vignette, which begins with Mildred enjoining Marge to watch shows aimed at self-improvement. They alight upon "Economy Corner," a cooking show "all about stretchin' leftovers and fixin' up new dishes to tempt your appetite and makin' the food look more pleasin' and things like that" (*LOOTF*, 103). But if they are initially awestruck by the "pretty kitchen with the oven in the wall and everything" in which the demonstrator prepares meals, this soon turns to disgust: for the recipe for "How to fix leftover stringbeans" requires a litany of prohibitively expensive ingredients (*LOOTF*, 103–4). In highlighting this irony, Mildred also exposes the fallacy of one of the central promises made by appliance manufacturers and advertisers of the "all-electric" kitchen: that they would help women save money (Strasser, 211). The promise made by refrigerator advertisements to white women in the 1930s, and to Black women in the mid-1950s and the 1960s—that electrically powered cold storage enabled the preservation of leftovers for longer, enabling the reworking of leftovers into exciting new configurations—is revealed to be contingent on access to a panoply of extra ingredients. The "pretty kitchen with the oven in the wall and everything" is an exclusive space, and the reuse of leftovers a privileged enterprise available only to those who can afford, in this case, real butter, heavy cream, chicken breasts, and sherry wine.

For Childress, then, the literary appliance is a supple object capable of signifying multiple, often contradictory, ideas. In revealing the different meanings ascribable to the vacuum cleaner, washing machine, electric iron, and refrigerator, Childress also suggests the potential for subject-object relations under consumer capitalism to be rewritten—and for the reification of Black Americans to be undone.

4. "Vacuum Cleaners and Crazy Things like That":[42] Paule Marshall's *Brown Girl, Brownstones* (1959)

Time-saving appliances in Paule Marshall's novel *Brown Girl, Brownstones* (1959) reflect the two central characters' fundamentally incompatible visions of of the world. Protagonist Selina Boyce's father, Deighton, an illegal immigrant from Barbados, is a daydreamer who has trained to no avail as a radio repairman, accountant, and trumpet player. In his eyes, domestic gadgets are either aspirational objects to furnish fantasies

[42] *BGB*, 76.

about a wealthy future that will never arrive, or, conversely, components of his wife's Taylorist kitchen, an implicitly white space whose efficiency is stultifying to the imagination. By contrast, for his wife, Selina's mother Silla, appliances are emblematic of the "machine age" to which one must adapt if one is to live, as well as facilitators of productivity even in the midst of personal grief or despair. These two visions are in turn racialized. Just as Deighton's various failed careers are linked to his alienation under white hegemonic capitalism, Silla's ease in her Taylorist kitchen, on the factory floor, and finally as a property owner and rentier, is linked to an ability to make herself at home in whiteness. The novel's time-saving appliances thus foreground the tension between imagination and pragmatism, and between male and female Black experiences of racism in America.

These issues are foregrounded early in the novel, when Selina's sister Ina seeks to prove that their father loves Selina less than he once loved her:

> "We'd go window-shopping downtown and he'd pick out things he was gonna buy me. . . . He'd pick out crazy things that I wouldn't want. . . lawn mowers and vacuum cleaners and crazy things like that. . . I remember once it was golf clubs. . . I didn't even know what they were for. That was our game. . ." Her voice trailed into a wistful silence and she stood tangled in the memory. (*BGB*, 75–6)

Ina's description of "lawnmowers and vacuum cleaners and crazy things like that" frames time-saving appliances as preposterous luxuries, vehicles for daydreams premised on her father's devotion to her, and for nostalgic yearning catalyzed by the *memory* of said daydreams. The appliances viewed from behind glass, and whose utility was frankly unfathomable for Ina as a child, bespeak a prosperous modernity out of reach, while the later recollection by the now-adolescent Ina of the games in which they featured bespeaks the irretrievability of both her childhood and the closeness she had with her daydreaming, impractical, father. The lawn mower and vacuum cleaner are laden with connotations both personal and sociopolitical, as well as being redolent not of time *saving* but of time's passage, and the racial dimension of techno-utopian modernity, wherein futurity is only accessible to those with the financial means.

The protagonists' engagements with property and consumer goods foreground the question of access, although the meanings of appliances specifically shift considerably over the course of this novel in line with both the characters' changing fortunes and the broader socioeconomic changes that took place during the period in which it is set. While published in 1959, Marshall's novel takes place between 1939 and 1947. In the beginning, Selina's family is renting one floor of a Brooklyn brownstone Silla aspires to own, in a part of Brooklyn from which white people have fled (*BGB*,

4). The potential for property ownership to counter racial inequality and aid social mobility is central to each of the novel's four sections. In Book I, Deighton inherits a plot of land in Barbados, and contrary to Silla's wishes, makes plans to move back there and build a magnificent house (*BGB*, 89). Ina is withering about this plan, explicitly equating it with his lawn mower and vacuum-cleaner daydreams (*BGB*, 90). In Book II, Silla attempts to persuade Deighton to sell the land to purchase their brownstone and rent it out. Book III sees Deighton and Silla both take jobs in the arms factories that opened in Williamsburg following the outbreak of the Second World War. Silla sells the land in Barbados without Deighton's knowledge, and he retaliates by spending all of the proceeds on Fifth Avenue in a move that recalls the game of make-believe he used to play with Ina: only instead of lawn mowers and vacuum cleaners, the "crazy things" he buys are expensive clothes and toys. He then irreparably injures his arm on the factory floor, leaves the family, and eventually drowns while being deported back to Barbados by ship after Silla reports him to the immigration authorities. Selina never forgives her mother for this, and Book IV, which takes place from winter 1946 to spring 1947, focuses on the distance between the two women, as Silla finally purchases the brownstone, evicts her neighbors, rents the rooms at a higher rate, and joins an organization that aims to elevate the status of Barbadian property owners by improving immigrants' access to credit. The value of time-saving appliances in turn changes in line with the position of their owners. The vacuum cleaner that in 1939 was a "crazy" thing for a woman of color to own by 1946 wakes Silla up every night, its whine a reminder of both her mother's status climbing and her insomnia (*BGB*, 199).

The time-saving appliances in *Brown Girl, Brownstones* also convey the transformative effects of mechanization, and the obliviousness of those most closely touched by it. Thus, when Silla tells Selina, "'I read someplace that this is the machine age and it's the God truth. You got to learn to run these machine to live,'" and then breaks off to rapturously admire the goods in a shop window, the link between industrial production and bounty is apparent to Selina and the reader, but not to her (*BGB*, 103). Similarly, the text reiterates connections to which Silla herself remains blithely unaware: that the "machine age" and the real estate investment opportunities seized upon by her and her first-generation Barbadian immigrant peers are linked, and that even when she becomes a landlord, white people will still associate her and her daughters with domestic workers and factory hands. What's more, from the perspective of 1959, Marshall and her first readers would also have been aware that many of the armament factories that created jobs during the Second World War were former appliance manufacturing plants. Those that first opened during the war would shift to producing appliances following the conflict's end, capitalizing on the demand that accrued between 1941, when restrictions on steel effectively stopped the production of all new appliances, and 1945, when these restrictions were lifted.[43] When Marshall describes Selina's visit to the factory where her mother works, the space she depicts is at once a site of weapons production, a metaphor for Fordism, and, more broadly, a retrospective account of the origins of the socioeconomic system inhabited by the novel's author and its first readers. Indeed, in light of the absence of any mention of the weapons being produced, the scene reads above all as a comment on the productivist paradigm itself:

> just as the noise of each machine had been welded into a single howl, so did the machines themselves seem forged into one sprawling, colossal machine. This machine-mass, this machine-force, was ugly, yet it had grandeur. It was a new creative force, the heart of another, larger, form of life that had submerged all others, and the roar was its heartbeat—not the ordered systole and diastole of the human heart but a frenetic lifebeat all its own. The workers, white and colored, clustered and scurried around the machine-mass, trying, it seemed, to stave off the destruction it threatened. They had built it but, ironically, it had overreached them, so that now they were only small insignificant shapes against its overwhelming complexity. Their movements mimicked its mechanical gestures . . . as if somewhere in that huge building someone controlled their every motion by pushing a button. And no one talked. . . . they performed a pantomime role in a drama in which only the machines had a voice. . . . Fleetingly she saw herself in relation to the machine-force: a thin dark girl in galoshes without any power with words. (*BGB*, 99)

Recalling the cinematography of Fritz Lang's *Metropolis* (1927) and the imagery of Aldous Huxley's *Brave New World* (1932), the passage conveys industrial capitalism's capacity to at once disempower, alienate, and inspire awe, and its cacophony to metaphorically and literally drown out anything and everything else.[44] But its concern with mechanization's effects on the individual and collective psyche also recalls the critiques leveled at it by Marshall's postwar critic contemporaries. Like these, it counters the rhapsodic celebrations of factory production that populated the postwar press and that framed American manufacturing as a "hard-won" achievement

[43] Maury Klein, *A Call to Arms: Mobilizing America for World War II* (London: Bloomsbury, 2013), 275; 696; May, 160.
[44] Fritz Lang, *Metropolis* (UFA, 1927); Aldous Huxley. *Brave New World* (London: Vintage, 2007 (1932).

FIGURE 4.2 James N. Keen. "Picture of the Week." *LIFE* (August 13, 1945): 27. Courtesy of Wright State University Libraries' Special Collections and Archives.

and time-saving appliances the products of the struggle for democracy itself. In particular, it provides a sharp counter to wartime news coverage of both weapons production and, later, the progress of "reconversion" (the shift from the manufacturing of weapons to consumer goods), which effectively served as free advertising for the companies that had successfully made the switch. Thus for example the caption of the "Picture of the Week" in the August 13, 1945, issue of *LIFE* informed readers that "At the Moraine, Ohio plant at General Motors shiny new Frigidaires and airplane propeller blades move along parallel assembly lines" (Figure 4.2). The new appliances would be available to civilians by early 1946 (27). This "news story" (in which the workers foregrounded were all white) extended the utopian rhetoric of the print advertisements that GM placed in *LIFE* throughout 1945, which promoted the manufacturers as a "peacetime builder" of appliances currently "busy in war work . . . to speed a complete and final victory."[45] Marshall's text challenges this mythos, portraying a factory floor where humans—and Black people in particular—are subjugated by machines in a process that appears to consume them entirely. Selina's visit to the factory enlivens her to the powerlessness of both children and adult workers against the forces of production. The juddering, life-like, "machine-mass" that drowns out human voices, deafens human ears, and negates human agency provides an apt metaphor for the consumer culture that exploded following the war's end, and which Selina and Silla themselves begin to witness in the novel's last section. The scene also draws attention to the relationship between manufacturing—be it of arms or of consumer goods—and the home, as evidenced by the description of Selina's discovery of her mother in the midst of these machines:

> Silla worked at an old-fashioned lathe which resembled an oversize cookstove, and her face held the same transient calm which often touched it when she stood at the stove at home. Like the others, her movements were attuned to the mechanical rhythms of the machine-mass. . . . Watching her, Selina felt the familiar grudging affection seep under her amazement. Only the mother's own formidable force could match that of the machines; only the mother could remain indifferent to the brutal noise. (*BGB*, 100)

On one level, Selina's comparison of Silla's workstation to the kitchen stove at home derives from her disorientation at seeing her mother doing something other than domestic work. But the comparison of the lathe to a cookstove and the "transient calm" of factory work to cooking is also a further reference to the novel's prime concern: the transformation of the boundaries between "home" and "work" during successive phases of capitalism, and the ramifications of this transformation for the individuals, and particularly immigrant racial minorities, involved. The reference to the factory as a kitchen is at once a reminder of Black American women's long-standing relegation to working in the kitchens of white people; the home's status as the original site of production prior to industrialization; the kitchen's own transformation following the introduction of Fordism and Taylorism into the home (which the novel references several times in Book I); and, finally, Silla's abiding desire to turn her *family's* home into a profit-generating enterprise as successful as any white capitalist's by purchasing it and letting out the rooms to high-income tenants. Silla's ability to make herself "at home" in the alienating site of paid factory work explicitly links her job to

[45] "Do You Want These Advantages in Your Next Refrigerator?" *LIFE* (September 17, 1945), 17.

a long history of exploitation of domestic labor, while foreshadowing the ease with which she will in turn transform her home into a place of work, and join the ranks of the capitalist class. In this way, Marshall exposes as naïve the claims made in *EBONY*'s jubilant editorial, "Goodbye, Mammy, Hello Mom" (March 1947), that the war had enabled "Negro mothers" to upgrade from working in "white kitchens" to "factories and shipyards" and finally to "their own" kitchens—as a result of which "the Negro mother has come home, come home perhaps for the first time since 1619 when the first Negro families landed at Jamestown, Virginia."[46] Silla's trajectory challenges this narrative of straightforward progress, suggesting the moral and ethical sacrifices that the Black American woman might have to make to attain access to an "all-electric" home of her own. Attaining the "good life" requires subscribing to capitalist values, and may well involve exploiting others.

The novel's frequent depictions of Silla's kitchen underscore that the machine age and the profit motive to which she is adapting are fundamentally white enterprises. Both in the opening pages of the novel and in the passage immediately following the factory scene, the kitchen is portrayed as clinical and blindingly white—a space of pragmatic, no-nonsense, efficiency whose underlying ethos as well as physical appearance exerts an unbearable pressure on the immigrant Black self to change (*BGB*, 18; 108; 116; 121). In the opening pages, Deighton "pause[s] uneasily at the kitchen door, shaken as always by the stark light there, the antiseptic white furniture and enamelled white walls" and "[t]he room seem[s] a strange unfeeling world which continually challenge[s] him to deal with it, to impose himself somehow on its whiteness" (*BGB*, 18). As Nickles has shown, the "all-electric" kitchen was a racialized space from its inception. Its positioning as nourishing white bodies and maintaining racially-coded hygiene standards contributed to the maintenance of white hegemony (Nickles 2002, 694; 705). The fact that Silla "st[ands] easily amid the whiteness" of her kitchen foreshadows her amenability to adapt to racial capitalism's strictures (*BGB*, 18).[47] Silla likewise receives the news she has successfully sold the Barbadian property against the backdrop of "the steam from the pots, the humming refrigerator and the remote surge of the March wind outside" (*BGB*, 108). Finally, her long wait for Deighton, after he disappears with the check from the property sale, occurs "[i]nside the kitchen [where] the

---

[46] "Goodbye Mammy, Hello Mom," *EBONY* (March 1947): 36–7, qtd. in Elaine Tyler May, 27.

[47] I use "racial capitalism" in the sense intended by Cedric J. Robinson in *Black Marxism: The Making of the Black Radical Tradition* (Chapel Hill, NC: U of North Carolina Press, 2000 [1983]), according to whom "[t]he development, organization, and expansion of capitalist society pursued essentially racial directions" and racialism in turn "permeate[d] the social structures emergent from capitalism" (2).

motor on top of the second-hand refrigerator turned over noisily" (*BGB*, 123). This emphasis on the machinery of the all-white kitchen that imposes its will on its inhabitants, and on the humming *noise* it generates and which the previous pages connected explicitly to a lack of individual agency, is significant. The humming refrigerator reminds the reader of the uneven effects of the machine age's transformation of the domestic sphere. Not only do some have better machines than others (in this case, the description of the second-hand refrigerator with a motor on the top allows us to identify the model to be the GE Monitor Top, launched in 1927, making Silla's at least a decade old). More importantly, some are better able than others to adapt to mechanization's encroachment: Silla's ease in the all-white kitchen even as she waits to hear whether her husband will return is countered by the news of Deighton's later accident in the factory, which the text frames as endemic of his powerlessness in the face of an industrial modernity coded as white. Thus, Selina imagines him helpless "amid that giant complex of pistons and power" and wonders: "Couldn't the machine have seen that he was already crushed inside? Couldn't it have spared him?" (*BGB*, 155).

A white woman's dehumanizing description of her former Barbadian servant in the novel's final chapter in turn underscores Marshall's broader preoccupation with the relationship between mechanization, institutional racism, and white hegemony. Like Mildred's employer in Childress's novel, the woman considered this servant to be "'just like one of the family,'" while her humility, good manners, and exceptional cleaning skills made her irreplaceable:

> "I've never been able to get another girl as efficient or as reliable as Ettie. When she cleaned, the flat was spotless. . . . We were heartbroken when she took ill. . . . She was so honest too. I could leave my purse—anything—lying around and never worry. You don't find help like that every day, you know. Some of them are . . . just impossible! . . . Oh, it's not their fault, of course, poor things! You can't help your color. It's just a lack of the proper training and education." (*BGB*, 288–9)

The woman's description of Ettie reinforces entrenched ideas about Black women's willingness to be reified—a mythos that scholars including Hartman have challenged by demonstrating the pivotal role that *resentment* of domestic servitude played in fueling Black women's resistance (234–6). Meanwhile the statement "I've never been able to get another girl as efficient or as reliable" recalls the copy of appliance ads of the 1930s, which framed appliances as more reliable than regressive Black servants in need of civilizing—as exemplified by Belden's 1936 ad for its electrical cords (Figure 4.3). This ad featured a gross caricature of an angry Black servant (huge lips, handkerchief, hoop earrings, and heavyset figure) tangled up in a vacuum-cleaner cord. The slogan, "Is Your Vacuum Cleaner Crippled with

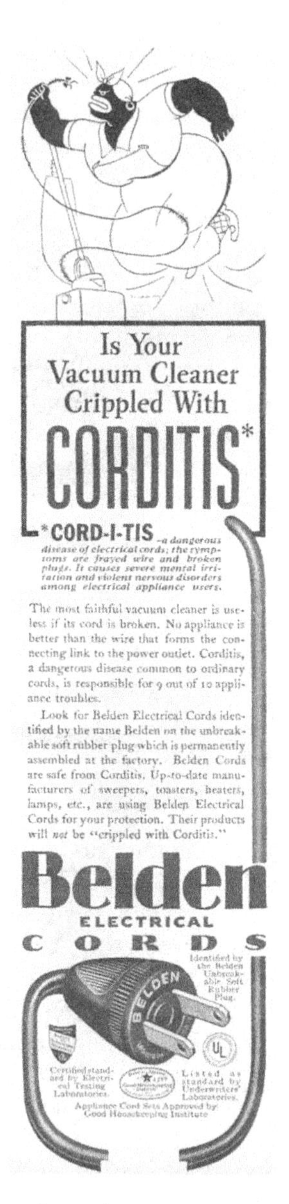

FIGURE 4.3 Belden Electrical Cords. "Is your Vacuum Cleaner Crippled with Corditis?" *Good Housekeeping* (April 1936): 259.

Corditis?" personified the vacuum cleaner while reducing the cantankerous servant to a symptom of the ailing appliance. The description of "corditis" as a "dangerous disease" resulting in "severe mental irritation and violent nervous disorders" among appliance users both contradicted the slogan and capitalized on the entrenched belief, discussed in the Introduction to this study, that Black servants were too feral to be allowed to use appliances unsupervised.

It is telling, then, that Marshall's novel ends in hard-won silence, as Selina walks through a housing project and imagines she hears "the garbled symphony of radios and televisions, children crying in close rooms: life moving in an oppressive round within those uniformly painted walls" before the project "recede[s] and she [i]s again the sole survivor amid the wreckage" (*BGB*, 310). The Black individual is only able to truly emerge from the cacophony of modernity, Marshall suggests, when she both extricates herself from the oppression of whiteness and distances herself from its entrapping technologies. Where, as discussed in Chapter 2 of this study, in "Oh Joseph I'm So Tired" (1981) Yates links the thrum of "all-electric" living to the stuff of life itself, Marshall hints at the suffocating quality of that thrum in a society that values some lives above others.

5. Conclusion

The texts examined in this chapter expose the racial dimension of time-saving appliances and domestic electrification, and the difference between these Black American writers' engagements with the mid-century advertising landscape and that of many of their white contemporaries. These texts enliven the reader to the story behind the time-saving appliance and its ad campaign, including that of the factory hands that produced it, and the slave labor it was initially designed to replace. They also highlight the disconnect between postwar advertisements for time-saving appliances, which situated these objects within a narrative of techno-utopian progress, and the inadequacy of such promises in the face of enduring racial inequality. These appliance depictions highlight domestic electrification's entanglement with the United States' fraught history of racial exploitation and violence, and with the subjugation of Black women in particular by a white patriarchal culture that treats them as inferior to white women. They raise questions about the limitations of equating representation in advertising with political representation, and access to consumer goods with social equality. The grotesque connotations ascribed to many of these gadgets draw attention to the paradox of eulogizing about mechanical domestic servants while dehumanizing human ones.

5

"Ever Think About Being Attacked by a [...] Vacuum Cleaner":[1]

Time-Saving Appliances in Sci-Fi, 1950–78

In June 1952, the magazine of popular technology and science *Popular Mechanics* ran a story titled, "A House to Make Life Easy" (Figure 5.1). Above a photograph of a one-story bunker-style home ran the caption, "House of the future? Home was designed by a writer of stories about a future world." The writer in question was Robert A. Heinlein, the by-then well-known science-fiction writer with a background in aeronautical engineering and real estate. The house was a property that Heinlein and his third wife, Virginia, had custom-designed in 1950 to reduce the time required to clean it, since, in his biographer Farah Mendleshohn's words, Virginia was "not a terribly domestic woman."[2] While the article left Virginia's resistance to housework unstated, it emphasized the property's science-fictional elements. Beginning with the provocative opening line, "In what kind of house will the captain of a space ship live during his stopovers on earth?" it went on to explain that "the engineering training that gives [Heinlein] a solid background for writing about the mechanics of space travel also has helped him in designing a house that's called extreme today but may become conventional before the twentieth century has run its

[1] James Tiptree, Jr., "Mama Come Home," in *10,000 Light Years from Home* (New York: Ace Books, 1978), 69. Henceforth, *MCH*.

[2] Farah Mendlesohn, "Heinlein's Intersitial Self," in *The Pleasant Profession of Robert A. Heinlein* (London: Unbound, 2019), N.P.

A HOUSE TO MAKE LIFE EASY

POPULAR MECHANICS
JUNE 1952
WRITTEN SO YOU CAN UNDERSTAND IT
VOL. 97 NO. 6

House of the future? Home was designed by a writer of stories about a future world

By Thomas E. Stimson, Jr.

IN WHAT KIND of house will the captain of a space ship live during his stopovers on earth?

It's too early to say yet, though probably it will contain some of the features of a residence just built by Robert A. Heinlein in Colorado Springs, Colo.

Heinlein is author of the movie *Destination Moon* and creator of the *Tom Corbett, Space Cadet* program on television. As a writer of science fiction his books *The Green Hills of Earth, The Puppet Masters* and others are on current book lists.

The engineering training that gives him a solid background for writing about the mechanics of space travel also has helped him in designing a house that's called extreme today but may become conventional

Author Heinlein relaxes on built-in divan beside raised fireplace. Note convenient cupboard at end of divan

65

There's everything to please a housewife in the kitchen, including an "office" with phone and typewriter

Below, "commuting" table is set with china in kitchen, then rolled through a wall to the dining area

66 POPULAR MECHANICS

FIGURE 5.1 Thomas E. Stimson. "A House to Make Life Easy." *Popular Mechanics* 97.6 (June 1952): 65–9. Copyright and reproduced with permission of the Heinlein Prize Trust and *Popular Mechanics.*

course" (Stimson, 65). Using rhetoric that Fabrizio Carli has identified as the defining characteristics of appliance advertising between the 1930s and the 1960s, wherein the home was marketed as a network of machines working in concert, the article listed features including air conditioning, a "compact" kitchen with "stove, sink and electric-dishwasher combination, automatic clothes washer, drier and refrigerator," and a "commuting" dining table that rolled through the wall between kitchen and dining room to facilitate setting and clearing the table (Figure 5.2).[3] This same home would inspire Heinlein's 1957 novel, *The Door into Summer*, about a military engineer's quest to create house-cleaning robots.

But time-saving appliances and automated homes appeared, as well, in a multitude of other sci-fi texts published over the next two decades, which similarly engaged with advertisers' promotion of the "all-electric" home's "science fictionality." This chapter examines the relationship between sci-fi and appliances promoted as "science fictional" via close readings of a

[3] Fabrizio Carli, *Elettrodomestici Spaziali: Viaggio Nell'Immaginario Fantascientifico Degli Oggetti Dell'Uso Quotidiano* (Rome: Castelvecchi, 2000), 71; 93. Translation my own. Stimson, 68–9; 228.

selection of scenes from texts by Judith Merril, Ray Bradbury, Margaret St. Clair, Kit Reed, James Tiptree, Jr. (the pseudonym for Alice B. Sheldon), Robert A. Heinlein, Philip K. Dick, Ira Levin, and Joanna Russ published between 1950 and the late 1970s alongside appliance ads of the same period. The significance of time-saving appliances in postwar sci-fi has been entirely overlooked in sci-fi scholarship, with the exception of Lisa Yaszek's seminal study, *Galactic Suburbia* (2008), which recovered the writing of early postwar sci-fi female writers dismissed by Joanna Russ as reproducing "present-day, white, middle-class suburbia," and, more recently, Caroline Edwards's work on sci-fi's engagements with female labor.[4] However, even Yaszek only attends to the most obvious appliance depictions in her chosen subgenre, while Edwards's work, in light of her broader concern with the future of work, focuses on the ramifications of automation, particularly with regard to time use, rather than on the objects themselves. By contrast, I am concerned with the mutual constitution of time-saving appliances in postwar sci-fi and their real-life counterparts. I argue that the rise of science fictionality as a mode of framing appliances in mid-century advertising arose from the very same sensibility that resulted in the exponential rise in sci-fi's popularity. Both mid-century appliance ads that deployed the narrative tropes of sci-fi and the sci-fi genre that responded to that appropriation spoke to an audience reeling from the proliferation of technological advancements of the previous decades, from the "all-electric" home to the nuclear bomb. In pursuing this line of enquiry, I intentionally circumvent questions of periodization and category. Following the time-saving appliance provides an alternative approach to the contested categories of "Weird," "Golden Age," or "New Wave."[5] It likewise allows us to include Ira Levin's *The Stepford Wives* on the basis of the text's concern with the science fictionality of the "all-electric" home and the politico-economic context that produced it, despite the novel's more usual categorization as horror or Gothic. These texts' very different

---

[4] Joanna Russ, "The Image of Women in Science Fiction," (1971), cited in Lisa Yaszek, *Galactic Suburbia: Recovering Women's Science Fiction* (Columbus, OH: Ohio State UP, 2008), 3–4; Caroline Edwards, "A Housewife's Dream? Automation and Domestic Labour in Feminist SF/F," *3rd Annual Meeting of the London Science Fiction Research Community*, Birkbeck, U of London, September 2019. While there isn't as yet published scholarship on time-saving appliances in sci-fi, as this book went into production, I discovered the PhD theses-in-progress of Kathryn Heffner, *Fandom is a Way of Life: Femmefans Write the Speculative Domestic*, and Nora Castle, *Food, Foodways, and Environmental Crisis in Contemporary Speculative Fiction*. See also the roundtable on "Science Fiction Kitchens" in the March 2022 special issue of *Science Fiction Studies* on "Food Futures."

[5] For a discussion of these categorizations, see Gerry Canavan and Eric Carl Link, *The Cambridge History of Science Fiction* (Cambridge UP: 2018), 1–10; 149–65; and 232–46; Mike Ashley, "The Time Machines: The Story of the Science-Fiction Pulp Magazines from the Beginning to 1950," *Utopian Studies* 12.2 (2001): 251–3; Adam Roberts, "The Golden Age SF: 1940–1960" and "The Impact of the New Wave: SF of the 1960s and 1970s," in *The History of Science Fiction* (New York: Palgrave Macmillan, 2016), 287–331; 333–81.

engagements with automation, domestic harmony, and temporality (as it relates to time travel, time's passage, *and* time saving) reflect not only the heterogeneity of the sci-fi genre but, more importantly, the suppleness of the time-saving appliance as a signifying object. In my focus on the relationship between textual responses to mid-century advertising rhetoric and mediated representations of subject-object relations, I likewise depart from recent sci-fi scholarship influenced by object-oriented-ontology (OOO), new materialism, and posthumanism, which tends to approach sci-fi texts in relation to the *effects* of objects in the absence of humans or human agency. As we shall see, apart from the very first story we examine, time-saving appliances in sci-fi are very much entangled in human stories and involved in the critique of social inequities.

1. Time-Saving Appliances at the End of the World: Ray Bradbury's "There Will Come Soft Rains" (1950) and Judith Merril's *Shadow on the Hearth* (1950)

Ray Bradbury's short story, "There Will Come Soft Rains," follows a day in the life of the gadgets in an "all-electric" home in 2026 whose inhabitants have been annihilated by the titular "rain" of nuclear fallout. In this post-apocalyptic future, temporality is recorded by and for objects alone, humans themselves having been designed out of the system, in a literalization of Le Corbusier's famous call for the integration of Taylorism into architecture, "The house is a machine for living in."[6] Thus at 7:09 "the breakfast stove g[ives] a hissing sigh and eject[s] from its warm interior" food for four absent people, which at 8:30 is "digested" by the sink.[7] At 9:15 a.m., a flurry of electric-powered robotic mice "suc[k] gently at hidden dust" before "popp[ing back] into their burrows" (*TWCSR*, 97). In the evening, the radio reads out a poem by the former owners' favorite poet, Sara Teasdale: "*There will come soft rains and the smell of the ground . . . And not one will know of the war, not one / Will care at last when it is done*" (*TWCSR*, 99, italicization in the original). And every hour, a talking clock announces the time. The rituals of meal preparation, disposal, and cleaning would continue forever, save for the chance fall of a tree bough that crashes through the kitchen window onto a bottle of cleaning solvent that spills onto the stove and ignites an unstoppable fire. The last machines to die are the appliances,

[6] Le Corbusier, *Towards a New Architecture* (New York: Dover Publication, 1986 [1923]), 107.
[7] Ray Bradbury, "There Will Come Soft Rains" (1950), in *The Stories of Ray Bradbury* (London and New York: Alfred A. Knopf, 2010), 96–101. Citations on 97 and 97. Henceforth, *TWCSR*.

which, as the flames rise, begin "making breakfasts at a psychopathic rate" before finally ceasing to work (*TWCSR*, 98). The story ends as the one surviving gadget, the clock, calls out the date.

Bradbury's fully automated kitchen resembles nothing more than a heightened version of the industrial research laboratories that GE, Westinghouse, GM, and Ford developed in the first decades of the twentieth century. Initially designed to test new appliances and conduct time-motion studies to determine the most efficient kitchen layouts, these labs became integral to manufacturers' promotion of corporate-sponsored science as a force for social good.[8] The spectacle of the industrial research lab was imbricated with a dynamic theory of history, according to which the corporate scientist's role was to respond to the needs of an ever-expanding marketplace and a "never-finished" society, wherein time itself served the needs of capital (Marchand and Smith, 154). Bradbury's erasure of the human and the civic, leaving only the machines intended to serve them, takes these ideas to their logical conclusion.

But Bradbury's story also parodies early postwar manufacturers' and housing associations' promotions of their products as capable of withstanding a nuclear attack—a strategy that both capitalized on nuclear fears and ensured they didn't prevent consumers from committing to long-term investments. While the speaking clock in the story ironically recalls the Doomsday Clock created in 1947 by the Bulletin of Atomic Scientists to communicate the likelihood of a human-made global catastrophe, Bradbury's sturdy kitchen gadgets anticipated the Gas Appliance Manufacturers Association's promotion, in 1955, of gas-powered appliances' greater capacity to survival nuclear attack than electrical appliances.[9] Meanwhile, the fact that the "blast-proof" objects in Bradbury's story are still vulnerable to a mundane falling tree branch challenges the fallacy of the early postwar era's equating of the home with safety and stability. This parodic dimension is heightened by the nature of the gadgets: the electrically powered mice that scuttle around the house are a horrific counter to the helpful mice in Walt Disney's animated film of Cinderella, which was released in cinemas nationwide in March 1950, two months prior to the story's publication in *Collier's* magazine.[10] Bradbury reimagines the rags-to-riches fairy tale of the pious beauty exploited by money-hungry women but helped by a benevolent

---

[8] Marchand and Smith, 150; George Wise, *Willis R. Whitney, General Electric, and the Origins of US Industrial Research* (New York: Columbia UP, 1985), esp. 177–9 and 214.

[9] Paul Boyer, *By the Bomb's Early Light: American Thought and Culture at the Dawn of the Atomic Age* (New York: Pantheon, 1994 [1985]), 64; R. C. Lisk, "Gas in the Atomic Age," *Gas Age* 115 (1955): 28; "'Operation Cue': Latest Photos of Atom Bomb Test," *Gas Appliance Merchandising* 27.7 (July 1955): 12–13.

[10] Clyde Geronimi, Hamilton Luske, and Wilfred Jackson, *Cinderella* (Walt Disney Productions, 1950).

natural world as a story of nature's belated revenge on the machines that threaten to replace it.[11]

Though also published in 1950 and set in an appliance-laden suburban home against the backdrop of nuclear war, Judith Merril's *Shadow on the Hearth* is diametrically opposed to "There Will Come Soft Rains" in its relentless emphasis on human—or more specifically, American—resolve in the face of the unthinkable, and on scientific gadgets' coterminous capacity to protect their "masters" from harm.[12] In this novel about Westchester housewife Gladys, her daughters Ginny and Barbie, and their Black maid Veda's survival of a nuclear attack that left the man of the house stranded in Manhattan, time-saving appliances join the Geiger counter to assist Gladys's suburban household-qua-frontier homestead stave off death by radioactive fallout. Where Yaszek reads Merril's text as espousing an idea of "radical motherhood" and anti-war activism rooted in critiquing an "inept masculine authority," following the time-saving appliance allows us to unearth the novel's broader affirmation of traditional gender norms and an American way of life that is to be defended at all costs against an abstract enemy with undefined motives (123; 132).

Four appliance depictions in the text stand out for our purposes. The first of these is in the opening chapter, as Gladys completes a seemingly infinite list of household chores that Veda (who has called in sick) would ordinarily do, and panics, while filling the washing machine, at the prospect of not completing them in time for a luncheon she has promised to attend (*SOTH*, 11–1). This account both foreshadows and accentuates the far greater race against time that occupies the narrative once the nuclear attack occurs. It is also revealed, later, that by preventing Gladys from attending the luncheon, the time-consuming nature of the chores saved her from exposure to radioactivity. In failing to save as much time as the ads claim, the washing machine paradoxically saves Gladys's life. The variously grounding, comforting, and protective attributes of Gladys's time-saving appliances are likewise reiterated throughout the rest of the novel. The second instance to note in fact occurs when the family gives shelter to Dr. Levy, a physicist being sought by the authorities due to his strident critiques of the government's failure to prepare for a nuclear attack. To shield him from the door-to-door patrollers, Barbie hides Dr. Levy in the dryer. Just as the washing machine ultimately affirms housework's greater importance than participation in civic life, the comical image of an electric dryer housing a physicist who knows (as the text repeatedly reminds the reader) all there is to know about electric and gas currents but has never done a laundry

[11] Ray Bradbury, *Fahrenheit 451* (New York: HarperCollins, 1993 [1953]), 27–9; 6).

[12] Judith Merril, *Shadow on the Hearth* (London: Sidgwick and Jackson, 1953 [1950]). Henceforth, *SOTH*.

helps circumvent tricky questions about the restriction of freedom of speech and movement during wartime. A similar act of domestication occurs when Ginny mistakes the emergency technicians in diving suits patrolling the area for "washing machine[s that] can walk"—an image that blurs the boundary between the domestic familiar and unknown beyond, with the result of simultaneously rendering strange the home, and domesticating the threat (*SOTH*, 97).

The third notable appliance depiction occurs in the central section of the text, which focuses not on nuclear fallout, the causes of the attack, or the identity of the perpetrators, but, rather, on a mundane gas leak from the house boiler (*SOTH*, 126–49). First detected by Veda (who has now joined the family) while doing more laundries, the leak threatens to blow up the whole house if Gladys turns on either the stove or, as various characters admonish her, any of her electric appliances (*SOTH*, 132; 135). Two chapters are devoted to Gladys's efforts to turn off the gas mains and the family members' evacuation of the gas-filled kitchen and preparation, in the hallway, of a dinner of waffles with an electric waffle iron, coffee with a Silex electric coffee maker, and hot chocolate on an electric hot plate (why they deem it safe to use this panoply of electric devices so soon after having been told not to remains unclear). The imminent threat of the house exploding stands in for the threat of nuclear annihilation, providing a challenge at once more fathomable for the reader, and resolvable by the characters. Where, in Bradbury's story, the gas fire started by the tree branch falling on the stove signals both nature's capacity to circumvent human-made schema and wreak destruction in even the most ordered systems and, too, the capacity of the home (symbolized in the gas stove flame) to harm as much as to shelter, Merril's story domesticates the threat of gas and flame, rendering them subservient to the housewife and her trusty army of time-saving appliances. Meanwhile, the positioning of the Black servant as a woman eager to devote herself to the family that employs her—and whose first response to the atomic alert is not to stay put but run to their assistance—affirms the entrenched stereotype of Black women's "grateful" acceptance of subservience, reducing her to an implement of her white "superiors" akin to the coffee maker or waffle iron.

Finally, it is noteworthy how the time-saving appliances in Merril's novel simultaneously mystify and domesticate the figure of the scientist. As Paul Boyer has shown, atomic physicists became celebrities in the early postwar era as a result of both the Manhattan Project's scientists' own efforts to prevent the dystopian scenarios made possible by their creation and the government and media's efforts to prevent mass panic (59–64). Focusing on the men who created the bomb and the ingenious inventions that might be powered by atomic energy helped neutralize the threat of atomic warfare, as well as to propagate an image of US science and ingenuity as both all-powerful and benevolent (61). Such domestication is evident in Merril's depiction of Dr. Levy as a scientist who understands domestic gadgets as much as he understands the effects of atomic fallout, and in the juxtaposition of his Geiger counter with Gladys' time-saving appliances. The references to domestic gadgets and their capacity to save the day effectively *set the stage* for the Geiger counter that only makes an appearance in the last third of the novel, so that the reader interprets the Geiger as just another friendly appliance—a problem-solver like the hotplate that replaces the gas stove, rather than an instrument with the terrifying capacity to reveal the presence of deadly levels of radioactivity. Framing the Geiger in this way enables Merril to present the atomic threat as something Americans, and specifically American women, could face bravely.

Where Bradbury's "all-electric" home critiques the techno-utopianism of the atomic age, Merril's depiction of women creatively making do with time-saving appliances and keeping the electric fires burning exemplifies the sentimental depictions of hardy, self-reliant white femininity ubiquitous to early postwar public service announcements about the bomb. While purportedly a warning against the potential ramifications of the nuclear arms race, Merril's novel enlists time-saving appliances in a manner that paradoxically reinforces what Kristina Zarlengo has identified as such announcements' incitement to white women to "imagine themselves as warriors in training."[13]

2. "All-Electric" Escapes: Margaret St. Clair, Eleanor Arnason, Kit Reed, and James Tiptree, Jr. (1950–87)

In contrast to those in Merril's novel, the time-saving appliances in the texts examined in this section exist as conduits between the mundane gender constraints that characterize the "real world" of the author (and first generation of readers) and a speculative future in which those constraints have been either amplified or entirely eradicated. In Margaret St. Clair's "New Ritual" (1953), Eleanor Arason's *Daughter of the Bear King* (1987), Kit Reed's "The New You" (1962) and "Cynosure" (1964), and James Tiptree, Jr.'s "Mama, Come Home" (1968), the time-saving appliance does not save minutes and hours of housework. Rather, it offers a literal escape into a different time, or throws into relief the archaic gender norms of the present.

[13] Kristina Zarlengo, "Civilian Threat, the Suburban Citadel, and Atomic Age American Women," *Signs* 24.4, *Institutions, Regulation, and Social Control* (Summer 1999): 925–58.

"New Ritual" (1953) opens with protagonist Marie's purchase of a huge second-hand freezer "better-looking [and] more useful" than her aging and distracted husband, Henry.[14] The appliance is soon revealed to be magic, replacing any item stored in it with a newer, better version. So Marie tries her luck, and pushes Henry in the freezer:

> For a while there were sounds of struggle. Henry thumped, heaved, beat on the sides of the chest. Marie, with tears running down her cheeks, remained seated on the lid. She noticed that from time to time the freezer motor made a sort of spitting noise, as if it might be over-exerting itself. At the end of two hours she raised the freezer lid. (*NR*, 180)

The passage's depiction of the effort involved in keeping the freezer lid closed and the time it takes to subdue Henry humorously counters the rhetoric of ease endemic to appliance advertising. The wish-fulfilling freezer is a time-saving device insofar as stuffing one's husband in it for two hours is less effort than buying him new dentures or filing for divorce, but it is not without its inconveniences. What's more, there is a violent dimension to Marie's shutting of the lid and the subsequent wheezing of the machine as it "over-exerts" itself. If this is not a magic freezer, then all Marie has done is lock her husband in a confined space in sub-zero temperature to die (which, granted, is one way to save time and get the marriage over with). That violence is accentuated by Marie's sister-in-law Bertha's suggestion, when she first purchased the freezer, that it might contain traces of the poisons the owner, an inventor, likely stored in it, and her comment that the owner "'bl[ew] his whole house up and kill himself. That freezer was about the only thing that was left'" (*NR*, 175). As well as explaining the source of the appliance's magical properties, this backstory, like the exploding houses and gadgets in Cheever discussed in Chapter 2, bespeaks the anxieties of the atomic age. But attending to the function of time-saving appliances, and refrigeration, in other popular culture forms and genres of this period allows us to identify a whole gamut of other resonances in Marie's magical freezer.

In particular, St. Clair's story subverts appliance manufacturers' early use, in the 1930s, of magic as a rhetorical tool to position themselves as God-like procurers of the "good life." This rhetoric originated with GE's exhibit of the General Electric Company Research Laboratory in 1933–4, which

[14] Margaret St. Clair, "New Ritual" (1953), in *The Best from Fantasy and Science Fiction. Third Series*, ed. Anthony Boucher and K. Francis McComas (New York: Doubleday, 1954). Originally published in *Fantasy and Science Fiction* (January 1953) under the pseudonym Idris Seabright. Henceforth, *NR*.

the company dubbed the "House of Magic."[15] Magic was likewise central to the exhibitions at the New York World's Fair in 1939, the most famous of which was GM's Futurama exhibit, which Marchand and Smith describe as "the most elaborate embodiment of corporate futurism ever devised" in its construction of "an entire consumer realm reshaped by science, technology, and free enterprise."[16] These exhibits were supplemented by advertorials in leading magazines, such as the president of Westinghouse's six-page manifesto, in *Popular Mechanics*, that urged the public not to "place any limits on the possibilities of electricity in the future." Private industry must be allowed to fully capitalize on "this invisible, omnipresent electric force."[17] Magic continued to feature in postwar ads, such as Frigidaire's promise to housewives: "You'll feel like a Queen in your kitchen surrounded by Frigidaire appliance magic."[18]

St. Clair's refrigerator endowed with actual magical properties parodies this rhetoric—while also countering the promise, implicit in such ads, that a new gadget could turn back time by transforming a tired housewife back into the beaming bride her husband first married. Instead, the story's conclusion posits the appliance as an escape from the constraints of space and time themselves. For months after Henry and Marie have *both* disappeared, Bertha receives a glossy picture postcard of an attractive, younger version of the couple "against a winter background," which suggests Marie did not stop at transforming her husband. Instead, she joined Henry in the freezer—and into a parallel, wintry, universe, where they will be eternally young and attractive (*NR*, 180). To appliances' promise of time saving and rejuvenation, St. Clair offers a refrigerator that does away with both time and mortality, in what amounts to a vision of domestic cryogenics that also subverts the form of the portal fantasy exemplified by C. S. Lewis's children's novel, *The Lion, The Witch, and the Wardrobe* (first published in 1950, three years before the publication of St. Clair's story). Joe Sutliff Sanders notes that in the usual formulation, adventures in the fantasy realm allow children to gain the experience necessary to transition into the adult world (although on occasion the door to go back to the magical realm might be left ajar).[19] But where the Pevensie children in Lewis's novel must eventually

---

[15] Marchand and Smith, 160–1; Dorothy Nelkin, *Selling Science: How the Press Covers Science and Technology* (New York, W.H. Freeman, 1987), 78, and John Burnham, *How Superstition Won and Science Lost: Popularizing Science and Health in the United States* (New Brunswick, NJ: Rutgers UP, 1987), 6–7.

[16] Marchand and Smith, 167. See also McGovern, 295–300.

[17] George H. Bucher, "The Electric Home of the Future," *Popular Mechanics* 72.2 (August 1939): 161–2.

[18] Frigidaire, "You'll feel like a Queen . . ." *LIFE* (September 14, 1959): 77.

[19] Joe Sutliff Sanders, "'Blatantly Coming Back': The Arbitrary Line between Here and There, Child and Adult, Fantasy and Real, London and UnLondon," in *China Miéville*, ed. Caroline Edwards and Tony Venezia (Gylphi Limited, 2015), 119–38.

return to England and grow up, St. Clair's story offers a *permanent* escape from the adult world for an adult woman whom that world has long infantilized via placating promises about time-saving gadgets. The freezer that offers not shortcuts for meal preparation but the chance to escape the constraints of linear time itself is the ultimate antidote to the escape-portal-qua-pedagogical tool, the infantilizing effects of consumer culture, and the rhetoric of time saving. In this giddy pastiche, St. Clair's fantastical refrigerator-qua-escape-portal splices the tropes of 1930s propaganda by GE and Westinghouse, mid-century appliance ads, 1950s sci-fi by male writers featuring cryogenics, and fantasy literature for children in a manner that exposes the ludicrousness of *all* of these forms.

The malfunctioning appliance as escape portal is also the catalyst for adventure in Eleanor Arnason's *Daughter of the Bear King* (1987). The novel opens with middle-aged Minneapolis housewife Esperance receiving an electric shock from her leaking washing machine, which transports her into "a world where magic work[s], where she [i]s a hero or—more correctly—a heroine."[20] Esperance—whose name signifies "hope" in French—is thus spirited away from the drudgery of "Blue Monday" (the name coined by housewives in the early twentieth century for the labor-intensive laundry day, which, prior to the invention of the washing machine, would have been done by hand and taken up the entire day) to a parallel world, and then back again.[21] A feminist activist herself, Arnason pushes to its extreme the trope of the housewife who escapes her dull life of housework through wild fantasies, established in classic second-wave feminist novels such as Sue Kaufman's *Diary of a Mad Housewife* (1967), discussed in Chapter 3, Ann Richardson Roiphe's *Up the Sandbox* (1970) and Sheila Ballantyne's *Norma Jean the Termite Queen* (1975).[22] The housewife who electrocutes herself with her washing machine to first escape reality and then change it is both a condemnation of the patriarchal structure that makes such an escape necessary and a comical subversion of the labour- and time-saving promises of washing machine ads: for neither death by electrocution nor teletransportation is exactly what washing machine advertisers had in mind.

The gadgets in Kit Reed's "The New You" (1962) and "Cynosure" (1964) by contrast enlist appliances to highlight the science-fictional quality of mid-century consumer culture itself.[23] In the first of these stories, "The New You" (1962), dumpy housewife Martha attempts to rekindle her husband Howard's interest in her by ordering a product that promises to make "'the

[20] Eleanor Arnason, *Daughter of the Bear King* (Seattle, WA: 2015 [1987]). Henceforth, *DOBK*.

[21] See Strasser, "Blue Monday," in *Never Done*, 104–24.

[22] Anne Richardson Roiphe, *Up the Sandbox!* (Greenwich, CN: Fawcett Crest, 1972 [1970]); Sheila Ballantyne, *Norma Jean the Termite Queen*. New York: Penguin, 1983 [1975]).

[23] Kit Reed, "The New You" (1962), and "Cynosure" (1964) in *Weird Women, Wired Women* (Hanover, NH: Wesleyan UP, 1998), 15–24; 25–33. Henceforth, *WWWW*.

Old You Melt Away'" (*WWWW*, 15). As in Bradbury's 1969 story, "I Sing the Body Electric" (discussed in the Introduction to this study), a coffin-shaped box arrives in the post. It contains not an "Electric Grandma" but a more attractive and polished version of Martha, who she calls Marnie, and who swiftly takes Martha's place. But because Martha-now-Marnie failed to read the product's instruction manual, the old her remains. And while delighted with her new self, Marnie grows frustrated with Howard, who suddenly appears too dumpy for the elegant parties to which she is now being invited. When Marnie discovers Howard has begun an affair with Martha, she orders a New Howard. But in an ironic twist of fate, New Howard *also* falls in love with Martha, and the two run away together, leaving the embittered Marnie and subdued Old Howard to live unhappily ever after.

A playful modern take on the myth of Pandora, Reed's story also exposes the fallacies of both advertising generally and 1950s appliance advertising specifically. In doing so, it reveals the ways in which such advertising conflated the housewife with her home, her implements, and her amorous duties as a wife. More specifically, the story's initial parenthetical description of the now-obsolete self that Marnie "stacked (like an old vacuum cleaner, as Marnie saw it, outmoded and unused) in the closet in the hall" illustrates in a very literal way what T. J. Jackson Lears terms the "therapeutic" ethos underlying early- and mid-century advertising, wherein replacing an old possession was framed as an act of self-transformation.[24] Moreover, the description highlights appliances' centrality to the development of a culture of disposal. After all, J. George Fredrick's concept of "progressive obsolescence" and his wife Christine Frederick's concept of "creative waste in spending" were conceived to incentivize the frequent replacement of household goods.[25] In this seemingly chance aside, Reed thus alights upon the imbrication of appliance marketing, planned obsolescence, and a self-improvement industry that indirectly emerged as a result of it. The obsolete self's refusal to stay hidden undermines the very tenets of the "therapeutic ethos" on which appliance ads of the period hinged. Martha's defiance of Marnie's efforts to poison and dispose of her, her subsequent "theft" of Marnie's husband and happiness, and the image of Marnie attempting and failing to stuff her obsolete self who looks "like an old vacuum cleaner" down the electric garbage "Dispose-al" unit subvert and reconfigure the

[24] *WWWW*, 18. T. J. Jackson Lears, "From Salvation to Self-Realization: Advertising and the Therapeutic Roots of the Consumer Culture, 1880–1930," in *The Culture of Consumption: Critical Essays in American History, 1880–1980*, ed. Richard Wightman Fox and T.J. Jackson Lears (New York: Patheon Books, 1983), 1–38; citation on 3.

[25] See Christine Frederick, *Selling Mrs. Consumer* (New York: Business Bourse, 1929), 79, qtd. in Rutherford, 150–1; Marchand, *Advertising the American Dream*, 156–7; Strasser, *Waste and Want*, 16.

narrative components of the mid-century appliance ad. Reed thus estranges the reader not only from the story's events, but from the formula they parody.

In broader terms, "The New You" reads as a speculative vision of how one might interrupt both mechanistic homogenization and a toxic logic of self-renewal. The lingering "Old You"—which results, crucially, from Marnie's neglect to read the manual—embodies the biological waste that remains when the replacement of self with machine is refused (or fails). This remaindered self is both a critique of the steep entry criteria for inter-categorical cyborg living (embodied in manuals whose inscrutable instructions the lay person is bound to ignore) and a suggestion of how cyborg living might be resisted: through human error that results in the strange coexistence of selves and their machine doubles in a manner reminiscent of Donna Haraway's utopianism. The totalizing tendencies of "technologically mediated societies" might be usefully resisted via what Haraway terms a "slightly perverse shift of perspective" involving "*pleasure* in the confusion of boundaries" (Haraway 15; 7, emphases in the original).

Such subversion is likewise evident in "Cynosure" (1964). As the first single mother in her suburban development, housewife Norma knows the importance of keeping up appearances: it is vital she prove she is "just as good as any of the housewives in the magazines," particularly to her neighbor Clarice Brainerd, gatekeeper of the neighborhood coffee morning to which Norma has never been invited. But Mrs. Brainerd's visits all follow an eerily formulaic negative trajectory. Upon arrival, she approvingly notices a clean surface. Norma replies with the name of the product she uses on it, only for Mrs. Brainerd to identify a spill and abruptly leave, uttering the name of a product whose ability to solve the aberration, she implies, might lead to Norma's invitation to the much-coveted coffee morning. The dialog consisting of identifications of dirt that sound like slogans recalls the stilted script of one genre of appliance and cleaning product television ads, in which a more experienced, generally older, woman sagely informs a young married couple that their outdated kitchen needs upgrading, or advises a disconsolate novice housewife about the best way to solve the problem of greyed laundry or greasy surfaces.[26] By introducing slogans and dialog patterns more commonly found in an appliance or cleaning product ad into what, by this point in the story, still appears to be a realist narrative, Reed conveys the inherent surrealness of the advertising testimonial. Mrs. Brainerd's halting, staccato words—which are in fact more artificial than

[26] See for example, Department of Agriculture's Office of Public Affair's public service announcement, "A Step Saving Kitchen" (1949); Westinghouse, "Stop! Don't Rinse Those Dishes! Gets you out of the kitchen after dinner to join in the family fun. You can be sure if it's Westinghouse—Westinghouse Dishwasher and Food Waste Disposer" (1953); Frigidaire, "That Mrs. Malard: So smart to own an automatic dishwasher" (1956); Kelvinator, "The Fabulous Foodorama by Kelvinator" (*ca.* 1950).

the words of an appliance spokesperson—and the description of her "mechanically articulated smile," amplifies this effect, suggesting she is not a woman like those in the ads but rather the woman-from-the-ads taken to her—*its*—extreme, automated conclusion (*WWWW*, 27).

This extremity renders the text disquieting long before the introduction of the weird gadget. In fact, a science-fictional appliance only features in the second of Norma's two attempts to provoke a different outcome by subverting the formula of the testimonial ad. The first, instead, merely involves Norma soliciting Mrs. Brainerd's advice on how best to clean the oven she has already scoured:

> ("I just wondered if you could tell me what to use," she said seductively, thinking that when Clarice Brainerd saw that Norma was worried about dirt in an oven that was cleaner than any oven on the block, she would be awed and dismayed, and she would have to invite Norma to the next day's morning coffee hour). (*WWWW*, 28)

This parenthetical irruption reveals Norma's disingenuous appropriation of the tenets of the appliance testimonial ad, and in particular the artificial premise on which such ads are based, wherein the "problem" of a stained or dirty surface has been manufactured for the purposes of narrating the product's benefits. The ensuing passage subverts the ending of cleaning product ads, where housewife and mentor are shown beaming at the newly cleaned appliance surface: here Mrs. Brainerd "spen[ds] a long time with her head in the oven," while Norma fights the "temptation to push her the rest of the way in, and turn up the gas" (*WWWW*, 28). The description incisively identifies the bizarreness of advertising narratives in which women variously drape themselves on, lean against, stick their necks into, and wildly open and close the doors of their appliances to demonstrate the ease with which they can be used and cleaned—while Norma's vision of herself gassing Mrs. Brainerd blasts apart the mentoring myth on which the testimonial ad depended, exposing not-so-normal Norma's state of mind.

In the last section of the story Reed combines the surreal elements of product slogans and advertisement testimonials with a further science-fictional element: a prohibitively expensive gadget that Norma orders after seeing a magazine ad promising that "your house can be the cynosure of your neighbourhood" (*WWWW*, 29). The gadget allows her to freeze wayward elements, such as her cat, dog, and daughter, and place them in picturesque positions, at once preventing them from wreaking havoc on just-cleaned spaces and turning them into cynosures in their own right—focal points worthy of attention and admiration. In this way, Reed exposes both the unrealistic expectations raised by appliance advertisements and the actual effort involved in living up to them—an effort that in fact involves impeding "living" altogether. The ideal appliance does not save time so much as *stop its passage*, thereby preventing the traces of breathing, eating, and defecation to accrue. However, the story's final dénouement radically upheaves these ideals: for when Mrs. Brainerd visits and is *still* dissatisfied, Norma uses the appliance to freeze her and to unfreeze her daughter and pets, whom she encourages to wreak havoc on the house. By forcing Mrs. Brainerd to watch as she and her household break all the rules of *Good Housekeeping*, choosing the chaos and unpredictability of life over the fixity and immobility of the sanitized living prescribed in its pages, Norma at once subverts housewife etiquette, the function of this particular appliance, and the function of time-saving gadgetry more broadly. The appliance is transformed into a tool for anarchic rebellion: for while it cannot dismantle the social structures and codes that deem Norma unworthy, it *can* disempower their ambassador. In turning the steel-like, mechanical Mrs. Brainerd into an actual object (that is, however, sentient, and can thus look on in horror at the dirt-strewn living space in which "it" is frozen), Norma is able to de-reify her*self*, in an act that anticipates Second-Wave Feminism's incitement to housewives to "self-actualize." If the ideal time-saving appliance under a patriarchal consumer capitalism is one that prevents signs of time's passage from sullying a living space, the ideal *anarchic* appliance is one that halts, if not patriarchal consumer capitalism, then its most vociferous ambassadors.

In contrast to these comical stories but perhaps reflecting the politically charged atmosphere of the late 1960s, the appliances in James Tiptree, Jr.'s "Mama Come Home" (1968) are brutally violent.[27] Set in an alternative version of the 1960s, "Mama Come Home" is narrated by a male CIA agent working in an advertising agency that is a cover for a top-secret government department established to find life beyond Earth. The agents eventually make contact with the Capellans, a species of giant females whose goal is to enslave Earth's men (*MCH*, 73). Technology's violent potential is central to this parody of patriarchal US imperialism, and, most notably, in the story's parenthetical description of the "blaze of pain" the narrator experiences when a Capellan rapes him: "(Ever think about being attacked by a *musth* vacuum cleaner:) [*sic*]" (*MCH*, 69–70). To postwar popular culture's ubiquitous depictions of women conflated with or reduced to appliances, Tiptree presents an extraordinary counterimage of an act of female violence as brutally efficient *as* a vacuum cleaner. The image of a vacuum cleaner that is either called "*musth*" or that makes the sound "*musth*" conjures latent fears about the violent potential of both the mechanical things used to clean the home and the women who wield them. But from another perspective, the

[27] James Tiptree, Jr., "Mama Come Home" (1968), in *10,000 Light Years from Home* (New York: Ace Books, 1978), 54–85. Henceforth, *MCH*.

description of rape as an "attack by a *musth* vacuum cleaner" reveals less about either the reification of women or the brutality of rape, than about the unimaginativeness of this particular ad man, who in seeking to describe an act of violence by a woman fails to conjure a metaphor from beyond the world of female-coded consumer goods. In this reading, the vacuum cleaner is just a stand-in for the inconceivable and inexpressible—which is not the experience of *alien* assault, but of *female* assault. This unimaginability (indeed, its alienness!) is alluded to by the colon at the end of the parentheses that leads to nothing. Tiptree's description of a man's incapacity to articulate assault by a woman forms part of a broader indictment of patriarchal capitalism—while suggesting the extent to which the dismissal of women as the "weaker" sex paradoxically leaves men vulnerable to attack by them.

The significance of Tiptree's vacuum cleaner analogy stands out all the more when read alongside the aerospace-inspired appliance designs that emerged in the late 1950s and 1960s, which were accompanied by a speculative, science-fictional, marketing language that aligned these objects with a streamlined future characterized by space exploration, the survival of atomic war—or both. Thus, for example, Westinghouse modelled its 1953 vacuum cleaner on a spaceship, and called it the "Rocket tank cleaner."[28] This futuristic ethos was exemplified by the short-lived popularity of "floating" appliances featuring hovercraft technology. The most famous of these, the spherically shaped Hoover Constellation vacuum cleaner, was launched in 1954 and featured a vinyl furniture guard around the middle resembling the ring around Saturn (Figure 5.2). The 1955 model contained an additional "Air-ride" feature that enabled the appliance to literally float on its own exhaust.[29] The replacement, in 1967, of the traditional housewife of the Constellation's original print ads with a woman wearing a space-suit-qua-pilot's outfit aligned housework with intergalactic exploration while divesting the appliance of its domestic connotations (Figure 5.3).

Frigidaire imitated this approach in 1965 with the launch of their "Space Age Refrigerators," which they supported with a two-year print campaign. In "Frigidaire Announces the Space Age Advance in Refrigeration," a group of female astronauts appeared to ride the "1966 Frigidaire Custom Imperial Nineteen Refrigerator" like a spaceship.[30] Callout images promoted the appliance's engineering worthy of a NASA spaceship. In "Another Space Age Advance," identical twin models wearing "Space Age fashions from *Harper's Bazaar*" promoted "The Gemini 19 New Refrigerator Freezer

[28] Gantz, *The Vacuum Cleaner,* 129.

[29] Gantz, *The Vacuum Cleaner*, 130–1.

[30] "Frigidaire Announces the Space Age Advance in Refrigeration," *LIFE* (November 19, 1965): 49 and Frigidaire Announces Space Age Refrigeration," *LIFE* (January 14, 1966): 7; *LIFE* (March 18, 1966): 15; and *LIFE* (June 24, 1966): 57.

FIGURE 5.2 Hoover. "New Hoover Constellation." *The Saturday Evening Post* (October 27, 1956): 7. Image courtesy of the Advertising Archives.

FIGURE 5.3 Hoover. "Hoover's Incredible Flying Machine." *LIFE* (August 25, 1967): 17. Image courtesy of the Advertising Archives.

Twin."[31] The name referred to the side-by-side "twin" refrigerator and freezer compartments as well as NASA's second human spaceflight program, Project Gemini, which ran from 1961 to 1966. Meanwhile "Frigidaire Refrigerators That Glide on Air" emphasized the range's optional add-on feature, the "Ride-Aire," which relied on the same principle as the Hoover Constellation.[32] Hooking a vacuum cleaner to a valve on the refrigerator's front created exhaust that "literally lift[ed] the refrigerator off the floor," allowing the housewife to move it with just "the touch of a finger" and easily clean behind it.[33] Tiptree's story about giant women raping men with

[31] Frigidaire, "Another Space Age Advance: The Gemini 19... New Refrigerator-Freezer Twin," *LIFE* (May 20, 1966): 31; *Better Homes and Gardens* 44 (1966): 429; *Harper's Bazaar* 99 (1966): 49. See also Archer, 168.

[32] Frigidaire Sales Brochure, "New! Frigidaire Refrigerators That Ride on Air! RIDE-AIRE" (November 18, 1966).

[33] Frigidaire, "The Ride-Aire," *House and Garden* 129 (1966): 66; *American Home* 69 (1966): 128; Author unknown, "Home Appliances: How Smart Can They Get?" *Popular Science* (March 1966): 99; 206. Frigidaire has denied permission to reproduce this pamphlet, but images can be found online on various websites devoted to vintage ads, as well as in Archer, *The Mid-Century Kitchen*; Jim Heiman, ed., *Mid-Century Ads* (Köln, Germany: Taschen, 2015); and Heimann, *All-American Ads of the 60s* (Köln, Germany: Taschen Icons, 2003).

the efficiency of a vacuum cleaner exposes the floating, spaceship-shaped Hoover and space-age refrigerator as quaintly retrograde. It likewise parodies the erotic origins of handheld appliances themselves, noted in the Introduction to this study, and the increasingly sexually explicit ads of the late 1960s discussed in Chapter 1. Tiptree's story playfully references each of these dimensions of the time-saving appliance, while suggesting that a truly radical future is not one in which women ride refrigerators into outer space or clean underneath their flying appliances. It is one in which appliances are able to eradicate patriarchy entirely.

The next section examines the ways in which Robert Heinlein and Philip K. Dick also, but in very different ways, play with both the temporal and gendered dimension of appliances in their time-travel narratives.

3. Parodies of Misogyny Through Time and Space: Robert Heinlein's *The Door into Summer* (1957) and Philip K. Dick's "The Adjustment Team" (1954) and *Ubik* (1969)

Heinlein's wry account, in *The Door into Summer*, of a male inventor intent on giving housewives the time-saving gadget they don't realize they need parodies the blinkered single-mindedness of the male engineer, and a culture in which the solution to domestic labor no one wants to do is not the redistribution of responsibilities between the sexes, but automation.[34] In order to truly appreciate the way in which time-saving appliances are paradoxically both vital to the novel's plot and effectively inconsequential to it, a detailed summary of this plot is necessary. *The Door into Summer* begins in the future—1970—and is narrated by an engineer born in 1940, "when everybody was saying that the individual was on the skids and the future belonged to mass man," and named after the original hero of individualism, Daniel Boone (*DIS*, 16). At the end of a war during which he developed cryogenic preservation for the military, Dan and his lawyer colleague, Miles, establish an enterprise to develop household robots from this same military technology. Dan, Miles, and their *femme fatale* bookkeeper-secretary (literally called Belle) set up shop in the Mojave Desert—where the military, and many of the manufacturing plants associated with the military-industrial complex, were indeed known to experiment during the

[34] Robert Heinlein, *The Door into Summer* (London: Orion/Gollancz, 2013 [1957]), 16. Henceforth, *DIS*.

Cold War.[35] They name their company *Hired Girl*, after their first vacuum-cleaner-like gadget. When Miles and Belle steal the company from under him in order to facilitate a takeover by a larger corporation, Miles goes to one of the many cryogenics labs that have emerged since the war's end and opts for a "cold sleep" of thirty years. When he awakens, *Hired Girl* no longer exists, while unskilled labor has been replaced by his once top-secret prototypes, which have been patented by one D. B. Davis. To find out how his signature ended up on these patents, what happened to his most cherished prototype, *Flexible Frank*, and why his company collapsed, Dan enlists the help of a time-travel scientist who enables him to go back to 1970 and—in true time-travel narrative fashion—discover that he himself, traveling back in time, was the one who filed the patents, stole *Flexible Frank* from Miles and Belle, dismantled the robot's parts, and buried them, before succumbing to the cold sleep—thus ensuring that *Hired Girl* would go out of business.

As a novel about an engineer fighting off corporate takeover but eulogistic about the benefits of military-backed science and of engineering's capacity to "solve" all of life's inequities and inconveniences, *The Door into Summer* is a profoundly contradictory text. Meanwhile the gender relations in the novel, including between Dan and Miles's nine-year-old stepdaughter Ricky, who Dan ends up marrying in 2000, are problematic to say the least, and it is unclear whether they are intended to be taken at face value. Even more puzzling is the contrast between the detailed descriptions, in the first thirty pages or so of the novel, of the gadgets Dan develops, which focus on the minutiae of housework and of assembling a machine capable of tackling anything from bathtub ring-scouring to martini-mixing, and the rest of the text, which all but abandons the question of household drudgery and automation until the very last pages. This interplay is particularly useful for our purposes, allowing us to consider the utility of time-saving appliances to the plot, to Heinlein's vision of rugged individualism, to his view of military spin-off technology, and to the text's concluding remarks about women's social role. The description of the robots' conception, which reveals the 1950s' near future to retain the same gender and racial stereotypes as the 1950s themselves, is particularly revealing. As Dan puts it:

> I didn't attempt to figure out a sensible scientific house; women didn't want one . . . housewives were still complaining about the Servant Problem long after servants had gone the way of the mastodon. I had

[35] Valerie Kuletz, *The Tainted Desert: Environmental and Social Ruin in the American West* (New York: Routledge, 1998), 10.

> rarely met a housewife who did not have a touch of slaveholder in her. (*DIS*, 18)

According to this account, women (understood here to mean *white* women) have no head for science and are fundamentally reactionary in their desires. What they really want is not time-saving gadgets, but to turn *back* time to when domestic work was delegated to servants or slaves. The explanation that the name *Hired Girl* was designed to invoke "thoughts of a semi-slave immigrant girl whom Grandma used to bully" reveals the appliance robot's main function to be the fulfillment of white women's antebellum fantasies, and the circumventing of both the inconvenience of slavery's end and the industrialization that saw working-class white women leave domestic service for better-paid factory work (*DIS*, 18). The white female consumer's irrational resistance to progress is reiterated in Dan's contemptuous description of housewives as "reactionaries" un-swayed by Le Corbusier's "'machines for living'" and in his dismissal of the "prattle" of "women's magazines [that] tal[k] about 'labor-saving in the home' and functional kitchens" but whose "pretty pictures sho[w] living-working arrangements essentially no better than those in Shakespeare's day" (*DIS*, 21).

The sardonic tone of Heinlein's novel, which often appears to parody the hard-boiled style of Raymond Chandler and James M. Cain, suggests that these views are intended to discomfit—and that Dan is, to some extent, a parodic figure. This is particularly apparent in the pages and pages of meticulous accounts of both Dan's gadgets and his design ethos. While reflecting Heinlein's commitment to "hard science fiction"—a subgenre he is credited with pioneering, and whose authors strove to incorporate scientifically accurate ideas into their narratives—these detailed descriptions also reveal Dan's near-fanaticism, and his perception of engineering as a higher calling.[36] The following, which is but a short excerpt of a three-page explanation, is indicative of this mindset. Having boasted all of the tasks *Hired Girl* can complete, Dan describes how he built the machine:

> I swiped the basic prowl patter from the "Electric Turtles" that were written up in *Scientific American* in the late forties, lifted a memory circuit out of the brain of a guided missile (that's the nice thing about top-secret gimmicks; they don't get patented), and I took the cleaning devices and linkages out of a dozen things, including a floor polisher used in army hospitals, a soft-drink dispenser, and those "hands" they

[36] Kathryn Cramer summarizes hard sci-fi as fiction in which "a relationship to and knowledge of science and technology is central to the work," and where science "provides the illusion of both realism and rationalism" ("Hard science fiction," *The Cambridge Companion to Science Fiction* (Cambridge: Cambridge UP, 2003), 186–96. Citation on 188).

> use in atomic plants to handle anything "hot." There wasn't anything really new in it; it was just the way I put it together. (*DIS*, 18–20)

Here and in the long, detailed, passages that follow, Dan elevates the status of the scientist to that of a cross between a social reformer and what a decade later Claude Lévi-Strauss would define as the *bricoleur* working against the odds. For Strauss, the *bricoleur* who "made do" with bits and pieces was diametrically opposed to the "engineer," whose "scientific mind" and access to resources enabled the latter to create a holistic totalizing system or discourse.[37] *Bricolage* later provided a foundation for Michel de Certeau's concept of the "tactic," an action enabling the disempowered to retain some form of agency to counter the "strategies" of those in power, a conceptual framework he based on military parlance.[38] The description of Dan's efforts to craft first *Hired Girl* and then the other robots is fascinating in its framing of this former military engineer as a downtrodden underdog working against the odds and inventing great products by stealth (*DIS*, 18). What's more, Dan's concern throughout the novel with affirming engineering as an art born of intuition and feeling goes hand in hand with the novel's broader framing of scientific innovation as social reform, and of the home as the place where such reform should begin. This idea is reinforced by Dan's description of *Flexible Frank*, a more sophisticated robot prototype than *Hired Girl* that is capable of identifying when and what household tasks require doing. Of particular note is his description of *Flexible Frank* as "look[ing] like a hat-rack making love to an octopus . . . but, boy, how he could polish silverware!" (*DIS*, 29). The description of the bizarre-looking machine recalls the nineteenth-century French poet Comte Lautréamont (the pseudonym for Isidore Lucien Ducasse)'s description of the "chance meeting of a sewing machine and an umbrella on an operating table," which the Surrealist artist Max Ernst appropriated to define the Surrealist aesthetic.[39] In referencing this famous Surrealist image, Heinlein (parodically) locates Dan within the category of artistic geniuses—and, indeed, among the quintessence of *bricoleurs*, who made it their lives' work to reimagine the world by reconfiguring its component parts.

---

[37] Claude Lévi-Strauss, *The Savage Mind* (Oxford and New York: Oxford UP, 2004 [1962]), 17–20.

[38] Michel de Certeau, *The Practice of Everyday Life*, transl. Steve Rendall (Berkeley: U of California Press, 1986), 35.

[39] Comte Lautréamont, *Maldoror*, transl. Guy Wernham (New York: New Directions, 1965 [1869]), 263, qtd. in Max Ernst, "What Is the Mechanism of Collage?" (1936), in *Theories of Modern Art: A Source Book by Artists and Critics*, ed. Herschel B. Chipp (Berkeley, CA: U of California Press, 1968), 437–28.

Heinlein's parody of the all-American hero reaches its apex in the novel's closing lines. Dan's reaction to Ricky's pregnancy, "'It just isn't *convenient* being a woman; something ought to be done and I'm convinced that some things can be done. There's that matter of leaning over, and also the backaches,'" reads as both a proto-feminist recognition of the feminine labors that time-saving gadgets cannot resolve and a parody of the engineer's God-like belief that he can solve any and all "design flaws," including the inconvenience of possessing a (female) body (*DIS*, 177–8, emphasis in the original). Heinlein's tongue-in-cheek depiction of a husband who sees his wife's pregnant body as primarily an engineering problem to be solved retrospectively alters the reader's perception of the description of reactionary housewives, revealing it to be a parody of the evangelical engineer for whom femininity and impracticality are synonymous (*DIS*, 177).

Time-saving appliances similarly expose fraught gender relations in Philip K. Dick's short story, "The Adjustment Team" (1954), and novel, *Ubik* (1969), although in a less comical manner than Heinlein's depictions. The vacuum cleaner and refrigerator I discuss here are but the most significant of the myriad appliance depictions scattered throughout Dick's work, and which have been almost entirely ignored (with the exception of Christopher Palmer's provocative reading of the robot-appliance in Dick's 1954 story, "Sales Pitch," whose incessant sloganeering forces the protagonist to flee both home and planet, as explicitly linking "the militarized . . . side of society, and the consumerist side").[40]

"The Adjustment Team" depicts a society in which teams of bureaucrats "adjust" sequences of events to ensure their smooth occurrence. The story opens with a clerk approaching the house of protagonists Ed and Ruth in order to "adjust" a sequence involving Ed's office.[41] This sequence is later revealed to be a real estate deal that will result in the discovery of a technology that will lead to the prevention of nuclear war. For the sequence to go to plan, the workers in Ed's office must be at the office by 9:00 a.m., so the adjustment team can freeze them in time without their knowledge and make the required adjustments to their surroundings. The clerk's job is to ensure Ed is punctual, but instead Ed is interrupted by a door-to-door insurance salesman and arrives at the office late. He finds the office interiors coated in dust, his colleagues frozen, and mysterious old men working, which he would not have discerned had he been frozen along with his colleagues. Ed only discovers all of this at the story's end, however, having previously assumed he was going mad—while Ruth suspects him of having

[40] Christopher Palmer, *Philip K. Dick: Exhilaration and Terror of the Postmodern* (Liverpool: Liverpool UP, 2003), 103.

[41] Philip K. Dick, "The Adjustment Team" (1954). https://en.wikisource.org/wiki/Adjustment_Team. Originally published in *Orbit Science Fiction 4* (September–October 1954). Henceforth, *AT*.

an affair. His efforts to disprove her suspicions without telling her about the adjustment team are interrupted by a vacuum-cleaner salesman whose arrival, the last sentences of the story imply, has been orchestrated by this same team.

Like Heinlein's novel, Dick's story is premised on a series of gendered assumptions whose constraining effects are exposed by the final twist. In other words, what at first appears to be a story that adheres to gender stereotypes is revealed to self-consciously *play* with those stereotypes as part of a broader comment on the sheer predictability of mid-century middle-class domestic and office life. More specifically, while the image of decrepit old men working in a temporally frozen office allegorizes the psychological state of the beleagured office worker, for whom time indeed appears to stand still, the doorstop sales reveal the temporality of middle-class domesticity to be indelibly shaped by commercial exchanges whose gendered construction renders them entirely foreseeable. In retrospect, the visit from the insurance salesman was *inevitably* going to derail Dan's timely arrival at work, since of course insurance (in contrast to household goods) is a subject for the man of the house to address. Likewise, the adjustment team's scheme to smooth out the ripples of the day's events via the vacuum-cleaner salesman relies on the formulaic nature of the doorstep appliance sale, which Dick describes in detail:

> He set down the vacuum cleaner and its attachments with a metallic crash. Rapidly, he unrolled a long illustrated banner, showing the vacuum cleaner in action. "Now, if you'll just hold this while I plug in the cleaner—" He bustled happily about, unplugging the TV set, plugging in the cleaner, pushing the chairs out of his way. "I'll show you the drape scraper first." He attached a hose and nozzle to the big gleaming tank. "Now, if you'll just sit down I'll demonstrate each of these easy-to-use attachments." His happy voice rose over the roar of the cleaner. "You'll notice—." (*AT*)

The ending's humor derives from the fact that the door-to-door appliance sales visit serves as the perfect foil not only for sexual advances (as depicted in Emily Arnold McCully short story discussed in Chapter 3, or in Kit Reed's 1974 parody of the Women's Liberation Movement, "Songs of War"), but for espionage.[42] Anticipating Graham Greene's 1958 satirical spy novel,

[42] "Songs of War" (1974) depicts a "college dropout" who becomes a vacuum-cleaner salesman only to realize that what housewives really want is a quickie. He soon replaces his pitch about the "Marvellous sweep with twenty attachments and ten optional features" to the pithier: "Want to screw?" (*WWWW*, 57). The text exposes the erotic subtext of doorstop appliance sales while playing on the erotic dimension of the vacuum cleaner itself, whose appendages and suctioning features recall those of the man touting it.

Our Man in Havana (whose vacuum-cleaner salesman protagonist accepts a job with MI6 to help finance his daughter's insatiable desire for consumer goods), "The Adjustment Team" posits the appliance sales representative as the quintessential everyman.[43] His demonstration's stiltedness is above suspicion because it is *supposed* to be scripted, while the regularity with which such sales representatives visited suburban households makes his sudden appearance entirely believable. The adjustment bureau's effort to hide their manipulation of linear time involves introducing a salesperson whose sales strategy hinges on taking up the *housewife's* time until she acquiesces to making a purchase, in a move that ironically results in consuming in advance the time she will later save by using the product. More to the point, attending to the gender norms on which the appliance salesman's visit hinges allows us to more fully appreciate the ingenuity of this foil. The doorstep appliance sale is the social exchange least vulnerable to chance insofar as not only the salesman's speech, but the housewife's reaction, follows a distinct formula that has no variables. Such a reading chimes with assessments of Dick's work as friendly to a "feminist reading, suggesting the deformation involved in capitalist social relations and the power of patriarchy," despite the author's own "often painful and hostile feelings about women."[44] One might even argue that (as in the case of David Foster Wallace, another male writer with a history of problematic behavior toward women), his own hostile feelings toward women are precisely what allow Dick to so accurately identify misogyny in culture at large. Put differently, Dick's capacity to critique Cold War containment culture's enforcement of suffocating gender norms is in keeping with the position of those postwar male writers such as Updike, Kerouac, Burroughs, Yates, and Carver whose incisive critiques of the formulaic quality of the era's prescribed gender norms, as mentioned elsewhere in this study, were bound up with their resentment toward the perceived emasculating and domesticating effects of that culture (indeed, the male protagonist's rage, in Dick's posthumously published early novel, *Voices from the Street,* when his wife's sister offers to give them the old Waring blender she has replaced with a newer model, uncannily recalls the scenes of emasculation-by-appliance in Yates).[45]

Dick's most famous appliance depiction, however, is the archaic, 1930s GE refrigerator that appears in one of the most surreal sequences in *Ubik*

---

[43] Graham Greene, *Our Man in Havana* (London: Vintage, 2006 [1958]).

[44] *Exhilaration and Terror of the Postmodern*, 86–7. Palmer's reading of Dick's short stories, which portray "horrible state[s] of affairs" that "exis[t] because women(feminism) wanted it" and "men have proved powerless in the face of women's withdrawal from nurture and kindliness" is particularly instructive (90).

[45] Philip K. Dick, *Voices from the Street* (London: Gollancz, 2014 [2007]), 43. The novel was written in the early 1950s.

(1969), where protagonist Joe Chip watches an ad for the titular substance, Ubik (*U*, 135). The ad's spokespeople promote Ubik's capacity to "'reverse'" the "'reversion of matter to earlier forms'" that is being experienced by people, such as himself, who are caught in the "'half-life'" between life and death (*U*, 135). Ubik can halt the disintegration of the material world perceived by these "'half-lifers'":

> A hard-eyed housewife with big teeth and horse's chin . . . bellowed, "I came over to Ubik after trying weak, out-of-date reality supports. My pots and pans were turning into heaps of rust. . . . But now I use economical new powerful today's Ubik, and with miraculous results. Look at this refrigerator." On the screen appeared an antique turret-top G.E. refrigerator. "Why, it's devolved back eighty years." "Sixty-two years," Joe corrected reflexively. "But now look at it," the housewife continued, squirting the old turret top with her spray can of Ubik. Sparkles of magic light lit up in a nimbus surrounding the old turret top and, in a flash, a modern six-door pay refrigerator replaced it in splendid glory. (*U*, 134)

Like Reed, St. Clair, and Heinlein before him, Dick playfully reappropriates the housewife trope and turns the fear of obsolescence on the one hand and death on the other into a problem that plagues only those caught between life and death, and that can be solved by a consumer good that makes old things new. In his Marxist analysis of the novel, Carl Freedman notes that *Ubik*'s "domination," or "constitution," by the commodity structure (where homes are equipped with talking doors and "pay refrigerators" that demand compensation to open), is exemplified by the thing "Ubik itself, the ultimate and universal commodity and the symbol of the ubiquity of the commodity structure."[46] But what of Ubik's specific *properties*? The fact that this spray *doesn't* resolve the dilemma of being caught between life and death in the first place but merely treats the surface issue of how things appear recalls the rhetoric of cleaning product advertising, exemplifying a capitalist process that, like housework, is "never done." Meanwhile, the old turret-top refrigerator communicates rather the opposite of what the housewife in the ad intends. After all, Joe's financial struggles throughout the novel have often left him with no money to pay his "pay refrigerator," making a 1930s model that opens without requiring payment a much more appealing prospect.

Dick enlisted this same GE refrigerator in *Ubik* in a letter to Claudia Bush six years after the novel's publication. Here he reflected upon a life-changing

[46] Carl Freedman, "Towards a Theory of Paranoia: The Science Fiction of Philip K. Dick," *Science Fiction Studies* 11.1 (March 1984): 15–24.

psychotic episode he had experienced in March 1974, which reinforced his belief that alongside the "vertical" time "we normally perceive" there exists a "horizontal, which is the axis along which the objects in *Ubik* regress."[47] Dick described his psychotic episode as a regression "along the horizontal (orthogonal) time axis," to "a former man, an adult of the same age as mine," but not a younger version of him:

> as in *Ubik* the present form (me an adult at 44 years old) rolled back to reveal the "crypte morphosis" concealed within, exactly as, say, the modern refrigerator rolled back to become . . . the old 1937 turret top G.E. The modern two-door freezer-refrigerator never was that old turret top, except along an entirely different form axis, that of cooling/storage appliances per se. As to why I regressed along the horizontal (orthogonal) time axis, which may be unique or nearly so in human experience—could be due to my having written/read *Ubik* and knowing about hypertime, or also, a current, unique weakening in some way of the vertical time force. (*TEOPKD*, 166)

From this perspective, the author's psychotic break was either influenced by the experience of writing about the hypertime of the refrigerator or it was, *itself*, an instance of time travel. This would be in keeping with Dick's remark, in an earlier letter, to Peter Fitting, that *he* was written by *Ubik*, rather than the other way around (*EOFLD*, 11). The turret-top refrigerator was the result of what elsewhere he called the "abolish[ment]" of the "press of time of everything" and a form of "revelation" (*EOFKD*, 3). Dick's choice of the refrigerator rather than any other object from the novel to illustrate this entropic process toward revelation is significant, as is the entirely *un*gendered, or gender-neutral, nature of the description. In contrast to its depiction in the novel, there is nothing here to suggest the refrigerator's long-standing association with housewifery: only its potential to describe the revelation experienced during the author's psychotic episode. The refrigerator would seem to stand, for Dick, as uniquely embodying the paradoxes of capitalist modernity and its reliance on unequal gender relations—as well as uniquely primed for decontextualization.

This becomes particularly apparent when one considers the refrigerator's significance in one of Dick's earliest works, *The Variable Man* (1953), in which an electric repairman from 1913 appears, by chance, in an unspecified future where the ability to repair old things has been lost, and his successful repair of a man's electric refrigerator, despite never having seen one before, results in the repairman's recruitment to work in the arms trade of this future

---

[47] *The Exegesis of Philip K. Dick*, ed. Pamela Jackson and Jonathan Lethem (New York: Houghton Mifflin Harcourt, 2011), 78. Henceforth *TEOPKD*.

society.[48] But where *The Variable Man* explicitly links built-in obsolescence, and the technological advances that made domestic electrification possible, to a capitalist project inextricable from military warfare, Dick's later, unpublished reflection desists from such a critique. This later text disassociates the time-saving appliance from the network of meanings with which it has long been linked, and from its function as an extender of the time-span of food, allowing it to transcend linear understandings of both time and space, and to enter the realm of the metaphysical—indeed, the divine.

4. "At Least She's Not in Love with Her Vacuum Cleaner":[49] Ira Levin's *The Stepford Wives* (1972)

Ira Levin's satirical vision of the extreme ends to which wealthy, conservative, white America might go to stamp out Second-Wave Feminism is perhaps the most famous treatment of the postwar housewife's conflation with her time-saving appliances. New Yorker Joanna Eberhart and her family move to the fictional suburb of Stepford where the men hold high-powered jobs in a cluster of local technology companies and spend their evenings at the Men's Association, while the women perform housewifery "like actresses in commercials" (*SW*, 49). When Joanna and one of the only other "normal" women in town, Bobbie Markowe, discover the housewives used to be feminists, they suspect their changed behavior to be caused by "'all those fancy plants on Route Nine'" where the Stepford men work in "'electronics, computers, aerospace junk,'" dumping "'crap ... into the environment'" (*SW*, 63). The novel's final pages instead reveal that far from being poisoned by pollutants, the women have been killed and replaced by robots developed by the Men's Association's leaders, who responded to the Women's Liberation Movement by using their experience in robotics, animation, and voice cloning to create machine-wives devoted to sex and housework. The novel ends with another newcomer, Ruthanne, the first and only Black woman in the community, running into the new machine-version of Joanna at the supermarket before going home to a husband who is happy to look after the kids while she works.

Levin's story about robot-housewives and collusion between employees of media and technology companies with implied military connections functions as an allegory for Cold War ideology's reliance on heteronormativity

---

[48] Philip K. Dick, *The Variable Man* (1953). https://www.gutenberg.org/files/32154/32154-h/32154-h.htm (accessed November 12, 2019).

[49] Ira Levin, *The Stepford Wives* (London: Constable and Robinson, 2011 [1972]), 40. Henceforth, *SW*.

and strict gender roles, suggesting the threat feminism posed to an entire system contingent upon female subjugation and racial inequality. The "All-American" housewife on which the Stepford wives are modeled is revealed to be both a product and a foundational element of the Cold War machine, akin to the Disney movies, television sitcoms, and household gadgets whose aim—beyond the profit motive—was to promote the American way of life.[50] That the cause of the deaths of the original Stepford wives is a carefully orchestrated conspiracy to ensure that this suburb remains unaffected by the sociopolitical transformations occurring in the United States' urban centers highlights the role that the idealization of white middle-class suburbia played in affirming a very narrow definition of "American values." Just as the postwar suburbs emerged as a means to protect white middle-class Americans from the twin threats of Black neighbors and nuclear attack, Stepford is reconfigured, by the Men's Association, to protect patriarchal values and whiteness from Second-Wave Feminism and Civil Rights. In this context, both actual appliances and the robot-wives-qua-appliances underscore the mechanistic dimension of the quotidian imagined in popular depictions of the "good life," and the relationship between those depictions and the sophisticated network of companies and government institutions involved in their promotion. The text's referral as much to the companies for which the husbands work as to the time-saving appliances the housewives use underscores their mutual imbrication. In one scene, for example:

> Joanna looked at the neat low modern buildings, set back from the road and separated each from the next by wide spans of green lawn: Ulitz Optics (where Herb Sundersen worked), and CompuTech (Vic Stavros, or was he with Instatron?), and Stevenson Biochemical, and Haig-Darling Computers, and Burnham-Massey-Microtech (Dale Coba—hiss!—and Claude Axhelm), and Instatron, and Reed & Saunders (Bill McCormick—how was Marge?), and Vesey Electronics, and AmeriChem-Willis. (*SW*, 67)

At this point in the novel, Joanna does not know about the robots, but the reader has been given enough clues to suspect. The list punctuated by asides to the men's involvement with these industrial conglomerates made up of different names, and the suggestion of the latters' interchangeableness, conveys the sheer scale of whoever or whatever is behind the mystery of the Stepford wives, and suggests the likely involvement of industry. The unusual

---

[50] For an account of Disney's role in promoting American values during the Cold War era, see Steven Watts, *The Magic Kingdom: Walt Disney and the American Way of Life* (Columbia, MO: U of Missouri Press, 1997). Watts notes that Disney "helped cement the Cold War consensus by mediating a host of jarring impulses: individualism and conformity, corporate institutions and small-town values, science and fantasy, consumerism and producerism" (289).

resemblance of the "wide spans of green lawn" outside the industrial plants to the green lawns of the Stepford homes, and the resemblance of the interchangeable nature of the tech companies (and the men who work for them) to the interchangeableness of the Stepford wives, combine to cement the link between the machines of industry, a mechanized domestic space, and the anonymous powers behind both.

Levin's text thus shows the way in which the image of the housewife "'in love with her vacuum cleaner,'" as Bobbie diagnoses the Stepford wives, is as much a product of the Cold War as the AI technologies and computer systems developed by military-backed manufacturers—while also calling attention to the military funding that the biggest appliance manufacturers (namely, Westinghouse, GE, and Frigidaire's parent company, GM) received to conduct research into nuclear, aerospace, and other defense technologies (*SW*, 40; Hine, 128). As mentioned in the Introduction to this study, consumer technology companies suspended production of consumer goods to manufacture weapons and military airplane and land vehicle parts during the Second World War; after 1945, many continued to supply the US government with defense aircraft and missiles (Hine, 128). By the late 1950s, they were aggressively promoting their defense hardware alongside their refrigerators and washing machines to counter Eisenhower's efforts to cut military expenditure (Hine, 128). Levin's robot-wives manufactured by employees of companies imbricated with the military-industrial complex are thus not just embodiments of Cold War ideology, but *appliance-qua-weapons* that perform both housework and the affirmation of a white hetero-patriarchal status quo.

That performativity is reiterated in a series of scenes in which Joanna visits different wives and competes with their time-saving appliances for their attention. Most notable among these is the description of Joanna's visit to the home of Kit Sunderson, who spends the entire visit doing housework against a backdrop of an "immaculate" kitchen, an "open dryer," and a "washer's round port [that] [i]s storming" (*SW*, 46–50). Joanna "watche[s] Kit open the refrigerator," then asks Kit about the now-defunct Women's Club, in response to which "Kit st[ands] at the lighted refrigerator, her back to Joanna" and replies with her back turned, before moving on to folding laundry from the dryer (*SW*, 47–8). The impression is not just of a commercial, as Joanna describes it, but of a woman interacting first and foremost with her machines: Joanna's visit appears more of an excuse for Kit to *use her appliances to serve coffee* than a social interaction in its own right. The encounter highlights a further level of reification, wherein the accoutrements of hosting are more important than the human beings they are intended to impress. And, of course, the scene is but one of many in which the machine-wife who has no time for anything but cleaning confirms both Schwartz Cowan's findings (that domestic mechanization paradoxically increased the amount of time women spent on housework), and what scholars such as Jane Elliott see as Second-Wave Feminism's reduction of gender inequality to the confinement of white women to the home.[51]

This narrative use of the time-saving appliance to highlight Stepford—and by extension, Cold War America's—elision of the social, and its atomizing of women, is important. Indeed, it marks one of the crucial differences between the novel and its two film adaptations, by Bryan Forbes in 1975 and Frank Oz in 2004, in which references to industry or government are replaced by an emphasis on the mechanistic qualities of the Stepford wives *themselves*, including their capacity to malfunction.[52] I will be returning to Oz's adaptation of *The Stepford Wives* in Chapter 7, as it exemplifies the depoliticizing nostalgic turn that I argue characterizes depictions of housewifery and the mechanized home in postmillennial advertising and a significant proportion of period dramas. The Forbes adaptation's depiction of what happens when a Stepford wife breaks, however, is worth examining here, as it masterfully conveys the extent of the housewife's reification. In the film's penultimate scene, Joanna stabs Bobbie in the stomach in order to prove she isn't human. The knife disrupts Robot-Bobbie's hardware, interrupting her coffee-making process. She begins moving haltingly back and forth between kitchen counter and table, pouring ground coffee on the floor instead of in the machine and repeating, increasingly slowly and mechanically, "'How could you do a thing like that. . . When I was *just* going to give you *co*ffee?'" She ends up in a corner of the kitchen, knocking against the stove and refrigerator while her internal mechanism slowly grinds to a halt.

The narrative decision to depict the interruption of the smooth functioning of the housewife-robot's processes lays bare what Bill Brown would term her/its "thingness," which he argues confronts us when objects "stop working for us . . . when their flow within the circuits of production and distribution, consumption and exhibition, [is] arrested."[53] Where an object is characterized by our use of it for its intended purpose, a "thing" is characterized by the object's failure or breakage. In a later essay, in which he

---

[51] While ultimately I read Levin's novel more sympathetically than Elliott, hers is the most useful reading, to my mind, of both the novel and the film's engagements with the politics of time—which includes both time-saving and pastoral narratives of linear historical progress, in which the passage of time inherently leads to increased profits, economic growth, improved living standards, and greater equality, as if these factors were interdependent rather than mutually exclusive. Notably, Elliott reads Levin and Forbes's representation of "the temporality of housework [a]s by nature a form of static time," and the works themselves as exemplifying popular feminist discourse's power "to offer the American national imagination a flexible yet ideologically charged vocabulary for allegorizing both the apparent loss of historical progress and the possibility of its retrieval" ("Stepford USA: Second-Wave Feminism, Domestic Labor, and the Representation of National Time," *Cultural Critique* 70 (Fall 2008): 32–62. Citations on 43 and 34).

[52] Bryan Forbes, *The Stepford Wives* (Columbia Pictures, 1975); Frank Oz, *The Stepford Wives* (Paramount, 2004).

[53] Bill Brown, "Thing Theory," *Critical Inquiry* 28.1 (Autumn 2001), 1–22, citation on 3–4.

built on Igor Kopytoff's account of the African slave as the first commodity, Brown elaborated further that "the commodity form itself depends on 'the conversion of things into persons and the conversion of persons into things'" and that "the spectral completion of commodity fetishism (where things appear to have lives of their own) is human reification (where people appear to be no more than things)."[54] If the robot-wife's robotness is revealed when she/it stops working, this is also an allegory for women's reification more broadly. The Cold War housewife's status as a human appliance whose value is contingent upon her capacity to make coffee and exchange pleasantries with her guest is exposed when she malfunctions and her capacity to perform these tasks fails. At the same time, however, such a depiction obscures two things. Firstly, the racial dimension of the commodity fetish: that only *some* humans ever experienced literal commodification, and that the white middle-class housewife, while reified to some extent, was never exploited to the extent of a slave or a Black woman servant (despite the claims of GE's infamous 1934 ad denouncing women's "enslavement," discussed in the Introduction to this study). Secondly, the racial*ized* dimension of the housewife figure: that the figure of the modern housewife was white.

By contrast, that racial dimension forms a vital, if ultimately underdeveloped, strand of Levin's original novel, which involves Ruthanne's perception of the Stepford wives' mechanical qualities as specifically *white*—and their devotion to housework as an excuse not to socialize with a Black woman. This element, which both film adaptations erase, enables the text to highlight the imbrication of Cold War capitalism with white supremacy. It is likewise noteworthy that the ending leaves unclear whether Ruthanne will ultimately become a Stepford wife like the others: while her husband's decision to move the family to Stepford indicates a desire to join the white middle classes, the couple's shared sense of alienation (tellingly, both interpret the Stepford wives' mechanistic behavior as racism) might buffer them against the Stepford project. If one reading of the novel then is that to sustain itself white patriarchal capitalism will subsume, or integrate, racial "others" within it, another is that Civil Rights has a chance to correct Second-Wave Feminism's failures. Betty Friedan famously denounced Levin's novel as a "rip-off of the women's movement."[55] But *The Stepford Wives*' explicit framing of the Stepford wives as products of US imperialism and inextricable from social constructions of whiteness is a valuable critique that has arguably stood the test of time far better than Forbes' white-washed horror film.

[54] Bill Brown, "Reification, Reanimation and the American Uncanny," *Critical Inquiry* 32 (Winter 2006): 175–207; citation on 178.

[55] Judy Klemesrud, "Feminists Recoil at Film Designed to Relate to Them," *The New York Times* (February 26, 1975): 29.

5. "[P]erhaps Some Defective Appliance Somewhere in Suburban Anytown": Joanna Russ's *The Female Man* (1975) and *The Two of Them* (1978)

In this last section, we examine time-saving appliances in Joanna Russ's *The Female Man* (1975), which follows four versions of the same woman who each inhabit alternate realities: angry feminist Joanna, who lives in Manhattan in 1969 and whose name at once situates the author herself in the novel, and playfully references the protagonist of *The Stepford Wives*; Jeannine, who inhabits a 1969 in which the Great Depression never ended and the absence of economic growth precluded the birth of Second-Wave Feminism; Janet, a police officer living in a future called "While away" where men don't exist; and Jael Reasoner, an assassin from a future in which the two sexes are locked in an endless war against each other for world domination.[56] The time-saving appliances in this text are a reminder of the material conditions that affected (some) white women's capacity to do something other than housework, while a self-induced electric shock is revealed to be the source of Joanna's psychic splitting. Surprisingly, the prominence of appliances in the novel has gone unnoticed, even by scholars concerned with the text's engagements with automation and the future of technology.[57] Thus, while Susana Martin persuasively reads Whileaway as a technological utopia and for Heather Hicks the novel "historicizes and complicates Donna Haraway's conception of contemporary female workers as 'cyborgs,'" neither considers the significance of the novel's focus on specifically *domestic* technology, or its temporal ramifications.

A passage early in the novel describes Jeannine's return from a visit to Janet's Whileaway to an endless list of chores, which she must perform with barely functioning appliances. The radiator leaks, and:

> there are . . . encrustations of ice inside the old refrigerator (it has to be propped open with a chair to defrost itself). . . . Of course nobody helps. . . . Milk goes back in the refrigerator—no, wait a minute, throw it out—. . . She has to pack and make the lunch. . . . That means things coming out of the icebox again and mopping the table again—leaving footprints on the linoleum again. (*FM*, 103–5)

[56] Joanna Russ, *The Female Man* (London: Orion/Gollancz, 2010 [1975]). Henceforth, *FM*.

[57] Susana Martin, "Revising the Future in *The Female Man*," *Science Fiction Studies* 32.3 (November 2005): 405–22; Heather Hicks, "Automating Feminism: The Case of Joanna Russ's *The Female Man*," *Postmodern Culture* 9.3 (1999).

In its enumeration of domestic drudgery, the passage clearly echoes the language, style, and rhetoric of Russ's second-wave feminist contemporaries, discussed in Chapter 3. But it differs in its emphasis: rather than decrying the gendered nature of time-saving appliances, Russ focuses on the laboriousness of housework prior to frost-free refrigeration. The thawing refrigerator that leaks water on the floor and spoils its contents, so that Jeannine's morning is ultimately consumed with disposing of rotten food and mopping, conveys the time taken up by domestic work and which Janet on Whileaway instead literally "whiles away." This attention to early refrigeration anticipates Russ's claims in her later essay, "Science Fiction and Technology" (1978), that the "technophobia" apparent in sci-fi by male writers reflected the vast differences between men and women's material conditions: for women, the "non-technological past" was far from idyllic.[58]

Where Jeannine awakens every morning to new layers of dirt requiring cleaning, Jael Reasoner lives in a self-cleaning smart home named "House" surrounded by an electrified fence and equipped with a kitchen consisting of "an armchair with controls like a 707's" that renders other appliances obsolete (*FM*, 179). "House" is assisted by "Telephone" and "Phonograph," the capitalization of whose names contributes to the impression they are alive (*FM*, 179). This impression is amplified by Jael's overt objectification of Davy, her robot manservant: where "Telephone" and "Phonograph" are attributed personhood, this machine-man has been reduced to an appliance whose brain receives electronic alerts from "House's" central computer whenever Jael wants sex. And where Jeannine's narrative involves a domestic space whose malfunctioning gadgets continuously threaten to revert her home to the preindustrial era, Jael's narrative suggests one of the more extreme potential outcomes of combining the pursuit of efficiency with the desire to destroy the patriarchy: a mechanized world in which men are either killed or turned into Stepford husbands.

While the description of Jael's home initially appears an indictment of mechanization's nefarious potential, attention to the essay by Russ just mentioned suggests the merits of a more nuanced interpretation. Here, Russ defined technophilia as stemming from possession of or proximity to power, and technophobia as the scapegoating of modern industrial society by those who feel they have a right to control it. Both are male. By contrast, "women, non-whites, the poor" become neither technophiles nor technophobes, having neither proximity nor a sense of entitlement to power. From this perspective, Jael's automated house appended with a male sex-bot reads as neither a condemnation nor a utopian daydream

---

[58] Joanna Russ, "Science Fiction and Technology as Mystification," *Science Fiction Studies* 5.3 (November 1978): 16.

of automation but, rather, a *parody* of the technophilia of sci-fi by white male writers (where the prime function of artificial intelligence is to create female robots to provide sexual pleasure), the techno-utopian discourse of mid-century architecture and domestic technology from which such fiction borrowed and to which it contributed, and the technophobia of certain conservative strains of sci-fi by white male writers (Aldous Huxley, Philip K. Dick, John Wyndham) for whom, according to Russ, technology posed a threat to individual agency.

If Jeannine's old refrigerator is a reminder of the very material need for certain kinds of domestic technologies that by 1975 would be taken for granted, the smart home equipped with a male sex robot in these final pages

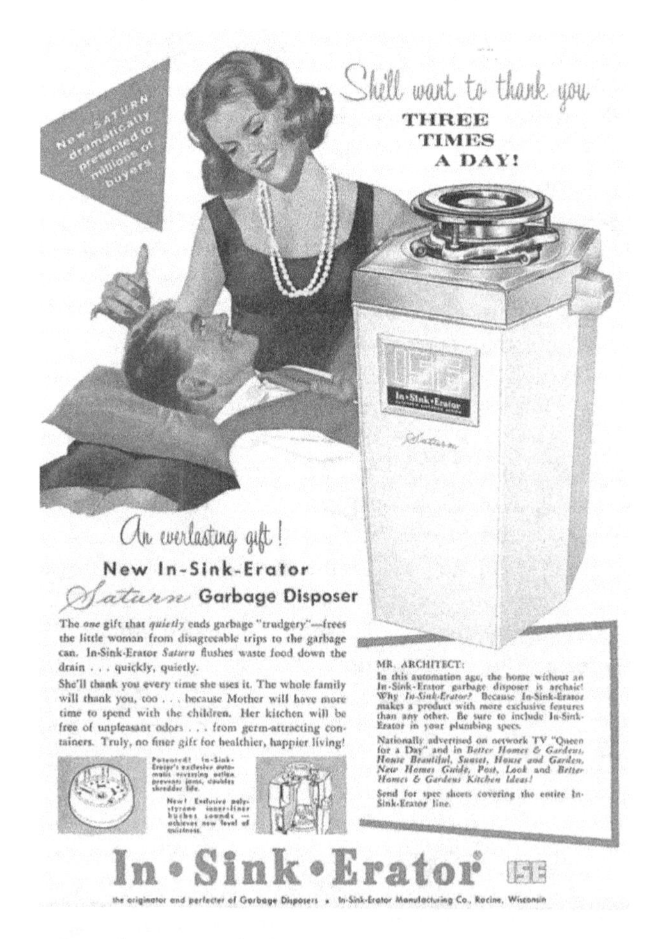

FIGURE 5.4 In-Sink-Erator. "She'll Want to Thank You THREE TIMES A DAY!" *The Architectural Forum* (August 1960): 227. Courtesy of In-Sink-Erator.

of the novel simultaneously inverts the trope of the mechanized housewife, and the femme-bot ubiquitous to sci-fi of the same period, and plays on the postwar era's reification of white middle-class women and conflation of them with their implements. In the early 1960s, In-Sink-Erator promised that if a man bought his wife a Saturn Garbage Disposer she would "want to thank [him] three times a day"—a quip whose double meaning hinged on the gadget's use after breakfast, lunch, and dinner, and the frequency with which the rested housewife would now want to have sex with her husband (Figure 5.4).[59] The foregrounding of the futuristically named Saturn over an illustration of a wife caressing her reclining husband's head obscured the bottom half of the man, and the wife's other arm, leaving to the imagination what she might be doing. By contrast, Jael's home is wired to do *all* the housework for her, and her man-appliance is wired to thank *her* . . . as many times a day as she likes. The self-cleaning house equipped with a vacuous male sex-bot responds both to the limitations of postwar appliances identified by Robert Heinlein's protagonist in *The Door to Summer* and to the objectification of housewives themselves by appliance advertising. Jael's reply to Janet, Jeannine, and Joanna's expressions of horror at this technology highlights the inevitability of women being blamed: "'Alas! those who were shocked at my making love that way [through anal penetration] to a man are now shocked at my making love to a machine; you can't win'" (*FM*, 192).

Finally, Russ mobilizes electrification a third way: to articulate Joanna's self-professed transformation into a "female man." This is the term Joanne uses, throughout the novel, to describe her embodiment of attributes, aspirations, and characteristics patriarchal society associates more commonly with those of the male gender and whose adoption is integral to women's liberation:

> To resolve contrarieties, unite them in your own person . . . take in your bare right hand one naked, severed end of a high-tension wire. Take the other in your left hand. Stand in a puddle. (Don't worry about letting go; you can't.) . . . When She sends the high voltage alone, well, we've all experienced those little shocks—you just shed it over your outside like a duck and it does nothing to you—but when She roars down in high voltage and high amperage both, She is after your marrow-bones; you are making yourself a conduit for holy terror and

[59] Feigning unawareness that the ad would appeal more to men than women, the company advertised its advertising strategy in the *NAHB Journal of Home Building* that same year, noting that "ONLY In-Sink-Erator talks the language of women—your best prospects—in big-space ads in magazines women read most . . . trust most. You know that a woman can make or break your sale" (*NAHB* 10.7–12 (1956)).

> the ecstasy of Hell. . . . Women are not used to power . . . but you are a strong woman, you are God's favorite, and you can endure. (*FM*, 134–5)

As in Eleanor Arnason's novel a decade later (which *The Female Man* likely inspired), a self-induced electric shock provides an allegory for the female protagonist's escape from gender constraints, conveying the shock, horror, pain, and ecstasy of such disavowal of established modes of being. This is reinforced by the statement that "Women are not used to power," which plays on the dual meaning of "power" as electric current, and as agency. Meanwhile the reference to "those little shocks" that "we've all experienced" and the higher voltage that renders one "a conduit for holy terror" is connotative of both the potentially brutal repercussions of self-assertion (electric-shock therapy) and the ecstasy of female orgasm—suggesting the erotic dimension of asserting one's dignity. Crucially, the transformation Joanna describes involves a rejection and transcendence of the very category of woman—and this is conveyed via the scene's elision of time-saving appliances, which Russ understands to be gendered objects. In allegorizing female emancipation as raw and untethered electric power (initially figured as a female-gendered current, but gradually divested of its pronouns), Russ "unplugs" both women and the idea of electricity from the network of signs and symbols of the postwar advertising landscape. In so doing, she extends the electrical imaginary beyond the strictures of the gender binary.[60]

Russ complicates these ideas in *The Two of Them* (1978), where protagonist Irene's longing to go back in time to 1953 centers on the image of an old Kelvinator:

> Only in a dream can one make the telephone ring over wires long since dismantled, on an instrument junked years ago, in a house long since torn down to make room for a parking lot, so that . . . the old Kelvinator next to the phone is a ghost [...] Young Mrs. Waskiewicz [Irene's long dead mother] stands in the kitchen in nineteen-fifty-three, looking out into the living room past the clunky old television set in its plastic case (new then)."[61]

[60] Jeanne Cortiel (212–14) and Amanda Boulter (151–66) provide particularly interesting readings of the rejection of gender categories in the novel, which usefully complicate interpretations of the novel as reinforcing transphobic stereotypes.

[61] Joanna Russ, *The Two of Them* (Middletown, CT: Wesleyan UP, 2005 [1978]), 116–17. Henceforth, *TOT*.

The passage reads as a comment on the nostalgic thrust of 1970s popular culture, which saw the release of the Broadway musical *Grease* (1972) and its cinematic adaptation (1978), *American Graffiti* (1973) and its TV series spin-off, *Happy Days* (1974–84), and magazine retrospectives on Marilyn Monroe, Elvis Presley, JFK, and what the June 16, 1972 cover story of *LIFE* magazine called "The Nifty Fifties."[62] The reference to the old Kelvinator and dead phone underscores the irretrievability of the past, which no time portal can access. More importantly, it underscores the distance between the cultural contexts of 1953, when the Kelvinator might have been old but the television was only recently invented, and the late 1970s, when such technologies have lost their futuristic charge, and the Vietnam War, the Pentagon Papers, Watergate, the Arab Oil Crisis, and frequent power outages have debunked the myth of undefeatable American ingenuity. Where Joanna in *The Female Man* moves through time and space and enlists different forms of electrification to forge a more equitable future for men and women, Irene's confrontation with the impossibility of going back is also a confrontation with the limits of the techno-utopianism originally embedded in the objects she longs to touch.

Russ's irretrievable Kelvinator is all the more compelling when examined alongside the appliance ads of the 1970s, which in contrast to the futuristic ads of earlier decades offset the triple threats of economic recession, Women's Liberation Movement, and Civil Rights by drawing on the past. A 1972 ad by Frigidaire featuring a sepia-toned photo of a crowd of people admiring a 1918 Frigidaire being pulled off the back of a horse-drawn carriage emphasized that "Antique Frigidaire refrigerators from decades ago can still be found in a number of homes. And they're not standing there as nostalgic memories."[63] GE ran a print campaign in 1978–9 in *LIFE*, *Better Homes and Gardens*, *House Beautiful*, *National Geographic*, and *EBONY* featuring four generations of white women standing alongside outdated refrigerator models—including the 1937 Monitor/Turret-Top model mentioned in *Ubik*—that for all their age were still running.[64] The fact that *EBONY*'s readers did not share

[62] Daniel Marcus, "The 1950s in the 1970s: Representations in a Cultural Revival," in *Happy Days and Wonder Years: The Fifties and the Sixties in Contemporary Cultural Politics* (New Brunswick, NJ: Rutgers UP, 2004), 9–35; Will Kaufman, *American Culture in the 1970s* (Edinburgh: Edinburgh UP, 2009); and Christine Sprengler, "Prone to Nostalgia: The 1950s in the 1970s," in *Screening Nostalgia: Populuxe Props and Technicolor Aesthetics in Contemporary American Film* (New York and Oxford: Berghahn Books, 2009), 46–8.

[63] Frigidaire, "In 1918 We Made the Only Frigidaire Refrigerator. We Still Do," *LIFE* (December 15, 1972): 83. Frigidaire denied permission to reproduce this ad, but it can be found online on various websites devoted to vintage ads.

[64] GE, "This 1937 GE Refrigerator's the Only One Mom's Ever Owned," *EBONY* (Aug. 1978): 53; "The Best Reason for Buying a New GE Refrigerator Is an Old GE Refrigerator," *EBONY*

the same heritage of appliance ownership as these white women went unacknowledged—while one wonders if the campaign itself was influenced by Dick's aforementioned depiction, in *Ubik*, of the "pay refrigerator's" regression back to a 1937 model. The irretrievable Kelvinator in Russ's novel at once challenges the techno-utopian optimism of earlier time-travel narratives, *and* the conservativism of the 1970s apparent in this period's appliance ads, while highlighting the culture of disposal that ads focused on product longevity seek to obfuscate: a product may well last forty years, but an entire media landscape exists to ensure the consumer disposes of it long before then. In so doing, Russ's text suggests the affinities between the concept of time travel and the accelerated lifespan of objects on which postwar consumerism depended—an acceleration inextricable from the commodification of time itself.

6. Conclusion

This chapter has traced the very different functions of time-saving appliances across a sample of sci-fi texts. Bradbury's "all-electric" home embodies the contradictions of a nation that celebrates time-saving solutions as much as the nuclear weaponry that threatens to render them redundant, while Merril's simultaneously expresses nuclear anxieties and neutralizes them. St. Clair's figuration of the time-saving appliance as a literal escape from reality parodies the rhetoric of magic enlisted by appliance manufacturers, while Reed subverts this same rhetoric and ultimately uses the time-*stopping* appliance as a weapon against the very norms it was meant to uphold. Tiptree's figuration of a man's rape by female aliens as an assault by a vacuum cleaner takes the conflation of housewives with their time-saving appliances to its most violent conclusion. Heinlein's depiction of an engineer on a time-traveling quest to rid the world of inefficiency reads as a parody of male ego—all the more so given the resemblance between the magazine stories about gadget-filled homes the protagonist decries and the article in *Popular Mechanics* about the home Heinlein himself designed. Likewise, Dick's time-warping doorstop appliance salesmen, and the framing of the ubiquitous all-encompassing commodity as a cleaning product capable of turning an outdated-appliance into the latest model, expose the "all-electric" home as embodying the most nefarious aspects of consumer capitalism. Finally, Russ's novels of the late 1970s complicate earlier critiques of the time-saving appliance as well as specific tropes

(May 1978): 132. Unfortunately, GE has denied permission to reproduce this ad, but it can be found online via the *EBONY* magazine archives, and on various websites including eBay.

common to sci-fi. Electricity both literally and figuratively is vital to the feminist project—while the reader attuned to the tropes common to time-travel narratives is primed to see through advertisers' efforts to conjure nostalgia for a past that never existed.

The time-saving appliances in these texts challenge Rita Felski's contention that "the vocabulary of modernity is the vocabulary of anti-home," revealing the extent to which the future of both the home and domesticity preoccupied mid-century sci-fi writers.[65] Attending to the imbrication of the literary appliances just discussed in networks of power (both literal and figurative), and their relation to specific discourses occurring at the time the texts in which they were published, provides important insights into one of sci-fi's enduring paradoxes: how a genre that for all its exploration of alternate universes, future societies, alien populations, and space travel, has yet to adequately resolve how the inhabitants of these temporally and spatially distant realities allocate and perform domestic labor.

[65] Rita Felski, *The Gender of Modernity* (Cambridge, MA: Harvard UP, 1995), 16.

6

"The Angel of Death Pushes a Vacuum Cleaner":[1]

Retrospective Appliances in Kurt Vonnegut and Don DeLillo, 1950–97

"There were many visions in the land, all fragments of the exploded dream, and some of the darkest of these visions were those processed in triplicate by our generals and industrialists," states David Bell, the narrating protagonist of Don DeLillo's first novel, *Americana* (1971).[2] According to Bell, "the dream of the good life" was merely a by-product of Cold War-era military-industrial collusion, "something else . . . left over for the rest of us, or some of the rest of us"—a qualifier that gestures to this "by-product's" exclusivity to the white middle classes (*A*, 129–30). This "left over" of imperialist aspiration, he notes, had great power:

> as a boy, and even later, quite a bit later, I believed all of it, the institutional messages, the psalms and placards, the pictures, the words. Better living through chemistry. The Sears, Roebuck catalog. Aunt Jemima. All the impulses of all the media were fed into the circuitry of my dreams. . . . One thinks of an image made in the image and likeness of images. (*A*, 129–30)

---

[1] Don DeLillo, "Baghdad Towers West," *Epoch* 17 (1968): 195–217. Citation on 198. Henceforth, *BTW*.

[2] Don DeLillo, *Americana* (London: Penguin, 2006 [1971]), 129. Henceforth, *A*.

Bell's articulation of the mutual constitution of corporate, military, and national identities chimes with Kurt Vonnegut's comments in an interview he gave that same year, where his quip that "'the Waring blender is not much help, the ABM [anti-ballistic missile] is not much help. . . . Maybe we could find better ways to comfort each other'" exposed the disingenuousness of Cold War America's framing of technology.[3] Both statements provide an apt starting point for analyzing the work of two authors for whom time-saving appliances provide a means to challenge official accounts of seminal events in the nation's history and, in broader terms, its sense of the past. As Theophilus Savvas notes, DeLillo's work exemplifies a tendency in post-1960s fiction to consider "history as an epistemological mode," and to "not just br[eak] down" the hierarchy between history and literature, but "question the very distinction between literature and history [on which] the hierarchy was necessarily premised."[4] Saavas's categorization provides a useful way into considering these authors' appliance depictions as obstacles intended to obstruct a tidy linear theory of history, techno-progressivism, and the manipulation of these by private enterprise.

The first three sections of this chapter focus on the depiction of time-saving appliances in a selection of texts by Vonnegut published between the early 1950s and 1990, with particular attention to *Slaughterhouse-Five* (1969). The influence on Vonnegut's work of GE, where his older brother worked as an atmospheric scientist, and in whose PR department he himself worked from 1947 to 1951, is well established—but the centrality to his fiction of GE's consumer products and the vision of "'Total Electric' living" promoted by *General Electric Theater*, for which he himself wrote two screenplays, remains overlooked.[5] My readings of Vonnegut reveal his fictional appliances to perform the opposite function of the didactic gadgets in the news stories he wrote for GE. They do this by challenging the narratives of American exceptionalism and triumphant linear progress on which the promotion of their real-life counterparts depended, and by unsettling GE and its competitors' claims to custodianship of the nation's history and future. Such critique is exemplified, perhaps, by the poem, "I have a kitchen / But it is not a complete kitchen / I will not be truly

---

[3] Richard Todd, "The Masks of Kurt Vonnegut" (1971), in *Conversations with Kurt Vonnegut*, ed. William Rodney Allen (Jackson, MS: UP of Mississippi, 1999 [1988]), 30–40. Citation on 39. Henceforth, *CWKV*.

[4] Theophilus Saavas, *American Postmodernist Fiction and the Past* (New York: Palgrave Macmillan, 2012), 2; 6.

[5] See in particular Ginger Strand, *The Brothers* Vonnegut; ch. 1 of Jerome Klinkowitz's *The Vonnegut Effect* (U of South Carolina Press, 2004) and *Kurt Vonnegut's America* (Columbia, SC: U of South Carolina Press, 2009); and Kevin Alexander Boon, *Kurt Vonnegut* (New York: Cavendish Square, 2013). The Ford Television Theater's *The Road Ahead* (1954) was based on Vonnegut's short story by the same title. Vonnegut also wrote the story for *D.P.* and the teleplay for *Auf Wiedersehen*, which aired on *General Electric Theater* in 1955 and 1958 respectively.

gay / Until I have a / Dispose-all," that a poet houseguest leaves scrawled "in what proved to be excrement" on the narrator's kitchen floor in *Cat's Cradle* (1963), and which foreshadows the novel's apocalyptic end.[6] Just as the pursuit of the thing that will "complete" the "all-electric" kitchen (the poem written in excrement) in fact devastates the current kitchen, the uncritical pursuit of progress by the atomic researcher at the "General Forge and Foundry Company" (who Vonnegut based on GE researcher and atomic theorist Dr. Irving Langmuir) results in the world-ending *ice-nine*.[7] Vonnegut provides a particularly interesting case for our purposes, insofar as his scathing indictment of time-saving appliances' use in obscuring inequality and exploitation coexists with an appreciation for the scientific processes that rendered them possible. This coexistence reflects a similar tension between his university studies in chemistry and his participation in its mystification while writing for GE, and between his upbringing in the 1930s, when, as he put it, "'Chemistry was [...] a magic word,'" and his first-hand experiences of war, when the Germans, too, "'had chemistry, and were going to take apart the universe and put it together again'" (*CWKV*, 34). These competing visions frequently lead Vonnegut to give greater credence to both technology in general and time-saving appliances in particular than some of his contemporaries. As he noted in "Science Fiction," an essay first published in 1965, "The feeling persists that no one can simultaneously be a respectable writer and understand how a refrigerator works."[8]

Sections 4–6 instead re-dress the absence of critical attention to the role of time-saving appliances in DeLillo—a near-silence that can be explained at least in part by DeLillo scholars' tendency to group his objects under the sign of either the commodity or its inverse, waste.[9] While these two tendencies have yielded important readings of the author's figuration of late capitalism's shaping of both subject-object and social relations, including

---

[6] Kurt Vonnegut, *Cat's Cradle* (London: Viking Penguin, 1986 [1963]), 53. Henceforth, CC.
[7] Susan Farrell, "A 'Nation of Two': Constructing Worlds through Narrative in the Work of Kurt Vonnegut," in *Imagining Home: American War Fiction from Hemingway to 9/11* (New York: Camden House, 2017), 77.
[8] Kurt Vonnegut, "Science Fiction," *The New York Times Book Review* (September 5, 1965): 87.
[9] See, for example, Stephen N. doCarmo, "Subjects, Objects, and the Postmodern Differend in Don DeLillo's *White Noise*," *LIT: Literature Interpretation Theory* 11.1 (2000): 1–33; Molly Wallace, "'Venerated Emblems': DeLillo's *Underworld* and the History-Commodity," *Critique* 42.4 (2001): 367–83. Notable examples of the vast scholarship on waste in DeLillo include Ruth Heyler, "'Refuse Heaped Many Stories High': DeLillo, Dirt and Disorder," *Modern Fiction Studies* 45 (1999): 987–1006; Joseph Dewey, Steven G. Kellman, and Irving Malin, eds., *Under/Words* (Newark: U of Delaware Press, 2002); Andrzej Antoszek, "'Who Will Clean Up All This Waste?' Post-Cold War America in Don DeLillo's *Underworld*," in *Post-Cold War Europe, Post-Cold War America*, ed. Ruud Janssens and Rob Kroes (Amsterdam: VU UP, 2004), 171–7; Mary Foltz, "Waste as Weapon: Fecal Bombing in Don DeLillo's Underworld," in *Contemporary American Literature and Excremental Culture: American Sh*t* (New York: Palgrave Macmillan, 2020), 179–218.

extensive demonstrations of how his work anticipated Baudrillard's theories of the "hyperreal" and the "simulacrum," and the ways in which domestic technology participates in rendering waste and dirt invisible, they also deny some important specificities.[10] I argue that DeLillo's appliance depictions communicate *more* than the interchangeability of human beings, their possessions, and the mediated images designed to whet consumer appetites. Rather, they remind us of the connections between the time-saving appliance, those communication devices that project commercial messages to promote its very sale, and the narrative formulae of those messages. To attend to the relations between DeLillo's time-saving appliances is to be confronted by the ways in which the refrigerator, toaster, vacuum cleaner, and so on are connected to each other both via the electric grid and in an artificial constellation of meaning centering on an abstract notion of family constructed by government, manufacturers and advertisers. As Baudrillard argued in *The Consumer Society*, published in French the year before *Americana*, objects' main function under consumer capitalism is to participate in an "infinite signifying chain" in which each object reinforces the need for the next associated object, and all reinforce the owner's status as an owner of both objects in the abstract, and of these *particular* objects.[11] DeLillo's appliance depictions not only support this reading, and Baudrillard's assertion that the purchase, obsolescence, and disposal of products under Fordism replaced day/night and biological birth and death as the most influential markers of time's passage. The subject-object relations depicted in his texts suggest the time-saving appliance's attraction lies in the intimation of immortality (or at least death deferral) inherent to the very promise of "time-saving." The appliances in my chosen texts reveal the atomization and alienation behind the façade of familial bliss on which both US Cold War ideology and the Cold War economy depended until the early 1970s—as exemplified by the description, in *End Zone* (1972), of a college football player called Norgene named after his uncle Gene, a military captain, and "'an old Norge refrigerator'" that was "'out on the back porch waiting to get thrown away,'" and whose death in an automobile accident is a reminder that, like his name, "nothing is too absurd to happen in America."[12] In exposing the marriage between the name of a military captain and an appliance manufacturer that during the Second World War

[10] See, for example, John N. Duvall, "From Valparaiso to Jerusalem: DeLillo and the Moment of Canonization," *Modern Fiction Studies* 45.3 Don DeLillo Special Issue (Fall 1999): 559–68; Marc Schuster, *Don DeLillo, Jean Baudrillard, and the Consumer Conundrum* (Amherst, NY: Cambria Press, 2008); and John Hodgkins, "An Epidemic of Seeing: DeLillo, Postmodernism, and Fiction in the Age of Images," in *The Drift: Affect, Adaptation, and New Perspectives on Fidelity* (London: Bloomsbury, 2013), 53–76.

[11] Jean Baudrillard, *The Consumer Society*, transl. C.T. (London and Los Angeles: Sage, 2017 [1998]). Originally published in French as *La Societé de Consummation* in 1970.

[12] Don DeLillo. *End Zone* (New York: Penguin, 1972), 13.

produced bullets and gun turrets, Norgene's origin story serves as an allegory for the military-industrial complex and the myths that obscured its workings (Gantz 2015, 172). I then complicate this argument by reading certain few of DeLillo's appliance depictions as marking a further shift in the history of the "all-electric" home that accompanied, and was indeed a result of, the supplanting of Keynesianism by neoliberalism, and the attendant shift from a culture of conformity to one of heightened individualism. Put differently, the intimation of immortality of "time-saving" is also an intimation of neoliberal "always on-ness"—as exemplified by the refrigerator itself, which is always running, and the *sound* of whose working embeds itself in the user's subconscious as a perpetual reminder of the network of production and consumption of which s/he is a part.[13]

1. "Nothing Would Do But It Be Followed by Miracles": Vonnegut's *Breakfast of Champions* (1973) and *Hocus Pocus* (1990)

In contrast to many of the appliance depictions examined in this study, Vonnegut's are supremely comical. The titular narrator of his 1987 novel, *Bluebeard: The Autobiography of Rabo Karabekian (1914–1988)*, explains the strident optimism of postwar consumerism as an inevitable result of the war's horrors, wherein "nothing would do but that it be followed by miracles": namely, instant coffee, DDT, and nuclear energy. The public's unwavering faith in technological progress, and the acceptance of "miraculous new fibers which could be washed in cold water and need no ironing afterwards!" as evidence that the war was "well worth fighting!" are traumatic responses—an effort to justify mass death and destruction.[14] In *Breakfast of Champions* (1973) and *Hocus Pocus* (1990), Vonnegut extends these ideas to critique the disproportionate influence of companies like GE on government policy and the reinforcement of narratives of American exceptionalism.

In *Breakfast of Champions*, Vonnegut enlists an advertising campaign by a company based on GE, the "Robo-Magic Corporation of America," to illustrate corporate America's reliance on the United States' foundational myths.[15] The unnamed narrator's opening clarification, that the writers of the Constitution that "became a beacon for freedom to human beings

---

[13] I am grateful to Stephen Shapiro for his insights into the relationship between refrigeration and neoliberal work during our conversations about this chapter.

[14] Kurt Vonnegut, *Bluebeard* (New York: Bantam Doubleday Dell, 1998 [1987]). Henceforth, *B*.

[15] Kurt Vonnegut, *Breakfast of Champions* (London: Vintage, 2000 [1973]), 54. Henceforth, *BOC*.

everywhere else" actually "used human beings for machinery," and his subsequent debunking of the lyrics of the national anthem, foreshadows his elucidation in the novel's last pages of the Robo-Magic Corporation's racist history (*BOC*, 11). The Robo-Magic washing machine's claims to emancipate white middle-class women by providing a mechanical alternative to their unreliable Black servants (a recurring promise in GE's early ads) is proven to be no different to the claims, by a nation founded on genocide and slave labor, to be a global model for humane government. The demystification of the "Robo-Magic Corporation of America's" slogan, "Good-bye Blue Monday," follows a similar structure. Having introduced the slogan in the novel's first pages as the single enduring aspect of an organization whose name and business have changed innumerable times since its founding, and as a statement inexplicably written "on a five-hundred-pound bomb . . . dropped on Hamburg, Germany" during the Second World War, Vonnegut only reveals the company's foundational purpose (manufacturing washing machines) in the novel's last pages (*BOC*, 42–3; 242). The appliance manufacturer's imbrication with weapons production underscores the frankly secondary importance of its original product concept. By the time the narrator explains the motto's genesis, it has already been tainted by its association with the bombing of Hamburg.

The narrator's demystification of this foundational narrative also warrants examining. The Robo-Magic motto "cleverly confused two separate ideas people had about Monday," he explains: Monday's negative associations for workers, and "that women traditionally did their laundry on Monday" (*BOC*, 243). The motto conflated these, suggesting that women hated doing laundry. This exposure of the truth behind the Robo-Magic's foundational myth reverberates with the "clever confusions" of US history clarified in the novel's opening pages, while highlighting a further level of exploitation. The narrator's claim that women "did [their laundry] any time they felt like it," including on Christmas Eve, when protagonist Dwayne H. Hoover's mother would announce that it was "'Time to do the N***** work,'" both underscores the continuous nature of housework, which as feminist historians have shown is "never done," and, too, the racism underlying white women's resentment of such work (*BOC*, 244).[16] Meanwhile, the narrator's recollection that when he was growing up, "The white men . . . called it *women's work*, and the women called it N***** work,'" is but one of many references in the novel, both implicit and explicit, to the washing machine's role in the transition from slave ownership and the employment of multiple servants to modern housewifery—and to negotiating a hierarchy which always sees Black women at the bottom (*BOC*, 245).

[16] See Strasser, *Never Done*; Cowan, *More Work for Mother*; and Cox et al., *Dirt*.

Via these remarks, Vonnegut throws into relief time-saving appliances' debt to nineteenth-century abolitionists, whose main reason for campaigning to end slavery, as the narrator argued in the novel's opening pages, was based not on humanitarian values but the belief that the nation's economic future depended on the "machines made of metal" that would replace "machines made out of meat" (*BOC*, 72). Indeed, as the narrator explains, Robo-Magic's founder Fred T. Barry predicted that "Robo-Magic appliances of various sorts would eventually do what he called 'all the N***** work of the world,' which was lifting and cleaning and cooking and washing and ironing and tending children and dealing with filth" (*BOC*, 245). This displacement was central to the Robo-Magic's original advertising campaign, in which a caricature of a Black maid with "eyes popping out in a comical way" looked with horror upon a washing machine being delivered to her employer's house (*BOC*, 245). A speech bubble revealed her thoughts: "'Feets, Get movin'! Dey's got theirselves a Robo-Magic! Dey ain't gonna be needin' us 'roun' here no mo''" (*BOC*, 245). Barry's manifesto and the ad copy featuring a gross imitation of Black patois communicated the washing machine's capacity to remove the "inconvenience" of Black people framed as backward.

The racist rhetoric of this fictional ad echoed that of actual appliance ads of the 1930s, which, as discussed in the Introduction to this study and Chapter 4, relied on the dehumanization and reification of Black Americans. GE's description of its Hotpoint mixer as "A servant with grand references" looking for "a job in your kitchen" (1933) implicitly positioned the time-saving appliance as a more reliable alternative to the new population of Black servants from the South whom white Northern women perceived to be too "primitive" to operate electrical appliances.[17] In Kelvinator's "Four Refrigerators in One Cabinet" (1935), the white woman of the house explained the attributes of her new refrigerator to her Mammy-like Black servant; the overlaying of an image of the adoring servant on the bottom left corner of a larger image of her white employer conveyed the former's lower status to both employer and appliance.[18] But Vonnegut's Robo-Magic ad most resembles a 1937 ad for GE's combined dishwasher, sink, and garbage disposal unit. The ad featured an illustration of a grinning, heavyset Black maid modeled on the enslaved Mammy archetype made famous by the logo of Aunt Jemima Pancakes (itself based on the titular character of a late-nineteenth-century minstrel song) and, later, by "Mammy" in the cinematic

[17] GE, "A Servant with Grand References Wants a Job in Your Kitchen!" *Good Housekeeping* (June 1933), 121; Hay, 115; Wolcott, 82.

[18] Kelvinator, "Yes, Mam, That's Right. We Sure Do Need *Four Refrigerators!*," *Good Housekeeping* (June 1935): 176. Unfortunately, Electrolux (which bought Frigidaire and Kelvinator in 1986) has denied permission to reproduce this ad, but it can be found online on various websites devoted to vintage print advertisements, as well as on my website, https://www.racheledini.com.

adaptation of *Gone With the Wind* (1939).[19] The Black maid standing over the unit and crowing, "'I'se Sure Got a Good Job NOW,'" positions the GE appliance as a *humane* purchase for the enlightened white housewife to bestow upon her grateful Black underlings.[20] Vonnegut's Robo-Magic ad renders explicit the subtext of "'I'se Sure Got a Good Job NOW'": be grateful, or be replaced. It is also significant that Vonnegut's stand-in for General Electric is a manufacturer of washing machines specifically, rather than appliances generally. For the washing machine provides a powerful allegory for propaganda's role in *laundering* reality. The Robo-Magic Corporation of America serves as a critique of corporate advertising's role in cleansing American imperialism of its negative associations in a rhetorical strategy that mirrors the nation's own history of ethnic cleansing of indigenous people. The machine that removes unseemly dirt to render clothing whiter than white is an apt allegory for an empire based on both racial othering (the treatment of indigenous people and ethnic minorities as "dirty" elements to be removed) and the *denial* of such othering.

Vonnegut enlists the Robo-Magic Company again in *Hocus Pocus* (1990) to critique the speed with which appliance manufacturers shifted to manufacturing weapons during the Second World War.[21] Narrating protagonist Eugene Debs Hartke recounts how Robo-Magic invested in researching "bomb-release mechanisms" so that by the war's end it "had gotten out of the washing-machine business entirely, had changed its name," and was making weapon parts (*HP*, 19). The appliance company's seamless transition from manufacturing domestic machinery to replace Black labor to manufacturing death machines exemplifies the "hocus-pocus" the novel seeks to expose. Indeed, the text next makes a direct connection between the seemingly benign domestic sphere and the state penal system. Following a prison break near his home, Eugene Debs Hartke (whose name is a nod to the famous socialist) invites three elderly convicts back to his house where a power outage obliges them to make a meal without the aid of appliances (*HP*, 222). Hartke's earlier quip, that the convicts have "at least" been spared "that great invention by a dentist, the electric chair" (a reference to dentist and inventor Alfred P. Southwick), reverberates in the following pages, ameliorating not only their life sentence but their more recent lot in a home divested of electrical comforts (Brandon, 15).

---

[19] See M. M. Manring, *Slave in a Box: The Strange Career of Aunt Jemima* (U of Virginia Press, 1998); Andrea Powell Wolfe, *Black Mothers and the National Body Politic: The Narrative of Positioning of the Black Maternal Body from the Civil War Period through the Present* (New York: Lexington Books, 2021); Micki McElya, *Clinging to Mammy: The Faithful Slave in Twentieth-century America* (Cambridge, MA: Harvard UP, 2007), esp. 15–37.

[20] GE, "I'se Sure Got a Good Job NOW," *Fortune* (January 1937): N.P. Unfortunately, GE has denied permission to reproduce this ad, but it can be found online via the *EBONY* magazine archives, and on various websites including eBay.

[21] Kurt Vonnegut, *Hocus Pocus* (London: Vintage, 2000 [1990]), 64. Henceforth, *HP*.

The unusual emphasis placed on the absence of electricity so soon after the detailed description of the prison riots has a leveling effect, resulting in the bizarre equating of malfunctioning appliances with civic unrest (*HP*, 221). Meanwhile the framing of the electric chair as an invention by a dentist refers back to the novel's opening pages, which recounted another character, Elias Tarkington's, invention of "a mobile field kitchen" that "with slight modifications, would later be adopted by the Barnum & Bailey Circus, and then by the German Army during World War I" (*HP*, 9). The malfunctioning "all-electric" home, electric chair, and mobile field kitchen used by both the circus and the German Army allegorize the connections between the vocabulary of electricity used in promoting the "all-electric" home, and its use by the state apparatus, corporate power, an entertainment company infamous for its central role in "mold[ing] contemporary ideologies concerning race, eugenics, and American exceptionalism," and the similarly imperialist project of the German Second Reich.[22] The language of electrical power is all too easily molded to fit imperialist aims—and the language of time-saving, to fit totalizing narratives of linear progress.

2. All-Powerful Vacuum Cleaners: Vonnegut's *God Bless You Mr. Rosewater* (1965), *Dead-Eye Dick* (1982), and *Galapagos* (1985)

The violent themes just described are especially evident in Vonnegut's depictions of one particular time-saving appliance: the vacuum cleaner, which surfaces in *God Bless You Mr. Rosewater* (1965), *Dead-Eye Dick* (1982), and, as an analogy, in *Galapagos* (1985). In the first of these, Fred Rosewater's wife Caroline's decision to leave her Electrolux around the house for him to trip on "like a pet anteater with a penchant for sleeping in doorways or on the staircase," and to "never put the vacuum cleaner away until she [i]s rich," parodies the more benign scenes of physical comedy involving appliances that featured in sitcoms and variety shows of the period.[23] The passage fuses slapstick, the stuff of sitcoms, elements of the comedy of errors, and a kind of anti-advertising ethos. One thinks, here, of Dick Van Dyke and Chuck McCann's portrayal of Laurel and Hardy as hapless vacuum-cleaner salesmen in "The Vacuum Cleaner," a sketch that aired on the *Chevy Showroom* in 1958, or the toast that in *Ozzie*

---

[22] Janet M. Davis, *The Circus and American Culture at the Turn of the Century*, Vol. 2 (Madison, WI: U of Wisconsin Press, 1998), 262.
[23] Kurt Vonnegut, *God Bless You, Mr. Rosewater* (London: Vintage, 1992 [1965]), 95; 98. Henceforth, *GBYMR*.

and Harriet (S13E05, 1958) jumps out of the toaster in alarm when Wally Plumstead uncharacteristically announces plans to get a job.[24] Or, indeed, Laura Petrie's quip in *The Dick Van Dyke Show* (S05E02, 1965), when her husband asks, "'What was that?,'" thinking he has heard the telephone ring: "'The refrigerator defrosting. You wanna answer it?'"[25] In these episodes, the appliance's personification is comical but benign, and either obscures or reaffirms the gender inequities between male and female characters. In Vonnegut's text, by contrast, the vacuum cleaner's conspiring with the frustrated housewife, while comical, underscores the novel's broader preoccupation with unfulfillment. The housewife here uses the Electrolux to express her "convic[tion] that she [i]s cut out for better things" and to *literally* save time by not vacuuming at all—making the Electrolux part of the mess itself (*GBMR*, 95).

The pregnant Mrs. Metzger in *Dead-Eye Dick* (1982) meanwhile is only saved from vacuuming when she is accidentally killed by the male narrator, who aimed a gun out of the window just to experience shooting.[26] The text positions Mrs. Metzger as a necessary casualty of a young man's rite of passage, while the assertion that her family on the floor below only "became worried" because "the vacuum cleaner went on running and running without being dragged around at all" conveys their conflation of her with her machine (*DED*, 72). The narrator's question, "What, incidentally, was a pregnant mother of two doing, operating a vacuum cleaner on Mother's Day? She was practically asking for a bullet between the eyes, wasn't she?," enlists the vacuum cleaner in blaming the victim in a manner that ironically plays on the inevitability of a woman being in the wrong—even after she is dead (*DED*, 76). The woman who dies while vacuuming—on Mother's Day, no less!—literalizes the postwar advertising landscape's image of the housewife wedded to her gadgets "until death do they part." A later description of Mrs. Metzger's daughter "who found her mother dead and vacuum cleaner still running so long ago," extends the traumatic effects of this murder from the narrator to the victim's daughter, thus reaffirming Mrs. Metzger's status as an appendage of other people's dramas (*DED*, 118). Meanwhile the placement of "mother dead" and "vacuum cleaner still running" alongside each other blurs the distinction between human and object—particularly since the latter has outlasted the former!

Vonnegut's most surreal vacuum cleaner however is in *Galapagos* (1985).[27] The novel recounts the events, beginning with a stock market crash and the

---

[24] "The Vacuum Cleaner," *The Chevy Showroom* Season 1, Episode 4 (July 24, 1958); "A Letter of Recommendation," *The Ozzy and Harriet Show* Season 13, Episode 5 (October 14, 1964).

[25] "A Farewell to Writing," *The Dick Van Dyke Show* Season 5, Episode 2 (September 22, 1965).

[26] Kurt Vonnegut, *Deadeye Dick* (New York: Random House, 1999 [1982]), 68–72. Henceforth, *DED*.

[27] Kurt Vonnegut, *Galapagos* (London: Flamingo, 1994 [1985]). Henceforth, *G*.

marooning of a nature cruise called *La Bahía de Darwin* off the Galapagos islands, that in 1986 resulted in the evolution of humans, over the next million years, into brainless fur-covered flipper-clad animals. It is narrated by the ghost of Leo Trout (son of Vonnegut's recurring character Kilgore Trout), who continues to haunt earth despite having died long ago, and who repeatedly refers to the death of specific characters as their facing "the blue tunnel into the afterlife." It is only in the novel's final pages, as Kilgore Trout's ghost attempts to cajole Leo back into the afterlife, that Leo elucidates that the blue tunnel is "what I liken to a vacuum cleaner," and that "If there is indeed suction within the blue tunnel, it is filled with a light much like that cast off by the electric stoves and ovens of the *Bahía de Darwin*"—appliances to which he has referred elsewhere in the novel to at once convey the ship passengers' self-sufficiency and the ludicrousness of their plight (*G*, 202). The passengers have, for example, stuffed a corpse into the ship kitchen's walk-in freezer (an event which the text references three times) and roasted a pet dog in the oven (*G*, 197; 203; 210; 195).

The figuration of the conduit to the afterlife as an illuminated vacuum cleaner contributes to the novel's broader parody of both Christian theology and the promises of "miraculous" results and "unparalleled power" so ubiquitous to appliance ads. Indeed, it throws into relief the parallels *between* theology and appliance advertising. Both claim to save—be it time, money, effort, or one's very soul—via a rhetoric that aligns cleanliness, electrical power, and godliness. Thus, Leo links his father's strength to his ability to "stand right in the nozzle and chat with me" regardless of the vacuum cleaner-like blue tunnel's suction (*G*, 202). In comparing the Godly light in the tunnel to the afterlife to electric lighting, Vonnegut playfully inverts the historical comparison of electricity to the otherworldly in a manner that conveys technology's elevation above the status of God.

This parallel is also evident in Leo's account of the ghost of his neighbor Naomi Tharp, who looked after him as a child, and who now enjoins him, from the end of the nozzle, to "'be a good boy now'" and "'come in here just like you used to come in through my kitchen door. . . . You don't want to be left out there for another million years'" (*G*, 202; 207). The image of the dead housewife urging the neighbor's son to crawl through the vacuum-cleaner nozzle to the kitchen of heaven delightfully parodies the didactic stories disseminated by both Sunday schools and the General Electric Home Economics Institute.

Leo's enlisting of appliance imagery a million years after human beings have lost the capacity to handle objects underscores the endurance of the "all-electric" home's symbolic charge. But more importantly, Leo's vacuum cleaner offers what neither Caroline Rosewater's implement of protest, nor Mrs. Metzger's witness to her own murder, nor any of the time-saving appliances in postwar ads can: direct access to the afterlife, where the very notions of time-saving, housework, or indeed dirt are presumably moot.

3. From House of Slaughter to House of Magic: Vonnegut's *Slaughterhouse-Five* (1969) and "Jenny" (*ca.* 1950)

Slaughterhouse-Five (1969) responds to the didacticism of GE, GM, and Ford's "all-electric" displays at the 1964 World's Fair by associating time-saving appliances not with a progress-filled future but rather with the corpses of wartime prisoners, the remains of Jewish concentration camp victims, and extra-terrestrial zoos in which Americans are held captive in "all-electric" homes for the entertainment of their alien hosts.[28] Attending to Vonnegut's repurposing of the objects of the "all-electric" home and the rhetoric used to sell it throws into relief the extent to which the text's humor is premised on the harrowing subversion of the narrative formulae of mid-century television sitcoms, and particularly the ridiculing of such programs' elevation of time-saving appliances to the status of characters.

Slaughterhouse-Five tells the story of Billy Pilgrim, a chaplain's assistant who the narrator, former GE publicity man Yon Yonson, met when the two were interned by the Germans in a labor camp in Dresden. Due to either a unique capacity to time travel or severe post-traumatic stress disorder, Pilgrim experiences time asynchronously. The reader thus follows him back and forth between his travel by freight train to Dresden, his survival of its bombing by taking shelter in the titular slaughterhouse, various psychiatric internments, and his capture by extraterrestrials from the planet Trafalmadore, where linear time does not exist. References to the "all-electric" home occur throughout the novel, each critiquing domestic electrification's status in the postwar American imagination, while revealing the links between the titular slaughter "house" and the "House of Magic" that GE professed to be (see Chapter 5). The top of a washing machine during a friend's party in 1961 is the site of Billy Pilgrim's "only" extramarital dalliance; the light on his daughter's Princess Telephone is the only witness to his nighttime kidnapping by the Trafalmadorians; a vibrating electric blanket called "Magic Fingers" lulls him whenever he is overcome by one of his inexplicable weeping fits; and for "marrying a girl nobody in his right mind would have married," he receives from her grateful father "an all-electric home" (*SF*, 33; 53; 45; 86). The blanket that appears to masturbate the unhappily married trauma survivor is especially comical when read alongside the ad copy for GE's Two-Control Automatic Blanket, which in describing it as the "'Happy Marriage' blanket," implied the object's power

[28] Kurt Vonnegut, *Slaughterhouse-Five* (London: Vintage, 2000 [1969]). Henceforth, *SF*.

to resolve differences beyond conflicting temperature needs.[29] The Pilgrims' appliances' involvement in illicit sex, kidnapping by aliens, the cure of unmentionable psychiatric disorders resulting from a war it has taken the narrator twenty-five years to write about, and a transactional marriage, fundamentally undermines their status as emblems of familial happiness or normalcy.

More broadly, time-saving appliances in *Slaughterhouse-Five* are framed as both participants in and symptoms of national delusion. This is most apparent in four interconnected scenes. In the first, Yonson visits his old war friend Bernard O'Hare to enlist help for his Dresden memoir. As the two men sit in the kitchen, Bernard's wife Mary "fixe[s] herself a Coca-Cola, ma[king] a lot of noise banging the ice-cube tray in the stainless steel sink," "mov[es] furniture around to work off her anger," and returns for another Coke, "tak[ing] another tray of ice cubes from the refrigerator [and] ban[ging] it in the sink, even though there was already plenty of ice out," before finally expressing the reasons for her rage:

> "You'll pretend [in your book that] you were men instead of babies, and you'll be played in the movies by Frank Sinatra and John Wayne or some of those other glamorous, war-loving, dirty old men. And war will look just wonderful, so we'll have a lot more of them." (*SF*, 10–11)

The housewife's tactic of trafficking to and from the refrigerator to express opposition to a system against which she has no power is rendered all the more harrowing given its resemblance to comparable appliance-centered gags in sitcoms such as *I Love Lucy* (1951–7), *Bewitched* (1964–72), *The Donna Reed Show* (1958–66), and the later *Rhoda* (1974–8). In these, the "cross" housewife comically performed her "annoyance" with her husband by banging pots, pans, and surfaces in the kitchen, before the inevitable reconciliation accompanied by a laugh track.[30] This similarity is particularly pronounced in Yonson's quip that "We tried to ignore Mary and remember the war," and his explanation to the reader: "So then I understood. It was war that made her so angry. She didn't want her babies or anybody else's babies killed in wars. And she thought wars were partly encouraged by

[29] GE, "'You're Never Too Cold... Never Too Warm,'" *Saturday Evening Post* (November 12, 1955): 97. Unfortunately, GE denied permission to reproduce this ad but it can be found online.

[30] In "Sales Resistance," Lucy attempts to resell a vacuum cleaner she impulsively purchased from a door-to-door salesman before Ricky finds out (*I Love Lucy*, S02E17, 1953). The arrival of Samantha's mother and aunt via the refrigerator is a recurring gag in *Bewitched*, playing on the stereotype of invasive in-laws. In "Parent's Day," Rhoda's mother deals with her anger by vacuuming in the middle of the night and wins arguments by drowning out dissenting views with her vacuum cleaner (Rhoda, S01E44, 1974). See also Kristi Rowan Humphreys, *Housework and Gender in American Television* (Lanham, MD: Rowman & Littlefield, 2016).

books and movies" (*SF*, 11). The phrasing of the latter, which adroitly—and intentionally—simplifies the source of Mary's pain, recalls nothing so much as the voice-over of *Leave It to Beaver* or *Ozzy and Harriet*, which (as discussed in Chapter 2), GE sponsored throughout the 1950s and 1960s, and which, contrary to Mary's interactions with the refrigerator, sought to portray the "all-electric" kitchen and its manufacturers in a favorable light. The novel's reduction of the housewife's anger against patriarchy's idealization of war to opposition to "babies being killed" and movies that "partly encourage" wars highlights the sitcom genre's reduction of gender tensions to sound bites. What others have read as Vonnegut's "gallows humour," "black humour," and "slapstick modernism" is in fact best understood as an ironic repurposing of the sitcom that in contrast to Cheever and Yates's efforts to reaffirm the power of literary realism serves, here, to expose postwar popular culture's concerted circumlocution of the topic of war in favor of formulaic narratives in which the worst that befalls a family is a comical squabble whose only casualty is a smashed ice cube.[31]

That Vonnegut is intentionally subverting the meanings of the "all-electric" home in his description of Mary's anger becomes apparent when one considers the references to the New York World's Fair of 1964 that bracket this scene. Having introduced his visit to Bernard as occurring in "whatever the last year was for the New York World's Fair," Yonson circles back to the event, noting that upon leaving the O'Hares' home he took his children to the Fair to "s[ee] what the past had been like, according to the Ford Motor Car Company and Walt Disney [and] what the future would be like, according to General Motors" (*SF*, 8; 13). As Michael Smith has shown, GE, GM, Ford, and Westinghouse's displays at the 1964 World's Fair, whose theme was "Understanding through Peace," were integral to the companies' efforts to position themselves as sponsors of the future.[32] Displays such as GM's "Futurama II," conceived by Disney engineers, were "three-dimensional advertisements that sold . . . ways of life receptive to the necessity of [the brands'] products" (Smith, 225). By situating objects in this "consumer-based narrative of progress," Smith argues, "time itself became commodified": time-saving appliances insinuated themselves into "leading roles" in a "pageant of progress" divested of any potentially threatening

[31] Jerome Klinkowitz, "How to Die Laughing: Kurt Vonnegut's Lessons for Humor," *Studies in American Humor* new series 3.26 (2012): 15–19; Will Kaufman, "What's So Funny about Richard Nixon? Vonnegut's 'Jailbird' and the Limits of Comedy," *Journal of American Studies* 41.3 (December 2007): 623–39; Joanna Gavins, *Reading the Absurd* (Edinburgh: Edinburgh UP, 2013), 112–18; William Solomon, *Slapstick Modernism: Chaplin to Kerouac to Iggy Pop* (Chicago, IL: U of Illinois Press, 2016), 179–206.

[32] Michael L. Smith, "Making Time: Representations of Technology at the 1964 Fair," in *The Power of Culture: Critical Essays in American History*, ed. Richard W. Fox and T.J. Jackson Lears (Chicago: U of Chicago Press, 1993), 223–44.

elements (226). Vonnegut's seemingly chance asides to the World's Fair function disavow such linear narratives of corporate-sponsored progress.

This disavowal is most apparent in *Slaughterhouse-Five*'s depiction of the "simulated Earthling habitat" in the zoo on Trafalmadore where Billy is held captive together with a starlet called Montana Wildhack (*SF*, 55; 81). The artificial home furnished with items "stolen from the Sears & Roebuck warehouse in Iowa City, Iowa," including a mint green gas range, refrigerator, and dishwasher, provides a life as good as that back home. The only drawback is that Montana, once pregnant, can only send Billy to the refrigerator to assuage her cravings for strawberries and ice cream, "since the atmosphere outside . . . was cyanide, and the nearest ice cream and strawberries were millions of light years away" (*SF*, 81; 130). The Trafalmadorians' edification of their public with a display home where they can watch authentic earthlings exercise, eat, excrete, and use their many gadgets, eerily recalls the colonialist strain of GM's portrayal of a world waiting to be civilized by US technology firms—not to mention the Dresden zoo that Vonnegut mentions toward the novel's end—and exemplifies what Greg Castillo has termed the "soft power" of mid-century design exhibits (Smith, 240; Castillo, xi). The Trafalmadores' claim that "'There isn't anything we can do about [our wars], so we simply don't look at them. We ignore them. We spend eternity looking at pleasant moments—like today at the zoo. Isn't this a nice moment?'" explicitly comments on corporate display culture's obscuration of violence and inequality and its depoliticization of new technologies (*SF*, 85). Meanwhile the home's protection of Billy and Montana from the deathly atmosphere beyond its walls reads both as an intertextual nod to the bomb shelter in *Cat's Cradle* (1963) equipped with a "short-wave radio" and "Sears, Roebuck catalogue" (*CC*, 164), and a reference to the real-life "Underground House" display at the World's Fair. This was a glorified, "all-electric," bomb shelter that the Fair's publicity brochures described as "providing protection from 'the hazards of modern living, including pollution, pollen, noise, and fallout'" (qtd. in Smith, 234). Just as the Underground House's promoters "domesticated the Bomb by assigning comparable 'annoyance status' to smog, rowdy neighbors, and thermonuclear war" (Smith, 234), and the bomb shelter in *Cat's Cradle* protected its inhabitants from the world refrigerated by *ice-nine* beyond, Billy and Montana's time-saving domestic gadgets obscure both the couple's status as prisoners and the lethality of the atmosphere beyond the walls of their home.

Vonnegut likewise parodies the strange temporality portrayed in GE's "Carousel of Progress" exhibit at the World's Fair, where audience members moved through a stage divided into different phases in the history of domestic electrification, via the Trafalmadorian show home's refrigerator, which is decorated with a whimsical illustration of a "Gay Nineties couple on a

FIGURE 6.1 "You'll Fall in Love with the BRIGHT NEW LOOK in Home Appliances!" *LIFE* (April 9, 1956): 29. © Whirlpool 2020. Reproduced with permission. Image courtesy of the Advertising Archives.

FIGURE 6.2 International Harvester. "Great New Kitchen Idea: New Decorator Refrigerator." © Whirlpool 2020. Image courtesy of the Advertising Archives.

FIGURE 6.3 Ralph Crane. "Far-Out Refrigerators: Even Pop Art Is Used to Dress Up New Models." *LIFE* (February 26, 1965): 55–6. © Getty Images.

FIGURE 6.4 Whirlpool. "The Refrigerator with a Thousand Faces." *LIFE* (June 23, 1967): 80. © Whirlpool 2020. Reproduced with permission.

bicycle built for two" that compensates for the inaccessible world beyond.[33] This colorful refrigerator also explicitly comments on the decorated refrigerator models that appliance manufacturers sought to popularize in the late 1950s and 1960s in order to overcome the challenges of market saturation. In 1956, for example, Admiral launched a line of refrigerators featuring "fashion front panels" on which the customer could either fix wallpaper to match their kitchen or choose from a selection of color panels provided by the manufacturer (Figure 6.1). International Harvester launched a range of "Decorator Refrigerators" whose fronts could be changed to match the housewife's mood in "just seven minutes" (Figure 6.2). In 1965, *LIFE* reported on Kelvinator's new line of "pop art refrigerators" retailing for "50% to 100% more than standard models" as part of the brand's "push to make the U.S. a nation of two-refrigerator families" (Figure 6.3). Meanwhile a 1967 ad by Whirlpool promoted a refrigerator into whose door frames housewives could "insert the material of your choice: curtain fabric, wallpaper . . . even a photo of your favorite husband" (Figure 6.4). The whimsical refrigerator in Billy and Montana's simulated home recalls both the nostalgic thrust of GE's Carousel of Progress and these decorated refrigerators. It also anticipates the pastoral scenes that widower Sanford Darling painted over his refrigerator as part of an effort to cover his entire home with nostalgic scenes reminiscent of his life with his deceased wife, and which *LIFE* magazine reported on in an illustrated four-page spread in 1971. Like the "refrigerator with a river view," as *LIFE* described it, the painted refrigerator on Trafalmador is a dreamspace. It promises to preserve an irretrievable past that (contrary to Darling's memories) is entirely mythical.[34]

Taken together, the references to the World's Fair and the appliances Vonnegut enlists to portray the O'Hares', Pilgrims', and Trafalmadorians' (simulated) domestic environments provide a powerful counternarrative to the glorified "all-electric" homes in GE's press releases and corporate displays. What's more, they appear to reverberate with echoes of Pilgrim and Yonson's experiences in Dresden. The fact that Billy Pilgrim finds himself, upon his arrival at the camp outside Dresden, digging through a pile of dead prisoners' overcoats "cemented together with ice" so that the guards are forced to "use their bayonets as ice picks, pricking free collars and hems . . . then peeling off coats," retrospectively imbues Mary O'Hare's ice-picking in the novel's opening scene with a harrowing quality (*SF*, 59). The description of Pilgrim's daughter Barbara's "set[ting of] the control of the electric blanket at the highest notch, which soon made Billy's bed hot enough to bake bread in," likewise refers back to his accidental burning of himself against the iron cookstove in the British prisoners' building

[33] Marchand and Smith, "Corporate Science on Display," 171.
[34] Author unknown, "Mr. Darling Paints his Dreamhouse," *LIFE* (June 25, 1971): 66–9.

in the Dresden prison camp, not to mention the candles "made from the fat of rendered Jews and Gypsies and fairies and communists, and other enemies of the State" that the prisoners use to light their way (*SF*, 95; 69–70). Finally, the Trafalmadorian model home equipped with a refrigerator but no means of escape recalls the meat locker "with no refrigeration" in the slaughterhouse where Billy and his fellow soldiers take shelter. If Billy Pilgrim is destined to relive the war through every subsequent encounter and hallucination, Vonnegut asks, too, that the reader detect the strange echoes of war in the so-called miracles of postwar modernity, and to recognize these to be products of the same atrocities Billy Pilgrim seeks to forget. He likewise invites the reader to experience how escaping death by taking shelter in a house for the slaughtering of animals might alter one's understanding of both the word "house" and the concept of the domestic. The novel *Slaughterhouse-Five* is a house of mirrors, in other words, in which the reader constantly flashes between both specific time periods and the different significations of time-saving gadgetry within them. What we might term this "spasticity of meaning" draws attention to GE's greatest sin in Vonnegut's eyes: the willingness to mystify science to commercial ends to obscure its violent and even genocidal uses.

I want to end this section by briefly discussing Vonnegut's unpublished early short story, "Jenny," which he wrote in the early 1950s.[35] "Jenny" recounts the story of George, an appliance repair-and-salesman for another stand-in for GE, the General Household Appliances Company (GHA). Twenty years ago, George replaced his wife Nancy with "Jenny," a refrigerator he equipped with Nancy's voice, and with whom he now travels across the nation to present GHA's wares. After recounting a series of comical in-store demonstrations, the short story ends with George visiting the deathbed of his ex-wife. She remonstrates him, diagnosing his replacement of her with "Jenny" as a misguided attempt to freeze time, and to remain suspended in an artificial version of his and Nancy's early relationship. While the story's last lines emphasize that there is still time for George to leave Jenny and "'pick up the pieces of [his] life,'" what stands out for a seasoned reader of Vonnegut's time-saving appliances, and of his later work, is the intimation of what *can't* be salvaged (*WMS*, 23). The ending suggests that manufacturers', retailers', and consumers' vested interest in artifice will lead to the inevitable extinction of genuine human relationships such as George and Nancy's messy, unphotogenic marriage. This is underscored by the story's twee narrative style, peppered with expressions such as "swell," "darn good," and "Sonny Jim," which creates a sense of dissonance between the events described and their effects on those involved. The appliance salesman's eventual commitment to live

[35] Kurt Vonnegut, *While Mortals Sleep: Unpublished Stories* (London: Vintage, 2011), 3–24. Henceforth, *WMS*.

FIGURE 6.5 Call-out from Kelvinator Foodarama ad, 1955. © Getty Images.

life "as a human being" thus feels less convincing, and indeed feasible, an end, than the future gestured at in the story's opening lines, which recount George's annual suggestion to GHA that the company make "'next year's refrigerator in the shape of a woman'" called the "Food-O-Mama" (*WMS*, 3). Taken alongside the raptness with which the audiences at George's in-store demonstrations later watch his interactions with Jenny, this suggestion reads as a prediction of the inevitable: Jenny and her relationship with George are merely prototypes.

Such a reading is all the more compelling when one considers that the name "Food-O-Mama" is a pointed reference to Kelvinator's "Foodarama," a side-by-side, two-door, refrigerator launched in 1955 (Figure 6.5). Ads for this enormous appliance invariably showed it with the doors splayed open and a small child reaching into its heaving shelves. Such compositions both demonstrated the amount of food the Foodarama could store, and aligned it with the maternal body, the open doors appearing to cradle the child it nurtured and fed. What's more, George's sketch of "a refrigerator shaped like a woman, with arrows showing where the vegetable crisper and the butter conditioner and the ice cubes and all would go," effectively anticipated Frigidaire's ad, "A Husband's Guide." Released in 1967, this ad featured a photo of a woman with annotations singling out the body parts that "your wife will use less" thanks to the new Frigidaire's labor-saving features.[36] Like Frigidaire's reduction of the housewife to her laboring parts, the personification of the refrigerator in "Jenny" dehumanizes the woman on which it is modeled, reducing femininity to the provision of food. The name "Food-O-*Ma*ma" renders explicit the connection between heaving refrigerator and maternal body gestured at in Kelvinator's Foodarama ads such as the one shown here, where the child appears at once cradled by, to take nourishment from, and to have been borne out of the gaping refrigerator. The story as a whole, while less sophisticated than Vonnegut's later work, takes the conflation of housewives with their machines to its logical conclusion—and in so doing throws into relief what is lost when utilitarianism is privileged at the expense of human feeling.

4. "That's a Vaculux, Isn't It?": DeLillo's *Americana* (1971)

Albeit in different ways to the Vonnegut texts just discussed, the "all-electric" home in DeLillo's *Americana* also exposes the mutual imbrication of corporate messaging and nationalist propaganda. Indeed, the novel's very title is arguably an ironic comment on the commodification of American heritage. While the term "Americana" broadly refers to things associated with US culture and folk music in particular, GE appropriated it in 1962 as the name for what would become its most famous series of appliances. The Americana collection remained on the market until the mid-1980s and was heavily advertised throughout this period via GE's longstanding agency, BBDO—a key competitor of Ogilvy (then called Ogilvy, Benson & Mather), where DeLillo worked from 1959 to 1964. Given DeLillo's own involvement in the industry at the time of the Americana collection's launch, it's not a stretch to assume he was aware of this cooption, and that the novel's title gestures to both a kind of historico-anthropological enquiry, and the subsumption of these by capitalist consumerism. Rather than through folk music, *Americana* tells the story of America through the thrum of its electrical appurtenances and commercial messaging. Dave Bell enlists time-saving appliances to reveal what lies beneath the "smoke and billboards" of the American Dream, and to expose the televised representations of the 1950s to be anything but authentic records of the period (*A*, 111). In approaching the text from this perspective, I necessarily depart from DeLillo scholars'

[36] Frigidaire, "A Husband's Guide to Parts of the Body Your Wife Will Use Less" (1968), *LIFE* (March 29, 1968): 24. Frigidaire denied permission to reproduce this ad, but it can be found in Jim Heimann, *Mid-Century Ads*, and online.

tendency to read *Americana* in relation to French New Wave cinema.[37] For all that Bell models himself on Godard, the dialog between father and son that forms the nucleus of his autobiographical film, and which replicates Bell's own conversations with his Madison Avenue ad man father, reveals advertising, not cinema, to provide the key to decoding his, and the nation's, recent past.

One scene in particular stands out for our purposes. It is a flashback to a traumatic event in Bell's adolescence in white middle-class suburban New York, when he discovered his mother in the kitchen, late at night, after the cocktail party she had just hosted:

> The house was dark except for the kitchen. I started in and then stopped at the doorway. My mother was in there. The refrigerator door was open. . . . She held a tray of ice cubes in her hands and she was spitting on the cubes. She disappeared behind the refrigerator door and I could hear her open the freezer compartment and slide the tray back in. I moved away as the freezer slammed shut. (*A*, 195)

Bell's mother's desecration of the freezer's contents in what amounts to the antithesis of good housekeeping provides a counter-image to her earlier role as hostess and her performances of motherhood elsewhere in the novel. It is also a counter to the idyllic representations of American family life in the commercial reels Bell's father watches each night in the family's darkened basement, convinced that "his purpose [is] to find the common threads and nuances of those commercials which had achieved high test ratings" (*A*, 84–5). Indeed, the scene evidences Bell's claim, earlier in the novel, that his mother, who was afflicted with an unnamed mental disorder and later died of cancer, "was not an advertising campaign and so he [Bell's father] did not know what to do with her" (*A*, 137). In the darkened house in the dead of night, the seemingly ideal housewife gives way to a filth-maker who acts out her unhappiness by sullying the very spaces she is entrusted with stewarding. The time-saving appliance becomes a partner in crime, shielding her deeds from view while undermining its own status as an emblem of wholesome maternal love and hygiene.

This sense of the illicit-come-to-light is exacerbated in the passage immediately following. Here Bell finds his mother in the pantry, where she embraces him and states "'It was only a matter of time,'" before the sound of his father's feet on the stairs interrupts them (*A*, 197). While scholars

[37] Mark Osteen, "Children of Godard and Coca-Cola: Cinema and Consumerism in the Early Fiction," in *American Magic and Dread: Don DeLillo's Dialogue with Culture* (Philadelphia, PA: U of Pennsylvania Press, 2000), 8–30; and David Cowart, "For Whom Bell Tolls: Don DeLillo's *Americana*," in *Don DeLillo: The Physics of Language* (Athens, GA: U of Georgia Press, 2002), 131–44.

have examined the Oedipal dimension of this scene and its relationship to the media landscape in which Bell has been raised, its significance as an early instance of the 1970s' fascination with the 1950s has gone unnoticed.[38] Indeed, the near-embrace between mother and teenage son in the shadow of the refrigerator debunks, in advance, the narrative of innocence that such films and television shows as *American Graffiti* (1973), its spin-off *Happy Days* (1974–84), and *Grease* (1978, based on the 1972 Broadway musical) sought to uphold. The 1950s were never as innocent as they claimed to be—and far from a bastion of pure maternal affection or source of physical nourishment and growth, the refrigerator at the heart of the 1950s home is revealed, here, to embody all of the era's repressed urges and frustrations.

The desecration of the ice tray followed by the thought of the desecration of the mother-son relationship undermines a series of myths central to the Bell family, and by extension the Eisenhower era. The tray's desecration counters the "dream of the good life" that Bell's mother instilled in him as a child via "charming little fables about Jesus" in which "Jesus was a blond energetic lad who helped his mother around the house and occasionally performed a nifty miracle" (*A*, 137–8). The juxtaposition of housework with the expression, "nifty miracles," echoes the formulae of mid-century ads, which resorted to storylines featuring animated appliances, elves, fairies, and other imaginary critters to personify their product benefits.[39] This affinity is indeed implied in the phrasing of Bell's acknowledgment that "It wasn't until much later that I realized she made [the fables] up," which echoes his earlier admission of the belatedness with which he stopped believing in Aunt Jemima (*A*, 138; 130).

The Bell family refrigerator and spit-laden ice tray also function as obverses to the object matter that it is Mr. Bell's job to incorporate into ads that, in his words, "'move the merchandise off the shelves,'" and that it is implied he was watching in the basement while the encounter between mother and son occurred (*A*, 85). They are the "something black (and somehow very funny) on the mirror rim of one's awareness" to which Bell refers in the soliloquy quoted at the outset of this chapter—the darkness that advertising seeks to obscure (*A*, 130). This encroaching darkness includes not only specific horrors alluded to throughout the text such as the Vietnam War, but the white hegemonic and patriarchal values on which the ideal of the "all-electric" kitchen and the nationalist ideology it upheld were based (*A*, 130). In describing his recreation of the pantry scene as "my

[38] Osteen; Douglas Keesey, *Don DeLillo* (New York: Twayne, 1993), 23; Tom LeClair, *In the Loop: Don DeLillo and the Systems Novel* (Urbana, IL: U of Illinois Press, 1987), 35–6, and Cowart, 242, ff. 2.

[39] Neuhaus, 41; 74; 150; Marchand, *Advertising the American Dream*, 229.

very own commercial, a life in a life," Bell identifies the relation between the original event and the televised commercial representations of the "all-American" family that his father helped produce, and which impede critical engagements with the postwar era (*A*, 317).

And, of course, the desecration of the ice tray is also a desecration of the feminine embodied in the ice tray itself, whose dainty size and easy-to-extract cubes, following its invention in the 1910s, feminized the once "manly" task of hacking at a block of ice or working an ice crank (the latter process of which we saw depicted in Yates's shorts story, "Oh Joseph I'm So Tired," discussed in Chapter 2, and in Kerouac's early poetry, discussed in Chapter 1). Manufacturers increasingly refined this process in the next decades. The Frigidaire QuickCube launched in the early 1930s, for example, featured a simple lever attached to the metal barriers dividing the ice into cubes that when pushed would make the cubes pop up.[40] The launch in 1955 of the Flip-Quick Ice Ejector—an ice tray installed upside down, whose cubes a lever would push into a bucket below—in pink and baby blue aluminum reinforced the object's function as a facilitator of graceful, feminine drink-making.[41] In spitting in the tray, Mrs. Bell spits in the proverbial face of such feminization.

The time-saving appliance is further demystified in the novel's closing pages, shortly after Bell has finished filming the reenactment of the pantry scene. Here, Bell sits clipping his fingernails while watching the maid clean his motel room:

> She reached past the door frame and dragged in a vacuum cleaner. . . . The machine crawled past me, eating my fingernails. . . . She got on her knees and was about to clean under the bed when she turned and looked at me. . . . I had no idea what time it was. . . . The hair of my belly and balls curled in the sheets in the hallway. She attached a small brush to the pipe and cleaned the blinds. "That's a Vaculux, isn't it? My father used to handle that account. That was years ago. He's growing a bread now. Just the thought of it makes me uncomfortable." "I just do my job," she said. She left quietly then, one more irrelevant thing that would not go unremembered. (*A*, 335)

The passage makes for uncomfortable reading in its positioning of the maid as ancillary to Bell's self-analysis. The sexualization of the (fictional) Vaculux sucking his pubic hair, coupled with the stream-of-conscious monologue about his father's handling of the Vaculux account, underscores

[40] Frigidaire, "'Super-Duty' Frigidaire with the Meter-Miser," *LIFE* (May 10, 1937): 78).

[41] Frigidaire, "Brilliant! This Convertible Beauty Changes Its Color to Please You—Serves Ice in a New 'dry-hands' Fashion," *LIFE* (November 21, 1955): 56.

Bell's objectification of this underpaid service worker. Indeed, in portraying Bell's side-lining of this woman as he focuses on planning the next stop in his travels, identifying the brand of vacuum cleaner, communicating his inherited connection to the brand, relating this to his father issues, and finally categorizing her as "one more irrelevant thing" that only one with as keen an eye such as him would be likely to remember, DeLillo highlights the limits of his protagonist's capacity to understand what he claims to be critiquing. It is likewise telling that the last appliance engagement in *Americana* involves a return to advertising, and a return to conceiving of the object over and above the person wielding it (as exemplified by the fact that only the vacuum cleaner is given a name). Eisenhower's America and its mechanical accoutrements remain illegible to those who came of age in it—and the men of this generation, if Bell is anything to go by, are destined to replicate the misogyny of their fathers, and to recognize brand names more quickly than their own destructive narcissism.

5. "Words to Believe and Live By":[42] DeLillo's *Underworld* (1997)

The passage in *Underworld* that concerns us brings together all of the themes discussed in this chapter thus far both figuratively, in its exploration of the deep symbology of the "all-electric" kitchen and its relation to postwar conceptions of temporality and historical progress, and, literally, in its montage-form, which splices references to brand-name appliances, recipes for quintessentially mid-century dishes, and a series of anxieties specific to the space age. We also find ourselves back in a setting eerily close to the kitchen-pantry scene in *Americana*, where, once more, a mother and son's relation to the "all-electric" kitchen conveys their atomization and alienation from one another, thus puncturing both the myth of the "all-American" family and the American exceptionalism for which it stands. Let's take a look.

It is October 8, 1957, four days after the Soviets' successful launch of Sputnik into space. In her "all-electric" kitchen, paradigmatic housewife Erica Deming fawns over the Jell-O parfaits she has made for this evening's dessert. In his bedroom, her son Eric, a future bomb-head, masturbates into a condom. And out in the breezeway, family patriarch Rick "simoniz[es] their two-ton Ford Fairlane convertible." The erotic charge of this latter expression chimes with that of the subject-object relations described throughout the rest of the scene. It also appears to link the Demings with the family in Arthur Miller's

[42] Don DeLillo, *Underworld* (London: Picador, 2011 [1997]), 520. Henceforth, *U*.

classic debunking of the postwar American Dream, *Death of a Salesman* (1949), where salesman Willie Loman nostalgically recalls his (similarly oversexed) son Biff's simonizing of the red Chevy in the late 1920s.[43] In the following pages, DeLillo juxtaposes Eric's sexual fantasies about missiles, satellites, space ships, and Jayne Mansfield's "thermoplastic" breasts, with Rick's careful polishing of the Fairlane, various unrelated product warnings akin to those found on aerosol cans, and Erica's besotted musings about her two-tone Kelvinator refrigerator and the Jell-O desserts it makes possible. The latter however are continuously interrupted by anxious thoughts about Sputnik, and about her son's treatment of her Jell-O antipasto salad as a "lickable female body part" (*U*, 521). Through this structure, DeLillo interlaces images evocative of mid-century advertising with insights into the internalization of Cold War propaganda. The characters' inner monologues betray the ease with which the self subsumes institutional claims to national superiority and corporate prowess into inchoate expressions of longing and rage. Where the refrigerator in *Americana* debunks the family ideal central to mid-century advertising, the Kelvinator refrigerator and automatic dishwasher in *Underworld* reveal such ads' psychic effects—the strange and unforeseeable ways in which, together with the "institutional messages, the psalms and placards" referenced by David Bell, they are subsumed into the subconscious, and contribute to the self's atomization (*A*, 129). DeLillo's portrayal of Erica's relationship to her gadgets highlights a series of clichés about the mid-century American kitchen, its electric accoutrements, the aproned white woman deploying them, and their unique vulnerability to manipulation into nostalgic reminiscence (as the Cold War memorabilia collector Marvin Lundy highlights elsewhere in the novel). Just as the time-saving appliance in the 1950s was inextricable from the messages promoting it, the time-saving appliance in post-Cold War recollections of the period, DeLillo shows, is all too easily subsumed into pastoral memories saturated with the imagery of mid-century ads, and divested of its links to the military-industrial complex, the subjugation of women, the erasure of Black or immigrant experience, the perpetuation of the myth of a "classless" America, or the upholding of heteronormative values.

This effort to demystify the "all-electric" kitchen is apparent in DeLillo's articulation of Erica and her son's respective affective responses to the refrigerator, which convey the former's internalization of mid-century ads and government propaganda, and the latter's internalization of the teachings of corporate science, from GE's "Progress Is Our Most Important Product" to DuPont's "Better Things for Better Living Through Chemistry (the title of the section in which the Demings' narrative unfurls)." The following

[43] *DOAS*, 13; *U*, 521. I am indebted to Peter Ward for drawing my attention to this earlier use of the expression in Miller's play.

passages reveal Erica and Eric to be in thrall to the same set of delusions as the young David Bell and his mother:

> One of Erica's favorite words in the language was breezeway. It spoke of ease and breeze and being contemporary and having something others did not. Another word she loved was crisper. The Kelvinator had a nice roomy crisper and she liked to tell the men that such-and-such was in the crisper. Not the refrigerator, the crisper. . . . There were people out there on the Old Farm Road, where the front porches sag badly and . . . the Duck River Baptists worship in a squat building that sits in the weeds on the way to the dump, who didn't know what a crisper was, who had iceboxes instead of refrigerators, or who had refrigerators that lacked crispers, or who had crispers in their refrigerators but didn't know what they were for or what they were called. (*U*, 516)

> [Eric] went into the kitchen and opened the fridge, just to see what was going on in there. The bright colors, the product names and logos . . . the general sense of benevolent gleam, of . . . a world unspoiled and ever renewable. But there was something else as well, faintly unnerving. . . . Maybe it was the informational flow contained in that endless motorized throb. Open the great white vaultlike door and feel the cool breezelet of systems at work, converting current into power, talking to each other day and night across superhuman spaces, a thing he felt outside of, not yet attuned to. . . . Except their Kelvinator wasn't white of course. . . . It was cameo rose and pearly dawn. (*U*, 517–18)

I have written elsewhere about the significance of Erica's infatuation with the "good things" made possible by Jell-O, and the refrigerator's affirmation, as Eric puts it, of the "unspoiled and ever renewable" nature of a world that he will one day have the security clearance to blow up (Dini 2016, 166–8). But the first of the two above-quoted passages also foregrounds the appliance's function in the performance of middle classness. To own a refrigerator instead of an icebox is to demonstrate wealth, knowledge, and fluency in the commodity's language. Indeed, while it is unlikely that knowledge of the nuances of the crisper was what Pierre Bourdieu had in mind when he articulated his theory of cultural capital, Erica Deming's intuitive sense of the importance of knowing the names of the refrigerator's component parts and their appropriate uses reveals this housewife's internalization of the gendered and class-based notions of "good taste" that appliance manufacturers seeded into ads for products that purportedly represented female emancipation and the end of class divisions.[44] The

[44] Pierre Bourdieu, *Distinction: A Social Critique of Good Taste*, transl. Richard Nice (Cambridge, MA: Harvard UP, 1984 [1979]).

upstanding purchaser as citizen, to use Lizabeth Cohen's term for mid-century America's designation of consumption as a form of patriotism, demonstrates her love of country by purchasing the appliance and then faithfully interpreting it in the manner prescribed by Madison Avenue and Uncle Sam—a manner that implicitly reproduces the class and gender inequalities that Cold War America claimed the "good life" planed away (9). A similar assimilation of institutional messages is likewise apparent in Eric's enraptured exploration of the refrigerator and his identification of the literal and metaphorical connections between domestic technologies, the electric grid that also powers the communication systems used by NASA, and the state power that funds the military research that makes possible these same technologies. Alongside the "tinsel glitter" and "benevolent" gleam of the refrigerator's food items there resides the intimation and possibility of other uses of technology—a point which DeLillo ironizes via Eric's hasty distinction between the "white vaultlike door" of the Cold War machine with which he associates the appliance and the disarming "cameo rose and pearly dawn" of the actual Kelvinator (*U*, 518).

But where Eric is excited by Sputnik, Erica is dismayed. Her heartbreak at what she interprets as a national failure expresses itself in revulsion toward the "new satellite-shaped vacuum cleaner" (obviously modeled on the Hoover Constellation discussed in Chapter 5) that, prior to the launch, she "loved to push across the room because it . . . seemed futuristic and hopeful"—a description that cleverly mimics what Kate Baldwin has termed Cold War appliance advertisers' framing of appliances as "prosthetic devices for the emotions" to "defra[y] the psychological and ideological costs of *Sputnik*" (*U*, 520; Baldwin, 139–40). The list of mid-century domestic vocabulary that follows immediately after this statement, "Stacking chairs Room divider Scatter cushions Fruit juicer Storage walls Cookie sheet," suggests what we might term the "domino effect" of such disillusion (*U*, 520). Sputnik has unleashed a tide of skepticism that threatens to strip the sheen of each of these mid-century domestic inventions and, more importantly, the sheen of the double-barrelled terminology that set these objects apart as pivotal components in the performance of modern American domesticity.

Meanwhile, in giving the three family members such similar names and revealing their identities solely through their relationship to the mechanized objects that hold them in such thrall—automobiles, missiles, and time-saving appliances—DeLillo conveys the flattening effects of Cold War conformity and its reduction of people (to misquote Marx) to appendages of their consumer goods. He suggests how such objects' abundant portrayal in mid-century media resulted not only in their disproportionate foregrounding in the consciousness of individuals, but in later recollections of the period. To remember the 1950s, DeLillo suggests, is to view a series of images in which one's familiars, or one's former self, are effectively crowded out by the objects around them, and by the mediated renditions of those objects.

One is reminded, here, of Martha Rosler's photomontage series, *House Beautiful: Bringing the War Home* (1967–72), whose juxtaposition of images of domestic interiors with scenes of war highlighted the distance between the rhetoric of family values, individual freedom, and safety espoused in popular representations of the American home and the horrors of the war happening overseas—not to mention the ludicrousness of the news media's juxtaposition of Vietnam War coverage with ads for household products (most of the images were taken from *LIFE* magazine).[45] In "Red Stripe Kitchen," armed soldiers prowled through a pristine kitchen, their posture easily confused with that of someone vacuuming and the missile in one of the soldier's hands easily confused with an appliance. In "Cleaning the Drapes," a housewife vacuumed curtains while soldiers huddled outside. Both works drew parallels between a domestic sphere equipped with "all-electric" conveniences and a war being waged with weapons produced by the same manufacturers as these gadgets. They also highlighted the complicity of those American women who, while purportedly believing in the sanctity of home and family, supported a war that destroyed the homes of countless Vietnamese. Like Rosler's photomontages—or, indeed, the gadget-ridden interior comprised entirely of cut-out magazine photos in British artist Richard Hamilton's collage, "Just What Was It That Made Yesterday's Homes So Different, So Appealing" (1956), in which a Hoover Constellation, male body builder, and bikini-clad woman all vie for the viewer's attention—DeLillo's literary montage confronts us with the entanglement of the mid-century home and its electrical appurtenances in the advancement of oppressive political ideologies.[46]

6. Neoliberalizing the "All-Electric" Kitchen: DeLillo's *Americana* (1971), *White Noise* (1985), and "Baghdad Towers West" (1968)

I have shown thus far how the DeLillean appliance, like the Vonnegutian one, exposes the fallacy of the myth of American exceptionalism and the "all-electric" home's role in its advancement. I have also shown how DeLillo enlists the time-saving appliance to expose the unique susceptibility to manipulation of the memory of the 1950s, which he ascribes to the

[45] Marth Rosler, *House Beautiful: Bringing the War Home* (1967-1972), in *Artists Respond: American Art and the Vietnam War, 1965–1972*, ed. Melissa Ho et al. (Princeton, NJ: Princeton UP, 2019), 93–9.

[46] Richard Hamilton, "Just What Was It . . ." (1956). Digital print on paper, 260 x 350 mm, Tate.

sustained propaganda effort by private industry and government during this decade that created the illusion of a national consensus on the meanings of "America," "family," and "home." In this penultimate section I want to turn instead to a key difference between Vonnegut and DeLillo's time-saving appliances. The latter, I argue, also articulate the emergence of a new, heightened atomization wherein the family is either absent, or reconfigured as an entity comprised of individuals isolated from each other. In doing so, DeLillo's time-saving appliances indirectly comment on the intensified individualization that social scientists have since ascribed to the restructuring of relations between citizens, states, and markets in the 1970s and 1980s. As David Harvey first argued in 1989, a crucial component of Fordism was the conceptualization of laborers as "worker-consumers" the calculation of whose pay and working hours took into account the need for discretionary spend and leisure time to enable them to participate in the consumer society.[47] The "all-electric" kitchen conceived under this system was a network of objects produced in a factory by laborers who, by the 1950s, were understood to also be its future consumers, and a network of symbols that signaled their owner's access to a postwar middle-class and female emancipation purportedly available to all. By contrast, the neoliberal kitchen to which certain few of DeLillo's texts gesture is characterized by the absence of social relations, and by the smooth flow of machines operating in a drama to which their owners, if they are even present, are mere spectators. Crucially, however, in interspersing these depictions with references to the mid-century or 1930s kitchen, DeLillo shows the neoliberal appliance to be but a *logical outcome* of the Fordist appliance, or, put differently, latent within it. In drawing this latter conclusion, I enlist Liam Kennedy and Stephen Shapiro's recent contention that "the cluster of macroeconomic ideas captured within the term Keynesianism and the ones under the term neoliberalism" were in fact "contemporaneous, and often interdependent, responses to the general economic crisis of the Great Depression and the socio-political catastrophe of the rise of the European . . . far-right, alongside the rising military aggression of Hirohito's Japan."[48] Particularly important for our purposes is their identification of neoliberal influences on US culture as early as the 1940s (9–10).

That DeLillo is concerned with not only dismantling the myth of the nuclear family central to the Eisenhower era but exposing the atomized individual it is likely to produce is particularly apparent in *Americana*,

[47] David Harvey, *The Condition of Postmodernity: An Enquiry into the Origins of Cultural Change* (Oxford: Blackwell, 1991 [1989]), 125–40.
[48] *Neoliberalism and Contemporary American Literature*, ed. Liam Kennedy and Stephen Shapiro, 6. In making these claims, Shapiro and Kennedy argue against Mitchum Huehls and Rachel Greenwald Smith's account in *Neoliberalism and Contemporary Culture* (Johns Hopkins UP, 2017), 1–20.

where DeLillo enlists electrification to portray Dave Bell as the prototypical neoliberal self. Thus, Bell dismisses Jennifer, a secretary from his office with whom he has just had sex, by impersonating a television announcer's closing comments for a show sponsored by "the Bell System"—a play on his name and the Bell Telephone Company (*A*, 42). The sardonic faux-announcement, "'Be back tomorrow night on behalf of the Bell System—communications for home, industry, and four-fifths of the universe—with another instalment of whatever it is we've been doing here, brought to you courtesy of the first family of telephones and electronics since time began'" at once crassly depersonalizes the encounter and allegorizes neoliberalism's treatment of corporations as individuals and vice versa (*A*, 42). Where Whitman sang the body electric to (however imperialistically) imagine a collective of selves connected across the nation, and articulated the endless permutations of the self as a body containing multitudes, Bell imagines the self as containing multiple *sub-corporations*, and society as a network of selves connected to, and powered by, a more-or-less-meaningless broadcast. Jennifer's whispered response to Bell's crassness, "'fascist,'" aptly describes the natural, if paradoxical, endpoint of such a trajectory (paradoxical insofar as, as Kennedy and Shapiro note, neoliberalism in the postwar era was partly driven by a desire to *prevent* fascism from reoccurring).[49] Bell's secretary Binky Lister's effort to dissuade him from embarking on a road trip across America by asserting that "'Nothing will be solved out there'"—on the American road—as "'It's just telephone poles stringing together the cities'" can be seen as a direct counterpoint to Gary Snyder/Japhy's comparison, in *On the Road* (discussed in Chapter 1), of the invisibility of "'the thing that bound us all together'" to the currents running through the telephone wires crossing the landscape (*OTR*, 308). Together with Bell's complaint, throughout the novel, that "Nothing connect[s]" (*A*, 196), Bell and Binky's repartee expresses the cynical underside to what we might term electrical utopianism—an optimism encompassing both the radical hopes of Kerouac or Piercy, *and* the hyper-capitalist visions sponsored by GE that, as the father in Bell's autobiographical film notes, were characterized by their circumscription, their promise of better machines to assist housework rather than the elimination of housework itself (*A*, 270). In this way, *Americana* posits "all-electric" living as augmenting capitalism's atomizing effects, and inextricable from the mediated images that promote it.

DeLillo's understanding of the "all-electric" home—and the kitchen in particular—as a site of contestation between Fordism and neoliberalism, or, more specifically, as a site in which the shift from one to the other in the 1970s and 1980s was most apparent, is most fully articulated in *White Noise* (1985). In one of the novel's most famous scenes, Jack Gladney

[49] Kennedy and Shapiro, 5; 8.

interprets the congealed mess in his garbage compactor as the (literally and figuratively) filthy consequence of his family, and US society's, consumption. He asks: "Did it belong to us? Had we created it? . . . Was this the dark underside of consumer consciousness?"[50] But shifting our focus from the compactor's contents to the compactor itself, and, in particular, to its relationship, described earlier in the same scene, with the freezer, yields a rather different interpretation to Gladney's:

> A strange crackling sound came off the plastic food wrap, the snug covering for half eaten things, the Ziploc sacks of livers and ribs, all gleaming with sleety crystals. A cold dry sizzle. A sound like some element breaking down, resolving itself into Freon vapors. An eerie static, insistent but near subliminal, that made me think of wintering souls, some form of dormant life approaching the threshold of perception. (*WN*, 258)

The freezer here is presented not as a preserver of life-giving sustenance, but rather a cryogenic chamber sustaining food in the suspended state between life and death, and an exemplification of what Gladney's colleague, the scholar of packaging Murray Suskind, earlier termed the "'American magic and dread'" apparent in advertising, tabloids, and the whirring sounds of the supermarket (*WN*, 19). The intimation of Freon, the chemical refrigerant that is vital to the refrigerator and freezer's function but toxic if inhaled, combined with Gladney's focus on animal organs and impression of "subliminal" static and "wintering souls," positions the freezer as a cross between a domestic morgue and an ancient burial ground. While amplifying the text's broader depiction of US culture as an extended exercise in denying the inevitability of death through the production and consumption of products ironically replete with more or less poisonous substances, Gladney's contemplation of his freezer compartment also affects our understanding of the garbage compactor. Attention to the freezer description reveals the compactor to be not a standalone object of signification but, rather, one component in a (literal and figurative) network of objects that appear to exist autonomously from their owners—and this scene to be merely a culmination of *White Noise*'s repeated figuration of the 1980s "all-electric" kitchen as a protagonist of a drama in which its owners are mere extras.

One thinks, here, of the novel's description, in the opening pages, of the "dreadful wrenching sound" of the garbage compactor and the churn of the washing machine as part of an "incidental mesh," as if the workings of one appliance somehow depend on those of the other (*WN*, 33). This foregrounding of time-saving appliances' interrelation with each other above the relations between the family members is again apparent in the

---

[50] Don DeLillo, *White Noise* (New York: Penguin, 1986 [1985]), 258–9.

kitchen scene following, which portrays the objects as participants in a kind of automated conspiracy from which Gladney and his son Heinrich are excluded:

> The refrigerator throbbed massively. I flipped a switch and somewhere beneath the sink a grinding mechanism reduced parings, rinds and animal fats to tiny drainable fragments, with a motorized surge that made me retreat two paces. I took the forks out of my son's hands and put them in the dishwasher. (*WN*, 101)

Throbbing refrigerator, grinding garbage compactor, and dishwasher appear at once animated and impervious to their users. Meanwhile, Henrich's remonstration, in the passage immediately following this description, regarding the inefficiency of his father's movements in the kitchen, both parodies the rhetoric of 1920s and 1930s time-motion studies and takes their philosophy to its logical, and absurd, conclusion:

> What do you save if you don't waste?" [Gladney asks]
> "Over a lifetime? You save tremendous amounts of time and energy," [Heinrich] sa[ys].
> "What will you do with them?"
> "Use them to live longer." (*WN*, 102)

The lure of scientific management, Heinrich implies, lies in the perceived equivalence of time-saving and life extension. At an unconscious level, the Fordist self—the self, that is, who has been socialized to abide by Fordist practices—buys into theories of rationalization due to a misguided assumption that the seconds, minutes, and hours saved will be tacked on to the end of their lives rather than being consumed by other activities, and in particular, more work. The "throbbing" refrigerator meanwhile reminds us that this is an object that is always on, always working, always productive—which suggests how the time saved by its appliance siblings will likely be spent. Gladney's deadpan comment to the reader following this exchange ("The truth is I didn't want to die first") reveals both the fallacy of such reasoning and its power. In its promise to save time and render waste invisible, the "all-electric" kitchen, according to DeLillo, also tacitly promises to eradicate death, and to replace it with endless *other* work. The throbbing refrigerator is a participant in the "white noise" of late capitalism that gives the novel its title, and that the text understands as the thrum of a society that aspires to endless productivity modeled on that of machines.

Examined in light of these earlier figurations, Gladney's late-night encounter with the contents of his freezer and garbage compactor reads as the culmination of the text's long-standing investment in exposing the "all-electric" kitchen as an uncanny, and indeed *Gothic* space—a haunted network of enmeshed objects promoted on the basis of their capacity to free up time to live better, longer, and more freely, but whose mechanisms, materials, and by-products are in fact redolent with connotations of death and imbricated in a system that promotes endless resource extraction and productivity in the name of boundless growth. What's more, the passage exposes these objects as engaged in a dialog on a frequency indiscernible to human ears, but which, DeLillo reminds us, is a product of human (and, more specifically, twentieth-century-US capitalist) activity. In this way, the text's figuration of the "all-electric" home functions, too, as an allegory for US capitalism more broadly. The mechanized domestic sphere whose inhabitants amount to mere guests is synecdochic of a body politic in which the interests of the demos are secondary to those of private companies, an (automated) financial system, and a value system that promotes productivity at the expense of everything else. As Stephen Shapiro notes, the always on-ness of the refrigerator "is like neoliberal[ism]'s constant marketplace, and it foreshadows later switched-on things, like the wireless internet."[51]

DeLillo's depictions of domestic automation and domesticity more broadly in his early short story, "Baghdad Towers West," similarly reflect on the future of a culture increasingly shaped by speculation, where the "all-electric" kitchen and the appurtenances of the "all-electric" home are neither status symbols nor sources of personal comfort but, rather, designed to inflate the value of properties intended as investments rather than dwellings. In this story about a man who takes on a New York luxury apartment lease, gets fired from his job for never getting out of bed, and ultimately decides to never leave the apartment again, the "all-electric" home in its luxury incarnation emerges as both the most extreme expression of neoliberalism and the only space that might resist it.

The titular luxury apartment block in Central Park West to which the narrator moves from the suddenly "historical" Gramercy Park is introduced as "a 40-story orgone box of glass and steel" that "promise[s] a new kind of mystery, electronic and ultramodern, in which the angel of death pushes a vacuum cleaner and all the werewolves are schnauzers" (*BTW*, 198). The "vast control panel" for the building's 24-hour surveillance system recalls a "launch site during countdown"—so much so that the narrator "wonder[s] if somewhere on that glittering panel there [i]s a button marked *abort*"—a figuration DeLillo repeated, three decades later, in his description of Erica Deming's "push button" kitchen (*BTW*, 198–9; *U*, 517). "Baghdad Towers West" portrays a new kind of "all-electric" home—not the suburban enclave rendered accessible to white people in the early postwar era but an atomized residence whose automated controls recall military weaponry. The figurations of the angel of death vacuuming and schnauzer-werewolves

---

[51] Email message, August 4, 2020.

take postwar anxieties regarding the feminization of culture to its logical conclusion: death itself has been domesticated, while the illicit thrills of the night have been neutered. They also contribute to the text's portrayal of luxury housing as the endpoint of narrative. The building the protagonist's roommates describe as "'the worst sort of unattractive spectacle one hears is rampant in America before one actually comes here,'" and that provides the perfect site for the narrator's self-obliteration, serves as allegory for a culture on its way to eradicating the human (*BTW*, 199; 200). Meanwhile, the protagonist's escape from the corporate world through endless sleep subtly references Georges Perec's novella, *A Man Asleep* (1967), in which a 25-year-old Parisian student removes himself from society by retreating to a bare apartment, where he watches the cracks on the ceiling and the drip of his hand-washed socks dry.[52] In locating his narrator's escape in a plush luxury dwelling (where socks are washed in a machine, thank you very much!), DeLillo suggests the impossibility of such escape for those raised on Madison Avenue's myths: there is little to distinguish the actions of this American youth from those of a jet-lagged businessman, sleeping until he has the energy again to clinch another deal.

More importantly, "Baghdad Towers West" articulates an important shift in the symbolic meaning of time-saving appliances, and the "all-electric" home, in line with urban gentrification and the rise of gated communities equipped with technology to prevent intrusion from unwanted "Others." The metaphor of the "angel of death pushing a vacuum cleaner" is inextricably connected to the actual kitchen that "hum[s] with power and a kind of stainless steel lust," the circuits that power the security cameras throughout the building, and the "air conditioning, dish washers [and] basement full of washers and dryers" singled out in one of the narrator's prior apartment viewings (*BTW*, 198). The image DeLillo presents the reader is the obverse of Kerouac, Piercy, and Yates's or indeed Whitman's visions of radical connectivity. Where these intimated the potential to connect selves to a grid envisaged as an allegory for collectivism, DeLillo's short story points to a future in which the nation's cities are punctuated by "all-electric" residences designed either as investments or as fortresses enabling total retreat from the social. In their intimations of neoliberalism, these depictions highlight a point implied by most of the literary appliances examined in this monograph. The "all-electric" home *always* contained the seed of its owners' destruction—for the truly efficient home is that whose inhabitants have no need for food, and who have pared themselves down to the point of creating no dirt or waste at all.

[52] Georges Perec, *Things: A Story of the Sixties with A Man Asleep*, transl. David Bellos (London: Vintage, 2011 [1965]).

7. Conclusion

In enlisting time-saving appliances to critique broader issues such as military warfare, the erosion of labor rights, the delusional rhetoric of corporate culture, the myth of American exceptionalism, and Cold War culture's enforcement of gender and racial inequality, Vonnegut reveals the imbrication of these objects in the maintenance of hegemonic power. Cumulatively, Vonnegut's time-saving appliances participate in an intertextual pageantry that dismantles GE's totalizing vision as much as do his recurring characters and settings. Where GE claimed that "Progress is Our Most Important Product," Vonnegut's gadgets recall Walter Benjamin's assertion that "There is no document of civilization that is not a document of barbarism."[53] DeLillo's time-saving appliances blast apart the myth of the "all-American" family—the myth on which the Eisenhower era was premised, and which served to obscure the violence of Vietnam, the nuclear arms race, and the military-industrial complex. In foregrounding brand names, sales messages, product materials, and the sounds or textures of appliances, over and above these objects' function or affective meaning for the owner—and in conflating sales message with affective meaning so that the two become indistinguishable from each other—DeLillo posits the time-saving appliance as the postwar era's most extreme commodity form. It is an object whose utilitarian function is ultimately secondary to its function as a symbol of the "good life" and a sign, for its owner, that all is well. The appliance depictions examined are but a small sample from an *oeuvre* replete with domestic gadgets, and particularly refrigeration, reflecting the author's decades-long concern not only with waste, but, as I have argued elsewhere, technologies of reclamation and preservation.[54] Indeed, one can trace a *direct link* from the time-saving appliances in *Underworld*'s depictions of the Demings' 1950s kitchen, and of a New York City plunged into darkness during the Great Northeast Blackout of 1965, to the power outage at the center of DeLillo's 2020 novel, *The Silence*.[55] DeLillo's oeuvre effectively traces the trajectory from corporate-sponsored electrical magic to breakage, using both to allegorize the social dysfunctions they mask. Without actually mentioning "smart" appliances or "smart" homes, DeLillo's premillennial fiction gestures to the imbrication of domestic electrification with networks of power and surveillance of which the public is only dimly aware—and serves as incubator for the more overt critiques of neoliberal electrification in his late postmillennial work.

---

[53] Walter Benjamin, "Theses on the Philosophy of History," in *Illuminations*, transl. Henry Zohn (London: Random House, 1999 [1955]), 248.

[54] Rachele Dini, "Review: Don DeLillo's *Zero K*." *European Journal of American Studies* (2016).

[55] *Underworld*, 621–37; Don DeLillo, *The Silence* (Picador, 2020).

7

"You Can *Overdo* Remembering Stuff":[1]

Anti-Nostalgic Appliances in Postmillennial Fiction

Within minutes we were in the bedroom.
I know this sounds bad.
Worst still to admit I'd said, *Sure,*
Come on over, when the man
called to inform me I was the lucky winner
of a ten-piece set of cutlery.
So the stranger with sharp knives arrived

in a green-plaid polyester blazer
with a silver Kirby vacuum cleaner
and a suitcase full of accessories.[2]

So begins Debra Marquart's poem, "Door-to-Door" (2013), which ends not in sex between the female speaker and Kirby salesman, but with her using the new knives to murder her violent boyfriend (lxxxii). In highlighting the erotic charge of the doorstep appliance purchase, a transaction that involves a stranger entering the home and, in this case, its most intimate space, the

[1] Lucy Ellmann, *Ducks, Newburyport* (London: Galley Beggar Press, 2019), 56. Henceforth, *DN*. All italics in the quotes from this novel are from the original.
[2] Debra Marquart, "Door-to-Door," *Narrative Magazine*. Poem of the Week, 2012–2013 (March 31, 2013).

poem's first lines recall several of the mid-century texts examined in this study. The sixty-nine subsequent lines however reveal that the events in question occurred not in the 1950s but in 1983, at what might be termed the twilight years of the myth of domestic electrification—after environmental concerns, and a decade defined by economic recession, skyrocketing electricity prices, power outages, and the move of manufacturing overseas, had tarnished time-saving appliances' proverbial shine. Meanwhile, the Kirby's trajectory conveys the transformation of gender relations under capitalism over the previous sixty years.

The poem's references to the temporal and cultural distance between the 1980s and the early postwar era are in fact matched by an equal emphasis on the distance between the 1980s and the 2010s from which the speaker is recalling the salesman's visit. Yes, the woman back in the 1983 of the poem's first half is less naïve than the housewives in mid-century ads and television shows, for whom a visit from an appliance salesman might well have been the high point of the week. But the woman in the 2010s of the poem's second half marvels at the naïveté of her 1983 self, who unquestioningly relinquished her data for the chance to win a prize, answered the door to anyone, allowed a stranger to take calls from his sales supervisor on her Princess Telephone, and tolerated a "brutish" boyfriend whose "brand of mean" a vacuum salesman could spot more easily than she (liv; xxxiii; xl; xlvii; xlviii). That distance between 1983 and 2010s is amplified by the speaker's explicit references, in the poem's second half, to the obsolescence, following the rise of the internet, of the objects, transactional methods, and social relations on which the events of the poem's first half were premised. In asserting she no longer "answer[s] a door . . . unless I know exactly who lurks / For me on the other side of the wall," the speaker conveys the legacy of domestic abuse, as well as the replacement with skepticism of the naïveté on which doorstep sales depended (liv–lvi). The ensuing statement, "Mostly I hope / nobody is forced to sell shit door-to-door in these inhospitable times," divests the appliance of its lure, reducing it to generic "shit," while suggesting a new cynicism (lvii–lxiii). It also gestures to the hardening of anti-immigrant, and particularly Latino immigrant, sentiment in the 2010s, and coterminous, and continued, rise of securitized domesticities.[3]

Marquart's poem differs from some of the more scathing critiques of the gendering of domestic mechanization examined in previous chapters, however. The comment, "I think about that Kirby sometimes," and subsequent lines, "I was not moved / to buy the machine. The princess phone / is in a landfill, returned to the elements by now, and the boyfriend, /

[3] Douglas Massey and Magaly Sánchez R, "Restrictive Immigration Policies and Latino Immigrant Identity in the United States," United Nations Development Programme Human Development Reports, October 11, 2013; Kyle Riismandel, *Neighborhood of Fear: The Suburban Crisis in American Culture, 1975–2001* (Baltimore, MD: Johns Hopkins UP, 2020), 8–9; 74–5; 179–80.

well, he got what he deserved," link the respective depersonalizations of the Kirby, Princess Telephone, and boyfriend, suggesting a connection between the speaker's indifference to the mid-century myth of time-saving gadgetry and her skepticism toward the equally powerful myth of male supremacy (lx; lxxv–lxxviii). However, the poem's last stanza *rehabilitates* the Kirby in a manner that exposes the difference between tool of patriarchal oppression, and tool for cleaning. First, the frank statement, "A Kirby is a good investment / I still maintain, if you have that kind of disposable income," highlights the harmlessness of the appliance itself, if divested of its gendered connotations (lxxix–lxxx). It is not the vacuum cleaner with attachments that ultimately maintains gender inequality, but the rhetoric around it, including the claims of its capacity to empower. What's more, the reader can infer exactly when the speaker's epiphanic realization of this harmlessness occurred from the poem's last lines: "the knives in the end proved worthless. The handles / cheaply made, and the blades not sharp enough / when it came time to use them" (lxxxi–lxxxiv). The discovery that the knives can't cut easily, thereby making the boyfriend's murder messy and laborious, is also a discovery about the falsity of the attributes ascribed to domestic goods more broadly—including the Kirby that, had she bought it, would not have been able to remove the bloody by-products of the killing.

Marquart's poem provides a useful way into discussing the links between the twentieth-century texts that we have examined thus far, and for considering the subsequent evolution of the time-saving appliance in postmillennial US literature. I have argued, thus far, that literary appliances—which is to say, fictive refrigerators, vacuum cleaners, washing machines, blenders, toasters, and the like—transformed the textual space in the twentieth century as much as their real-life counterparts transformed the domestic. The advent of time-saving appliances provided a new vocabulary for imagining social connectivity on the one hand and for justifying gender, class, and racial oppression on the other hand, and offered new ways of conceiving the relationship between the individual, home, family, and nation—not to mention the world and (in the case of sci-fi) universe(s) beyond. The authors that seized upon these opportunities revealed the time-saving appliance's suppleness as a signifying object, exposing its potential to symbolize liberation for some and oppression for others—and for these meanings to shift over time. Crucially, these writers enlisted time-saving appliances to comment on both contemporary shifts in the conceptualization and valuation of time, and their eras' relation to the past and the future.

Indeed, the close readings I have put forward reveal an abiding tension between past and future, tradition and progress, and nostalgia and futurism that has been inherent to the promotion of time-saving appliances since these objects' inception, and that is palpable across the literary responses to their initial appearance, subsequent saturation of the mass market, and eventual ubiquity. This tension reflects a contradiction inherent to time-saving appliances themselves, and which numerous of the texts discussed imply. While a direct result of advances in knowledge and the discovery of new manufacturing materials and processes, and while often promoted as bringing about a new and ultimately unknowable future, the impetus behind the creation of the "all-electric" home was, by and large, a *conservative* one, stemming from a desire to keep women in the home, to maintain a white hegemonic culture, and to affirm the United States' superiority over other nations. The promotion of time-saving appliances as obedient servants in the 1920s; components of a complex kitchen-factory in the 1930s; rewards for wartime frugality in the 1940s; sleek, stylish embodiments of the American "good life" (and capitalism's superiority over communism) in the 1950s; reasons for women to ignore the feminists and stay home in the 1960s and 1970s; and symbols of wholesome family values coded white and hetero and the durability of US manufacturing in the 1970s, 1980s, and 1990s (Civil Rights, Second-Wave Feminism, gay liberation movement, and outsourcing all be damned), is testament to the paradoxical emphasis on tradition and nostalgia in popular depictions of the "all-electric" home alongside claims of its "modernity" or intimation of a "space age," "atomic," or "digital" future.

This chapter extends the ideas discussed thus far to a selection of appliance depictions in writing published since 1991, including David Wojnarowicz's memoir, *Close to the Knives* (1991); Joan Didion's essay, "Sentimental Journeys" (1991); A. M. Homes's *Music for Torching* (1999); Charles H. Johnson's "Dr. King's Refrigerator" (2005); Catherynne M. Valente's *The Refrigerator Monologues* (2017); Lucy Ellmann's *Ducks, Newburyport* (2019); and Mattilda Bernstein Sycamore's *The Freezer Door* (2020), which are either set in the recent past or challenge long-standing assumptions on which American imperialism is based. Like Richard Yates's revision of the 1930s in "Oh Joseph, I'm So Tired" (discussed in Chapter 2), Joanna Russ's recollection of the 1950s in *The Two of Them* (Chapter 5), and Kurt Vonnegut and Don DeLillo's revisions of the Second World War and early postwar era (Chapter 6), these texts cast the past in a new light.

I read these texts in relation to some of the more prominent political upheavals of the last thirty years, and the coterminous rise, in popular culture, of nostalgic depictions of the mid-century home. Without claiming a direct link between latter and former, I argue that the proliferation of images of white housewives and 1950s appliances since the 1990s, like the popularization of mid-century design more broadly, is ascribable not only to the neutralizing effects of time's passage, which renders the past ripe for mythologization, but to a political landscape that has thrust, once more, the question of what constitutes "home" and "family" at the center of public discourse. The phenomena my chosen texts enlist appliances to discuss include the AIDS epidemic of the 1980s and early 1990s, the rise of gun violence since the late 1990s, the subprime mortgage crisis of 2007 and global recession of 2008–10, the rise of economic precarity, in-work poverty and homelessness, the rise of climate change-related natural disasters, and the growth of radical movements in an increasingly polarized political discourse. In these texts, the time-saving appliance is foregrounded in a more explicit, and cynical, way than in the texts discussed thus far—as evidenced by its presence, in some instances, in the very title. The anti-nostalgic time-saving appliances in end-of-millennial and postmillennial literature confirm the protagonist of *Ducks, Newburyport*'s conclusion that "you can *overdo* remembering, sometimes" (*DN*, 56). They reflect an abiding effort to challenge nostalgic accounts of the last three quarters of a century, and, perhaps, a recognition that as advertising grows subtler, more insidious, and more far-reaching, a more robust and explicit rebuttal is needed.

1. End-of-Millennial Luxury Appliances: David Wojnarowicz and Joan Didion

In 1992, the Coalition for the Homeless launched an ad campaign featuring an image of a corrugated cardboard box under the statement: "Something's wrong when Frigidaire and Westinghouse do a better job of housing the homeless than New York City."[4] The ad was a reference to the use of refrigerator boxes as shelters by the city's growing homeless population. Whether intentionally or not, the ad echoed similar statements that David Wojnarowicz and Joan Didion had each made, the year prior—the one, in his memoir of Reagan's America's response to the AIDS crisis, *Close to the Knives*; the other, in an essay in *The New Yorker* about the four Black men and one Latino man, known as the "Central Park Five," who were wrongly convicted of the rape of a white female jogger.[5] Like the ad, Wojnarowicz and Didion's texts alighted upon the contrasting fates of refrigerator and person to critique the valuation of property over people.

Wojnarowicz's description of a "skinny bum with red bare feet—once somebody's little baby—crawl[ing] into a box that once contained a refrigerator" also gestured, however, to the hypocrisy of an administration that claimed commitment to so-called family values (*CTTK*, 72). Occurring in a text that presented the Reagan administration's treatment of the AIDS crisis as an opportunity to stamp out homosexuals, Wojnarowicz's portrayal of the bum-once-somebody's-baby in an appliance box allegorized the violent ends to which heteronormativity is prepared to go to "preserve" itself. Meanwhile, Didion's essay described the self-righteous anger of middle- and upper-class New Yorkers to the "Central Park Five" as an expression of a "growing and previously inadmissible rage" against the "uneasy guilts that

[4] Chris Smith, "Poster Boy," *New York Magazine* (April 27, 1992): 20.

[5] David Wojnarowicz, *Close to the Knives: A Memoir of Disintegration* (Canongate, 2016 [1991]); Joan Didion, "Sentimental Journeys" (1990), in *We Tell Ourselves Stories in Order to Live: Collected Nonfiction* (New York: Alfred A. Knopf, 2006), 685–727. Henceforth, *CTTK* and *SJ*.

came to mind in a city where entire families slept in the discarded boxes in which new Sub-Zero refrigerators were delivered, at twenty-six hundred per, [*sic*] to more affluent families."[6] Denouncing the Central Park Five, Didion argued, was a circuitous way for the wealthy to voice anger at the effect of homeless people living in refrigerator boxes on their properties' curb appeal.

The brand Didion identified was also significant: the Sub-Zero is among the most expensive refrigerators on the market (in 2020, the largest model retailed for $17,965).[7] It became a status symbol in the 1980s and 1990s among the nation's elite due to its unusually large size, capacity to preserve food at lower temperatures, and purported potential to increase the value of one's property—so much so that a *New York Times* opinion piece published in 1998 about the rise of luxury rentals criticized its absence from Trump Tower's penthouse.[8] Retrospective accounts of New York City's rapid gentrification in the 1980s and 1990s, and of growing social inequality in America today, similarly frame the Sub-Zero as a symbol of obscene wealth.[9] This impression wasn't helped by the brand's introduction, in 1998, of a series of smaller units to fit in bedrooms or bathrooms, designed to eliminate the need for millionaires to cross 15,000 square feet to the kitchen for a snack.[10] Wojnarowicz's "box that once contained a refrigerator" and Didion's Sub-Zero convey how under financial capitalism the time-saving appliance's central function is not to save time but to enhance a property's accrual of value *over* time, while its discarded encasings provide shelter to those whom this economic system has displaced.

In "Living Close to the Knives," Wojnarowicz further enlisted an appliance to describe his rancor as his lover and mentor, Peter Hujar, lay dying of an AIDS-related illness:

> I talk inside my head . . . of need [*sic*] for something to suddenly and abruptly take place, like that last image of some Antonioni film where the young woman looks at the house that her father built and because of her gaze it explodes . . . the entire contents of the family refrigerator

---

[6] Citation on 721.

[7] 48" PRO Refrigerator/Freezer PRO4850 $17,965, *2020 Sub-Zero United States Distributor Price List*, 46. Based on the Bureau of Labor Statistics consumer price index, according to which 2020 prices are 88.5 percent higher than in 1991, the same refrigerator in 1991 would have cost $7,401.45.

[8] Tracie Rozhon, "Turf; Now, the Six-Figure Rent (Yes, Rent)," *New York Times* (January 8, 1998).

[9] Geoffrey Gilbert's *Rich and Poor in America: A Reference Handbook* (Santa Barbara, CA: ABC Clio, 2008) opens with a description of the life of America's wealthiest, who enjoy cold beverages from a "Sub-Zero PRO 48 refrigerator costing $12,000," which a minimum-wage worker "does not earn in a year" (1). William B. Irvine's *On Desire: Why We Want What We Want* (Oxford: Oxford UP, 2006), lists the Sub-Zero alongside luxury watches as emblematic of the insatiable desires of the ultra-rich (16).

[10] Patricia Leigh Brown, "Public Eye; The Fridge Flees the Kitchen," *The New York Times* (July 9, 1998), F1.

> lovingly spilling out toward the eye in rage, a perfect rage that I was beginning to understand . . . wanting . . . [to] create shockwaves that would cause all the manufacturing of the preinvented world to go tumbling down. (*CTTK*, 95–6)

Wojnarowicz was referring, here, to the climactic closing scene in Michelangelo Antonioni's cult film, *Zabriskie Point* (1970), in which the protagonist imagined the explosion of the desert home owned by her boss, a real estate developer ravaging the landscape with his luxury resorts.[11] The seven-minute sequence of household objects spiraling in the air illustrated the youth counterculture's rejection of bourgeois values, war, and white supremacy, while the exploding refrigerator flinging its contents across the sky countered the televisual images of plenitude with which this generation had grown up. Wojnarowicz's text incorporates Antonioni's imagery into his indictment of what he describes, elsewhere, as a genocide. The "entire contents of the family refrigerator lovingly spilling out toward the eye in rage" simultaneously embodies the anger of a population left to die, and the violence underlying the images of home and family that Reagan propagated throughout his time as ambassador for GE and his subsequent political career. The reference to the "preinvented world" links the refrigerator to those policy makers who, as Wojnarowicz puts it elsewhere, "can read instruction manuals from front to back and then follow them to the letter," and who see gay people as expendable but will fund the development of "laser[s to be] discharged from a device the size of a refrigerator" (*CCTK*, 147; 38).

2. From "The New Domesticity" to the #Tradwife: Time-Saving Appliances, Nostalgia, and White Nationalism

The depictions of time-saving appliances examined in the next sections extend Wojnarowicz and Didion's critical stance to critique the nostalgia for the mid-century home apparent in popular culture of the last three decades. The contradictions inherent to such nostalgia are exemplified by *International Flights*, a coffee cup collection launched by upmarket Italian coffee brand Illy in 2002. These featured a series of images by the aptly-pseudonymised artist Norma Jeane (Marilyn Monroe's real name) of flying washing machines against a sky-blue background. Seemingly without irony, the accompanying press release claimed the collection was inspired by the exploding house in *Zabriskie Point*.[12] It did not acknowledge that linking a product aimed at

[11] Michelangelo Antonioni, *Zabriskie Point* (Metro-Goldwyn-Meyer, 1970).

[12] Norma Jeane and Illy, *International Flights*. 2002. www.normajean-contemporary.com.

the bourgeoisie to one of the most memorable images of the bourgeoisie's destruction might be something of a contradiction in terms. Instead, the press release explained that the washing machines depicted were not photos of actual machines, but of model appliances intended to resemble an appliance-shaped refrigerator magnet. *International Flights* thus offered the customer a commodity bearing a mechanical reproduction (a silkscreened image) of a mechanical reproduction (a miniature model) of a washing machine intended to resemble a mechanical reproduction (a magnet) designed to decorate a machine surface (a refrigerator door). Not content with this Baudrillardian game, the press release made a direct link between the "liberated and at the same time dream-like effect" of the flying "consumer icons blown up" in *Zabriskie Point* to the cessation of time afforded by a coffee break: "Time suspended, a moment we devote to ourselves."

The clinical detachment of *International Flights* was paradigmatic of a broader shift in the popular depiction of time-saving appliances and the domestic sphere between the 1980s and the early 2000s. As discussed in Chapters 5 and 6, the nostalgic construction of mid-century America actually dates back to the 1970s, which saw the release of a spate of films and television shows set in the 1950s, as well as earth-toned appliance ads that positioned time-saving appliances as historical icons (Marcus, 9–35; Sprengler, 46–8). This nostalgia gained pace at the millennium's turn, with television shows such as *The Wonder Years* (1988–93) and *That Seventies Show* (1998–2006), and several dozen films, the vast majority of which either portrayed mid-century America in a sentimental light, or affectionately satirized it.[13] *All* of them featured scenes in kitchens bedecked with mid-century appliances. Indeed, vintage appliances in this period became a staple of television shows set in the present, as well—from Elaine Benes's vintage Hotpoint in *Seinfeld* (1989–98) and the Bundys' vintage GE Americana in *Married With Children* (1987–97), to Monica Geller's vintage International Harvester refrigerator, KitchenAid,

[13] Neal Marlens and Carol Black, *The Wonder Years* (1988–1993); Mark Brazill, Bonnie Turner, and Terry Turner, *That Seventies Show* (FOX, 1998–2006). The following is a non-exhaustive list of nostalgic and/or mid-century period films released between 1980 and the early 2000s: Lawrence Casdan, *The Big Chill* (Columbia, 1983); Robert Zemeckis, *Back to the Future* (Universal, 1985); David Lynch, *Blue Velvet* (De Laurentiis, 1986); Emile Ardolino, *Dirty Dancing* (Vestron, 1987); John Waters, *Hairspray* (New Line Cinema, 1988); Tim Burton, *Edward Scissorhands* (20th Century Fox, 1990); Oliver Stone, *The Doors* (Tri-Star, 1991) and *JFK* (Warner Bros, 1991); Robert Zemeckis, *Forrest Gump* (Paramount, 1994); Betty Thomas, *The Brady Bunch Movie* (Paramount, 1995); Ron Howard, *Apollo 13* (Universal Pictures, 1995); Jocelyn Moorhouse, *How to Make an American Quilt* (Universal, 1995); Tim Fywell, *Norma Jean and Marilyn* (HBO, 1996); Gary Ross, *Pleasantville* (New Line Cinema, 1998); Peter Weir, *The Truman Show* (Paramount, 1998); Hugh Wilson, *Blast from the Past* (New Line Cinema, 1999); Sofia Coppola, *The Virgin Suicides* (Paramount, 1999); James Mangold, *Girl, Interrupted* (Columbia, 1999); Mike Newell, *Mona Lisa Smile* (Sony, 2003); Peyton Reed, *Down with Love* (20th Century Fox, 2003). For incisive analyses of these and other works, see the essays in *Was It Yesterday?: Nostalgia in Contemporary Film and Television*, ed. Matthew Leggatt (New York: SUNY Press, 2021).

and upright Hoover and the vintage GE that appeared in Joey Tribbiani's kitchen in S06E20 in *Friends* (1994–2004), Joey Potter's vintage Frigidaire in *Dawson's Creek* (1998–2003), and, later, Lily Aldrin and Marshall Eriksen's (unspecified) vintage fridge in *How I Met Your Mother* (2005–14).[14]

The proliferation of mid-century appliances in late millennial television and film coincided with a broader revival in mid-century interior design, propelled in part by Cara Greenberg's coining of the term "mid-century modern" in the first retrospective book of the style, published in 1984.[15] "The 50s are back in vogue," concluded the *New York Times* in their analysis of the book's success, just as *LIFE* had a decade and a half earlier.[16] Renewed interest in mid-century culture likewise fueled Hamilton Beach's relaunch, in 1983, of its DrinkMaster in a range of pastel colors, under the slogan, "Full of Old-fashioned Flavour!"[17] Home cooking and kitchen design experienced a resurgence in interest in this same period, as so-called post-feminists argued that the movement had achieved its aims and women could now enjoy domestic pursuits as hobbies, and as the New Right called for a return to "traditional family values."[18] Stockbroker-turned-lifestyle entrepreneur Martha Stewart's *Martha Stewart Living* magazine, launched in 1990, amplified the period's repositioning of housework as a choice, an art, and a source of pride for white middle-class women.[19] Responding to these shifts, AT&T launched the Signature Princess Telephone in 1993 in homage to the original 1959 model (though with a touchtone dial, like the 1963 model).[20] KitchenAid extended its Model K Standing Mixer range in 1994 to include such colors evocative of the 1950s as Empire Red, Cobalt Blue, and Pastel Yellow, while in 1997 Italian appliance brand SMEG

---

[14] Larry David and Jerry Seinfeld, *Seinfeld* (NBC, 1989–1998); Michael G. Moye and Ron Leavitt, *Married With Children* (Fox, 1987–1997); David Crane and Martha Kaufman, *Friends* (NBC, 1994–2004); Kevin Williamson, *Dawson's Creek* (The WB, 1998–2005); Craig Thomas and Carter Bays, *How I Met Your Mother* (CBS, 2005–14).

[15] Cara Greenberg, *Mid-Century Modern Design* (Three Rivers Press, 1984).

[16] Suzanne Slesin, "Design Bookshelf; Some Attractive New Volumes Look Forward, Others Back," *The New York Times* (December 13, 1984): C10; Misc. Authors, "A *LIFE* Special: Nostalgia," *LIFE* (February 19, 1971): 39–78; Author Unknown, "The Nifty Fifties," *LIFE* (June 16, 1972): 38–46.

[17] "Take if from Mick, You Can't Pick a Better Premium than the Hamilton Beach DrinkMaster!" *Survey of Buying Power* (1983): 7.

[18] See Michell M. Nickerson, *Mothers of Conservatism* (Princeton, NJ: Princeton UP, 2012), 172.

[19] See Margaret Talbot, "Money, Time, and the Surrender of American Taste: Les Trés Riches Heures de Martha Stewart," *New Republic* (May 13, 1996); Sarah Abigail Leavitt, *From Catharine Beecher to Martha Stewart* (U of North Carolina Press, 2002), 195–206; Charlotte Brunsdon, "The Feminist in the Kitchen," in *Feminism in Popular Culture*, ed. Joanne Hollows and Rachel Moseley (London: Bloomsbury, 2006).

[20] Signature Princess Telephone, 1993; After Henry Dreyfuss Associates (United States); USA; compression-molded abs plastic, metal, electronic components; H x W x D: 10.5 x 21.5 x 10 cm (4 1/8 x 8 7/16 x 3 15/16 in.); Cooper Hewitt, Smithsonian Design Museum; Gift of AT&T; 1994-50-1.

launched a series of luxury "retro" refrigerators modeled on 1950s designs, and in summer 2001 Waring launched the Deluxe Waring 60th Anniversary blender, modelled on its 1935 design, and in a color it called "retro green."[21] 2001 also saw the launch of Nostalgia Appliances, a brand that claimed to offer "a unique way of looking towards an innovative future while holding on to the best parts of what came before." Its inaugural Vintage Hot Air Popcorn Maker, followed by "retro" s'mores and cotton candy makers, hot dog toasters, hot dog steamers, and tortilla bowl makers, claimed to capture "that familiar comfort of our favorite childhood foods, a style from a bygone era, [and] a memory we have or wish we had." (As this book went to press, the brand was celebrating its twentieth anniversary—which is to say, its twenty-year strategy of selling gadgets that had never existed before as both historical and timeless).[22] An article published in the January 2002 issue of *Popular Science* titled "High Tech vs. Retro Tech," which compared this new-old design to Oster's Y2K-inspired digitally-enhanced "In2itive Blender/Food Processor," identified the crucial dilemma for appliance design at the turn of the millennium: whether to promise the future, or a return to the past.[23]

The latter would appear to have won out. For the cult of the mid-century appliance gained pace in the 2000s and 2010s, buoyed by the rise of reality cooking programs and the proliferation of television shows either set in, or evocative of, the 1950s, which first box sets and then streaming services made available to audiences vastly larger than analog television was ever able.[24] Thus, the KitchenAid and Kenwood KMixer have vied for the

---

[21] Smith and Kraig, 432; "FAB28—History of FAB Fridges," SMEG Website, N.D.; "'Mix a Delicious Daiquiri in this Waring 60th Anniversary Blender,'" *Bloomberg Markets* 10. (June 2001): 110. See also Suzanne Mazur-Stommen, "'Appliances, Kitchen,'" in *The Encyclopedia of Consumption and Waste: The Social Science of Garbage,* Volume 1, ed. Carl A. Zimring and William L. Rathje (London: Sage, 2012), 28–29, but esp. 29.

[22] Nostalgia Appliances website, https://nostalgiaproducts.com/pages/about and https://nostalgiaproducts.com/collections/all.

[23] Author Unknown, "High Tech vs. Retro Tech: Can Microchips Make the Perfect Piña Colada?" *Popular Science* (January 2002), 8.

[24] The following is a non-exhaustive list of shows either set in or nostalgic for mid-century America: Marc Cherry, *Desperate Housewives* (ABC Studios, 2004–2012); Matthew Weiner, *Mad Men* (AMC, 2017–12); Andy Devonshire et al., *The Great British Bake-Off* (BBC Studios/Channel Four, 2010–); Michelle Ashford, *Masters of Sex* (Showtime, 2013–16); Carlton Cuse et al., *Bates Motel* (A&E, 2013–17); Bill Burr and Michael Price, *F is For Family* (Netflix, 2015–21); Stephanie Savage, *The Astronaut Wives Club* (Disney/ABC, 2015); John McNamara, *Aquarius* (NBC, 2015–16); Amy Palladino, *The Marvellous Mrs. Maisel* (Amazon Prime, 2017–); Joe Penhall, *Mindhunter* (Netflix, 2017–19); Dahvi Waller, *Mrs. America* (FX/Hulu, 2020); Scott Frank and Allen Scott, *The Queen's Gambit* (Netflix, 2020); Evan Romansky and Ryan Murphy, *Ratched* (Netflix, 2020). Time-saving appliances feature especially prominently in *Desperate Housewives*, whose pilot episode opens with Martha Huber visiting Mary Alice Young's house to investigate the sound of a gunshot, with the excuse of returning Mary Alice's blender. When Martha finds her dead, she keeps the blender. In S01E8, Mary Alice's husband bludgeons Martha with the same blender after discovering Martha had been blackmailing Mary Alice. In S0318, Karen McCluskey is revealed to have been hiding her husband's corpse in the basement freezer in order to keep receiving his pension

position of star protagonist of *The Great British Bake Off* (2009–), while guests on the reality cooking show *Girl Meets Farm* (2018–) are instructed to dress in outfits that will complement host Molly Yeh's pistachio green SMEG refrigerator.[25]

The rise of mid-century period film and television coincided with the renewed interest in vinyl and turntables, and the growing popularity of vintage consumer goods, including clothes, automobiles, dishware, appliances, and print ads, which social media sites such as Pinterest (founded in 2009), Instagram (2010), and TikTok (2016) propelled into a global phenomenon. One thus finds entire social media accounts dedicated to vintage appliances, appliance ads, and appliance manuals and cookbooks, YouTube channels showcasing how to restore vintage mixers, and fan sites for specific appliance brands or types (https://monitortop.freeforums.net/ for the GE Monitor Top, http://www.automaticbeyondbelief.org/ for the Sunbeam Toaster, https://sunbeammixmasterlove.tumblr.com for Sunbeam mixers, https:// kitchenaidworld.com/ for the KitchenAid Standing Mixer, https://www.vacumland.org/ for vintage vacuum cleaners, and so on), the latter of which one can purchase via eBay, Etsy, and independent online antiquarians.

Manufacturers have seized upon this enthusiasm. While one aspect of the industry has gone truly sci-fi by investing in research and development in the growing field of "smart appliances"—that is, appliances connected to the internet, which users can operate remotely via their mobile phones or tablets like a drone, and which can feed back data regarding usage patterns to the manufacturer to gain insight into consumer habits—another aspect has followed SMEG, KitchenAid, and Waring back into the past.[26] Thus, alongside robot vacuum cleaners and refrigerators like the AI-enhanced LG ThinQ that assist the user's diet goals, there have emerged brands such

checks. Appliances and nostalgia become more prominent from S05 (which aired in 2010) onwards. Bree publishes a nostalgic cookbook, and Lynette pitches a marketing campaign to her with the tagline, "Let Mrs. Van De Kamp Turn Your Oven into a Time Machine"—which Bree vetoes due to its liability to encourage children to climb into their mothers' appliances (S05E04). Elsewhere, appliances are used to denote class, and classist views: in S08E15, Lynette describes her son's having a child out of wedlock as evidence she is becoming "white trash": "I'm two weeks away from having a washing machine on the porch."

[25] Andy Devonshire et al., *The Great British Bake-Off* (BBC Studios/Channel Four, 2010); Molly Yeh, *Girl Meets Farm* (Food Network, 2018–). I am indebted to Sheila Liming for drawing my attention to the SMEG refrigerator's protagonism on Yeh's show. The press made much of the Kenwood KMix mixer's supplanting of the KitchenAid in S06 of *GBBO*: "The Great British Bake Off MIXER scandal: Enraged viewers take to Twitter as much loved KitchenAids are replaced with the 'inferior' Kenwood kMix," *Daily Mail* (August 6, 2015); "Great British Bake Off: Mystery of the Missing KitchenAid Mixers," *Daily Telegraph* (August 6, 2015).

[26] Adrienne So, "The Best Robot Vacuums," *WIRED* (July 16, 2020); Shoshana Zuboff, *The Age of Surveillance Capitalism: The Fight for a Human Future at the New Frontier of Power* (London: Profile, 2019), 233–8; 477–8.

as Big Chill, Swan, North Star, Chambers, and Unique, which specialize in 1950s-style appliances.[27] Some of the industry's leaders have also launched or extended their own "retro" ranges. In 2014, SMEG launched a range of "retro" toasters, blenders, standing mixers, and kettles to match its refrigerators; the following year, KitchenAid launched the "KitchenAid Iconic Fridge Freezer," whose design explicitly recalls that of the standing mixer, and whose name gestures to a nonexistent longevity, heritage and iconicity (the brand having never manufactured refrigerators before).[28] It also extended its range of colors to include pink, coral, and other whimsical hues. And in 2018 it launched a limited edition of its mixer in pale blue to commemorate the brand's centenary—despite the fact that the *mixer's* centenary won't be until 2037. An accompanying advertorial in *The Daily Mail* revealed a "newly unearthed collection" of print advertising images from its archives, while a television and digital campaign celebrated "countless memories made, countless more to come" to capitalize on the popularity of vintage ad collecting.[29]

While the press has ascribed the popularity of mid-century design to the lure of nostalgia during times of socioeconomic upheaval, the above-discussed examples demonstrate that this nostalgic thrust predated both 9/11 and the 2007–8 global financial crisis by several decades.[30] It is more likely that 9/11 and the financial crisis merely augmented the longing identified by Fredric Jameson, four decades ago, in the Whitney Museum talk and *New Left Review* article that what would become *Postmodernism: The Cultural Logic of Late Capitalism* (1991)—whereby popular depictions of the 1950s "refract" "the desperate attempt to appropriate a missing past . . . through the iron law of fashion change and the emergent ideology of the generation."[31] To this we might add that in the age of AI, "retro" appliances

[27] Josh Mears, "Diet-Friendly Fridges," *Trendhunter* (January 10, 2012).

[28] Laura Neilson, "SMEG Launches a Small Appliance Line," *Food Republic* (October 30, 2014); Maud Goodhart, "Design Classic: The Smeg FAB28 Refrigerator by Vittorio Bertazzoni, *Financial Times* (March 20, 2015); Stephanie Linning, "Collection of Retro KitchenAid Images Reveals How the Must-have Mixer Has Evolved from a Housewife's Gadget to a Bake Off Hero – as the Brand Celebrates Its 100th Anniversary," *Daily Mail Online* (February 2, 2019).

[29] Stephanie Linning, "Collection of Retro KitchenAid Images Reveals How the Must-Have Mixer Has Evolved from a Housewife's Gadget to a Bake Off Hero - as the Brand Celebrates Its 100th Anniversary," *Daily Mail Online* (February 2, 2019); KitchenAid, "Celebrating 100 Years of Making," *Progressive Electrical* (May 31, 2019): 4. At the time of writing, the campaign remains live on the brand's Japanese website: "Making History: 1919-2019. Explore a century of innovation and inspiration in the kitchen," https://www.kitchenaid.jp/en_jp/100year/history.html.

[30] Stuart Elliot, "Warm and Fuzzy Makes a Comeback," *New York Times* (April 6, 2009), N.P.; Stuart Elliott, "In Commercials, the Nostalgia Bowl," *The New York Times* (February 7, 2010), N3; Ruth La Ferla, "Longing for No Nostalgia," *The New York Times* (July 30, 2010), N.P.; Gabe Johnson, "Nickelodeon Nostalgia," *New York Times* (July 21, 2011), N.P.; Mike Daisey, "Against Nostalgia," *The New York Times* (October 6, 2011); Mark Hayward, "The Economic Crisis and After: Recovery, Reconstruction and Cultural Studies," *Cultural Studies* 24.3 (2010): 283–94.

[31] Fredric Jameson, "Postmodernism and Consumer Society," Whitney Museum Lecture, Autumn 1982; "Postmodernism, or, the Cultural Logic of Late Capitalism," *New Left Review*

have an additional appeal: they don't collect their owners' data to sell to third parties.[32] While a replica of an object that its first users would have found exciting, new, and futuristic, the "retro" appliance is, ironically, aimed at technophobes, and at those for whom the future is very scary indeed. The vintage appliance in turn offers the durability that newer models are perceived to lack, as attested by the ubiquity, on collectors' forums, of the complaint that "they just don't make them like they used to!"—a statement that gestures, however, to disillusionment with far more than shortened product lifecycles.

One could equally argue that the amplification of nostalgia in the 2010s was less a response to growing public interest in the past or response to financial uncertainty, than a phenomenon orchestrated by ad campaigns by brands terrified at the prospect of declining sales—and whose consultants were well-versed in postmodern theory. This would be in line with my own experience, while employed by a London-based market research company in the 2010s, where what we called the "nostalgia trend" was largely an incitement to clients to produce sepia-tinted ads in order to weather the recession. Put simply, one watches and purchases what is on offer—and in the last decade, it has been difficult to find homewares, furniture, or clothing that *don't* pay homage to the period 1940–75. Likewise, as Horkheimer and Adorno noted over seventy years ago in their claim that "the prepared ear can always guess the continuation after the first bars of a hit song and is gratified when it actually occurs," the pervasion of such design motifs across product categories and, crucially, across price bands has inculcated a new generation into what amounts to a formula for good taste.[33] While the "retro" blender functions to some extent as an emblem of self-expression for those who define themselves in relation to their passion for old things and past times, items like standing mixer-shaped earrings, or appliance-patterned sheets or kitchen accessories are arguably more indicative of the *ubiquity* of mid-century style. Thus what might have begun as a response to or anticipation of a collective need for reassurance quickly became the decade's defining style by mere default (as suggested by the recent proliferation in articles on how to choose a "retro" refrigerator).[34] Indeed, as attested by the obnoxious PTA mother who in *Modern Family* (S08E09, 2016) puns that her vintage toaster

I.146 (July/August 1984): 66–8; *Postmodernism: Or, The Logic of Late Capitalism* (Durham, NC: Duke UP, 1991), 19.

[32] For a discussion of smart appliance manufacturers' monetization of user data collected, see Zuboff, *The Age of Surveillance Capitalism* (London: Profile, 2019), 233–8.

[33] Theodore Adorno and Max Horkheimer, "The Culture Industry: Enlightenment as Mass Deception," in *Dialectic of Enlightenment*, transl. Edmund Jephcott; ed. Mieke Bal and Hent de Vries (Stanford UP, 2002 [1947]), 94–136. Citation on 99.

[34] Brittney Morgan, "The Best Retro Refrigerators You Can Buy," *House Beautiful* (January 29, 2020); Samuel J. Tan, "Top 5 Best Retro Fridge Freezers," *Colour My Living* (n.d.); Author Unknown, "7 Brands that Make Colorful Retro Style Refrigerators," *Designrulz* (n.d.); Tom Morgan, "Retro Fridge Freezer Buying Guide," *Which?* (n.d.); Luke Edward Hall, "The

collecting is a "crumby hobby," and who describes the school principal as "hotter than a vintage Sunbeam Toastrite," collecting vintage appliances has itself become something of a postmillennial cliché.[35]

Identifying the ramifications of this cult of the mid-century appliance is more straightforward. Very simply, it risks reinscribing long-standing myths that have, for nearly a century, projected the experiences of white middle-class protestant Americans in the 1950s as universal. Thus, Emily Matchar's interpretation, in *Homeward Bound: Why Women Are Embracing the New Domesticity* (2013), of her generation's "love of . . . vintage KitchenAids" as a rejection of "all-out careerism" only makes sense if one ignores those twenty- and thirty-something who do not have high-pressure "careers" so much as underpaid, precarious, low-skilled jobs, and for whom work is a necessity, not a choice.[36] The ascription, in a 2019 article in *The Atlantic*, of the popularity of KitchenAid standing mixers among this demographic to the economic uncertainty faced by a generation of renters in precarious employment, for whom the "traditional" markers of adulthood—marriage, home ownership, raising a family—remain inaccessible, was likewise based on the belief in a halcyon past in which all Americans were able to own their home.[37] What's more, the prescription of a $299 to $999 KitchenAid to alleviate existential angst fails when applied to anyone who isn't middle class or wealthy.[38] And yet echoes of this argument can nevertheless be found in media coverage of the renewed popularity of both baking and nostalgia during the first Covid-19 lockdown in spring 2020, not to mention KitchenAid's 2020 campaign, #MakeItTogether.[39]

Tyranny of Twee Kitchenalia," *Financial Times* (July 19, 2019); Merlisa Lawrence Corbett, "Best Technology for the Mid-century Modern Look," *Chicago Tribune* (February 18, 2021).

[35] "Snow Ball," *Modern Family* S08E9 (December 14, 2016), 13'03; 13'30.

[36] Emily Matchar, *Homeward Bound* (New York: Simon & Schuster, 2005), 5.

[37] Amanda Mull, "The New Trophies of Domesticity," *The Atlantic* (January 29, 2020).

[38] Figures are for the KitchenAid 4.3 L Classic Stand Mixer 5K45SS, 6.9 L Professional Stand Mixer 5KSM7990X, and Artisan Mini 3.5 Quart Tilt-Head Stand Mixer JSM3316XBM and taken from the KitchenAid US website.

[39] Jenny G. Zhang, "Quarantine Baking in Times of Crisis," *Eater* (March 13, 2020); Catherine Clifford, "Why Everyone Is #Quarantinebaking Their Way Through the Coronavirus Pandemic." CNBC (March 28, 2020); Katherine Gammon, "Kneading to Relax?" *The Guardian* (April 19, 2020); "Americans Have Baked All the Flour Away: The Pandemic Is Reintroducing the Nation to its Kitchens," *The Atlantic* (May 12, 2020). Sean Gammon and Gregory Ramshaw, "Distancing from the Present: Nostalgia and Leisure in Lockdown," *Leisure Sciences* (June 24, 2020); Alexandra Marvar, "Stress Baking More than Usual?" *The New York Times* (March 30, 2020); Katja Brunk et al., "How Coronavirus Made Us Nostalgic for a Past That Held the Promise of a Future," *The Conversation* (July 14, 2020); Oscar Rickett, "We Were Already Knee-Deep in Nostalgia: Coronavirus Has Just Made It Worse," *The Guardian* (April 20, 2020). KitchenAid's #MakeItTogether campaign was promoted as "inspir[ing] consumers and fuel[ing] their creativity as they hunker down at home," and capitalized on the surge in online searches for how to make bread (Larissa Faw, "KitchenAid's Data-Driven #MakeItTogether Campaign," *MediaPost* [April 24, 2020]).

In line with Sventlana Boym's definition of nostalgia—from the Greek words "*nóstos*" ("return home") and "*álgos*" ("longing")—as a "longing for a home that no longer exists or *has never existed*," the time-saving appliance in these accounts emerges as a symbol of a particular kind of domesticity in narratives that once more take the experiences of the white middle class to be representative of an entire generation, and that compare the conditions of those born after 1980 to one subset of their forerunners: the most privileged.[40] One wonders, too, whether Black, Latina, and other ethnic minority women, who continue to make up the majority of domestic workers in the United States, feel the same kind of affection toward the KitchenAid or retro-looking vacuum cleaner as their white counterparts.[41]

Appliance manufacturers themselves have contributed to this mystification of the past both in the launch of "iconic" product designs (most notably, 1950s-style microwaves, when the first domestic microwave did not become available until the 1970s!) and in the "brand history" pages of their websites which, as Jameson said of nostalgic media, "approac[h] the 'past' through stylistic connotation, conveying 'pastness' by the glossy qualities of the image, and . . . '1950s-ness' by the attributes of fashion."[42] The aestheticization of the 1950s on which the appliance industry currently capitalizes is necessarily premised on an essentialized version of the past and on the negation of these objects' contribution to the circumscription of women within the home and the suppression of professional cleaners' wages, not to mention a consumer-focused understanding of the value of science, technology, and the natural world.

The question of whose history the time-saving appliance embodies, and of who would actually benefit from a return to the 1950s, brings us to the most problematic aspects of what I call postmillennial nostalgia: its treatment of the gains made by Civil Rights, feminist, and gay activists as either guaranteed or regrettable. The second position is apparent in ironic appliance depictions such as those in the 2004 remake of Ira Levin's *The Stepford Wives*, discussed in Chapter 5. A title sequence featuring original footage of appliance ads from the 1940s and 1950s in which women dance with their gadgets (including those discussed in Chapter 2 of this study!), and a later scene in which Glenn Close's character leads the housewives in an exercise class involving dance moves named after appliances, neutralizes the concept of housewife-as-appliance that is only gestured at in Levin's original novel—*by rendering it explicit*. The distance of time between the movie

---

[40] Svetlana Boym, *The Future of Nostalgia* (New York: Basic, 2001), xiii. Emphasis added.

[41] See "Domestic Workers Are at Risk During the Coronavirus Crisis: Data Show Most Domestic Workers Are Black, Hispanic, or Asian Women." Economic Policy Institute Working Economics Blog (April 8, 2020). Mary Romero's now-canonical study, *Maid in the USA* (London: Routledge, 2002 [1992]), provides an incisive analysis of the lives of Latina immigrant domestic workers.

[42] *Postmodernism*, 19.

and both the early postwar era, when the housewife myth had the power to truly oppress, and the Women's Liberation Movement that promised to relegate it to obscurity, makes the aerobics class a comical novelty, a stance heightened by Nicole Kidman's rendition of Joanna as a caricature of the moody, all-black wearing, workaholic New Yorker. But from a critical feminist perspective, the credit sequence and aerobics scene affirm that the future envisaged by Levin has in fact arrived—not in the form of robot women, but in the transformation of feminist critique into ironic references to housewifery premised on the mistaken assumption that women in the twenty-first century have nothing to lose.

It is likewise disconcerting how quickly the tendency Matchar referred to as the "New Domesticity," already evident in characters such as *Desperate Housewives*' (2004–12) gun-toting, anti-immigrant homemaker Bree Van de Kamp, has evolved into the #tradwife movement, a crusade calling for white women to return to the domestic sphere and devote themselves to procreation in order to preserve the white race.[43] The movement's influence within the United States can be traced back to the aforementioned anti-feminist backlash of the 1990s, and, indeed, that of the 1980s and 1970s before that. Most notably, it is traceable back to the conservative activist Phyllis Schlafly, whose anti-feminist campaigning against the Equal Rights Amendment (ERA) in the 1970s contributed to the rise of the New Right, and who argued in her newsletter for housewives, *The Phyllis Schlafly Report*, that "The great heroes of women's liberation are not the straggly-haired women on television talk shows and picket lines, but Thomas Edison who brought the miracle of electricity to our homes to . . . run all those labor-saving devices."[44] While not all of these #tradwives align themselves with white supremacy as explicitly as their US counterparts, the movement as a whole—like Schlafly's Eagle Forum in the 1970s—is premised on the idealization of white femininity, the erasure of nonwhite women, and a skewed understanding of the postwar era that appears gleaned entirely from Second World War propaganda, 1950s ads, and postwar American television shows—or the Pinterest pages devoted to these—and that ignores the unevenness of access to goods and services in the period (or indeed the fact that the 1950s consumer boom reached the United States a full decade earlier than in other countries).

[43] Annie Kelly, "The Housewives of White Supremacy," *New York Times* (June 1, 2018), SR1. See also the interview with Nicole Jorgenson on the white nationalist radio show Radio 3-Fourteen: "How the Migrant Invasion Made Me Become a Trad Wife," Radio 3Fourteen (April 19, 2017); Seyward Darby, *Sisters in Hate: American Women on the Front Lines of White Supremacy* (New York: Hachette, 2020); Julia Ebner, *Going Dark: The Secret Social Lives of Extremists* (London: Bloomsbury, 2020).

[44] Kelly, SR1; Phyllis Schlafly, "What's Wrong with 'Equal Rights' for Women?" *The Phyllis Schlafly Report* 5.7 (February 1972): 1–4; *Debating the American Conservative Movement: 1945 to the Present*, ed. Donald T. Critchlow and Nancy MacLean (New York: Rowman & Littlefield), 197–201, citation on 199; Ginia Bellafante, "At Home with Phillis Schlafly," *The New York Times* (March 30, 2006), F.1.

Unsurprisingly, images of time-saving appliances feature heavily both in #tradwife blogs and social media accounts, where they once more stand out as paragons of wholesome love of hearth, husband, and nation that any claims to irony fail to truly undermine, and in media coverage of the movement.[45] Thus, the illustration by Na Kim accompanying Annie Kelly's 2018 piece on the #tradwives in the *New York Times* featured a Hoover ad of a housewife vacuuming superimposed on the statement "The Future is Female," which the vacuum nozzle appeared to erase. One of *The Daily Mail*'s stories about a prominent UK #tradwife featured a photograph of her in the company of her electric iron and KitchenAid mixer; another showed her posing with a mid-century upright vacuum cleaner.[46] The tongue-in-cheek disclaimer in an Instagram post plugging the article, "I swear I've never met that vacuum cleaner before in my life, I had to rush home to apologize to my faithful old Henry!," drew on the long-standing trope of the housewife married to her appliance, in which sexual desire is sublimated into a subject-object relation that reaffirms the housewife's subordination to her function as housekeeper and caregiver.[47] The difference, of course, is that *this* housewife also earns money from her persona in the way of product endorsements and paid subscribers to her YouTube channel, while the explosion of press stories about her "lifestyle" in the space of one week in January 2020, which served as plugs for the Darling Academy under the coverage of news, suggests she hasn't abandoned her marketing career after all.[48] As Catherine Rottenberg and Shani Orgad noted, far from rejecting neoliberal values, the #tradwives have capitalized on them.[49]

The account of the battle between Schlafly and second-wave feminists including Gloria Steinem, Shirley Chisolm, Betty Friedan, Bella Abzug, and Jill Ruckelshaus over the ERA put forth in the 2020 mini-series *Mrs. America* provides a corrective to the nostalgic currents just discussed.[50] Over the course of the eight episodes, Schlafly's nostalgic calls for the preservation of traditional gender roles reveal the distance between conservative rhetoric

---

[45] See, for example, Miranda Christou, "#Tradwives: Sexism as Gateway to White Supremacy," *OpenDemocracy* (March 17, 2020) and Sally Howard, "'I Want to Submit to my Husband like a 50s Housewife': Inside the Controversial UK Tradwife Movement," *Stylist* (December 2019).
[46] Monica Greep, "'Tradwife' Who Believes in Submitting to her Husband," *Daily Mail* (January 23, 2020).
[47] The Darling Academy, "Cleaning Up the Mess," *Instagram* (January 25, 2020), https://www.instagram.com/p/B7vODBKnUvm/?utm_source=ig_embed.
[48] Author Unknown, "#Tradwife: Submitting to my Husband like It's 1959," *BBC* (January 17, 2020); Polly Phillips, "I'm Proud to Be a Tradwife and Don't Regret Being Paid a 'wife bonus' by My Husband," *The Daily Telegraph* (January 21, 2020); Rebecca Flood, "Wild Wifestyle," *The Sun* (January 21, 2020); Monica Greep, "'Tradwife' Who Believes . . ." *Daily Mail Online* (January 23, 2020); Sadie Nicholas, "Darling, I'll Do Anything to Make You Happy!" *Daily Mail Online* (January 24, 2020); Jack Malvern, "Tradwife Is There to Serve," *The Times* (January 25, 2020).
[49] Catherine Rottenberg and Shani Orgad, "Why the Rise of the Domestic 'Tradwife' Tells Us More about Modern Work Culture than Feminism," *Prospect* (February 10, 2020).
[50] Dahvi Waller, *Mrs. America* (FX on Hulu, April 15 to May 27, 2020).

and reality. Like the #tradwives mentioned earlier, Schlafly is positioned as a woman who has built a career on telling women to forego theirs. Moreover, in contrast to the playfully ironic montage of dancing appliances in the title sequence of Oz's *The Stepford Wives*, the animated title sequence of *Mrs. America* portrays historical change as hard-won, and easily undone. The parade of housewives vacuuming up the text of the ERA as quickly as it emerges from Gloria Steinem's typewriter in this title sequence conveys that progress is a narrative involving colliding interests whose resolution is never assured. The soundtrack to this sequence—Walter Murphy's "Fifth of Beethoven," to which Glenn Close's housewife-minions do their washing-machine dance in *The Stepford Wives*—makes it all the more compelling to read *Mrs. America* as a corrective to Frank Oz's rose-tinted version of the past. In this version, appliances are oppressive maintainers of the status quo one would do well to resist romanticizing.

British playwright Laura Wade's play, *Home, I'm Darling* (2018), about a woman whose decision to give up her job, redecorate her home with vintage homewares, and live according to what she calls "'fifties values,'" similarly exposes how mid-century America's projection of itself both domestically and abroad has warped subsequent generations' understanding of the period—including those far from the United States' shores.[51] In an interview, Wade explained the play was a rebuttal of the "'fetishised domesticity'" of the 2000s and 2010s, which she ascribed to the deterioration of working conditions and the lack of child care support for working mothers.[52] In a nod to both *Death of a Salesman* and the mid-century sitcoms discussed in Chapters 2 and 6 of this study, an authentic 1950s refrigerator that doesn't actually work takes pride of place in Judy's kitchen, and is referenced throughout the play, which culminates with a rant by Judy's mother, who upon noticing the refrigerator yells: "'The fifties didn't even look like this in the fifties. You're living in a cartoon'" (*HID*, 37; 42; 62; 64; 74; 82). And in a nod to both the cult of the mid-century appliance, and the formulaic unhappy marriages of mid-century fiction, Judy's husband Johnny tells her, "'It's like the woman I love has been vacuumed out from inside of you'" (*HID*, 101). Whether the play's title is intended to be an ironic nod to the earlier-mentioned Darling Academy or not, the overarching narrative certainly highlights the dangers of nostalgia in its references to the mistreatment of Black, disabled, and gay people in the period Judy claims was so humane.

Like *Mrs. America* and *Home, I'm Darling*, the texts by Homes, Johnson, Valente, Ellmann, and Sycamore discussed in the next sections reappropriate

---

[51] Laura Wade, *Home, I'm Darling* (London: Oberon Books, 2019 [2018]), 39. Henceforth, *HID*.
[52] Emine Saner, "Recipe for Disaster: What's Behind the Rise of 50s-style Domesticity?" *The Guardian* (July 2, 2018).

time-saving appliances to challenge postmillennial popular culture's reduction of mid-century America to a celebration of white middle-class housewives waltzing with their refrigerators.

3. "She Decided to Grill the House":[53] A. M. Homes's *Music for Torching* (1999)

A. M. Homes's *Music for Torching* begins with the partial fulfillment of Antonioni's destructive fantasy in *Zabriskie Point.* Marketing executive Paul and housewife Elaine Weiss attempt to escape the boredom of white suburbia by setting fire to their (nonelectric) outdoor grill, hoping it will burn down their Westchester home. But the attempt only results in a semi-destroyed living room, no electricity, and a charred smell that will ultimately require professional cleaners to purify the air with a mega vacuum cleaner-like appliance that "'suck[s] the air out of the house and refill[s] it with something better'" (*MFT*, 161). The insurance company having found no sign of arson, repair to the damage will be reimbursed, thereby allowing the couple to undertake refurbishments for free. These are enthusiastically endorsed by the neighbors, who, in what Homes describes as a "postmodern barn raising," shower the Weisses with renovation advice, including the recommendation to install a Sub-Zero refrigerator (*MFT*, 47). Over the rest of the novel, the Weisses contend with the psychological legacy of a destructive act for which there appear to be no material consequences. That is, until the day after the renovation's completion and the housewarming party the neighbors throw them, when the seven-year-old son of one of Paul's lovers comes to school with a gun and a bomb made of aerosol cans of cleaning fluid strapped to his chest, and murders Sammy (*MFT*, 355). The catastrophe that the neighbors tell the Weisses throughout the novel "'could have happened to any one of us'" is not the fire they survived but a violent act by a child from within the community (*MFT*, 306).

Time-saving appliances (both electric and non) advance *Music for Torching*'s plot and serve as heavy-handed metaphors for the protagonists' alienation and cloistered privilege—from the (nonelectric) grill that starts the fire and the electric dishwasher whose loading punctuates both the novel's first and penultimate chapters, to the Weber Kettle grill Paul and Elaine receive the night before their son is murdered and which Elaine compares to a wrecking ball (*WFT*, 305). But these objects also participate in the text's sustained semi-parodic homage to the mid-century suburban novel and its descendants' obsessive concern with the annihilation of home

[53] A. M. Homes, *Music for Torching* (London: Granta, 1999), 36. Henceforth, *MFT.*

and family. In deploying time-saving appliances to illustrate the tensions at the novel's heart—exemplified by Elaine's vision of her husband telling people, "'There were hot dogs in the freezer, but instead of grilling them she decided to grill the house'"—Homes highlights both the myopia of mid-century literary depictions of the home as "enslaving" white middle-class women and "neutering" white middle-class men, *and* the endurance of the social norms that such fiction sought, in however limited a way, to challenge (*MFT*, 36).

This is apparent in the text's references to iconic literary depictions of appliances, the home-as-appliance, and automated women, from the portrayal of Elaine's neighbor, Pat Nielson, as a Stepford wife, to the mélange of mid-century sound bites that comprise Pat's reply to Elaine's query about why she married a man when she prefers women: "'I've made myself a wonderful life. . . . Nothing matters to me more than being normal. That's what I wanted most, a good life'" (*MFT*, 157–8). Meanwhile, the broken appliances that plague Elaine throughout the novel, which in fact opens with her mumbled prayer about the dishwasher, "'Hope it's fixed, hope it doesn't flood, hope the gasket isn't gone,'" recall housewife Gertrude Lockhart in Cheever's *The Wapshot Chronicle* (see Chapter 2) whose malfunctioning home drives her to suicide (*MFT*, 2). The stakes in each of Homes's homages however are far higher than anything imagined by Cheever, as evidenced by *Music for Torching*'s very structure, which subverts the tidy closure of *The Wapshot Chronicle*. Where the latter begins and ends with a priest's prayer for God's protection from postwar America's many explosive devices, the resemblance of the housewarming cookout in *Music for Torching*'s penultimate chapter to that in the opening, like the reference to the dishwasher loading in both scenes, gives the reader the sense of a *false* ending, leaving them unprepared for the school shooting to come.

Homes's homage to the appliance writing of earlier decades also highlights Westchester's, and by extension white suburbia's, resistance to the cultural shifts of the previous three decades. This is apparent in the novel's echoes of Yates's *Revolutionary Road*, which include not only Paul's serial infidelity and inexplicable success in a marketing job he barely understands, or his and Elaine's desire to transcend their suburban surroundings, but the positioning of the home itself as a coconspirator in the maintenance of conformity. The description of the "glow" of Pat and her husband George Nielson's illuminated house as "spill[ing] across the lawn, onto the neighbors' grass and brushing against the very foundations of other people's homes" recalls the hostile animism of the Wheelers' home (*MFT*, 145). Similarly, descriptions such as that of a neighborhood cookout where "men hover around the grill" while "the women bathe in the cold blue fluorescent light of the kitchen," a self-help pamphlet titled "'The Fear Index—Are you afraid of the vacuum cleaner?,'" and the home of a neighbor decorated with "the colors of 1957, of Ozzie and Harriet," portray Westchester as a community stuck in a past that never existed

(*MFT*, 10; 226; 278). Indeed, the mere half-dozen details in the novel that betray its end-of-millennial setting actually highlight the continuity between the 1950s and the 1990s as much as they situate the novel in the latter. Just as Elaine's subscription to *Martha Stewart Living* merely underscores the renewed appetite for "homemaking" in the 1990s, the popularity in the Weisses' neighborhood of "safety suites" that are effectively updated fallout shelters draws attention to the endurance of mid-century norms in the most privileged pockets of the United States at the end of the millennium (*MFT*, 267).

The text's juxtaposition of these mid-century images with the characters' critical commentary, which is infused with the rhetoric of queer, feminist, Marxist, and critical race theory, in turn exposes the ease with which such theories are subsumed by the very systems they seek to dismantle. Thus, when Pat's offer to remove a stain from Elaine's shirt leads to them unexpectedly having sex on the kitchen floor against a backdrop of working appliances, an encounter that might have radically reconfigured both the characters' social relations and the narrative possibilities of the suburban domestic novel is just as quickly neutralized. For Pat is "horrified" to notice "crumbs stuck to Elaine's ass" and immediately "lick[s] them off, sucking the crumbs from Elaine, from the floor, and swallowing them like a human vacuum cleaner. 'I sweep,' she says, wiping dust off her mouth. 'I sweep every day'" (*MFT*, 108). Even as they defy heteronormativity and break the marriage covenant, both women remain trapped in their respective roles, the one alternating between self-doubt and consternation, the latter scrambling to demonstrate her excellence as a hostess. Meanwhile Elaine's dismissal of her friend Liz's pursuit of a degree in women's studies, which involves writing papers on "'The Male Gaze as (Dis)played in Your Grocer's Dairy Case,'" reads as an exposure of feminist theory's limits (*MFT*, 117). Where Allen Ginsberg's fantasy, in "A Supermarket in California" (1956), of Walt Whitman "poking . . . among the / meats in the refrigerator aisle and eyeing the grocery boys," queered the postwar supermarket, his depiction of "Aisles / full of husbands! Wives in the avocadoes, babies in the tomatoes!" highlighting the role of the nuclear family in upholding capitalist consumer values, and where Marilyn French's PhD students in *The Women's Room* (1977) excitedly imagined the disruptive possibilities of studying "'the filthy refrigerator'" (see Chapter 3), Homes shows a new generation desensitized to critique.[54] In imagining Liz "writing a paper on 'The Burning House,' finding some sociocultural explanation for what happened," Elaine forecloses the very interpretation of the novel's events that I have been advancing, exemplifying what Martin Paul Eve has termed the tendency in contemporary fiction since the so-called postmodern turn to anticipate how it will be read by a university-educated

[54] Allen Ginsberg, *Howl and Other Poems* (San Francisco: City Lights, 1965 [1956]), 23–4, lines ix–x; vi–vii; *WR*, 250.

audience fluent in critical theory.[55] Such a tendency is arguably exemplified by DeLillo's *White Noise*, whose appliance depictions interspersed with whimsical analysis, as shown in Chapter 6, suggested that by the twilight of the twentieth century, critique of the "all-electric" home was effectively preprogrammed into it (and to whose "most photographed barn in America" Homes's earlier-quoted description of the "postmodern barn raising" appears to pay homage[56]). But Homes amplifies it. For example, Elaine's sarcastic reply, while loading the washing machine, to Paul's question, "'Aren't you supposed to separate the coloreds from the whites?,'" with the tight-lipped "'Segregation ended,'" simultaneously draws attention to the absence of people of color in the couple's neighborhood, the endurance of gendered divisions of labor (Paul does no housework), the whiteness of the literary tradition into which the novel has self-consciously placed itself, and, most importantly, the rise of an educated white middle class fluent in the language of oppression but ultimately compliant with white hegemonic norms (*MFT*, 8). A comparable ironic distancing is apparent in the depiction of Elaine and Pat's second sexual encounter, in Pat's laundry room:

> with Elaine on top of the washer, clinging to the control panel as the machine frantically vibrate[s] beneath her, whipping through the spin cycle, and then with Pat bare-assed on the dryer, tumbling, hot. Elaine remembers looking up at a shelf filled with cleaning products—Downy, Fantastik, Bon Ami—each item suddenly charged with intention, desire—housewife homoerotica. (*MFT*, 157)

While echoing the scenes of illicit laundry room lust discussed earlier in this study from Billy Pilgrim's dalliance with his neighbor in *Slaughterhouse-Five* (1969) to Norma Jean's vision, in *Norma Jean the Termite Queen* (1975) of the housewife who orgasms at her washing machine's effectiveness, Elaine's recollection of her abandonment to desire differs in its infusion with the vocabulary of cultural studies, and a self-conscious awareness of the moment's resemblance to countless pornographic fantasies, including those in the *Neighborhood Women* movies her husband watches in secret. Elaine understands this encounter to be based on an amalgamation of appliance clichés.

But Homes's critique of critique, as it were, is most apparent in the claim, by a male guest at the housewarming barbecue, that moving a TV to the backyard is "'a radical gesture'" that "'play[s] the interiority of the back against the exteriority of the front'" by "'substituting private space for public'" (*MFT*, 307). While recalling professor of packaging Murray

[55] *MFT*, 117. Martin Paul Eve, *Literature Against Criticism* (Cambridge: Open Book Publishers, 2016).
[56] *WN*, 12; 128.

Suskind's equally absurd claims in *White Noise*, the statement also stands out in its inaccuracy. The concept of the backyard conceived by the planners of postwar suburbia hinged precisely on the interplay of interior and exterior, and on the transformation of the back exterior of the home into a blend of living room, kitchen (represented by the outdoor grill) and Great Plain for the pioneering male to civilize via his lawn mower.[57] Homes's depiction of an asinine male academic striving to impress a woman with a high theory-infused analysis of the domestic sphere that at once misrepresents the history of the subject described and divests the word "radical" of any meaning exposes end-of-millennial cultural studies' formulaic and acritical properties. The response of an elderly neighbor, "'Whatever you do, don't marry him.... He'll reduce you to rubble,'" gestures to both the misogynistic tendencies of a particular kind of male intellectual, and the destructive consequences of a critical discourse empty of *actual* critique (*MFT*, 307). In these depictions, Homes conveys her awareness of the theoretical lenses through which the novel is likely to be approached, exposes theory's limits, and highlights the constrictive effect of the domestic ideal that continues to shape end-of-millennial relations among the most privileged. In sarcastically asking, "Does it matter more that Elaine tipped the grill or that she fucked Pat for breakfast?" Homes's text challenges John Updike's famous assertion that "'something quite intricate and fierce occurs in homes'" and that it is "'without doubt worthwhile to examine what it is.'"[58] She suggests, instead, the destructiveness bred by insularity.

4. "The Whole Universe Is in Our Refrigerator!":[59] Charles H. Johnson's "Dr. King's Refrigerator" (2005)

It is late at night on December 1, 1954, "exactly one year before Rosa Parks refused to give up her bus seat," and Martin Luther King, Jr., a newly married graduate student in his first pastorate at Dexter Avenue Baptist Church in Montgomery, Alabama, is behind on writing the coming Sunday's sermon (*DKR*, 23). Overcome by food cravings, he goes to the kitchen, where upon observing the myriad items inside the refrigerator, he is reminded of the

[57] In *Cold War Hothouses*, Snyder argues that by the 1950s "the kitchen, dining, and playroom are physically joined together and, with the backyard, constitute the largest 'room' of the suburban dwelling" (140).

[58] Jane Howard, "Can a Nice Novelist Finish First?" *LIFE* (November 4, 1966), 74–82. Citation on 74.

[59] Charles H. Johnson, "Dr. King's Refrigerator," in *Dr. King's Refrigerator* (New York: Simon & Schuster, 2011 [2005]), 21–32. Citation on 28. Henceforth, *DKR*.

showbread that, in Exod. 25:30, God instructs Moses to display in the Temple in Jerusalem:

> All of human culture, history, and civilization laid unscrolled at his feet, and he had only to step into his kitchen to discover it. No one people or tribe, living in one place on this planet, could produce the endless riches for the palate that he'd just pulled from his refrigerator. He looked around the dishevelled room, and he saw in each succulent fruit . . . a fragile, inescapable network of mutuality in which all earthly creatures were codependent, integrated, and tied in a single garment of destiny. (*DKR*, 27)

Upon hearing his expostulation that "'The whole universe is in our refrigerator!'" Martin's wife assumes he is drunk (*DKR*, 28; 29). But when he explains that he "'had a *revelation* tonight,'" of which "'ministers only get maybe one or two . . . in a lifetime,'" she "[g]racefully, like an angel, or the perfect wife in the book of Proverbs . . . place[s] her hand on his cheek," and goes quietly to bed (*DKR*, 30). The story ends with Martin "holding a very spiritually understood grapefruit in one hand and an ontologically clarified head of lettuce in the other," before putting the items back on the refrigerator shelves and deciding that "while his sermon c[an] wait until morning, his new wife definitely should not" (*DKR*, 31).

In this comical account of a young, overworked PhD student and a patient wife who has sacrificed her career to observe him discover the unity of humankind in a grapefruit, the refrigerator emerges as the source of an entire pacifist worldview that the man who later became the leader of the Civil Rights movement would describe in his famous "I Have a Dream" speech at the March on Washington (*DKR*, 24). Indeed, the text playfully suggests that it was the image of integration embodied in these refrigerated foods from different nations rather than the events of the Montgomery bus boycott that inspired his vision of a future in which "'the glory of the Lord shall be revealed and all flesh shall see it together.'"[60] This comedic speculation is complicated, however, by the story's references to the shortcomings of the young pastor's vision. The portrayal of Coretta Scott King (who, tellingly, is never even named) recalls her own statement, in 1986, "'I am made to sound like an attachment to a vacuum cleaner'" rather than an activist and woman in her own right who, as Jeanne Theoharis notes, "helped shape [King's] antipoverty work and his opposition to the war in Vietnam."[61] Meanwhile the description of these food items as paradigmatic of "a fragile, inescapable network of mutuality" recalls the principle of "complex interdependence"

---

[60] Dr. Martin Luther King, Jr, "I Have a Dream" (March on Washington for Jobs and Freedom, Lincoln Memorial, Washington D.C., August 28, 1963). The citation is from Amos 5:34.

[61] Qtd. in Jeanne Theoharis, *A More Beautiful and Terrible History: The Uses and Misuses of Civil Rights* (Boston, MA: Beacon Press, 2018), 156; 157.

in international relations articulated by Joseph Nye and Robert Keohane in 1977, according to which state cooperation would result from the decline of military force as a policy tool and the coterminous rise of economic interdependence between nations.[62] The items in Dr. King's refrigerator are both symbols of that economic interdependence, and reminders of its fragility—a point inescapable for Johnson's first readers (the story was published three and a half years after 9/11).

The refrigerator in Johnson's story thus conveys an obliviousness specific to male youth, and an optimism specific to pre-1960s America. Prior, that is, to Second-Wave Feminism, which for all its erasure of Black women's experience called into question the legitimacy of wives' relegation to serving their husbands; prior to the height of the Vietnam War; prior to the violence wreaked against anti-segregationists; and prior to the environmentalist and anti-globalization movements that revealed year-round access to seasonal and exotic fruits to be reliant on the disproportionate consumption of fossil fuels, and on the exploitation of natural resources and labor of the poorest nations.[63] Indeed, the complexity of Johnson's story lies in its enlisting of a time-saving appliance, and of specific food items, that lend themselves to both utopian and dystopian readings. The corn and squash "introduced by Indians to Europe in the fifteenth century," which Martin perceives to be emblematic of the generosity on which the United States was founded, stand out to the postmillennial reader as emblems of the forceful removal of indigenous tribes from their land in the name of the same "civilizing" efforts that would lead to the refrigerator's positioning, in historical accounts of domestic modernization as recent as 2015, as a gift to other backward nations (Anderson, 4–5; Rees, 187). One is reminded, here, of Diletta DiCristofaro's analysis of the refrigerator that in Matthew Sharpe's novel, *Jamestown* (2007), is powered by Pocahantas's life energy, as a "metaphor for the bodies of the colonized powering capitalist accumulation and white comfort."[64] Likewise, Martin's interpretation of the mingling of food items from such countries as China, Tibet, Mexico, Italy, and Japan as symbolizing a humanity "integrated, and tied in a single garment of destiny," exposes his short-sightedness, given these nations' historical conflicts with one another. Indeed, one could argue that it is not the specific places he invokes that expose

[62] Joseph Nye and Robert Keohane, *Power and Interdependence: World Politics in Transition* (New York: Little Brown and Company, 1977). I am grateful to Giovanni Dini for pointing out the links between the text and Nye and Keohane's ideas.

[63] See Willa Zehn, "Exports," in *The SAGE Encyclopedia of Food Issues*, ed. Ken Albala (London: Sage, 2015), 423–8; Tara Garnett, "Where Are the Best Opportunities for Reducing Greenhouse Gas Emissions in The Food System (Including the Food Chain)?" *Food Policy* 36 (2011): 23–32.

[64] Matthew Sharpe, *Jamestown* (New York: Soft Skull Press, 2007), 322, qtd. in Diletta DiCristofaro, *The Contemporary Post-Apocalyptic Novel: Critical Temporalities and the End Times* (New York: Palgrave Macmillan, 2019), 104.

his vision's fallaciousness, but the invocation of nations and states in the first place, the history of which is also, inherently, one of violence and oppression.

The language Johnson uses to describe the pastor's vision of the brotherhood of mankind in his fridge is also important, recalling the broader rhetoric of World Federalism that emerged in the immediate aftermath of the Second World War, and the co-option of such rhetoric by food, drink, and appliance manufacturers to capitalize on the growing market for international foods and the rise of air travel—from Edison's 1958 cookbook *Around the World Cookery with Electric Housewares* (discussed in Chapter 2), to *LOOK* magazine's invitation to readers to "eat your way around the world . . . from the home base of an American kitchen."[65] Johnson's story comments on postwar consumer culture's reliance on the lure of other countries, and on postwar America's reliance on the notion of the so-called melting pot, even as it excluded entire demographics from access to the most basic rights. By mimicking this rhetoric, Johnson highlights the disparity between capitalist imperialism's egalitarian conceptualization of all nations, peoples, and things as potential commodities, and the exploitation, oppression, and jingoistic suspicion on which such a system is premised, and which it obscures. Through his depiction of the pacifist vision of a man who would ultimately be assassinated for his views, Johnson conveys both the simplicity of the principles of equality and collaboration, and the extent of the United States' failure to uphold them.

Finally, by situating the young Martin's revelation in the mid-century home, Johnson's text challenges the nostalgic narratives advanced by the period television shows and films released in the 1990s/2000s, many of which, as I argued earlier, transformed the fraught class, gender, and race struggles of the postwar era into self-congratulatory stories of American triumph. Indeed, read alongside these depictions (from which Black characters were almost entirely absent), "Dr King's Refrigerator" reads as a parody of the obscurantism of nostalgic narratives that capitalize on the temporal distance between their audience and the time period portrayed in order to excise the period's more problematic aspects. By (playfully) attributing the source of the Civil Rights movement's leader's ethos to the time-saving appliance that mid-century America celebrated as embodying the quintessence of American ingenuity and whiteness in the same whimsical tone as these later cinematic and televisual accounts of white American exceptionalism, Johnson exposes the absurdity of both mid-century techno-utopianism and turn-of-millennium amnesia. In placing the leader of the Civil Rights movement in dialog with the most celebrated appurtenance

[65] Lesley Blanch, "Food for Americans from Around the World," *LOOK* (September 20, 1955), qtd. in Sylvia Lovegren, *Fashionable Food: Seven Decades of Food Fads* (Chicago: U of Chicago Press, 2005 [1995]), 198.

of the "all-electric" home, Johnson asks us to consider the ramifications of reducing mid-century America to a story about happy appliances, obedient wives, and genius husbands—or of limiting our efforts at reparation to expanding these narrative formulae to include Black people. His portrayal of the refrigerator as host to a "network of mutuality" provides an alternative symbology centered on communalism, multiculturalism, and an endless, constellatory openness to counter the symbology of containment advanced by postwar US government and manufacturers. How different might this period have looked, Johnson suggests, had Americans read the "all-electric" home through an empathic lens like that of his fictional Dr. King?

5. "Creating an Entire Superhero Universe to Make a Point":[66] Catherynne M. Valente's *The Refrigerator Monologues* (2017)

In 1999, Gail Simone responded to episode 54 of *Green Lantern*, "Forced Entry" (1994), in which Kyle Rayner finds his girlfriend's corpse stuffed in a refrigerator, by launching *Women in Refrigerators*, a website cataloging the deaths of female characters in superhero comics.[67] Catherynne M. Valente's 2017 novella about six women who meet in the afterlife after having been killed to advance the plots of their superhero boyfriends responded to the election of a man with a history of alleged rape and sexual assault as president by paying homage to both Simone's idea and Eve Ensler's iconic feminist play, *The Vagina Monologues* (1994), on which its title riffs.[68] The treatment of the "fridging" motif in the last of these origin stories, "Happy Birthday, Samantha Dane," renders explicit what Simone's critique only implied: entombing a female character in a refrigerator literalizes women's circumscription within the domestic sphere, and their long-standing conflation with the kitchen's appurtenances.

"Happy Birthday, Samantha Dane" reimagines *Green Lantern*'s Alexandra DeWitt as a photographer living in New York City during the Occupy Movement (2011–12). Samantha lives with Jason, a countercultural artist whose anti-capitalist, anti-racist graffiti, which follow the Dadaist ethos of "ephemerality," only lasting a few days before the City removes them, have gained a degree of permanence thanks to her photographic documentation

[66] Catherynne M. Valente, "Acknowledgements," in *The Refrigerator Monologues* (New York: Simon & Schuster, 2018), n.p. Henceforth, *TRM*.
[67] Ron Marz, Darryl Banks and Romeo Tanghal, "Forced Entry," *Green Lantern* 3.53 (August 1994); Gail Simone, Women in Refrigerators, https://www.lby3.com/wir/ (accessed October 28, 2019).
[68] Eve Ensler, *The Vagina Monologues* (London: Virago, 1994).

of his process in a wildly successful series ironically titled *The Gallery System Is a Noose Around the Neck of the Artist* (*TRM*, 125). The couple's life is upended when Jason discovers a button emblazoned with the motto, "The Wages of Sin Are Reaganomics," that grants him the power to temporarily turn his graffiti into living entities (*TRF*, 124). After Jason drops everything to join a group of other New York City superheroes, known collectively as the "Avant Garde," who use their superpowers to wreak revenge on the wealthy, Samantha is obliged to abandon her art to financially support them both (*TRM*, 134). A millionaire patron of the arts tempts her into allowing her pieces to be mass produced in exchange for funding—only for her to discover he is a supervillain out to destroy the Avant Garde by making Faustian pacts with artists that they must fulfill within twenty-four hours "'or the despair will make [them] pitch [themselves] out a window'" (*TRM*, 140). It is not despair that kills Samantha, however, but one of Jason's fellow superheroes, whom the villain's spirit possesses before murdering her and stuffing her, naked, in the refrigerator. Here Samantha realizes that avenging her will make Jason famous: "I belong in the refrigerator. Because the truth is, I'm just food for a superhero. He'll eat up my death and get the energy he needs to become a legend" (*TRM*, 144).

As this summary suggests, Valente's version of "Forced Entry" explicitly connects women's marginalization within comics to their treatment within countercultural politics, the art world, and US culture more broadly. Samantha's overnight demotion from co-artist to breadwinning caregiver once Jason joins the Avant Garde recalls less the narrative trajectory of male superheroes' female sidekicks than the position of the wives and lovers of countercultural artists associated with the New York scene in the 1960s and 1970s, who, like their foremothers in the French Surrealist movement, provided free labor as cooks, cleaners, childminders, muses, and secretaries before being forgotten.[69] Valente thus pointedly critiques the willingness of anti-capitalists to exploit when it suits them. The bargain Samantha makes with a villain whose rallying cry is that "'Reaganomics *saved* this country'" reads as a comment on the lack of options available to women artists, particularly in the aftermath of the 2007–8 global financial crisis that sparked the Occupy Movement against whose backdrop the story's events take place, and whose effects, studies have shown, disproportionately

[69] Linda Nochlin, "Why Have There Been No Great Women Artists?" *Artnews* (January 1971); Miriam Schapiro and Melissa Meyer, *Heresies: Women's Traditional Arts: The Politics of Aesthetics* (Winter 1978): 66–9. For a more recent assessment of women in art, see Maura Reilly, "Taking the Measure of Sexism: Facts, Figures, and Fixes," *ArtNEWS* (May 26, 2015). For insight into mid-century male New York artists' propensity for love affairs, see Russ Wetzsteon, *Republic of Dreams: Greenwich Village: The American Bohemia, 1910–1960* (New York: Simon & Schuster, 2002), 105–212.

affected women.[70] Meanwhile, the suicide of those who make a deal with the villain gestures both to the self-loathing of artists who sell out and to the fate of debtors unable to keep up with their payments to creditors. Valente renders her "fridged" female protagonist a casualty of both a debt-based economy and the historical tendency to privilege so-called male genius above the work or well-being of women, be they wives, lovers, or artists in their own right.

The literary appliance's susceptibility to co-option by formulaic narratives that uphold patriarchal capitalist values is implied in the story's very opening, where Samantha's comments, to the food items in the refrigerator, "it's just you and me, extra chunky peanut butter," appear to caricature the attitude of a lonely housewife binge-eating while her husband is at work (*TRM*, 122). It is likewise implied in the text's reference to Andy Warhol—the artist most closely associated, after Marcel Duchamp and Jean Tinguely, with incorporating domestic machines into art, but also criticized for representing popular culture uncritically—and to a photo that Samantha took of the Avant Garde, which is now "stuck on the outside of this refrigerator with a MOMA magnet" (*TRM*, 133). The latter description simultaneously conveys Samantha's subsumption by the Avant Garde superhero group (and, by extension, women artists' subsumption by a male-centric countercultural art scene); the Avant Garde movement's subsumption by the establishment; and the subsumption of time-saving appliances like the refrigerator into once-radical art works now valued at millions. From a different perspective, the refrigerator that stands for female oppression also points to a radical alternative to a long-since commodified counterculture—an escape route that leaves behind the art market, MOMA, and in-fighting Avant Garde artists who view themselves as superheroes. Just as the story's end suggests Jason's aesthetic of the ephemeral is *entirely in keeping* with an accelerationist culture constantly in search of new stimuli, Samantha's refrigerator-tomb is revealed to be an "escape" from the very notion of art as an investment, and from a culture industry that invests only in clichés (*TRM*, 147). Samantha's reunion, in the novella's final pages, with the other dead heroines gestures toward an open-ended future, in which she and her peers might create new narratives for themselves, unconstrained by the formulae of DC comics but also, I would argue, those of the mid-century realist fiction, television shows, and films that the text's references to refrigerators and kitchens implicitly challenge. The refrigerator thus functions as a kind of portal to another universe—a more radical version, in

[70] *TRM*, 139, emphasis in the original. See "Jobs: A Function of Demand," in *The State of Working America*, 12th edition, ed. Lawrence Mishel, Josh Bivens, Elise Gould, Heidi Shierholz (Ithaca: Cornell UP, 2012). See also Hilary Wething, "Job Growth in the Great Recession Has Not Been Equal between Men and Women," Economic Policy Institute Blog (August 26, 2014).

its dispensation of both linear time and *men*, of the freezer in Margaret St. Clair's "New Ritual" discussed in Chapter 5.

6. ". . . the Fact That There's Also the Vacuuming":[71] Lucy Ellmann's *Ducks, Newburyport* (2019) and the Trump-Era "All-Electric" Kitchen

A 1,000-page, one-sentence long inner monologue by an academic turned seller of home-baked goods that is occasionally interrupted by the story of a female mountain lion searching the Ohio wilderness for her cubs, Lucy Ellmann's *Ducks, Newburyport* (2019) reveals the kitchen's fundamental porosity. This is thanks to not only various digital devices that provide Ellmann's housewife-narrator instant insight into events occurring beyond her kitchen window but the infinitude of her own imagination, which is capable of transcending time and geographical distance as she bakes. In contending with issues as various as sexual assault, the legacy of slavery, the inescapability of social media, the lure of the kitchens in Nancy Meyers's romcoms, DuPont's role in the bombing of Hiroshima and Nagasaki, police brutality, reproductive rights, #tradwives, school shootings, and her husband's love of the clothes dryer, *Ducks, Newburyport* brings together all of the themes we have discussed thus far. But it also expands on them, taking the time-saving appliance's amenability to reinterpretation to its most extreme conclusion via a veritable avalanche of 103 references to domestic gadgets.[72] All of the time-saving appliances are connected to each other by virtue of the novel's very structure, wherein each sentence clause is linked by the expression "the fact that" without ever concluding, and wherein the narrative itself is propelled by the narrator's free associations between words, ideas, and events. But Ellmann's time-saving appliances are *also* connected by their shared narrative function: illustrating patriarchal white supremacy's capacity to withstand seemingly seismic cultural shifts,

[71] *DN*, 19.

[72] Refrigerator: 37. Fridge: 98; 104; 118; 222; 249; 309; 310; 475; 486; 629; 714; 888; 890; 895; 907; 933; 975; 983; 987 (three times); 988. Vacuum cleaners/vacuuming: 17; 19; 21; 85; 99; 148; 439; 442; 443; 610; 752; 920; 997. Freezer: 323; 413; 454–6; 617; 656; 710; 823; 891; 961; 979; 898. Dishwasher: 24; 26; 57; 59; 103; 110; 111; 610; 617; 662; 936. Kitchen/oven timer: 182; 964; 965; 976; 977; 981; 983. Mixer with kneading function: 42; 58; 76; 181; 273; 374; 717. Washing machine: 46; 231; 232 (three times); 272; 730. Dryer: 232; 353 (twice); 656; 752. Oven: 182 (twice); 189; 190; 372; 474; 967; 972. Stove: 98; 184; 415; 372; 474. Toaster oven: 84; 132. Microwave: 415. Apple-peeling machine: 752. Self-cleaning house: 638–9. Garbage disposal unit: 863.

and exposing the white middle-class housewife as a socially constructed figure designed to uphold gender, race, and class inequality. Consider, for example, the following passage:

> the fact that I don't take *any* pride in housework, as far as I know . . . houseproud Hausfrau, housewife, homemaker . . . the fact that nothing you do seems innocent anymore, the fact that even baking a pie has many ramifications, the fact that the more you bake the more you brood . . . stay-at-home moms, the fact that when I vacuum I wonder if movie stars ever vacuum, or aliens on other planets, the fact that it's pretty unlikely we're the only creatures in the universe bothered by dust after all, the fact that aliens probably think we're real slobs not to Swiffer our moon more . . . the fact that I don't know if sci-fi books ever get into how to clean up on other planets. (*DN*, 20–1)

Through this depiction of the networks of associations that constellate out from particular words, objects, slogans, literary genres, titles, and tropes, Ellmann demonstrates the potentially infinite imagination of a figure that US culture since the 1950s has positioned as entirely focused on hearth and family at the expense of everything else, including herself. In contrast to this caricature, Ellmann's protagonist contains multitudes. She is the daughter of academics, sister to a (now deceased) housewife much more organized than her, mother of four, wife, baker, ex-university lecturer of Ohio history, romantic comedy lover, foodie, begrudger of housework, Democrat, homebody, and a woman who has never recovered from the premature death of her mother. She is also neighbor to a Trump-supporting handyman called Ronny, who in the novel's final pages holds her and her children at gunpoint, shoots up the refrigerator and oven timer, and shovels raw cookie dough in his mouth while berating her for being a tease. In exposing the reader to each of these aspects of its unnamed protagonist, the novel tells the story of Trump's America, revealing the perspective from behind the kitchen sink to encompass the concerns of an entire nation, not to mention the world beyond. In turn, Ellmann takes the idea of the time-saving appliance as a networked object to its most extreme conclusions. The time-saving appliance in this text is shown to be an object plugged into a grid whose energy consumption has an ecological effect, and, too, a participant in a semiotic chain that radiates different meanings.

For one thing, the novel abounds with references not only to the appliances in the narrator's home but to those of friends, relatives, her childhood home, and her daydreams, and to those that furnish the homes in her favorite popular media. The latter include the rusty refrigerator in the pickup truck in which Cary Grant makes an escape in *North by Northwest* (1959), and the lyric, "*Picking on a wishbone from the Frigidaire*" from Dean Martin and Line Renaud's 1955 cover of "Two Sleepy People" (*DN*, 222; 474–5; 865). As well as enlivening the reader to "the fact that I probably learnt most of my housekeeping methods from movies," these references to fictitious appliances draw attention to the novel's place within a long tradition of popular film, television, and fiction in which electrically powered objects similarly communicate period-specific tensions around gender, race, class, and sexuality (*DN*, 475). Indeed, while the novel's reviewers were quick to compare Ellmann to Virginia Woolf, James Joyce, Thomas Pynchon, and David Foster Wallace, *Ducks, Newburyport* is actually more indebted to mid-century popular culture and second-wave feminist fiction (no less given Ellmann's remarks, in an interview, that she only read *Mrs. Dalloway* following reviewers' comparisons, and has never read Foster Wallace).[73] Such a reading is all the more compelling when one considers that Ellmann's mother, after whose hometown of Newburyport, Massachusetts, the book is named, was the pioneering feminist literary studies scholar Mary Ellmann.

Of particular note are *Ducks, Newburyport*'s multiple references to Rachel Carson's *Silent Spring* (1962), which helped launch the environmental movement in the United States, the trope of the Stepford wife, and the themes of the "mad housewife" novel (*DN*, 305; 349; 526; 916; 956). Ellmann's text also reflects the influence of Shirley Jackson's two memoirs of her life as a mother of four and faculty wife, *Life Among the Savages* (1953) and *Raising Demons* (1957), and Ruth Franklin's 2016 biography of Jackson—a point which the author herself confirmed in a Twitter exchange with me.[74] Like Jackson, who in her first memoir acknowledged her "wholehearted" fear of "such hazardous appliances as a toaster and an electric coffee pot," Ellmann's narrator frets about how many children die of suffocation every year playing in old freezers, the "millions of food poisoning cases a year" caused by "crockpots and slow cookers," the housewife in 1912 whose oven exploded when she opened it to check on her cherry pie, and her own narrow escape from a falling buckeye that "could've *killed* me, or at least . . . sent me sliding headfirst right over to the stove, where the oven door could have jolted open, dumping a red-hot

[73] Nora Krug, "Lucy Ellmann Interview: 'A Woman Writing a Long Book Is Considered Audacious, If Not Outrageous,'" *The Independent* (September 23, 2019). Comparisons between Ellmann and Foster Wallace, Joyce, and Pynchon were made in the following articles: John Warner, "Ducks, Newburyport," *Chicago Tribune Online* (September 3, 2019); D.J. Taylor, "*Ducks, Newburyport*," *The Times* (September 20, 2019); Sarah Ditum, "Lucy Ellmann's 1000-page Novel . . .," *New Statesman* (September 25, 2019); Ammar Kalia, "I Wish More People Would Read *Ducks, Newburyport*," *The Guardian* (May 6, 2020); Ellmann, *Thinking About Women* (Boston, MA: Thomson Learning, 1970 [1968]).

[74] Shirley Jackson, *Life Among the Savages* (New York: Penguin, 1997 [1953]). Henceforth, *LATS*. Portions appeared in *Charm*, *Collier's*, *Good Housekeeping*, *Harper's*, *Mademoiselle*, *Woman's Day*, and *Woman's Home Companion* between 1948 and 1952. Shirley Jackson, *Raising Demons* (New York: Penguin, 2015 [1957]). Henceforth, *RD*. Portions appeared in *Woman's Day* and *The New Yorker* between 1953 and 1956. Ruth Franklin, *Shirley Jackson: A Rather Haunted Life* (New York: W.W. Norton, 2016). Lucy Ellmann, Twitter post, June 14, 2020, 4:42 p.m., https://twitter.com/FictionAtelier/status/1272192691544231937.

tarte tartin right on top of my head" (*LAS*, 148; *DN*, 979; 550; 323; 190; 372–3; emphases in the original).

On one level, these appliance-centered anecdotes highlight domestic comedy's long-standing reliance on appliance-based disasters that make the housewife the butt of the joke (see Chapters 1, 2, 5, and 6 of this study).As the narrator puts it elsewhere, "I don't want to be Lucille Ball and have to make a fool of myself every week on TV for a living" (*DN*, 957). On another, they foreshadow the violent sequence at the novel's end, which is narrated in a style that underscores the simultaneous absurdity and horror of being held at gunpoint for not being more generous with one's baked goods. But most importantly, these anecdotes convey the "all-electric" home's simultaneous incapability of withstanding the threat of unchecked violence in a country with lax gun laws, and embodiment *of* violence in the form of the long-standing exploitation, and oppression, of white women and racial minorities. In particular, the juxtaposition of appliance anecdotes with references to "Ain't I a Woman?" (1851), Sojourner Truth's famous speech to white suffragettes in Akron, Ohio, and such comments as "Katherine Hepburn was into eugenics, the fact that a major lightbulb has gone in the downstairs hallway," indirectly points to the mutual imbrication of systemic racism, patriarchy, and a domestic sphere historically constructed as white and middle class (467; 638).

The novel foregrounds time-saving appliances' racial dimension in the very first pages. Here, the sudden memory of the narrator's deceased sister Abby's pristine fridge leads to her recognition "that sometimes I misspell 'refrigerator'" (*DN*, 37). This is followed by a meditation on how "OoJ stands for obstruction of justice, which is something Trump gets up to all the time"—a point that conveys how the failure to hold the highest office in the country to account empties the vocabulary of justice of meaning (*DN*, 37–8). The juxtaposition of these thoughts with "*Imitation of Life*, Lifting As We Climb [the slogan of the National Association of Colored Women], the fact that Abby was a *queen* of housekeeping, whereas I'm a slob" (*DN*, 38), indirectly points to the sharp differences between the heritage of white housewifery with which the protagonist and her sister must contend, and that of their Black peers—as well as white women's complicity in upholding white hegemonic capitalist norms. *Imitation of Life* is the title of Fannie Hurst's 1933 novel about a white woman and her Black housekeeper, and its two film adaptations of 1934 and 1959.[75] In the original novel, the white woman monetizes her housekeeper's recipe for waffles, building an instant waffle mix business whose profits the servant renounces, preferring

[75] Fannie Hurst, *Imitation of Life* (Durham, NC: Duke UP, 2015 [1933]); John M. Stahl, *Imitation of Life* (Universal Pictures, 1934); Douglas Sirk, *Imitation of Life* (Universal Pictures, 1959).

servitude. The first film has the housekeeper become a millionaire in her own right. The second removes this subplot altogether. Ellmann's reference to a title that could equally refer to Hurst's original novel or to the two cinematic adaptations, each of which offers different endings for its Black protagonist, suggests the potential for reparation. In broader terms, the sheer number of permutations and divagations between "fridge" and "slob" (not to mention the reference to a grassroots organization that successfully transformed the place of Black people in many communities across the United States, albeit via a questionable rhetoric of "uplift"), enacts the sense of open-endedness, and of individual and collective agency even in the bleakest of politico-economic landscapes, upon which the entire novel is premised.[76] The history of Black and white women's relationships to each other and to the structures of patriarchal capitalism, this passage suggests, needn't define the future. And the kitchen is as good a place as any to radically rethink one's place in the social fabric.

This notion of connectivity is foregrounded in the passages about the mountain lion that interrupt the protagonist's main narrative (*DN*, 407). But the mutual imbrication of wilderness and civilization is most vividly expressed in the narrator's alternation between eulogizing the benefits of her time-saving appliances and wondering about their potentially devastating ecological effects. In the opening pages, she describes her reliance on her "Candy-Apple Red, 7-quart kneading machine," noting, "I could make do without a different *color* 7-quart kneading machine, but I sure couldn't make all this cinnamon roll dough without *some* kind of kneading machine, and it wouldn't be as much fun if it wasn't Candy-Apple Red," and, "I bet that mixer's paid for itself by now, or I sure hope so anyway, the fact that these things are so expensive, the fact that some cost thousands" (*DN*, 42–3). The kneading machine, which is most likely the KitchenAid Pro Line 7 Quart Bowl-Lift Standing Mixer in Candy-Apple Red, emerges as both vital to the protagonist's baking business and a source of comfort, its bright color and sleek design rendering more pleasurable the labor that "people have no idea . . . goes into making a cinnamon roll."[77] Meanwhile its description as a purchase based on desire rather than a careful cost-benefit analysis recalls Shirley Jackson's deliberations, in *Life Among the Savages*, regarding whether she might justify the purchase of an electric mixer (*LATS*, 81; 83; 84).

---

[76] In *Beyond Respectability: The Intellectual Thought of Race Women* (Chicago, IL: U of Illinois Press, 2017), Brittney C. Cooper notes the fraught history of the expression "lifting as we climb," which "reinforced" the "divisive class politics" in the Black community following the rise of Jim Crow, wherein uplift" was premised on, in the words of Kevin Gaines, "placing a moral stigma on poverty" (51).

[77] *DN*, 42. While the color "Candy-Apple Red" is used by a number of manufacturers, as far as I am aware KitchenAid is the only appliance brand to use it for its red appliance range. See "All Stand Mixers, Candy Apple Red." kitchenaid.com.

In giving so much narrative space to the time-saving appliance, Ellmann challenges our conception of what is "valuable" versus "trivial," while complicating binary accounts in which a standing mixer embodies either familial loyalty or capitalist patriarchal exploitation. To the narrator's earlier acknowledgement that "I'm wallowing in domesticity here and I know it's stupid, hand-knitted baby blanket, toaster oven," this paean to the mixer affirms the validity of domesticity, recalling Gertrude Stein's hymn to the Mixmaster discussed in the Introduction to this study (*DN*, 84). These affirmations are undermined however in a later portrayal of the kneading machine as a participant, together with the household's other time-saving appliances, in the devastation of the natural world—and of GE, Whirlpool, Kenmore, and SMEG as among the country's most polluting companies (*DN*, 556; 996). Thus the narrator frets about her daughter Stacy's anger at her "car-driving and meat-eating and sugar-eating and consumerism and I don't know *what* all, my kneading machine, I guess, and the freezer, the washer and dryer," before reflecting on "the fact that Stonewall Jackson and John Brown both came from around here," and "Stonewall Jackson taught a slave how to read . . . so well, the slave read something about the Underground Railroad and took off for Canada," and "the fact that at least our *washer* is eco, which is something" (*DN*, 230–2). Through this page-long account of Stacy's disgust at the machines on which the household relies, Ellmann conveys the transformation of the time-saving appliance's meaning since the birth of the environmental movement in the 1960s, and the distance between its embodiment of both emancipation and gender conformity for second-wave feminists, and its embodiment of unchecked consumption in the face of dwindling energy resources for Stacy's generation. Meanwhile the seamless transition between the reference to Stonewall Jackson's involvement in the Underground Railroad and the emphasis on the washing machine's ecological credentials performs the historical understanding of the interchangeability of enslaved Black American and mechanical object.

I mentioned earlier that *Ducks, Newburyport*'s greatest debt is to Shirley Jackson's two memoirs, which contrasted with her Gothic fiction, presenting the home in whimsically comical terms, and her own role within it as centered entirely on housework while her academic husband worked in their study. To a postmillennial reader, and particularly one who has read Franklin's biography of Jackson, these depictions read as sanitized accounts of parenthood and marriage, while the absence of any reference in either memoir to Jackson's own writing career appears a concerted attempt to appeal to a particular kind of white middle-class female readership. These impressions are amplified by the time-saving appliances—and particularly a malfunctioning refrigerator—in the two memoirs, which function as characters in their own right, participating in various comedies of errors.

At first glance, *Ducks, Newburyport*'s comical accounts of mundane domestic incidents appear to pay tribute to these memoirs. But its juxtaposition of references to Shirley Jackson's own unhappy marriage with discussions of the unequal division of domestic labor and the narrator's children's infinite demands on her energy reveals a further purpose: to expose the account of domestic life advanced in her predecessor's memoirs as a myth. Comments like "Shirley Jackson never complained about anything much, including her husband, who did play around a bit, with his students," that "he sort of bullied her into writing, to help make ends meet," and that her own husband "is not like Shirley Jackson's husband," cast Jackson's narratives in a negative light, while highlighting the narrator's own convoluted ways of justifying the division of labor in her own home (*DN*, 106; 107; 106).[78] The final sequence in Ellmann's novel, wherein the "Make America Great Again" hat-wearing Ronny breaks into the protagonist's kitchen, likewise challenges Jackson's portrayal, in her memoirs, of the home as insulated from national or global politics. Indeed, it suggests that Jacksons's novel *We Have Always Lived in the Castle* (1963), which ends with the two sisters at the novel's center fending off a mob of townspeople and failing to prevent a fire from wrecking their house, is a more accurate account of both McCarthy's America, and of the American home's imbrication with the very violence, conflict, and threat from which entire industries have sought to protect it.

This challenge is especially apparent in the difference between Jackson's and Ellmann's refrigerators. *Raising Demons* features a forty-page-long comical description of Jackson's five-year-old daughter Sally's belief in her own paranormal powers to fix the refrigerator's faulty door and the family's subsequent discovery of a Freon leak, in this same appliance, that nearly blows up the entire house—a crisis averted thanks to the purchase of a new refrigerator (*RD*, 154–98). The refrigerator in *Ducks, Newburyport* by contrast is replete with DuPont filter jugs (necessary for making Ohio's toxic chemical-laden tap water potable [*DN*, 975]). After Ronny's invasion, it is covered in bullet holes that "look more spectacular than they are . . . like Jack Lemmon's double bass in *Some Like it Hot*" (*DN*, 987). Ellmann's narrator's fear that the liquid leaking from the fridge as a result of the bullet holes might be "something *worse* than water, like some nasty carcinogen" reads differently to the actual threat posed by the Freon leak in Jackson's text, given that water has proven to be toxic *throughout* Ellmann's novel (for example, two pages are devoted to listing all of Ohio's polluted waterways [*DN*, 326–7]). Ellmann's protagonist's later comparison of her incontinence during Ronny's attack to the leaking fridge extends the novel's concern with the historical association of women with leaky vessels, and historical conflation of women with their implements—the latter of which

[78] These assertions are borne out by, and perhaps derived from, Ruth Franklin's excellent biography of Jackson mentioned earlier, esp. 91; 98; 287; 298–9; 239.

arises earlier in the shooting sequence, when she notes that "it's weird but I remember thinking that that kind of timer's now very hard to get, the fact that he accused me of playing hard-to-get" (*DN*, 968; 964–5). In contrast to Jackson's comical appliances, Ellmann's reference to the family's newly acquired fear of "every noise, such as the *new* kitchen timer," whose sound "remind[s] me we could have been *killed*," reveals the transformation of her "all-electric" home into a site of trauma (*DN*, 976; 981).

7. "Everything Melts":[79] Anti-Normative Appliances in Mattilda Bernstein Sycamore's *The Freezer Door* (2020)

Mattilda Bernstein Sycamore's memoir, *The Freezer Door* (2020), comprises a hundred or so vignettes of Sycamore's life as an activist and sex worker in 1990s San Francisco and a writer in postmillennial Seattle. The text juxtaposes accounts of sex in public toilets and parks with mini-manifestoes against the assimilation of gay people into mainstream culture, the commodification of gay pride, gentrification, the shrinking of the welfare state, and militarization. In among these different narratives are wedged four (very funny) dialogs between an ice cube who "want[s] to be fluid," and an ice tray:

> Explain gentrification to me, says the ice cube. Crushed ice, says the ice cube tray . . .
> The only open relationship is the open door, says the ice cube tray.
> Are you trying to scare me with a metaphor, asks the ice cube . . .
> What do you do when you're not in the freezer, asks the ice cube.
> You don't want to know, says the ice cube tray . . .
> Explain violence to me, says the ice cube.
> Someone turns off the electricity, says the ice cube tray.
> What is the meaning of life, asks the ice cube.
> There's no future for us, says the ice cube tray. But sometimes I like living in denial.
> Explain nihilism to me, says the ice cube. Everything melts, says the ice cube tray.
> What is it like to gamble, asks the ice cube. Open the freezer door, says the ice cube tray. (*TFD*, 31–40)

[79] Mattilda Bernstein Sycamore, *The Freezer Door* (South Pasadena, CA: Semiotext(e), 2020), 40. Henceforth, *TFD*.

Sycamore personifies the ice cube as a non-binary thinker, while the ice tray sees the world in categories. Though humorous by dint of involving inanimate household objects, these dialogs are tinged with tragedy. The ice tray's claim "there's no future for us" echoes Sycamore's descriptions elsewhere about the agony of coming of age as a genderqueer person at the height of the AIDS crisis. The equating of an open relationship with the open freezer door that will result in the ice cube's decimation echoes her detailed descriptions of both homophobic violence and the legacy of the AIDS crisis, when to be polyamorous was, indeed, to risk death. And, of course, the ice cube's identification with fluidity articulates Sycamore's own struggle for acceptance as a self-proclaimed "genderqueer faggot queen" who goes by female pronouns in a culture defined by categories.[80] Crucially, Sycamore articulates these ideas via two objects that, as we have seen throughout this study, are deeply imbricated with the history of US imperialism, and a Cold War containment culture premised on the reinforcement of rigid gender roles. Via this ice cube who longs to escape the clutches of the ice tray and freezer, Sycamore skewers a whole host of values, associations, and ideals central to the American project—a project that she has, throughout her writing and activism, challenged.

This is a writer, after all, who disagreed with opposition to Don't Ask, Don't Tell, the policy introduced under Bill Clinton to prevent military applicants from being asked about their sexual orientation. She argued that gay people should be campaigning not to be allowed into the military, but for its disbanding.[81] And she has written candidly, both in this memoir and her other texts, about the sexual abuse she suffered, throughout her childhood, at the hands of her psychiatrist father.[82] When I interviewed her, Sycamore noted that for her, the suburbs will always be linked to the trauma of incest, and the violence of communities such as the wealthy suburbs of Washington, DC, where she grew up, in which the horrific acts that occur behind closed doors are sanctioned by the perpetrators' wealth—and in which privacy becomes a means to cloak abuse.[83] The freezer door at the center of her text is thus a provocation. Like the refrigerators in *Close to the Knives*, to whose author, David Wojnarowicz, Sycamore's memoir is dedicated, electrical cold storage in this text stands for the violence at the heart of the American project. But the freezer *door* offers an escape from this violence, and a more redemptive vision, ultimately, than Wojnarowicz's destructive lasers "the size of a refrigerator" and Antonioni-influenced fantasies of exploding

---

[80] Mattilda Bernstein Sycamore, Email Interview with Rachele Dini, March 5, 2021.

[81] "Does Opposing 'Don't Ask, Don't Tell' Bolster US militarism? A Debate with Lt. Dan Choi and Queer Activist Mattilda Bernstein Sycamore," *Democracy Now!* (October 22, 2010).

[82] Lara Mimosa Montes, "An Interview with Mattilda Bernstein Sycamore," *Believer Mag* (January 14, 2021).

[83] Mattilda Bernstein Sycamore, Email Interview with Rachele Dini, March 5, 2021.

refrigerators (*CTK*, 38; 72). It is a portal *out* of the private, the hidden, and the repressed—a means to access a radical openness and vulnerability premised on the rejection of categories, rules, and restraint.

The freezer door is the counterpoint, in fact, to the "Seattle Freeze," an expression used to describe the coldness of Seattleans, and which she notes might sound like "some kind of cute local popsicle flavour," but is actually "the gentrified gaze, the suburban imagination in the urban environment, the white picket fence in the eyes" (*TFD*, 220). This description echoes Sarah Schulman's description of yuppiedom in *The Gentrification of the Mind: Witness to a Lost Imagination* (2012)—a key influence for Sycamore.[84] In this book about the displacement of radical queer communities in New York City during the AIDS crisis, Schulman describes the "industrial minimalism" of a yuppie restaurant on Avenue A as "a bit like the inside of a refrigerator" (32). Sycamore's freezer door offers *an escape* from the cloistered, alienating chill of both the homogeneity of yuppiedom described by Schulman, and the Seattle Freeze—a chance to melt, mingle, and confuse the borders between selves.

Because the threat of the open freezer door is simultaneously the threat of dissolution, disclosure, and revelation. Sycamore's paean to melting might remind the reader of Marx and Engels's famous articulation of capitalism's incessant pursuit of greater efficiencies, which comes at the expense of human relations: "all that is solid melts into air."[85] The reader might also be reminded of Zygmunt Bauman's description of neoliberalism as "liquid" capitalism—defined by the frictionless flow of capital enabled by digital financialization.[86] But Sycamore's concept of melting is not so much a comment on either neoliberalization or its effects on social relations (even and despite her scathing commentaries on gentrification) but, rather, a *reappropriation* of liquidity, and of the interstitial state between liquid and solid, as metaphors for queer liberation. The open freezer door is not a metaphor for the catalyst of a liquid capitalism freed of human elements but, rather, a radical queer embodiment that allows, as Ahmed describes it (and as already cited in our discussion in Chapter 1 of the freezer in Kerouac), the "extending [of] bodies into spaces that create new folds, or new contours of what we could call livable or inhabitable space" (11).

---

[84] Sarah Schulman, *The Gentrification of the Mind: Witness to a Lost Imagination* (Berkeley, CA: University of California Press, 2012). Schulman is listed in Sycamore's acknowledgments (276) and referenced in a discussion of gentrification elsewhere in the memoir (125).

[85] *The Communist Manifesto*, 223. I presented these ideas to the members of the department of Contextual Studies at the University of St Gallen in March 2021. I am grateful to Dieter Thomä for his questions about the connections between Sycamore's fluidity, Marx, and Bauman and to Christa Binswanger for her questions about the relationship between Sycamore's text and Ahmed's ideas.

[86] Zygmunt Bauman, *Liquid Times: Living in an Age of Uncertainty* (Cambridge: Polity, 2007), 3; 121.

To open the freezer door is to disclose to the world the doubts housed inside it (personified in the ever-questioning ice cube, who relentlessly imagines different ways of being). And it is to disclose the different forms of control, coercion, and constraint on which the dream of America depends—personified in the tray that constrains the cubes in their boxes so reminiscent of mid-century suburban houses. Nor is it a coincidence that anytime the ice cube suggests the appeal of polyamory, of living between the states of solid and liquid, or of venturing outside the freezer, it is met with reminders of the dangers of such experimentation. While the freezer is revealed to be a closeted space where the desires of the non-conforming are put on ice, the freezer *door* is revealed to be a liminal space, a boundary between the inside of the cold storage unit and the exterior that if opened for too long negates the controlling functions of the freezer itself. The freezer door is a space of potentiality. The possibility of opening the freezer door is the possibility of transformation—and whether to melt is to be destroyed or to be transfigured is revealed to be subjective.

But while Cold War America looms as large over this text as the AIDS epidemic, the majority of the domestic spaces Sycamore describes are postmillennial ones. Likewise, her invocation of time-saving appliances to illustrate the effects of skyrocketing rents, rising homelessness, and a property market that discriminates against minorities, complicates a binary reading of these objects as symbols of domesticated militarism or heteronormativity. Her accounts of living in buildings with shared, barely functioning washing machines, and apartments equipped with outdated kitchen appliances, remind us that beyond their entanglement in semiotic systems, appliances are also objects that perform practical functions; that access to these objects is confined to those who can afford them; and that in the twenty-first century, a functioning stove and refrigerator are seen, by many, as basic necessities. By drawing the reader's attention to the absence of these necessities in her, and her peers', homes, Sycamore conveys the widening gap between the wealthy gay white men who have escaped into Seattle's gated communities, and the conditions of those who resist such assimilation. Resistance, she reminds us, involves sacrifice. A life of activism is often a life on the breadline. And gay assimilation is not the same as queer liberation. In describing the landscaped gardens of gated communities as militarized spaces and as the "new suburbs," and the leaf blowers that keep these areas pristine as embodiments of the social cleansing that gentrification entails, Sycamore links the commodification of LGBTQ+ pride to a new kind of containment culture, and shows the speed with which the project of US capitalism subsumes dissidence.

But again, Sycamore's loving descriptions of the time-saving appliances she eventually came to own provides a redemptive alternative to either disavowing home comforts or becoming a sell-out. Her nuanced depictions, like the image of the freezer door, allow us to linger in the space between ideological positions. The following passage is especially telling:

> I could describe the whole horrible process that gets me into the middle-class dream I never aspired to, but I'd rather tell you about the feeling of waking up in this new place . . . where I have a kitchen that I can hardly believe. . . . All the cabinets, there are so many cabinets. I don't have to keep my blender on a chair anymore. I spend my whole life in the kitchen, preparing all my food so I don't get sick. And still getting sicker. But it's nice to have a kitchen with room to dream. (*TFD*, 209)

Sycamore extricates time-saving appliances from their connotations of middle classness and reclaims the dream of sweetly scented laundry and gleaming kitchen surfaces from the jaws of an advertising landscape beholden to the military-industrial complex. The reference to the unspecified sickness that necessitates cooking from scratch in turn challenges the long-standing equation of the "all-electric" kitchen with physical fitness, and healthy American bodies redolent of the health, strength, and fortitude, of the state.[87] Sycamore divests the "all-electric" kitchen of its associations with an American Dream coded hetero, binary, and middle-class, and repopulates it with the dreams of a genderqueer person striving to overcome the infirmities of her body, and to imagine beyond the narrow confines of what America claims is possible.

The scene is all the more poignant in its homage to the tropes of mid-century appliance ads such as those discussed throughout this study, and in its recovery of the queer subtext of certain industrial films of the period. In particular, it recalls the Bell Telephone Company's film, *Once upon a Honeymoon* (1956), discussed in Chapter 2. Here, a board meeting of guardian angels looks down from heaven upon a suburban couple of newlyweds who have had to put off their honeymoon while the husband

[87] Here I am thinking about Shanon Fitzpatrick's work on the image of American athleticism promoted abroad in print magazines in the early twentieth century ("*Physical Culture's* World of Bodies: Transnational Participatory Pastiche and the Body Politics of America's Globalized Mass Culture," in *Body and Nation: The Global Realm of U.S. Body Politics in the Twentieth Century*, ed. Emily S. Rosenberg and Shanon Fitzpatrick (Duke UP, 2014): 83–108; Kristina Zarlengo's analysis of the role of public service announcements in encouraging housewives to see themselves as "warriors in training," cited in Chapter 5, and Rachel Louise Moran's work on the trajectory from early-twentieth-century "scientific mothering" to postwar investment in promoting physical fitness to win the Cold War (Rachel Louise Moran, *Governing Bodies: American Politics and the Shaping of the Modern Physique* [Philadelphia, PA: U of Pennsylvania P, 2018]). I'm also thinking of Reagan's own embodiment of masculine fitness, free enterprise, family values, and "all-electric" living throughout his time at GE. In our email interview, Sycamore explained that she suffers from a range of illnesses including fibromyalgia and chronic fatigue syndrome caused by the trauma of the abuse she suffered in childhood.

finishes writing a musical number called "The Wishing Song." They send a camp, bespectacled angel to help. From his perch on the roof of the couple's house, he observes the young housewife despair at the state of her outdated appliances and then make up a song about all of the gadgets she wishes she owned. In response, he showers fairy dust down on the house, new appliances appear, her song is a hit with her husband's producer, and the couple can go on their honeymoon and, it is implied, *finally* consummate their marriage. The Bell Telephone Company connects newlyweds to their dreams and helps maintain the sparks that make for healthy, hetero relationships.

And yet the community of male angels up on high gestures to other modes of living—be it the musical theater community or non-heteronormativity more broadly. The existence of this community is *what renders the honeymoon necessary.* Where the new appliances will free up the new wife's time and the *song* about appliances will ensure the husband is able to take time off for the honeymoon, the honeymoon will ensure he doesn't veer off with a fairy dust-wielding Broadway angel. You could even complicate this, and see the board room of angels as embodying corporate masculinity, and the camp guardian angel as the queer rogue element that fits in neither the heavens of corporate America nor the everyday drudgery of the home—in which case the task of the honeymoon is to ensure that the suburban husband doesn't end up in this queer in-between space (a space akin to Sycamore's freezer door) either. Sycamore's summary of the pleasures of appliance ownership, "Have a kitchen with room to dream," reminds us of *all the other kinds of dreams* that these time-saving might engender, and that indeed pullulated below the surface of ads produced at the height of the Eisenhower era. In refusing to describe the middle-class dream she never wanted, and instead lingering on the dreams and imaginative energies latent within objects long linked to the American project, Sycamore reveals time-saving appliances themselves to have long-standing repressed queer associations.

The Freezer Door beautifully complicates the appliance narratives discussed throughout this chapter, and throughout this study. The ice cube tray, in this context, is akin to the constraining little boxes of suburbia, and to the gated communities and gentrified neighborhoods she describes as militarized landscapes premised on the same principles of exclusivity and racial segregation as the postwar suburbs. Leaving the freezer door open, or pulling the plug on the freezer, function as metaphors for both a politics of radical hope, and for queerness itself—a chance to challenge what she sees as the suburbanization of the urban imagination. To open the freezer door is to allow the ice inside to melt, and to become "fluid," as Sycamore herself describes the ideal state of being. At the same time however her starry-eyed descriptions of her long-standing aspiration to own her own washing machine, and to have a kitchen with functioning appliances, remind us of the unevenness of access to the material benefits of these objects. They also retrospectively queer the narratives, in mid-century appliance ads, of housewives longing for a new refrigerator, and reveal the powerful queer subtext that underlay these narratives all along.

8. Conclusion

Homes, Johnson, Valente, Ellmann, and Sycamore's appliance depictions warn us of the consequences of taking at face value the object stories put forth in the admittedly beautiful period television shows, movies, and coffee table books about mid-century design, the mid-century kitchen, and mid-century advertising that have proliferated over the last two decades. They invite us to scrutinize the pastoral images associated with mid-century time-saving appliances—and to recognize the obfuscating qualities of both the claims of "futurity" first used to sell them a century ago, and those of "iconicity" and historicity used to sell them today.

I make these claims as someone who has long been enthralled with mid-century popular culture. I was raised on a diet of Hayley Mills Disney films, the soundtracks to *American Graffiti* (1973), *Grease* (1978), and *Forrest Gump* (1994), my mother's *Enciclopedia della Fanciulla* (1963–5; *The Young Lady's Encyclopedia*), and *L'America Del Rock* (1994), a series of retrospective compilations of US rock spanning 1950 to 1990 that the Italian newspaper *Le Repubblica* released in twelve monthly instalments, and which I studiously collected. Raised between Tuscany and the Midwest by Italian emigrés, I was attuned to the "Americanness" of the microwave oven, which my mother to my great frustration refused to buy, thinking it dangerous. I had an unusual fondness for upright vacuum cleaners, insisted my father equip my Barbies' apartment complex (a stack of cardboard boxes) with electric lighting, and was fascinated by the crock pot owned by the Quimby family in Beverley Cleary's *Ramona and her Mother* (1979).[88] I also came of age at the turn of the new millennium, as the cult of the mid-century appliance was gaining pace—which manifested itself, in my case, in an assiduous aspiration to own a pink Princess Telephone and pink SMEG refrigerator, whose ads I cut out from *La Repubblica*'s women's supplement, *D*, and pasted in my diary. The critiques I have put forward thus come from a place of simultaneous appreciation of, and exasperation at, the seductiveness of mid-century appliance nostalgia and the complex gender politics it obscures.

To my mind, the cover image of this monograph—a cropped version of Patty Carroll's photo installation, "Cooking the Goose," and part of her series, *Anonymous Women: Domestic Demise* (2016–2019), captures

[88] Beverly Cleary, *Ramona and her Mother* (Oxford: Oxford University Press, 1990 [1979]), 76–81.

this duality.[89] This image, which I discovered after Penguin used it for the cover of the 2021 reissue of Shirley Jacksons' second memoir, *Raising Demons*, literalizes the mid-century housewife's simultaneous conflation and entanglement with her kitchen gadgets. Like "May All Your Appliances Be White," another installation from the same series featuring a stark white female mannequin being throttled by a multitude of equally white appliances in a pale blue and white kitchen, "Cooking the Goose" forces the viewer to confront the violent underside of the idea of domestic femininity and feminine domesticity that lurks at the heart of the American Dream. The pink kitchen consuming its housewife in an apparent reimagining of Sylvia Plath's horrific suicide and the assemblage of alabaster mannequin and appliances that appears to embody the undiluted desires of white supremacy act as correctives to the postmillennial nostalgia for mid-century appliances. At the same time, the visually arresting qualities of these compositions enlivens us to the reasons for the pervasiveness of this nostalgia and our powerlessness against it. Simply put, and quite apart from the uncertainties of our own present, the mid-century "all-electric" kitchen is a thing of beauty.[90] It is all too easy to lose ourselves in its sheen.

I also want to emphasize that the texts discussed in this chapter are but a small sample of the proliferation of postmillennial fiction that depicts time-saving appliances ironically to critique heteronormativity, class inequality, the rigidity of bourgeois values, and the distance between media portrayals of the mid-century "all-electric" home and the lived experiences of actual Americans. One could, indeed, write an entire book on this genre alone, which I expect will continue growing in light of the continued popularity of mid-century design. Such a study might include the upright vacuum cleaner with which Alison Bechdel and her siblings strive to appease their closeted gay father's obsessive desire for a perfect house in her memoir, *Fun Home: A Family Tragicomic* (2006); the outdoor pile of broken appliances that foreshadows Hurricane Katrina's decimation of the Black working-class protagonists' home in Jesmyn Ward's *Salvage the Bones* (2011); Christina Nichol's use of the "all-electric" American home to comically allegorize globalization's effects on post-Soviet Georgia in *Waiting for the Electricity* (2014); and Jen Beagin's darkly comedic depictions of an otherwise cynical, and anti-materialist, twenty-something house cleaner's sentimental

[89] Shirley Jackson, *Raising Demons* (New York: Penguin, 2021). Patty Carroll, *Anonymous Women: Domestic Demise*, with text by Bruce Thorn (Savanna, GA: Aint-Bad, 2020), and https://pattycarroll.com/anonymous-woman-demise/.

[90] See also, Rachele Dini, "Things of Beauty: The Politics of Postmillennial Nostalgia for Midcentury Design," *Ancillary Review of Books* (June 21, 2021), https://ancillaryreviewofbooks.org/2021/06/21/things-of-beauty-the-politics-of-postmillennial-nostalgia-for-mid-century-design/ and Rachele Dini, Sophie Scott-Brown, and Sonia Solicari, "Mid Century Modern," BBC Radio 3, Free Thinking, June 23, 2021. https://www.bbc.co.uk/programmes/m000x709

attachment to her vintage upright Eureka vacuum cleaner in *Pretend I'm Dead* (2015) and its sequel, *Vacuum in the Dark* (2019).[91]

Finally, I am thinking of Michael D. Snediker's eloquent prose poem collection, *The Apartment of Tragic Appliances* (2013)—a "pile-up" of poem fragments that the preface invites us to imagine as an apartment full of broken appliances rented by a gay man called Persephone, and which, the speaker suggests, are best read through a (Walter) Benjaminian lens: if "'allegories are, in the realm of thoughts, what ruins are in the realm of things,'" Persephone "lives in an allegory and thinks ruinously."[92] Snediker asks us to consider what we might gain from contemplating appliances that fail to save us time—that break, cause fuses to blow, or stun us with an electric shock. What might we gain from seeing time-saving appliances not as allegories for either technological progress or traditional family values, but for a culture hell-bent on believing myths long-since debunked? Might the washing machines, refrigerators, and vacuum cleaners that lie in landfill—for no, most appliances are not disposed of responsibly—serve as a different kind of allegory to that imagined by GE, GM, and Westinghouse?

The centrality of time-saving appliances to these different texts' decimation of the American Dream reflects both the endurance of appliances as icons of American exceptionalism, and the coterminous capacity for such iconicity to be radically reclaimed.

---

[91] Alison Bechdel, *Fun Home: A Family Tragicomic* (New York: Jonathan Cape, 2006), 36; 43; 50; Jesmyn Ward, *Salvage the Bones* (London: Bloomsbury, 2011), 102; 189; 239; 258; Christina Nichol, *Waiting for the Electricity* (New York: Overlook, 2014), 192–213; Jen Beagin, *Pretend I'm Dead* (London: Oneworld, 2015), 23; 64–5, and *Vacuum in the Dark* (London: Oneworld, 2019), 145; 149; 180; 194–5.

[92] "Appliqué," in Michael D. Snediker, *The Apartment of Tragic Appliances* (Brooklyn, NY: Peanut Books, 2013), n.p.

Conclusion:

"All-Electric" Narratives after 2020, and the "Use" of Time-Saving

In this book, I have argued that the depiction of time-saving appliances in US literature of the last century, and particularly since 1945, provides insight into the transformation of the nation's conceptualization of home, family, work, and time itself. The texts I have examined enlist time-saving appliances, and the dizzying array of connotations used to sell them, to either challenge or uphold hegemonic values. The by turns sentimental, erotic, disappointing, absurd, nostalgic, and horrific gadgets in these texts challenge the attributes ascribed by advertisers to time-saving appliances and the "all-electric" home over the course of the last century, as well as audiences' expectations of how these objects might improve their lives. In so doing, they also transform the literary forms and genres in which their authors operated. By tracing the representation of time-saving appliances across specific authors' oeuvres and across specific genres, I have unearthed new ways of reading them—and exposed unexpected connections between writers of very different political persuasions.

Following the time-saving appliance has enabled us to discover Jack Kerouac's hidden affection for the refrigerator and the differences between his and his fellow Beats' gendered understandings of appliances more broadly, as well as to read the icebox in William Carlos Williams's iconic poem, "This is just to say . . ." as a melancholy swan song to nonelectric cold storage rather than an embrace of modern refrigeration. It has enabled us to uncover hitherto unexplored aspects of John Cheever's atomic anxieties; Richard Yates's engagements with mid-century media; Kurt Vonnegut's critiques of GE and the military industrial complex's leveraging of the nation's past; Don DeLillo's debunking of mid-century America's self-mythologizations; Marge Piercy's feminism; the narrative function of domestic technology in sci-fi; and Ralph Ellison, James Baldwin, Toni Morrison, Alice Walker, Alice Childress, and Paule Marshall's different aesthetic approaches to challenging white hegemony. What's more, following the time-saving appliance has enabled us to identify salient differences between US writers' understanding of the political symbology of time-saving gadgetry, and to recognize the appliance depictions of celebrated white heterosexual male writers to be instances of a much wider, heterogeneous, discourse, rather than representatives of it.

Following the time-saving appliance has also enabled us to trace how these objects have been used, throughout their history, to promote regressive values, and to position new social norms as "traditional" or "historical," even as they promised novelty, progress, and change. Likewise, excavating overlooked ads that portray Black servants as by turns unreliable, replaceable, or in need of educating in the ways of "all-electric" living has enabled us to challenge retrospective accounts of the time-saving appliance as emancipatory. General Electric, Kelvinator, and Frigidaire's denial of permissions to reproduce these ads in this book helps explain their absence from popular histories of advertising and is a further reminder of the influence these corporations still have on the public's perception of the history of both housework and commercial cleaning products and gadgets.

Finally, attending to the vocabulary of currents and connectivity in the work of certain of these writers has enabled us to identify the ways in which they resisted the individualism propagated by the electric utilities and appliance industries since electricity was first harnessed for human use. The networks of humming gadgets in these texts suggest a recurring effort to re-imbue the concepts of electricity, home, and time itself with collectivist connotations—to imagine alternative forms of community and kinship in which energy sources are shared rather than hoarded, dwellings are erected for living rather than capital accrual, and time is spent in imaginative pursuits rather than underpaid, round-the-clock wage labor. What's more, the time-saving appliances in these texts ask us to consider what we *mean* by "time-saving." What happens to that saved time? Who benefits from it? And is that saving worth the exploitative labor practices on which these objects' manufacturing is premised, and the decimation of the environment in which it results?

The questions raised by the texts discussed in this study are far from resolved. And indeed it might be argued that it is only now, as we enter the third decade of the twenty-first century and approach the centenary of time-saving appliances' entry into the mass market, that we can appreciate the multifarious, often contradictory, meanings that the appurtenances of the "all-electric" American home have garnered. Likewise, as we hurtle toward a future in which "all-electric" living appears less and less sustainable and in which the need for time-saving appliances, in the absence of a human race to use them, could be up for debate, we are primed to examine from a more critical distance the different mythologizations of these objects and the complex interplay of literary responses these elicited. The division of household labor, the exploitation of professional cleaners (and the enduring tendency of these roles to be filled by immigrant women and women of color), and the environmentally devastating consequences of technologies manufactured by underpaid and often underage laborers in unsafe conditions only to end up in landfill where they are mined for spare parts, again by children, are pressing concerns for anyone committed to living in a more just society.[1]

So, too, are the ramifications of equipping our homes with smart appliances that have the capacity to harvest our data, providing manufacturers free insight into how to sell us more stuff, and whose female gendering reaffirms that housework is women's work, even when done by machines (of which Amazon's Alexa and Toshiba's "Femininity" appliance range are perhaps the most heinous examples).[2] As Jennifer Gabrys notes, so-called enabling smart technologies generate "distinct ways of life," where what Deleuze terms a "'microphysics of power' is performed through everyday scenarios": subjects' actions "have less to do with individuals exercising rights and responsibilities, and more to do with operationalising the cybernetic functions of the smart city."[3] The ramifications of such a worldview, and of such subject-object relations, should give us pause. And this is not to mention the consequences of an industry that values convenience and aerodynamic design at the expense of environmental sustainability—as seen, most recently, in Dyson's announced plans to devote all R&D resources to the development of wireless models powered by lithium batteries whose safe disposal is difficult if not impossible, or by recent research demonstrating that the reduction in household energy consumption enabled by smart home

---

[1] See: Sally Howard, *The Home Stretch: Why It's Time to Come Clean About Who Does the Dishes* (New York: Atlantic Books, 2020); Jennifer Gabrys, *Digital Rubbish: A Natural History of Electronics* (Ann Arbor: Michigan UP, 2011), 81 and 141; "Tragedies of Globalization: The Truth Behind Electronics Sweathops," goodelectronics.og/Chinalaborwatch.org (July 12, 2011); Lorella Fava, "Child Labour: An Unspoken Truth of the Electronic Waste Industry," *Paper Round, BPR Group* (September 17, 2019); Amit Kumar et al., "E-waste: An Overview on Generation, Collection, Legislation and Recycling Practices," *Resources, Conservation and Recycling* 122 (July 2017): 32–42; "Yunhui Zhang et al., "Blood Lead Levels among Chinese Children: The Shifting Influence of Industry, Traffic, and E-Waste over Three Decades," *Environment International* 135 (February 2020).

[2] William Mitchell and Federico Casalegno, *Connected Sustainable Cities* (Boston, MA: MIT Mobile Experience Lab Publishing, 2008), 59. Astoundingly, while the authors enumerate "Femininity's" "foodstuffs management functionality" that "suggests recipes based on family preferences," they make no mention of the gendered dimension of the system's name or its associations.

[3] Jennifer Gabrys, "Programming Environments: Environmentality and Citizen Sensing in the Smart City," in *Smart Urbanism: Utopian Vision or False Dawn?*, ed. Simon Marvin, Andrés Luque-Ayala, and Colin McFarlane (London: Routledge, 2016), 88–107. Citation on 96. For a discussion of the uses of smart appliances such as the Roomba vacuum cleaner in data harvesting see Zuboff, *The Age of Surveillance Capitalism*, 233–8; 477–8.

energy systems that allow users to turn off the heating or specific appliances remotely is outweighed by the electricity required to run them.[4]

The often-harrowing story of our time-saving' deployment in advancing questionable ideologies and agendas, which the texts we have discussed reveal, provides a cautionary tale against taking at face value the placating rhetoric around smart technology. And it suggests the merits of approaching with skepticism military technologies that effectively domesticate warfare. As Giorgio Mariani notes, military drones "carry out the main business of war—that is, killing—as their 'pilots' sit in front of a computer screen, perhaps sipping on their morning coffee [before] get[ting] in their cars and driv[ing] back home to their spouses and kids."[5] Where appliance manufacturers during the Second World War positioned themselves as "peacetime makers" thanks to their contribution to weapons production, and Cold War-era manufacturers described time-saving appliances and defense weaponry as collaborators in the protection and advancement of the American way of life, contemporary discussions around smart technology risk conflating the convenience of turning off the oven remotely from the office with bombing the enemy from one's home. What's more, as J. D. Schnepf argues in her analyses of magazines such as *Martha Stewart Living* and *Vogue*'s representations of women using drones in the home, the drone itself has become a powerful means to feminize and domesticate the War on Terror.[6] Amazon's launch of the Halo wristband—a fitness tracker that also informs the user if "their tone of voice is 'overbearing,' or 'irritated,'" is of a piece with this and other new technologies.[7] Where the domestic drone updates the figure of the Cold War housewife-as-warrior for the twenty-first century "Forever Wars," the tone-policing Halo provides a further means to monitor and control women's behaviour—effectively shrinking the distance between them, the Alexa, and Levin's Stepford wife.

The importance of being vigilant to the ethical issues time-saving appliances so often obscure has been further amplified by the Covid-19 crisis in ways that we have yet to fully grasp. The higher death toll among

---

[4] Michelle Fitzsimmons, "Dyson Is Done with Corded Vacuums," *TechRadar* (March 6, 2018); Amit Katwala, "The Spiralling Environmental Cost of our Lithium Battery Addiction," *WIRED* (August 5, 2018); Mary H. J. Farrell, "The Problem with Cordless Sticks? The Battery," *Consumer Reports* (June 25, 2020); Jean-Nicolas Louis, Antonio Calo, Kauko Leiviskä, and Eva Pongrácz, "Environmental Impacts and Benefits of Smart Home Automation: Life Cycle Assessment of Home energy Management System," *Science Direct* 48.1 (2015): 880–5. For a discussion of the environmental impact of data centers and smart technology, Nathan Ensmenger, "The Cloud Is a Factory," in *Your Computer Is On Fire,* ed. Thomas S. Mullaney, Benjamin Peters, Mar Hicks and Kavita Philip (Boston, MA: MIT Press, 2021), 29–50.

[5] Giorgio Mariani, *Waging War on War: Peacefighting in American Literature* (Chicago: U of Illinois Press, 2015), 191.

[6] J. D. Schnepf, "Domestic Aerial Photography in the Era of Drone Warfare," *Modern Fiction Studies* (Summer 2017): 270–87.

[7] Geoffrey A. Fowler and Heather Kelley, "Amazon's New Health Band Is the Most Invasive Tech We've Ever Tested," *The Washington Post* (December 10, 2020), n.p.

Black people has further revealed the ramifications of a broader history of structural racism, while the higher death toll (at the time of writing) among Americans than in any other nation has been interpreted by some critics as evidence of the human toll of the neoliberal policies of the last half century.[8] Early figures likewise indicate the disproportionate impact of the closure of schools and day cares on women, who overnight found themselves balancing work with childcare.[9] The response to these figures has followed a recognizable template, as exemplified by the controversy that came to be known as #cleanergate, when certain white middle-class feminists in the press decried as sexist the plea for households to pay their cleaners to stay at home.[10] By claiming that women were reliant on professional cleaners, these white feminists at once universalized the experience of white middle-class women; reinforced the assumption that men and children were incapable of housework; and implied that working-class women, women of color, and immigrant women's safety was worth sacrificing for the sake of their wealthier white sisters' convenience. The narrative was uncannily reminiscent of Judith Merril's 1952 novel, *Shadow on the Hearth*, in which the Black servant Veda is praised for risking exposure to nuclear fallout to assist her white female employer, and the long-standing treatment of domestic cleaners as little more than living appliances (see Chapters 3–6).

We should likewise pay attention to the gendered and classist discussion of the Covid home. For many, the home during lockdown has become an omnipresent space in which all aspects of living take place, including work. Whereas the word "appliance" codes domestic, the home office now competes with the kitchen as a site of appliance use—while for those with no home office, laptop and kitchen gadgets coexist on the kitchen table. While on one level this takes us back to preindustrial forms of domesticity, wherein work and "living" took place within the same four walls, the "always on-ness" of these appliances—and our employers' ability to contact us at all times, via multiple channels—takes us into an entirely new territory. And that's without considering the effects of #cleaninfluencers—(primarily female) social media users with thousands of followers and endorsed by

[8] David Barsaim, "Noam Chomsky: What History Shows Us About Responding to Coronavirus," *Lithub.com* (May 28, 2020). According to CNN's reporting of the Johns Hopkins University Center for Systems Science and Engineering's figures, as of May 22, 2021, the United States has recorded 589,393 deaths by Covid (180 per 100,000 people). The countries with the second and third highest death count are Brazil (446,309; 211 per 100,000 people), and India (295,525; 22 per 100,000 people).

[9] Helen Lewis, "The Coronavirus Is a Disaster for Feminism," *The Atlantic* (March 19, 2020); Harriet Walker, "It's Like *The Handmaid's Tale*," *The Times* (April 20, 2020); Helen Carroll, "Desperately Happy Housewives!" *Daily Mail* (April 19, 2020); Donna Ferguson, "'I Feel like a 1950s Housewife': How Lockdown Has Exposed the Gender Divide," *The Observer* (May 3, 2020); Eleanor Margolis, "Stop This Retro Nonsense . . ." *The Guardian* (April 23, 2020).

[10] Rosie Cox, "#Cleanergate: Domestic Workers and the Intimate Geographies of Lockdown," *Geography Directions RGS-IBG* (June 8, 2020).

corporations to "inspire" people in lockdown to "take control" of their living spaces and hygiene via a combination of self-help and militaristic rhetoric.

Perhaps more importantly, the reporting of early findings that sales of time-saving appliances, like domestic goods more broadly, have benefited from the lockdown obscures the vast differences between those with the funds and space for new gadgets.[11] It should likewise concern us that workers' and students' capacity to fulfill their obligations during lockdown is contingent on their ability to access broadband or to afford home computers and the higher utility bills that result from spending more time at home.[12] Such issues underscore once more the social ramifications of private ownership of utilities, bringing us back, full circle, to the debates of the 1920s and 1930s. If, as Ian Bogost suggests, the selling out of chest freezers in March 2020 in response to fears of food shortages is indicative of a wider shift toward pandemic-fueled stockpiling, this should be cause for more than a little concern, given the likely ramifications for those without the space or means to afford such cold storage solutions (let alone the cost of the electricity to power them).[13]

The media commentary around the technological transformation of the home during Covid feels especially uncanny when placed alongside the popular accounts of domestic time-saving technology discussed throughout this study. One hears, in these new accounts, echoes of the stories that proliferated in *Good Housekeeping*, *Popular Mechanics*, and *LIFE*. Indeed, *Playboy*'s pronouncement, in the introduction to "Leisure in the Seventies" (December 1970), that "This is the decade . . . when the American home will begin to emerge as a total environment . . . where modern man can live completely . . . we may never need to leave home" could well have been written in 2021.[14] One wonders how much our discussions of "future" technologies merely recapitulate the same wishes—and whether the whimsical framing of these narratives merely serves to obscure their more nefarious aspects, such as the erosion of privacy and home/work balance that is likely to result if the surveillance technology being trialed to monitor employees working from home becomes commonplace.[15]

---

[11] Romita Majumdar, "Lockdown Drives Demand for Home Automation Appliances," *LiveMint* (June 16, 2020); Angie Tran, "How Appliance and Electronics Brands Are Winning," *AdRoll* (May 20, 2020).

[12] Olga Khazan, "America's Terrible Internet Is Making Quarantine Worse," *The Atlantic* (August 17, 2020).

[13] Aimee Ortiz, "Freezers Sell Out as Consumers Stock Up," *The New York Times* (March 21, 2020), qtd. in Ian Bogost, "Revenge of the Suburbs," *The Atlantic* (June 19, 2020).

[14] Alan Adelson, "Leisure in the Seventies: At Home," *Playboy* (December 1970): 143; 162; 336–8.

[15] Sophia Maalsen and Robyn Dowling, "Covid-19 and the Accelerating Smart Home," *Big Data and Society* (July 28, 2020).

As I write this, the death count of Covid victims continues to climb. In an uncanny echo of MAGA hat-wearing Ronny's invasion of the narrator's home in *Ducks, Newburyport*, Trump supporters stormed the US Capitol in January 2021, announcing they were "taking back their house."[16] And critics across the spectrum note that while Trump may have been unseated, Trumpism is only just beginning. Meanwhile, the climate emergency is only growing more urgent. 2020 was the hottest year on record, and the first half of 2021 saw a two-week power outage in Texas. It is thus difficult, in May 2021, not to see *Ducks, Newburyport* as a warning—and its images of appliances that by turns explode, suffocate small children, electrocute housewives, and act as landing pads for the bullets of angry white supremacists as an allegory for a nation or world in disarray. Then again, perhaps we should be grateful to have access to warnings this eloquent.

Indeed, perhaps the best way to read the literary texts we have discussed throughout this study is not only as anti-advertisements that challenge the promises made by time-saving appliance advertisers and proponents of American exceptionalism but as alternative *manuals*—as how-*not*-to guides, warning us of the dangers of too rigorously believing the "myths and placards," as DeLillo's Dave Bell describes, the imperialistic stories with which the United States so loves to lull itself to sleep. These short stories, novels, and poems provide guidance far more useful than GE, Westinghouse, GM, or Ford's appliance pamphlets ever could. In telling the story of misbehaving, recalcitrant, and melancholy gadgets that systematically fail to save their owners any time at all, they provide a much-needed corrective to the swirling mire of myths with which twenty-first century-subjects are saturated. They encourage us to listen out for the crackling murmur of incipient shock and dysfunction, and to look beyond the glamor of soft curves and smooth veneers. We would do well to heed their invitation.

[16] The 2020 presidential campaign featured an unusual number of stories about appliances, likely due to the fact that much of the country was in lockdown. Among the most salient stories are follows: the RNC's branding of Nancy Pelosi as "Marie Antoinette" for owning a $24,000 refrigerator after Pelosi appeared on *The Late Show* via Zoom and shared her ice-cream preferences; a study published in the *New York Times* that asked readers to guess whether a person was a Trump or Biden supporter based on the contents of their fridge (whose surprising results simultaneously revealed and subverted readers' classist assumptions); and, in the last days of the presidential campaign, Trump's reiteration of his promise to "make appliances great again" with renewed fervor. See: David Boyer, "GOP Mocks 'Nancy Antoinette' After Pelosi Shows Off High-End Freezer Full of Ice-Cream," *The Washington Times* (April 16, 2020); John Keefe, "Can You Tell a 'Trump' Fridge from a 'Biden' Fridge?"—*The New York Times* (October 27, 2020); Author unknown, "'Make Dishwashers Great Again?' Trump Brings Reform to Popular Appliances," *Fox59.com* (October 29, 2020); Todd C. Frankel, "Trump's Big Policy Win: Stronger Showers, Faster Dishwashers. It's Something Almost Nobody Wanted," *Washington Post* (December 30, 2020).

BIBLIOGRAPHY

Archival Materials

Adelson, Alan. "Leisure in the Seventies: At Home." *Playboy*. December 1970. 143; 162; 336–8.
Admiral. "There Are Others That Are New, but None so Truly Modern! It's Food Heaven!" *LIFE*. March 13, 1950. 65.
Author Unknown. "Home Appliances: How Smart Can They Get?" *Popular Science*. March 1966. NP.
Author Unknown. "Microwave Mastery: Tasteful Presents." *Working Mother*. December 1987. 137–49.
Author Unknown. "Mr. Darling Paints his Dreamhouse." *LIFE*. June 25, 1971. 66–9.
Author Unknown. "'Operation Cue': Latest Photos of Atom Bomb Test." *Gas Appliance Merchandising* 27.7 (July 1955): 12–13.
Author Unknown. "The New Domesticated American Male." *LIFE*. January 4, 1954. 42–5. Citation on 44.
Author Unknown. "The Nifty Fifties." *LIFE*. June 16, 1972. 38–46.
Author Unknown. "The Right Place: Where to Put your Microwave Oven." *Working Mother*. December 1987. 144–5.
Beaudine, William. *Design for Dreaming*. MPO Productions/GM, 1956.
Bird, Harry Lewis. *This Fascinating Advertising Business*. New York: Bobb-Merrill, 1947.
Blanch, Lesley. "Food for Americans from Around the World." *LOOK*. September 20, 1955. NP.
Brown, Donald H. *Young Man's Fancy*. Edison Electric Institute, 1952.
Bucher, George H. "The Electric Home of the Future." *Popular Mechanics* 72.2. August 1939. 161–2.
Champion, Gower. *Once Upon a Honeymoon*. Jerry Fairbanks Productions/Bell Systems, 1955. Prelinger Archives.
Church, Ruth Ellen. *Mary Meade's Magic Recipes for the Electric Osterizer*. Indianapolis and New York: Osterizer/Bobbs-Merrill Company, 1952.
Crosley. "A Care-free Kitchen Is the Heart of your Home so Set your Heart on a Crosley Shelvador." *LIFE*. March 2, 1953. 57.
DeBoth, Jessie M. *Frigidaire Frozen Delights*. Dayton, OH: Frigidaire Corporation, 1927. Alan and Shirley Brocker Sliker Collection, Michigan State University Library. Shortened henceforth to ASBSC, MSUL.
Department of Agriculture Office of Public Affairs. "A Step Saving Kitchen." 1949. Television ad.
Edison Electric Institute. *Around the World Cookery with Electric Housewares*. New York: Home Service Committee, 1958. ASBSC, MSUL.

Edison General Electric. *The Kitchen of Her Dreams*. Chicago: Edison GE Appliance Company, Inc and Hotpoint, 1920. ASBSC, MSUL.

Electric Light & Power Companies. "Try Telling the Lady She'll Have to Start Washing by Hand." *LIFE*. June 11, 1971. 2.

Federal Communications Commission. *Activities of Regulatory and Enforcement Agencies Relating to Small Business: Hearings Before Subcommittee No. 6 of the Select Committee on Small Business Part 2*. Washington: US Government Printing Office, 1966.

Frigidaire. "Another Space Age Advance: The Gemini 19… New Refrigerator-Freezer Twin." *LIFE*. May 20, 1966. 31.

Frigidaire. "Brilliant! This Convertible Beauty..." *LIFE*. November 21, 1955. 56.

Frigidaire. "Frigidaire Announces the Space Age Advance in Refrigeration." *LIFE*. November 19, 1965. 49.

Frigidaire. "Frigidaire Announces Space Age Refrigeration." *LIFE*. January 14, 1966. 7.

Frigidaire. *Frigidaire Refrigerators That Ride on Air!*. November 18, 1966.

Frigidaire. *How to Stay in Love for Years....* Dayton, OH: G.M. Corporation, 1947.

Frigidaire. "In 1918 We Made the Only Frigidaire Refrigerator. We Still Do." *LIFE*. December 15, 1972. 83.

Frigidaire. "Inexpensively the Frigidaire Provides ...." *Ladies' Home Journal*. April 1932. NP.

Frigidaire. "Is Your Wife Getting Muscles Where She Used to Have Curves?" *LIFE*. November 10, 1967. 3.

Frigidaire. "Now—the Refrigerator Made for Once-a-Week Shopping." *LIFE*. January 15, 1951. 47.

Frigidaire. "'Super-Duty' Frigidaire with the Meter-Miser." *LIFE*. May 10, 1937. 78.

Frigidaire. "That Mrs. Malard: So Smart to Own an Automatic Dishwasher." 1956. Television ad.

Frigidaire. "The Ride-Aire." *American Home* 69. 1966. 128.

Frigidaire. "You'll Feel Like a Queen ..." *LIFE*. September 14, 1959. 77.

Frigidaire. "Your Frigididaire Dishwasher Turns You On." *LIFE*. December 1, 1967. 22.

GE. "25% to 50% More Food Space in the General Electric Refrigerator!" *LIFE*. October 16, 1950. 26.

GE. "A Servant with Grand References Wants a Job in Your Kitchen!" *Good Housekeeping*. June 1933. 121.

GE. "For $179.95, You Can Keep Your Mother out of Scrapes." *LIFE*. April 18, 1969. 17.

GE. "How Wonderful . . . This Automatic Sleeping Comfort!" *LIFE*. September 2, 1946. 25.

GE. *Instructions and Recipes: General Electric Portable Mixer*. Bridgeport, CN: General Electric Company Appliance and Merchandise Department, 1947. ASBSC, MSUL.

GE. "Live Better Electrically." *GE Theatre*. 1950.

GE. "Some Frank Talk about our Just-A-Minute Oven." *Playboy* (December 1971): 323.

GE. "The Best Reason for Buying a New GE Refrigerator is an Old GE Refrigerator." *EBONY*. May 1978. 132.

GE. "The Finest Refrigerators General Electric Ever Built!". 1934.
GE. "The Food He Eats Is the Man He'll Be." *Ladies' Home Journal*. October 1929. NP.
GE. *The New Art*.... Nela Park, Cleveland, OH: General Electric Kitchen Institute, 1934. ASBSC, MSUL.
GE. *The "Silent Hostess" Treasure Book*. Cleveland, OH: General Electric, 1930. Reprinted 1931. ASBSC, MSUL.
GE. *The Small Appliances Most Women Want Most*. Bridgeport, CN: General Electric Company Appliance and Merchandise Department, 1947. Automatic Ephemera Appliance Archive.
GE. "This 1937 GE Refrigerator's the Only One Mom's Ever Owned." *EBONY*. August 1978. 53.
GE. "You Shall Not Enslave Our Women!" *Woman's Home Companion*. 1933. 58–9.
GE. "You're Never Too Cold... Never Too Warm." *Saturday Evening Post*. November 12, 1955. 97.
Gibson. "Gibson Market Master: Space for an Extra Cart of Fresh Food." *LIFE*. November 7, 1955. 116.
Gillies, Mary Davis. *What Women Want in their Kitchens of Tomorrow*. New York: McCall Corporation, 1944.
Gold, Herbert. "What It Is, Whence It Came." In "The Beat Mystique." *Playboy*. February 1958. 20–1.
Goldstein, Betty. *UE Fights for Women Workers: End Rate Discrimination, End Job Segregation!* United Electrical, Radio and Machine Workers of America, 1952.
Hamilton. "How a New Hamilton Washer and Dryer...." *LIFE*. September 19, 1969. 81.
Hamilton Beach. "Take It from Mick, You Can't Pick a Better Premium than the Hamilton Beach DrinkMaster!" *Survey of Buying Power* (1983): 7.
Herrick. "Food Keeps BEST in the Herrick—the Aristocrat of Refrigerators." *House Beautiful*. 1922. 51.
Herrick. *Herrick, The Aristocrat of Refrigerators*. Waterloo, IA: Herrick Refrigerator Company, 1926.
Hoover. "Hoover's Incredible Flying Machine." *LIFE*. August 25, 1967. 17.
Hoover. "Meet a Home that Is Shortening the War." *LIFE*. October 11, 1943. 18.
Hoover. "New Hoover Constellation." *Saturday Evening Post*. October 27, 1956. 7.
Hoover. "The Biggest Refrigerator News in Years! New Wonderwall Insulation Adds 50% More Food Space." *EBONY*. June 1960. 127 and *EBONY*. July 1960. 25.
Hotpoint. "Bride's Wish Comes True!" *Better Homes and Gardens*. February 1940. NP.
Howard, Jane. "Can a Nice Novelist Finish First?" *LIFE*. November 4, 1966.
Ivens, Joris. *Power and the Land*. Rural Electrification Administration, 1940.
Johnson, John S. "Why Negroes Buy Cadillacs." *EBONY*. September 1949. 34.
Kelvinator. "Take this Ad to your Kitchen..." *LIFE*. August 21, 1950. 1.
Kelvinator. "The Fabulous Foodarama by Kelvinator". ca. 1950. Television ad.

Kelvinator. "When You Said 'I Have 4 Refrigerators' I Thought You Were Joking." *Good Housekeeping*. March 1935. NP.
Kelvinator. "Why the Aristocrat of Refrigerators Costs You Less to Own." *LIFE*. May 3, 1937. 92.
Kelvinator. "Yes, Mam, That's Right. We Sure Do Need *Four Refrigerators!*" *Good Housekeeping*. June 1935. 176.
Kelvinator. "Kelvinator's New WonderWorkers for Your Kitchen!" *LIFE*. March 20, 1950. 57.
"L'Aspirateur SAMY: Ce que toute Femme désire." *Vendre*. Month unkown 1958. Page unknown.
Lisk, R. C. "Gas in the Atomic Age." *Gas Age* 115.1955. 28.
Lloyd, Norman. *A Word to the Wives*. TelAmerica, Inc, 1955.
Misc. Authors. "A *LIFE* Special." *LIFE*. February 19, 1971. 39–78.
Norge. "Norge Designs Refrigerators for the Woman Who Wants Everything." *EBONY*. July 1965. 18.
Norge. "Norge Extras Give You the 15 lb. Washer that Keeps this Promise." *EBONY*. April 1965. 22.
Norge. "Only Norge Dispensomat Washer pre-loads..." *EBONY*. November 1959. 25.
Osterizer. *Osterizer Recipes for 8-Speed Push-Button Models*. Milwaukee, WI: John Oster Manufacturing Co, 1963.
Osterizer. "Press on to Exotic Drinksmanship." *Playboy*. June 1966. 68.
Osterizer. "Secret of Success in Drinksmanship." *Esquire*. June 1967. 60.
Parton, Margaret. "Sometimes Life Just Happens." *The Ladies' Home Journal* 79. October 1962. 28–33.
Philco. "1,386 Salads from Now..." *EBONY*. May 1964. 153.
Philco. "LET ME TELL YOU About Our Career Opportunities." *EBONY*. March 1968. 128.
Proctor-Silex. "Frozen Passion." *EBONY*. May 1972. 34.
Signature Princess Telephone, 1993; After Henry Dreyfuss Associates (United States); USA; compression-molded abs plastic, metal, electronic components; H x W x D: 10.5 x 21.5 x 10 cm (4 1/8 x 8 7/16 x 3 15/16 in.); Cooper Hewitt, Smithsonian Design Museum; Gift of AT&T; 1994-50-1.
Sunbeam. "... And No other Mixer has the Advantages of Sunbeam Automatic Mixmaster." *Life*. September 17, 1945. 19.
Sunbeam Mixmaster Mixer, ca. 1955; USA; chrome-plated metal, molded glass, molded plastic; H x W x D: 32 x 25 x 34 cm (12 5/8 x 9 13/16 x 13 3/8 in.); Cooper Hewitt, Smithsonian Design Museum; 1993-150-1-a/h.
Weedman, Frances. *Manual of Miracle Cookery*. Chicago: Edison General Electric Appliance Co., 1935. ASBSC, MSUL.
Westinghouse. "Free! $23,000.00 in Electrical Prizes Westinghouse 'Advise-A-Bride' Contests." *LIFE*. April 22, 1940. 69.
Westinghouse. "If Our Hand Wash Agitator Can Wash This Pucci Scarf..." *EBONY*. April 1973. 27.
Westinghouse. *Modern Ways for Modern Days*. Mansfield, OH: Westinghouse Electric Corporation, 1920. ASBSC, MSUL.

Westinghouse. "New Streamline Beauty! New Economy! New Convenience!" *Good Housekeeping*. June 1935. 193.
Westinghouse. "Spending Big Money on Clothes, That's not Pearl's Idea of a Thrill." *EBONY*. April 1977. 21.
Westinghouse. "Stop! Don't Rinse Those Dishes!". 1953. Television ad.
Westinghouse Atomic Power Divisions. "Westinghouse Is GO." *EBONY*. October 1968. 38.
Westinghouse Atomic Power Divisions. "Westinghouse Is NOW." *EBONY*. August 1968. 162.
Westinghouse Electric Corporation Careers. "I Want to Shape the Future." *EBONY*. June 1988. 151.

Rest of Book

Adkins, Lisa. *The Time of Money*. Redwood City, CA: Stanford UP, 2018.
Adorno, Theodore and Max Horkheimer. *Dialectic of Enlightenment*. Translated by Edmund Jephcott. Redwood City, CA: Stanford UP, 2002 (1947).
Ahmed, Sarah. *Queer Phenomenology: Orientations, Objects, Others*. Durham, NC: Duke UP, 2006.
Albala, Ken, ed. *The SAGE Encyclopedia of Food Issues*. London: Sage, 2015.
Aldair, Gene. *Thomas Alda Edison: Inventing the Electric Age*. Oxford: Oxford UP, 1996.
"All Stand Mixers, Candy Apple Red." kitchenaid.com.
Altieri, Charles. "Presence and Reference in a Literary Text: The Example of Williams' 'This is Just to Say.'" *Critical Inquiry* 5.3. Spring 1979. 489–510.
Alworth, David. *Site Reading: Fiction, Art, Social Form*. Princeton, NJ: Princeton UP, 2015.
Anderson, Oscar Edward. *Refrigeration in America*. Princeton, NJ: Princeton UP, 1953.
Antonioni, Michelangelo. *Zabriskie Point*. Beverly Hills, CA: Metro-Goldwyn-Meyer, 1970.
Archer, Sarah. *The Mid-Century Kitchen: America's Favorite Room from Workspace to Dreamspace*. New York: Countryman Press, 2019.
Arnason, Eleanor. *Daughter of the Bear King*. New York: Avon, 1987.)
Arnold McCully, Emily. "How's Your Vacuum Cleaner Working?" *The Massachusetts Review* 17.1 (Spring 1976): 23–43.
Ashley, Mike. "The Time Machines: The Story of the Science-Fiction Pulp Magazines from the Beginning to 1950." *Utopian Studies* 12.2. 2001. 251–3.
Asim, Jabari. *The N Word: Who Can Say It, Who Shouldn't, and Why*. New York: Houghton Mifflin, 2007.
Atashi, Laleh. "The Status of William Carlos Williams in American Modernism." *Messages, Sages, and Ages* 3.3. 2016.54–63.
Auchincloss, Eve and Nancy Lynch. "An Interview with Norman Mailer." In *Conversations with Norman Mailer*, edited by J. Michael Lennon, 39–51. Jackson: UP of Mississippi, 1988.

Austin, Roger. *Playing the Game: The Homosexual Novel in America*. Indianapolis and New York: Boobs-Merrill, 1977.

Author Unknown. "Tradwife: Submitting to my Husband like It's 1959." *BBC*. January 17, 2020.

Author Unknown. "7 Brands That Make Colorful Retro Style Refrigerators." Designrulz. ND.

Author Unknown. "High Tech vs. Retro Tech: Can Microchips Make the Perfect Piña Colada?" *Popular Science*. January 2002. 8.

Author Unknown. "A Letter of Recommendation." *The Ozzy and Harriet Show*. S13E05. October 14, 1964.

Author Unknown. "Make Dishwashers Great Again?'" *Fox59.com*. October 29, 2020.

Author Unknown. "Tragedies of Globalization: The Truth Behind Electronics Sweatshops." goodelectronics.og/Chinalaborwatch.org. July 12, 2011.

B, Stephen. "Joanna Russ 1937–2011." *Bad Reputation*. May 10, 2011. badreputation.org.uk/2011/05/10/joanna-russ-1937-2011.

Bailey, Blake. *A Tragic Honesty: The Life and Work of Richard Yates*. New York: Picador, 2003.

Baille, Justine. *Toni Morrison and Literary Tradition: The Invention of an Aesthetic*. London: Bloomsbury, 2013.

Bakke, Gretchen. *The Grid: The Fraying Wires Between Americans and Our Energy Future*. London: Bloomsbury, 2016.

Baldwin, James. *Just Above My Head*. New York: Penguin, 1994 (1979).

Baldwin, James. *Nobody Knows My Name: More Notes of a Native Son*. London: Penguin, 1991 (1964).

Baldwin, James. *Tell Me How Long the Train's Been Gone*. New York: Penguin, 2018 (1968).

Baldwin, Kate. "Cold War, Hot Kitchen: Alice Childress, Natalya Barnskaya, and the Speakin' Place of Cold War Womanhood." In *Globalizing American Studies*, edited by Brian Edwards and Dilip Parameshwar Gaonkar, 135–54. Chicago: U of Chicago Press, 2010.

Baldwin, Kate. *The Racial Imaginary of the Cold War Kitchen: From Sokol'niki Park to Chicago's South Side*. Lebanon, NH: Dartmouth College Press, 2016.

Baldwin, Neil. *To All Gentleness: William Carlos Williams, the Doctor-Poet*. Cambridge, MA: Atheneum, 1984.

Ballantyne, Sheila. *Norma Jean the Termite Queen*. New York: Penguin, 1983 (1975).

Banks, Nina. "Black Women's Labor Market History Reveals Deep-Seated Race and Gender Discrimination." Economic Policy Institute Working Economics Blog. February 19, 2019.

Barnstone, Tony. "William Carlos Williams and the Cult of the New." *William Carlos Williams Review* 36.2 (2019): 89–125.

Barthes, Roland. *The Rustle of Language*. Translated by Richard Howard. Oxford: Blackwell, 1986.

Baudrillard, Jean. *Selected Writings*, edited by Mark Poster. Stanford, CA: Stanford UP, 1988.

Baudrillard, Jean. *The Consumer Society* (1970). Translated by C.T. London and Los Angeles: Sage, 2017 (1998).

Baxandell, Rosalyn and Elizabeth Ewan. *Picture Windows: How the Suburbs Happened*. New York: Basic Books, 2000.

Beagin, Jen. *Pretend I'm Dead*. London: Oneworld, 2015.

Beagin, Jen. *Vacuum in the Dark*. London: Oneworld, 2019.

Bechdel, Alison. *Fun Home: A Family Tragicomic*. New York: Jonathan Cape, 2006.

Bellafante, Ginia. "At Home with Phillis Schlafly." *The New York Times*. March 30, 2006. F.1.

Belletto, Steve, ed. *The Cambridge Companion to the Beats*. Cambridge: Cambridge UP, 2013.

Benjamin, Walter. *Illuminations*. Translated by Henry Zohn. London: Random House/Pimlico, 1999 (1955).

Bennett, Jane. *Vibrant Matter: A Political Ecology of Things*. Durham, NC: Duke UP, 2010.

Berger, John. *Ways of Seeing*. New York: Penguin, 2008 (1972).

Bird, William L. *"Better Living": Advertising, Media, and the New Vocabulary of Business Leadership, 1935–1955*. Evanston: Northwestern UP, 1999.

Boon, Kevin Alexander. *Kurt Vonnegut*. New York: Cavendish Square, 2013.

Boscagli, Maurizia. *Stuff Theory: Everyday Objects, Radical Materialism*. London: Bloomsbury, 2014.

Boulter, Amanda. "Unnatural Acts: American Feminism and Joanna Russ's *The Female Man*." *Women: A Cultural Review* 10.2 (June 19, 2008): 151–66.

Bourdieu, Pierre. *Distinction: A Social Critique of Good Taste*. Translated by Richard Nice. Cambridge, MA: Harvard UP, 1984 (1979).

Bouson, J. Brooks. *Jamaica Kincaid: Writing Memory, Writing Back to the Mother*. New York: SUNY Press, 2006.

Boyd, Janet and Sharon J. Kirsch. *Primary Stein: Returning to the Writing of Gertrude Stein*. Lanham, MD: Rowman and Littlefield, 2014.

Boyer, David. "GOP Mocks 'Nancy Antoinette' After Pelosi Shows Off High-End Freezer Full of Ice-Cream." *The Washington Times*. April 16, 2020.

Boyer, Paul. *By the Bomb's Early Light: Atomic Thought and Culture at the Dawn of the Atomic Age*. Chapel Hill: U of North Carolina Press, 2005 (1983).

Boym, Svetlana. *The Future of Nostalgia*. New York: Basic, 2001.

Bradbury, Ray. *The Stories of Ray Bradbury*. London and New York: Alfred A. Knopf, 2010.

Brautigan, Richard. *Revenge of the Lawn*. New York: Pan Books, 2014 (1974).

Brewer, Priscilla J. *From Fireplace to Cookstove: Technology and the Domestic Ideal in America*. Syracuse, NY: Syracuse U Press, 2000.

Brewer, Rose M. "Theorizing Race, Class, and Gender: The New Scholarship of Black Feminist Intellectuals and Black Women's Labor." *Race, Gender & Class* 6.2 (1999): 29–47.

Briganti, Chiara and Kathy Mezei. *The Domestic Space Reader*. Toronto: U of Toronto Press, 2012.

Brodkin, Karen. *How Jews Became White Folks and What That Says about Race in America*. New Brunswick, NJ: Rutgers UP, 1998.

Brooks, James L., Allan Burns, Charlotte Brown, David Davis et al. "Parent's Day." *Rhoda*. S01E44. September 30, 1974.
Brown, Bill. *A Sense of Things: The Object Matter of American Literature*. Chicago: U of Chicago Press, 2004.
Brown, Bill. "Reification, Reanimation and the American Uncanny." *Critical Inquiry* 32. Winter 2006. 175–207.
Brown, Bill. "Thing Theory." *Critical Inquiry* 28.1(Autumn, 2001): 1–22.
Brown, Patricia Leigh. "Public Eye; The Fridge Flees the Kitchen." *The New York Times*. July 9, 1998. F1.
Bruegmann, Robert, ed. *Art Deco Chicago: Designing Modern America*. New Haven, CT: Yale UP, 2018.
Brunk, Katja et al. "How Coronavirus Made Us Nostalgic for a Past that Held the Promise of a Future." *The Conversation*. July 14, 2020.
Bryant, Marsha. "Ariel's Kitchen: Plath, *Ladies' Home Journal*, and the Domestic Surreal." In*The Unravelling Archive: Essays on Sylvia Plath*, edited by Anita Plath Helle, 119–38. Ann Arbor: U of Michigan Press, 2007.
Bryant, Marsha. "Plath, Domesticity, and the Art of Advertising." *College Literature* 29.3 (Summer 2002): 17–34.
Bryant, Miranda. "The Washing Machine 'Liberates Women.'" *The Independent*. March 8, 2009.
Burnham, John. *How Superstition Won and Science Lost: Popularizing Science and Health in the United States*. New Brunswick, NJ: Rutgers UP, 1987.
Burroughs, William. *Naked Lunch: The Restored Text*, edited by James Grauerholz and Barry Miles. London and New York: Harper Perennial, 2005 (1959).
Burroughs, William. *The Wild Boys: A Book of the Dead*. New York: Penguin, 2012 (1971).
Burroughs, William and Daniel Odier. *The Job: Interviews with William S. Burroughs*. London: Penguin, 2008 (1969).
Bush, Kate. "Mrs. Bartolozzi." Track#4 on *Aerial*. EMI Records, 2005.
Cage, John. "Variations VII." New York, October 15, 1966.
Cage, John. "Water Walk." *Lascia o Raddoppia*. RAI 1, Milan, February 5, 1959.
Calonne, David Stephen, ed. *Conversations with Gary Snyder*. Jackson: UP of Mississippi, 2017.
Campbell, John. "Electricity Distribution is Holding Nigeria Back." *Council on Foreign Relations*. July 3, 2018.
Canavan, Gerry and Eric Carl Link. *The Cambridge History of Science Fiction*. Cambridge: Cambridge UP, 2018.
Carli, Fabrizio. *Elettrodomestici Spaziali: Viaggio nell'Immaginario Fantascientifico degli Oggetti dell'Uso Quotidiano*. Rome: Castelvecchi, 2000.
Carlisle, Nancy Camilla and Melinda Talbot Nasardinov. *America's Kitchens*. Gardiner, ME: Historic New England, 2008.
Carroll, Helen. "Desperately Happy Housewives!" *Daily Mail*. April 19, 2020.
Carroll, Patty and Bruce Thorn. *Anonymous Women: Domestic Demise*. Savannah, GA: Ain't Bad, 2020.
Carver, Raymond. *What We Talk About When We Talk About Love*. London: Vintage, 2003 (1981).

Cassady, Carolyn. *Jack Kerouac: A Biography*. New York: Penguin, 1990.
Cassady, Neal. *Collected Letters, 1944–1967*. London: Penguin, 2004.
Casdan, Lawrence. *The Big Chill*. Los Angeles, CA: Columbia, 1983.
Castillo, Greg. *Cold War on the Home Front: The Soft Power of Midcentury Design*. Minneapolis: U of Minnesota Press, 2010.
Chambers, Jason. *Madison Avenue and The Color Line: African Americans and the Advertising Industry*. Philadelphia: U of Pennsylvania Press, 2008.
Charlton-Jones, Kate. *Dismembering the American Dream: The Life and Work of Richard Yates*. Tuscaloosa: U of Alabama Press, 2014.
Chauncey, George. "Lots of Friends at the YMCA: Rooming Houses, Cafeterias, and Other Gay Social Centers." In*The Gender and Consumer Culture Reader*, edited by Jennifer Scanlon. 49–70. New York: New York UP, 2000.
Cheever, John. "From the Seventies and Early Eighties: Excerpts from a Diary." *The New Yorker*. August 4, 1991.
Cheever, John. *The Collected Stories of John Cheever*. London: Vintage, 2010 (1977).
Cheever, John. *The Wapshot Chronicle*. London: Vintage, 1998 (1954).
Cheever, John. *The Wapshot Scandal*. London: Vintage, 2003 (1959).
Cheever, Susan. *Home Before Dark*. New York: Simon and Schuster, 1984.
Cherry, Marc. *Desperate Housewives*. ABC Studios, 2004–2012.
Childress, Alice. *Like One of the Family: Conversations from a Domestic's Life*. Boston: Beacon Press, 2017 (1956).
Christou, Miranda. "#Tradwives: Sexism as Gateway to White Supremacy." *OpenDemocracy*. March 17, 2020.
Clarke, Jackie. "Work, Consumption and Subjectivity in Postwar France: Moulinex and the Meanings of Domestic Appliances 1950s–70s." *Journal of Contemporary History* 47.4 (October 2012): 838–59.
Cleary, Beverly. *Ramona and Her Mother*. Oxford: Oxford University Press, 1990 (1979).
Clifford, Catherine. "Why Everyone Is #Quarantinebaking Their Way Through the Coronavirus Pandemic." CNBC. March 28, 2020.
Cockburn, Cynthia and Susan Ormrod. *Gender and Technology in the Making*. London: Sage, 1993.
Coe, Lewis. *The Telegraph: A History of Morse's Invention and Its Predecessors in the United States*. Jefferson, NC: McFarland, 2003.
Cohen, Lizabeth. *A Consumer's Republic: The Politics of Mass Consumption in Postwar America*. New York: Alfred A. Knopf, 2003.
Cole, David John, Eve Browning, and Fred E. H. Schroeder, eds. *Encyclopedia of Modern Everyday Inventions*. Westport, CN: Greenwood Press, 2003.
Collins, Robert G. "From Subject to Object and Back Again: Individual Identity in John Cheever's Fiction." *Twentieth Century Literature* 28.1 (Spring 1982): 1–13.
Combahee River Collective. "A Black Feminist Statement." In*The Second Wave: A Reader in Feminist Theory*, edited by Linda Nicholson, 63–70. New York: Routledge.
Connor, Steven. "Thinking Things." http://www.stevenconnor.com/thinkingthings/.
Coontz, Stephanie. *A Strange Stirring: The Feminine Mystique and American Women at the Dawn of the 1960s*. New York: Perseus, 2011.

Coontz, Stephanie. *Marriage, A History: How Love Conquered Marriage*. London: Penguin, 2005.

Coopee, Todd. *Light Bulb Baking: A History of the Easy-Bake Oven*. Ottawa, ON: Sonderho Press, 2013.

Cooper, Brittney C. *Beyond Respectability: The Intellectual Thought of Race Women*. Chicago: U of Illinois Press, 2017.

Coppola, Sofia. *The Virgin Suicides*. Los Angeles, CA: Paramount, 1999.

Corbett, Merlisa Lawrence. "Best Technology for the Mid-century Modern Look." *Chicago Tribune*. February 18, 2021.

Cortiel, Jeanne. *Demand My Writing: Joanna Russ, Feminism, Science Fiction*. Liverpool: Liverpool UP, 1999.

Cosgrove, Lisa and Robert Whitaker. *Psychiatry Under the Influence: Institutional Corruption, Social Injury, and Prescriptions for Reform*. New York: Palgrave Macmillan, 2015.

Cowan, Ruth Schwartz. *A Social History of American Technology*. New York: Oxford UP, 1997.

Cowan, Ruth Schwartz. *More Work for Mother: The Ironies of Household Technology from the Open Hearth to the Microwave*. New York: Basic Books, 1983.

Cowart, David. *Don DeLillo: The Physics of Language*. Athens: U of Georgia Press, 2003.

Cox, Rosie. "#Cleanergate: Domestic Workers and the Intimate Geographies of Lockdown." *Geography Directions* RGS-IBG. June 8, 2020.

Cox, Rosie. "House/Work: Home as a Space of Work and Consumption." *Geography Compass* 7.12 (2013): 821–31.

Cox, Rosie et al., eds. *Dirt: The Filthy Reality of Everyday Life*, 37–74. London: Profile Books, 2011.

Cramer, Kathryn. *The Cambridge Companion to Science Fiction*. Cambridge: Cambridge UP, 2003.

Crane, David and Martha Kaufman. *Friends*. NBC, 1994–2004.

Crenshaw, Kimberlé. "Demarginalising the Intersection of Race and Sex: A Black Feminist Critique of Antidiscrimination Doctrine, Feminist Theory and Antiracist Politics." *University of Chicago Legal Forum*. 1989. Iss. 1, Article 8.

Crenshaw, Kimberlé. "Mapping the Margins: Intersectionality, Identity Politics, and Violence Against Women of Color." *Stanford Law Review* 43.6 (July 1991): 1241–99.

Critchlow, Donald T. and Nancy MacLean, eds. *Debating the American Conservative Movement: 1945 to the Present*. New York: Rowman&Littlefield.

Cross, Gary. *Kids' Stuff: Toys and the Changing World of American Childhood*. Cambridge, MA: Harvard UP, 1997.

Cureton, Richard. "Readings in Temporal Poetics: Four Poems by William Carlos Williams." *Style* 51.2 (2017): 187–206.

Cuse, Carlton, Kerry Ehrin, and Anthony Cipriano. *Bates Motel*. A&E, 2013–2017.

Daisey, Mike. "Against Nostalgia." *The New York Times*. 6 October 2011.

Daly, Jennifer, ed. *Richard Yates and the Flawed American Dream: Critical Essays*. Jefferson, NC: McFarland, 2017.

Darby, Seyward. *Sisters in Hate: American Women on the Front Lines of White Supremacy*. New York: Hachette, 2020.
David, Larry and Jerry Seinfeld, *Seinfeld*. NBC, 1989–1998.
Davidson, Michael. *Guys Like Us: Citing Masculinity in Cold War Poetics*. Chicago: U of Chicago Press, 2004.
Davis, Angela. *Women, Race and Class*. New York: Vintage, 1983 (1981).
Davis, August. "Reading the Strange Case of Woman-as-Appliance: On Transfigurations, Cyborgs, Domestic Labour and the Megamachine." *Transfigurations: Transational Perspectives on Domestic Spaces* 29 (2015): 356–76.
Davis, Janet M. *"Instruct the Minds of All Classes": The Circus and American Culture at the Turn of the Century*, Vol. 2. Madison: U of Wisconsin Press, 1998.
de Beauvoir, Simone. *The Second Sex*. Translated by H. M. Parshley. New York: Alfred A. Knopf, 1997 (1949).
de Certeau, Michel. *The Practice of Everyday Life*. Translated by Steve Rendall. Berkeley: U of California Press, 1986.
Delany, Samuel. "The Legendary Joanna Russ, Interviewed by Samuel R. Delany," 2007.
Delap, Lucy. "Housework, Housewives, and Domestic Workers: Twentieth-Century Dilemmas of Domesticity." *Home Cultures* 8.2 (2011).
DeLillo, Don. *Americana*. London: Penguin, 1971.
DeLillo, Don. "Baghdad Towers West." *Epoch* 17 (1968): 195–217.
DeLillo, Don. *End Zone*. New York: Penguin, 1972.
DeLillo, Don. *The Silence*. London: Picador, 2020.
DeLillo, Don. *Underworld*. London: Picador, 2011 (1997).
DeLillo, Don. *White Noise*. New York: Penguin, 1986.
Denniston, Dorothy Hamer. *The Fiction of Paule Marshall: Reconstructions of History, Culture, and Gender*. Knoxville: U of Tennessee Press, 1995.
Dercon, Chris. "Kerry James Marshall and the Invisible Man." *032c*. May 9, 2017. https://032c.com/kerry-james-marshall. Accessed October 20, 2019.
Deutsche, Tracy. *Building a Housewife's Paradise: Gender, Politics, and American Grocery Stores in the Twentieth Century*. Chapel Hill: U of North Carolina Press, 2010.
Devonshire, Andy et al. *The Great British Bake-Off*. BBC Studios/Channel Four, 2010–.
Dewey, Joseph, Steven G. Kellman, and Irving Malin, eds. *Under/Words: Perspectives on Don DeLillo's* Underworld. Newark: U of Delaware Press, 2002.
Díaz, Eva. *The Experimenters: Chance and Design at Black Mountain College*. Chicago: U of Chicago Press, 2015.
Dick, Philip K. "The Adjustment Team" (1954). https://en.wikisource.org/wiki/Adjustment_Team.
Dick, Philip K. *The Exegesis of Philip K. Dick*, edited by Pamela Jackson and Jonathan Lethem. New York: Houghton Mifflin Harcourt, 2011.
Dick, Philip K. *The Variable Man*. 1953. https://www.gutenberg.org/files/32154/32154-h/32154-h.htm.
Dick, Philip K. *Voices from the Street*. London: Gollancz, 2014 (2007).
DiCristofaro, Diletta. *The Contemporary Post-Apocalyptic Novel: Critical Temporalities and the End Times*. New York: Palgrave Macmillan, 2019.

Didion, Joan. *We Tell Ourselves Stories in Order to Live: Collected Nonfiction.* New York: Alfred A. Knopf, 2006.

Dini, Rachele. *Consumerism, Waste, and Re-use in Twentieth-Century Fiction: Legacies of the Avant-Garde.* New York: Palgrave Macmillan, 2016.

Dini, Rachele. "The House Was a Garbage Dump: Waste, Mess, and Aesthetic Reclamation in 1960s and 70s 'Mad Housewife' Fiction." *Textual Practice.* August 2018.

Dini, Rachele. "Review: Don DeLillo's *Zero K.*" *European Journal of American Studies.* 2016.

Dini, Rachele. "Things of Beauty: The Politics of Postmillennial Nostalgia for Midcentury Design." *Ancillary Review of Books.* June 21, 2021. https://ancillaryreviewofbooks.org/2021/06/21/things-of-beauty-the-politics-of-postmillennial-nostalgia-for-mid-century-design/.

Dini, Rachele, Sophie Scott-Brown, and Sonia Solicari. "Mid Century Modern." BBC Radio 3. Free Thinking. June 23, 2021. https://www.bbc.co.uk/programmes/m000x709.

Dire Straits. "Money For Nothing." Track#2 on *Brothers in Arms.* 1985.

Dire Straits. "Money For Nothing." Directed by Steve Barron. 1985.

Ditum, Sarah. "Lucy Ellmann's 1000-page novel ..." *New Statesman.* September 25, 2019.

doCarmo, Stephen N. "Subjects, Objects, and the Postmodern Differend in Don DeLillo's *White Noise.*" *LIT: Literature Interpretation Theory* 11.1 (2000): 1–33.

Donaldson, Scott. *John Cheever: A Biography.* New York: Random House, 1988.

Douglas, Ann. "Holy Fools: The Beat Generation and the Cold War." *Reviews in American History* 41.3 (September 2013): 525–32.

Dreifus, Claudia. "Chloe Wofford Talks About Toni Morrison." *New York Times.* September 11, 1994. 73.

Duvall, John N. "From Valparaiso to Jerusalem: DeLillo and the Moment of Canonization." *Modern Fiction Studies* 45.3 Don DeLillo Special Issue (Fall 1999). 559–68.

Dyer, Joyce, Jennifer Cognard-Black, and Elizabeth MacLeod Walls, eds. *From Curlers to Chainsaws: Women and their Machines.* East Lansing: Michigan State University, 2016.

Editorial Board. "Make Dishwashers That Clean Again: The Energy Department Wants to Give Consumers an Appliance Choice." *Wall Street Journal* (October 13, 2019).

Edwards, Caroline. "A Housewife's Dream? Automation and Domestic Labour in Feminist SF/F." 3rd Annual Meeting of the London Science Fiction Research Community. LSFRC. U of London, Birkbeck, September 2019.

Ehrenreich, Barbara. *The Hearts of Men: American Dreams and the Flight from Commitment.* New York: Anchor Press, 1983.

Elliott, Jane. *Popular Feminist Fiction as American Allegory: Representing National Time.* New York: Palgrave, 2008.

Elliott, Jane. "Stepford USA: Second-Wave Feminism, Domestic Labor, and the Representation of National Time." *Cultural Critique* 70 (Fall 2008): 32–62.

Elliott, Stuart. "In Commercials, the Nostalgia Bowl." *The New York Times.* February 7, 2010. N3.

Elliott, Stuart. "Warm and Fuzzy Makes a Comeback." *New York Times*. April 6, 2009.

Ellison, Ralph. *Invisible Man*. New York: Penguin, 2001 (1952).

Ellison, Ralph. *Three Days Before the Shooting...*, edited by John Callahan and Adam Bradley. New York: The Modern Library, 2010.

Ellmann, Lucy. *Ducks, Newburyport*. London: Galley Beggar Press, 2019. Henceforth, *DN*.

Ellmann, Lucy. Twitter post, June 14, 2020, 4:42 p.m., https://twitter.com/FictionAtelier/status/1272192691544231937.

Ellmann, Mary. *Thinking About Women*. Boston, MA: Thomson Learning, 1970 (1968).

Elmwood, Victoria A. "The White Nomad and the New Masculine Family in Jack Kerouac's *On the Road*." *Western American Literature* 42.4 (Winter 2008): 335–61.

Energy Conservation Program: Energy Conservation Standards for Dishwashers, Notification of Petition for Rulemaking, 83 Fed. Reg. 17768 (proposed March 21, 2018).

Engles, Tim. *White Male Nostalgia in Contemporary American Literature*. New York: Palgrave Macmillan, 2018.

Ensler, Eve. *The Vagina Monologues*. London: Virago, 1994.

Ernst, Max. "What Is the Mechanism of Collage?" (1936), in *Theories of Modern Art: A Source Book by Artists and Critics*, edited by Herschel B. Chip, 427–8. Berkeley: U of California Press, 1968.

Ettling, John. *The Germ of Laziness: Rockefeller Philanthropy and Public Health in the New South*. Cambridge, MA: Harvard UP, 1981.

Eve, Martin Paul. *Literature Against Criticism*. Cambridge: Open Book Publishers, 2016.

Evelyn, Kenya. "Trump Rails Against Refrigerators and Promises Cleaner Dishes." *The Guardian* (January 15, 2020).

"FAB28—History of FAB Fridges." Smeg Website, ND.

Farrell, Mary H. J. "The Problem With Cordless Sticks? The Battery." *Consumer Reports*. June 25, 2020.

Farrell, Susan. *Imagining Home: American War Fiction from Hemingway to 9/11*. New York: Camden House, 2017.

Fava, Lorella. "Child Labour: An Unspoken Truth of the Electronic Waste Industry." Paper Round. September 17, 2019.

Faw, Larissa. "KitchenAid's Data-Driven #MakeItTogether Campaign." *MediaPost* (April 24, 2020).

Felski, Rita. *The Gender of Modernity*. Cambridge, MA: Harvard UP, 1995.

Ferguson, Donna. "'I Feel like a 1950s Housewife': How Lockdown has Exposed the Gender Divide." *The Observer*. May 3, 2020.

Filippelli, Ronald L. and Mark D. McColloch. *Cold War in the Working Class: The Rise and Decline of the United Electrical Workers*. New York: State U of New York Press, 1995.

Fitzgerald, F. Scott. *The Great Gatsby*. New York: Penguin, 1985 (1925).

Fitzpatrick, Shanon. "Physical Culture's World of Bodies: Transnational Participatory Pastiche and the Body Politics of America's Globalized Mass Culture." In *Body and Nation: The Global Realm of U.S. Body Politics in the*

Twentieth Century, edited by Emily S. Rosenberg and Shanon Fitzpatrick. Durham, NC: Duke UP, 2014.
Fitzsimmons, Michelle. "Dyson is Done with Corded Vacuums." *TechRadar*. March 6, 2018.
Flood, Rebecca. "Wild Wifestyle." *The Sun*. January 21, 2020.
Foltz, Mary. *Contemporary American Literature and Excremental Culture: American Sh*t*. New York: Palgrave Macmillan, 2020.
Forbes, Bryan. *The Stepford Wives*. Columbia Pictures, 1975.
Fox, Richard W. and T. J. Jackson Lears, eds. *The Power of Culture: Critical Essays in American History*. Chicago: U of Chicago Press, 1993.
Fowler, Geoffrey A. and Heather Kelley. "Amazon's New Health Band Is the Most Invasive Tech We've Ever Tested." *The Washington Post*. December 10, 2020. NP.
Frank, Scott and Allen Scott. *The Queen's Gambit*. Netflix, 2020.
Frankel, Todd C. "Trump's Big Policy Win: Stronger Showers, Faster Dishwashers. It's Something Almost Nobody Wanted." *Washington Post*. December 30, 2020.
Franklin, Ruth. *Shirley Jackson: A Rather Haunted Life*. New York: W.W. Norton, 2016.
Frederick, Christine. *Selling Mrs. Consumer*. New York: Business Bourse, 1929.
Freeberg, Ernest. *The Age of Edison: Electric Light and the Invention of Modern America*. New York: Penguin, 2013.
Freedgood, Elaine. *The Ideas in Things: Fugitive Meaning in the Victorian Novel*. Chicago and London: Chicago University Press, 2006.
Freedman, Carl. "Towards a Theory of Paranoia: The Science Fiction of Philip K. Dick." *Science Fiction Studies* 11.1 (March 1984): 15–24.
Freeman, Fred, Lawrence J. Cohen and Carl Reiner. "A Farewell to Writing." *The* Dick Van Dyke Show S05E02. September 22, 1965.
Freeman, James. "The Dishwasher Rebellion." *Wall Street Journal* (June 27, 2018).
French, Marilyn. *The Women's Room*. London: Virago, 2004 (1977).
Friedan, Betty. *The Feminine Mystique*. New York: Dell, 1974 (1963).
Fywell, Tim. *Norma Jean and Marilyn*. New York: HBO, 1996.
Gabrys, Jennifer. *Digital Rubbish: A Natural History of Electronics*. Ann Arbor: Michigan UP, 2011.
Gabrys, Jennifer. "Programming Environments." In *Smart Urbanism: Utopian Vision or False Dawn?* edited by Simon Marvin, Andrés Luque-Ayala, and Colin McFarlane, 88–107. New York: Routledge, 2016.
Gammon, Katherine. "Kneading to Relax? How Coronavirus Promoted a Surge in Stress Baking." *The Guardian*. April 19, 2020.
Gammon, Sean and Gregory Ramshaw. "Distancing from the Present: Nostalgia and Leisure in Lockdown." *Leisure Sciences*. June 24, 2020.
Gansky, Carroll. "Refrigerator Design and Masculinity in Postwar Media, 1946–1960." *Studies in Popular Culture* 34.1 (Fall 2011): 67–85.
Gantz, Carroll. *Refrigeration: A History*. Jefferson, NC: McFarland, 2015.
Gantz, Carroll. *The Vacuum Cleaner: A History*. Jefferson, NC: McFarland, 2012.
Garcia, Rebecca. "EPCA Reform to Make Dishwashers Great Again." *Loyola Consumer Law Review* 31.1 (January 14, 2019): 114–27.

Garnett, Tara. "Where Are the Best Opportunities for Reducing Greenhouse Gas Emissions in the Food System?" *Food Policy* 36 (2011): 23–32.
Gavins, Joanna. *Reading the Absurd*. Edinburgh: Edinburgh UP, 2013.
Genter, Robert, ed. *Late Modernism: Art, Culture, and Politics in Cold War America*. Philadelphia and Oxford: U of Pennsylvania Press, 2011.
Genter, Robert, "'Mad to Talk, Mad to Be Saved': Jack Kerouac, Soviet Psychology, and the Cold War Confessional Self." *Studies in American Fiction* 40.1 (2013): 27–52.
Geronimi, Clyde, Hamilton Luske, and Wilfred Jackson. *Cinderella*. Walt Disney Productions, 1950.
Gilbert, Geoffrey. *Rich and Poor in America: A Reference Handbook*. Santa Barbara, CA: ABC Clio, 2008.
Gillan, Jennifer. *Television and New Media: Must-Click TV*. New York: Taylor & Francis, 2010.
Gilmore, Paul. *Aesthetic Materialism: Electricity&American Romanticism*. Stanford, CA: Stanford UP, 2009.
Ginsberg, Allen. *Howl, and Other Poems*. San Francisco, CA: City Lights, 1956.
Gold, Herbert. "What It Is, Whence It Came." *Playboy* (February 1958): 20–1.
Goodhart, Maud. "Design Classic: The SMEG FAB28 Refrigerator by Vittorio Bertazzoni. *Financial Times*. March 20, 2015.
Gore, Dayo F. *Radicalism at the Crossroads: African American Women Activists in the Cold War*. New York: New York UP, 2011.
Graham, Laurel D. "Domesticating Efficiency: Lillian Gilbreth's Scientific Management of Homemakers, 1924–1930." *Signs: Journal of Women in Culture and Society* 23.3 (1999): 633–75.
Grandoni, Dino and Paulina Firozi. "The Energy 202: Trump Wants to Make Dishwashers Great Again. The Energy Department Has a New Rule for That." *The Washington Post*. January 17, 2020.
Greenberg, Cara. *Mid-Century Modern Design*. New York: Three Rivers Press, 1984.
Greene, Eric M. "The Mental Health Industrial Complex: A Study in Three Cases." *Journal of Humanistic Psychology* (February 15, 2019).
Greene, Graham. *Our Man in Havana*. London: Vintage, 2006 (1958).
Greenwood, Jeremy Greenwood et al. "Engines of Liberation." *The Quarterly Journal of Economics* 72.1 (January 2005): 109–33.
Greep, Monica. "'Tradwife' Who Believes in Submitting to her Husband." *Daily Mail*. January 23, 2020.
Greer, Germaine. *The Female Eunuch*. London: Fourth Estate, 2006 (1970).
Gregory, Andy. "Trump Renews Attack on Lightbulbs, Dishwashers, Fridges, Toilets and Showers: President Vows to Make Appliances Great Again." *The Independent*. January 15, 2020.
Haddox, Thomas F. "Whitman's End of History: 'As I Sat Alone By Blue Ontario's Shore,' Democratic Vistas, and the Postbellum Politics of Nostalgia." *Walt Whitman Quarterly* 22. 1 (2004): 1–22.
Hale, Grace. *Making Whiteness: The Culture of Segregation in the South, 1890–1940*. New York: Vintage, 1999.
Hall, Luke Edward. "The Tyranny of Twee Kitchenalia." *Financial Times*. July 19, 2019.

Hamilton, Richard. "Just What Was It…". 1956. Digital print on paper. 260 x 350 mm. Tate.
Hankin, Emily. *Buying Modernity? The Consumer Experience of Domestic Electricity in the Era of the Grid.* U of Manchester, 2013. PhD Thesis.
Haralovich, Mary Beth. "Sitcoms and Suburbs: Positioning the 1950s Homemaker." *Quarterly Review of Film and Video* 11.1 (May 1989): 61–83.
Haraway, Donna J. *Simians, Cyborgs, and Women: The Reinvention of Nature.* New York: Routledge, 1991.
Harris, O. "Cold War Correspondents: Ginsberg, Kerouac, Cassady, and the Political Economy of Beat Letters." *Twentieth Century Literature* 46.2 (2000. 171–92.
Hartman, Saidiya. *Wayward Lives, Beautiful Experiments: Intimate Histories of Social Upheaval.* New York: W.W. Norton, 2019.
Harvey, David. *The Condition of Postmodernity: An Enquiry Into the Origins of Cultural Change.* Oxford: Blackwell, 1991 (1989).
Hay, Vanessa. *Unprotected Labor; Household Workers, Politics, and Middle-Class Reform in New York, 1870–1940.* Chapel Hill: U of North Carolina Press, 2011.
Hayward, Mark. "The Economic Crisis and After: Recovery, Reconstruction and Cultural Studies." *Cultural Studies* (March 24, 2010): 283–94.
Heimann, Jim. *Mid-Century Ads.* Köln: Taschen, 2015.
Heimann, Jim. *The Golden Age of Advertising: The 50s.* Köln: Taschen, 2001.
Heinlein, Robert. *The Door into Summer.* London: Orion/Gollancz, 2013 (1957).
Heinze, Andrew. *Adapting to Abundance: Jewish Immigrants, Mass Consumption, and the Search for American Identity.* New York: Columbia UP, 1990.
Herring, Scott. *The Hoarders: Material Deviance in Modern American Culture.* Chicago: U of Chicago Press, 2014.
Heyler, Ruth. "'Refuse Heaped Many Stories High': DeLillo, Dirt and Disorder." *Modern Fiction Studies* 45 (Winter, 1999): 987–1006.
Hicks, Heather. "Automating Feminism: The Case of Joanna Russ's *The Female Man.*" *Postmodern Culture* 9.3 .1999. 237–52.
Higginbotham, Evelyn Brooks. "African-American Women's History and the Metalanguage of Race." *Signs: Journal of Women in Culture and Society* 17.2 (Winter, 1992): 253–4.
Hine, Thomas. *Populuxe.* New York: Alfred A. Knopf, 1986.
Hines, John. *Voices in the Past: English Literature and Archaeology.* Cambridge: D.S. Brewer, 2004.
Ho, Melissa et al., eds. *Artists Respond: American Art and the Vietnam War, 1965–1972*, edited by Melissa Ho et al. Princeton, NJ: Princeton UP, 2019.
Hodgkins, John. *The Drift: Affect, Adaptation, and New Perspectives on Fidelity.* London: Bloomsbury, 2013.
Hogeland, Lisa Maria. *Feminism and Its Fictions.* Philadelphia: U of Pennsylvania Press, 1998.
Holliday, Laura Scott. "Kitchen Technologies: Promises and Alibis, 1944–1966." *Camera Obscura* 16.2 (2001): 78–131.
Hollows, Joanne and Rachel Moseley, eds. *Feminism in Popular Culture.* London: Bloomsbury, 2006.

Homes, A. M. *Music for Torching*. London: Granta, 2013 (1999).
hooks, bell. *Ain't I a Woman? Black Women and Feminism*. New York: Routledge, 2015.
Horowicz, Daniel. *Betty Friedan and the Making of the Feminine Mystique: The American Left, the Cold War, and Modern Feminism*. Amherst: U of Massachusetts Press, 1998.
Howard, Ron. *Apollo 13*. Universal Pictures, 1995.
Howard, Sally. "'I Want to Submit to my Husband like a 50s Housewife': Inside the Controversial UK Tradwife Movement." *Stylist*. December 2019.
Howard, Sally. "Living in the Past: Lifestyles of Bygone Eras." *The Guardian*. May 31, 2020.
Howard, Sally. *The Home Stretch: Why It's Time to Come Clean about Who Does the Dishes*. New York: Atlantic Books, 2020.
Howell, John Harris. *The Right to Manage: Industrial Relations Policies of American Business in the 1940s*. Madison: U of Wisconsin Press, 1982.
Hoy, Sue Ellen. *Chasing Dirt: The American Pursuit of Cleanliness*. New York and Oxford: Oxford UP, 1996.
Huehls, Mitchum and Rachel Greenwald Smith, eds. *Neoliberalism and Contemporary Culture*. Baltimore, MD: Johns Hopkins UP, 2017.
Hughes, Langston. *Langston Hughes and the Chicago Defender: Essays on Race, Politics and Culture 1942–62*, edited by C. C. De Santis. Chicago and Urbana: U of Illinois Press.
Hughes, Langston. *The Collected Poems of Langston Hughes*, edited by Arnold Rampersad and David Roessel. New York: Vintage, 1995.
Humphreys, Kristi Rowan. *Housework and Gender in American Television: Coming Clean*. Lanham, MD: Rowman & Littlefield, 2016.
Hurst, Fannie. *Imitation of Life*. Durham, NC: Duke UP, 2015 (1933).
Huxley, Aldous. *Brave New World*. London: Vintage, 2007 (1932).
Innes, Sherrie A. *Dinner Roles: American Women and Culinary Culture*. Iowa City, IA: U of Iowa Press, 2001.
Innes, Sherrie A. *Kitchen Culture in America: Popular Representations of Food, Gender, and Race*. Philadelphia: U of Pennsylvania Press, 2001.
Irvine, William B. *On Desire: Why We Want What We Want*. Oxford: Oxford UP, 2006.
Isendstadt, Sandy. "Visions of Plenty: Refrigerators in America around 1950." *Journal of Design History* 11.4. 1998. 311–21.
Jackson, Shirley. *Life Among the Savages*. New York: Penguin, 1997 (1953).
Jackson, Shirley. *Raising Demons*. New York: Penguin, 2015 (1957).
Jackson, Shirley. *Raising Demons*. New York: Penguin, 2021 (1957).
James, Selma and Mariarosa dalla Costa. *The Power of Women and the Subversion of the Community*. Bristol: Pétroleuse Press, 1973.
Jameson, Fredric. "Postmodernism and Consumer Society." Whitney Museum Lecture, Autumn 1982.
Jameson, Fredric. "Postmodernism, or, the Cultural Logic of Late Capitalism." *New Left Review* I.146. July/August 1984. 66–8.
Jameson, Fredric. *Postmodernism: Or, The Logic of Late Capitalism*. Durham, NC: Duke UP, 1991.

Janssens, Ruud and Rob Kroes, eds. *Post-Cold War Europe, Post-Cold War America*. Amsterdam: VU UP, 2004.

Jeane, Norma and Illy. *International Flights*. 2002. http://www.normajeane-contemporary.com/.

Johnson, Charles H. *Dr. King's Refrigerator: And Other Bedtime Stories*. New York: Simon & Schuster, 2011 (2005).

Johnson, David K. *The Lavender Scare*. Chicago: U of Chicago Press, 2006.

Johnson, Gabe. "Nickelodeon Nostalgia." *New York Times*. July 21, 2011.

Jones, Claudia. "An End to the Neglect of the Problems of the Negro Woman!" *Political Affairs* 28. 1949. 51–67.

Jones, Sophie A. "Richard Yates's Autofictions and the Politics of Canonization." In *Richard Yates and the Flawed American Dream: Critical Essays*, edited by Jennifer Daly, 87–107. Jefferson, NC: McFarland, 2017.

Jonnes, Jill. *Empires of Light: Edison, Tesla, Westinghouse, and the Race to Electrify the World*. New York: Random House, 2003.

Jorgensen, Janice, ed. *Encyclopedia of Consumer Brands, Volume 3: Durable Goods*. Detroit, MI: Gale/St James Press, 1994.

Jorgenson, Nicole. "How the Migrant Invasion Made Me Become a Trad Wife." *Radio 3Fourteen*. April 19, 2017.

Juffer, Jane. *At Home with Pornography: Women, Sexuality, and Everyday Life*. New York: NYU Press, 1998.

Jurca, Catherine. *White Diaspora: The Suburb and the Twentieth-century American Novel*. Princeton, NJ: Princeton UP, 2001.

Kalia, Ammar. "I Wish More People Would Read *Ducks, Newburyport* by Lucy Ellmann." *The Guardian*. May 6, 2020.

Kaplan, Amy. "Manifest Domesticity." *American Literature* 70.3(September 1998):581–606.

Katwala, Amit. "The Spiralling Environmental Cost of our Lithium Battery Addiction." *WIRED*. August 5, 2018.

Kaufman, Sue. *Diary of a Mad Housewife*. Harmondsworth: Penguin, 1971 (1967).

Kaufman, Will. *American Culture in the 1970s*. Edinburgh: Edinburgh UP, 2009.

Kaufman, Will. "'What's so Funny about Richard Nixon? Vonnegut's 'Jailbird' and the Limits of Comedy." *Journal of American Studies* 41.3(December 2007): 623–39.

Keefe, John. "Can You Tell a 'Trump' Fridge from a 'Biden' Fridge?" *The New York Times*. October 27, 2020.

Keenaghan, Eric. "Vulnerable Households: Cold War Containment and Robert Duncan's Queered Nation." *Journal of Modern Literature* 28.4, Poetry (Summer, 2005): 57–90.

Keesey, Douglas. *Don DeLillo*. New York: Twayne, 1993.

Keith, Tamara. "Trump Vs. Toilets (and Showers, Dishwashers, and Lightbulbs)." *NPR* (December 27, 2019).

Kelly, Annie. "The Housewives of White Supremacy." *New York Times*. June 1, 2018.

Kennan, George F. "The Sources of Soviet Conduct." *Foreign Affairs* 4.25 (July 1947): 566–82.

Kennedy, Liam and Stephen Shapiro, eds. *Neoliberalism and Contemporary American Literature*. Hanover, NH: Dartmouth College Press, 2019.

Kennedy, Randall. *Nigger: The Strange Career of a Troublesome Word*. New York: Pantheon, 2001.

Kerouac, Jack. *Book of Sketches 1952–1957*. London: Penguin, 2006.

Kerouac, Jack. *On the Road: The Original Scroll*. London: Penguin, 2007.

Kerouac, Jack. *Selected Letters, 1940–1956*, edited by Ann Charters. New York: Penguin, 1996.

Kerouac, Jack. *The Dharma Bums*. London: Mayflower, 1969 (1958).

Kerouac, Jack. *The Town and the City*. London: Penguin, 2000 (1950).

Kesey, Ken. *One Flew Over the Cuckoo's Nest*. London: Penguin, 2005 (1962).

Kincaid, Jamaica. *My Garden. Book*. New York: Farrar, Strauss, Giroux, 1999.

King, Dr. Martin Luther. "I Have a Dream." March on Washington for Jobs and Freedom. Lincoln Memorial, Washington, DC. August 28, 1963.

KitchenAid. "Celebrating 100 Years of Making." *Progressive Electrical*. May 31, 2019. 4.

KitchenAid. "Making History: 1919–2019. Explore a Century of Innovation and Inspiration in the Kitchen." https://www.kitchenaid.jp/en_jp/100year/history.html.

Klein, Maury. *A Call to Arms: Mobilizing America for World War II*. London: Bloomsbury, 2013.

Klemesrud, Judy. "Feminists Recoil at Film Designed to Relate to Them." *The New York Times*. February 26, 1975. 29.

Klinkowitz, Jerome. "How to Die Laughing: Kurt Vonnegut's Lessons for Humor." *Studies in American Humor* 3.26. 2012. 15–19.

Klinkowitz, Jerome. *Kurt Vonnegut's America*. Columbia: U of South Carolina Press, 2009.

Klinkowitz, Jerome. *The Vonnegut Effect*. Columbia: U of South Carolina Press, 2004.

Kocela, Christopher. *Fetishism and Its Discontents in Post-1960 American Fiction*. New York: Palgrave Macmillan, 2010.

Krug, Nora. "Lucy Ellmann Interview." *The Independent*. September 23, 2019.

Kuletz, Valerie. *The Tainted Desert: Environmental and Social Ruin in the American West*. New York: Routledge, 1998.

Kumar, Amit, Maria Holuszko, and Denis Crocce Romano Espinosa. "E-waste: An Overview on Generation, Collection, Legislation & Recycling Practices." *Resources, Conservation and Recycling* 122 (July 2017): 32–42.

Kummings, Donald D., ed. *A Companion to Walt Whitman*. Oxford and New York: Wiley-Blackwell, 2009.

Kusmer, Kenneth L. *Down and Out, On the Road: The Homeless in American History*. Oxford and New York: Oxford UP, 2002.

Kusmer, Kenneth L. and Joe W. Trotter, eds. *African American Urban History since World War II*. Chicago: U of Chicago Press, 2009.

La Ferla, Ruth. "Longing for No Nostalgia." *The New York Times*. July 30, 2010.

Lang, Fritz. *Metropolis*. Beverly Hills, CA: United Film Artists, 1927.

Langlois, Shawn. "How Come Trump Knows So Much about Dishwashers? 'Women Tell Me,' He Says." *Marketwatch*. December 19, 2019.

Larrabee, Eric. "Rosebuds on the Silverware." *Industrial Design* 2 (February 1955): 62–3.

Latour, Bruno. *We Have Never Been Modern*. Translated by Catherine Porter. Cambridge, MA: Harvard UP, 1993.

Lautréamont, Comte. *Maldoror*. Translated by Guy Wernham. New York: New Directions, 1965 (1869).

Le Corbusier, *Towards a New Architecture*. New York: Dover Publication, 1986 (1923).

Leavitt, Sarah Abigail. *From Catharine Beecher to Martha Stewart: A Cultural History of Domestic Advice*. Chapel Hill: U of North Carolina Press, 2002.

LeClair, Tom. *In the Loop: Don DeLillo and the Systems Novel*. Urbana, IL: U of Illinois Press, 1987.

Leggatt, Matthew, ed. *Was It Yesterday?: Nostalgia in Contemporary Film and Television*. New York: SUNY Press, 2021.

Leibman, Nina C. *Living Room Lectures: The Fifties Family in Film and Television*. Austin: U of Texas Press, 1995.

Lévi-Strauss, Claude. *The Savage Mind*. Oxford and New York: Oxford UP, 2004 (1962).

Levin, Ira. *The Stepford Wives*. London: Constable and Robinson, 2011 (1972).

Levinson, Marc. *The Box: How the Shipping Container Made the World Smaller and the World Economy Bigger*. Princeton, NJ: Princeton UP, 2008.

Lewis, Helen. "The Coronavirus is a Disaster for Feminism." *The Atlantic*. March 19, 2020.

Lewis, Sinclair. *Babbitt*. New York: Signet / New American Press, 1964 (1922).

Lidwell, William and Gerry Manacsa. *Deconstructing Product Design*. Beverly, MA: Rockport, 2009.

Liebermann, Jennifer. *Power Lines: Electricity in American Life and Letters, 1882–1952*. Boston, MA: MIT Press, 2017.

Linning, Stephanie. "Collection of Retro KitchenAid Images Reveals ..." *Daily Mail* Online. February 2, 2019.

Lipsitz, George. *The Possessive Investment in Whiteness: How White People Profit from Identity Politics*. Philadelphia, PA: Temple UP, 1998.

Litvinova, Tatyana. "John Cheever's *The Brigadier and the Golf Widow*." In *Soviet Criticism of American Literature in the Sixties: An Anthology*, edited by Carl R. Proffer, 24–6. New York: Ardis, 1972.

Lovegren, Sylvia. *Fashionable Food: Seven Decades of Food Fads*. Chicago: U of Chicago Press, 2005 (1995).

Lupton, Ellen, ed. *Mechanical Brides: Women and Machines from Home to Office*. Princeton, NJ: Princeton Architectural Press, 1993.

Lynch, David. *Blue Velvet*. Wilmington, NC: De Laurentiis, 1986.

Lyons, Bonnie and Marge Piercy. "An Interview with Marge Piercy." *Contemporary Literature* 48.3. Fall 2007. 327–44.

Maalsen, Sophia and Robyn Dowling. "Covid-19 and the Accelerating Smart Home." *Big Data and Society*. July 28, 2020.

Magloughin, Andrew. "Secretary Perry Can Make Dishwashers Great Again." Freedomworks.org. April 4, 2018.

Maher, Jr., Paul. *Kerouac: The Definitive Biography*. New York: Taylor Trade Publishing, 2004.

Maher, Jr., Paul. *Why Are We in Vietnam?* New York: Random House, 2017 (1967).

Maines, Rachel P. *The Technology of Orgasm: 'Hysteria,' the Vibrator, and Women's Sexual Satisfaction*. Baltimore, MD: Johns Hopkins UP, 1999.

Malvern, Jack. "Tradwife Is There to Serve." *The Times*. January 25, 2020.

Mangold, James. *Girl, Interrupted*. Los Angeles, CA: Columbia, 1999.

Manring, M. M. *Slave in a Box: The Strange Career of Aunt Jemima*. Charlottesville: U of Virginia Press, 1998.

Mao, Douglas. *Solid Objects: Modernism and the Test of Production*. Princeton, NJ: Princeton UP, 1998.

Marchand, Roland. *Advertising the American Dream: Making Way for Modernity, 1920–1940*. Berkeley: U of California Press, 1992.

Marchand, Roland. *Creating the Corporate Soul: The Rise of Public Relations and Corporate Imagery in American Big Business*. Berkeley: U of California Press, 1998.

Marchand, Roland and Michael L. Smith. "Corporate Science on Display." In *Scientific Authority and Twentieth-Century America*, edited by Ronald G. Walters, 148–82. Baltimore, MD: Johns Hopkins UP, 1997.

Marcus, Daniel. *Happy Days and Wonder Years: The Fifties and the Sixties in Contemporary Cultural Politics*. New Brunswick, NJ: Rutgers UP, 2004.

Margolis, Eleanor. "Stop This Retro Nonsense about Lockdown Being a Return to Domestic Bliss for Women." *The Guardian*. April 23, 2020.

Mariani, Giorgio. *Waging War on War: Peacefighting in American Literature*. Chicago: U of Illinois Press, 2015.

Marlens, Neal and Carol Black, *The Wonder Years*. ABC, 1988–1993.

Marling, Karal Ann. *As Seen on TV: The Visual Culture of Everyday Life in the 1950s*. Cambridge, MA: Harvard UP, 1994.

Marquart, Debra. "Door-to-Door." *Narrative Magazine*. Poem of the Week, 2012–2013. March 31, 2013.

Marshall, Garry and Jerry Belson. "Lucy The Disk Jockey." *The Lucy Show*. S03E26. April 12, 1965.

Marshall, Paule. *Brown Girl, Brownstones*. Eastford, CT: Martino Fine Books, 2014 (1959).

Marshall, Paule. *Reena and Other Stories*. New York: Feminist Press at CUNY, 1983.

Martin, Susana. "Revising the Future in *The Female Man*." *Science Fiction Studies* 32.3 (November 2005): 405–22.

Martinez, Manuel Luis. *Countering the Counterculture: Rereading Postwar American Dissent from Jack Kerouac to Tomás Rivera*. Madison: U of Wisconsin Press, 2003.

Marvar, Alexandra. "Stress Baking More than Usual?" *The New York Times*. March 30, 2020.

Marx, Karl and Friedrich Engels. *The Communist Manifesto*. London: Penguin Classics, 2015 (1848).

Marz, Ron, Darryl Banks and Romeo Tanghal. *Forced Entry*: *Green Lantern* 3.53 (August 1994): NP

Matchar, Emily. *Homeward Bound: Why Women Are Embracing the New Domesticity*. New York: Simon & Schuster, 2005.

Mazur, Susan. "Appliances, Kitchen." In: *Encyclopedia of Consumption and Waste*. Edited by Carl A. Zimring and William L. Rathje, 28–29. London: Sage, 2012.

McCarthy, Anna. *The Citizen Machine: Governing by Television in 1950s America*. New York: The New Press, 2010.

McCarthy-Miller, Beth. "Snow Ball." Modern Family S08E9. December 14, 2016.

McClintock, Ann. "Soft-Soaping Empire: Commodity Racism and Imperial Advertising." In *Travellers' Tales: Narratives of Home and Displacement*, edited by George Robertson et al., 128–52. London and New York: Routledge, 1994.

McDuffie, Erik S. *Sojourning for Freedom: Black Women, American Communism, and the Making of Black Left Feminism*. Durham, NC: Duke UP, 2011.

McElya, Micki. *Clinging to Mammy: The Faithful Slave in Twentieth-century America*. Cambridge, MA: Harvard UP, 2007.

McGaw, Judith A. "No Passive Victims, No Separate Spheres: A Feminist Perspective on Technology's History." In *In Context: History and the History of Technology*, edited by Stephen H. Cutcliffe and Robert C. Post, 172–91. Bethlehem PA: Lehigh UP, 1989.

McGovern, Charles F. *Sold American: Consumption and Citizenship, 1890–1945*. Chapel Hill: U of North Carolina Press, 2006.

McMahon, Arthur W. and Miles F. Shore. "Some Psychological Reactions to Working with the Poor." *Arch Gen Psychiatry* 18.5 (May 1968): 562–8.

McNamara, John. *Aquarius*. NBC, 2015–2016.

Mears, Josh. "Diet-Friendly Fridges." *Trendhunter*. January 10, 2012.

Mendlesohn, Farah. *The Pleasant Profession of Robert A. Heinlein*. London: Unbound, 2019.

Mercury, Freddy. "I Want to Break Free." Dir. David Mallett, 1984.

Merril, Judith. *Shadow on the Hearth*. London: Sidgwick and Jackson, 1953 (1950).

Metzger, T. H. *Blood and Volts: Edison, Tesla, and the Electric Chair*. New York: Autonomedia, 1996.

Miles, Barry. *Allen Ginsberg: Beat Poet*. London: Virgin Books, 2010 (1989).

Miles, Barry. *William Burroughs: A Life*. London: Weidenfeld & Nicholson, 2014.

Miller, Arthur. *Death of A Salesman*. London: Penguin, 2000 (1949).

Miller, Henry. *The Henry Miller Reader*. New York: New Directions, 1959.

Millett, Kate. *Sexual Politics*. New York: Columbia UP, 2016 (1970).

Mimosa Montes, Lara. "An Interview with Mattilda Bernstein Sycamore." *Believer Mag*. January 14, 2021.

Mishel, Lawrence, Josh Bivens, Elise Gould, and Heidi Shierholz, eds. *The State of Working America*. 12th edn. Ithaca, NY: Cornell UP, 2012.

Mitchell, Joni. "The Last Time I Saw Richard." 1971. Track#10 on *Blue*. Reprise, 1971.

Mitchell, William and Federico Casalegno. *Connected Sustainable Cities*. Boston, MA: MIT Mobile Experience Lab Publishing, 2008.

Mock, Michelle. "The Electric Home and Farm Authority, 'Model T Appliances,' and the Modernization of the Home Kitchen in the South." *The Journal of Southern History* 80.1 (February 2014): 73–108.
Mohun, Arwen. *Steam Laundries: Gender, Work, and Technology in the United States and Great Britain, 1880–1940*. Baltimore, MD: Johns Hopkins UP, 1999.
Mohun, Arwen and Roger Horowitz, eds. *His and Hers: Gender, Consumption and Technology*. Charlottesville: U of Virginia Press, 1998.
Moorhouse, Jocelyn. *How to Make an American Quilt*. Universal City, CA: Universal, 1995.
Moran, Joe. "The Author as a Brand Name: American Literary Figures and the 'Time' Cover Story." *Journal of American Studies* 29.3 (December 1995): 349–63.
Moran, Rachel Louise. *Governing Bodies: American Politics and the Shaping of the Modern Physique*. Philadelphia: U of Pennsylvania Press, 2018.
Moran, Richard. *Executioner's Current: Thomas Edison, George Westinghouse, and the Invention of the Electric Chair*. New York: Vintage Books, 2003.
Morgan, Brittney. "The Best Retro Refrigerators You Can Buy." *House Beautiful*. January 29, 2020.
Morgan, Robin, ed. *Sisterhood Is Powerful: An Anthology of Writings from the Women's Liberation Movement*. New York: Random House, 1970.
Morgan, Tom. "Retro Fridge Freezer Buying Guide." Which? ND.
Morrison, Toni. *Love*. London: Vintage, 2004 (2003).
Morrison, Toni. *Paradise*. London: Vintage, 1999 (1997).
Morrison, Toni. *Tar Baby*. London: Vintage, 2004 (1981).
Morrison, Toni. *The Bluest Eye*. London: Vintage, 1994 (1970).
Morrison, Toni. "The Work You Do, the Person You Are." *The New Yorker*. June 5–12, 2017.
Moye, Michael G. and Ron Leavitt. *Married with Children*. Fox, 1987–1997.
Mull, Amanda. "Americans Have Baked All the Flour Away: The Pandemic is Reintroducing the Nation to its Kitchens." *The Atlantic*. May 12, 2020.
Mull, Amanda. "The New Trophies of Domesticity." *The Atlantic*. January 29, 2020.
Mullaney, Thomas S., Benjamin Peters, Mar Hicks, and Kavita Philip, eds. *Your Computer Is On Fire*. Boston, MA: MIT Press, 2021.
Mullen, Bill V. and James Smethurst, eds. *Left of the Color Line: Race, Radicalism, and Twentieth-Century Literature of the United States*. Chapel Hill: U of North Carolina Press, 2003.
Murphy, John. *The Telephone: Wiring America*. New York: Chelsea House/ Infobase Publishers, 2009.
Napasteck, Martin. *Richard Yates Up Close: The Writer and His Works*. Jefferson, NC: McFarland, 2012.
Napelee, Dan. "On the Road: The Original Scroll, Or, We're Not Queer, We're Just Beats." *The Explicator* 69.2 . 2011. 72–5.
Nebeker, Frederik. *Dawn of the Electronic Age: Electrical Technologies in the Shaping of the Modern World, 1914 to 1945*. Oxford: Wiley-Blackwell, 2009.
Neilson, Laura. "SMEG Launches a Small Appliance Line." *Food Republic*. October 30, 2014.

Nelkin, Dorothy. *Selling Science: How the Press Covers Science and Technology*. New York, W.H. Freeman, 1987.
Neuhaus, Jessamyn. *Housewives and Housework in American Advertising*. New York: Palgrave Macmillan, 2011.
Newell, Mike. *Mona Lisa Smile*. Culver City, CA: Sony, 2003.
Nichol, Christina. *Waiting for the Electricity*. New York: Overlook, 2014.
Nicholas, Sadie. "Darling, I'll Do Anything to Make You Happy!" *Daily Mail*. January 24, 2020.
Nickerson, Michell M. *Mothers of Conservatism: Women and the Postwar Right*. Princeton, NJ: Princeton UP, 2012.
Nickles, Shelley. "More Is Better: Mass Consumption, Gender, and Class Identity in Postwar America." *American Quarterly* 54.4 (December 2002): 581–622.
Nickles, Shelley. *Object Lessons: Household Appliance Design and the American Middle Class, 1920–1960*. PhD thesis. U of Virginia, 1999.
Nickles, Shelley. "'Preserving Women': Refrigerator Design as Social Process in the 1930s." *Technology and Culture* 43.4 (October 2002): 693–727.
Nightingale, Carl H. *On the Edge: A History of Poor Black Children and Their American Dreams*. New York: Basic Books, 1993.
Nixon, Sean. "Life in the Kitchen: Television Advertising, the Housewife and Domestic Modernity in Britain, 1955–1969." *Contemporary British History* 31.1(2017): 69–90.
Nochlin, Linda. "Why Have There Been No Great Women Artists?" *Artnews*. January 1971.
Nye, David E. *American Illuminations: Urban Lighting, 1800–1920*. Cambridge, MA: MIT Press, 2018.
Nye, David E. *Consuming Power: A Social History of American Energies*. Cambridge, MA: MIT Press, 1997.
Nye, David E. *Electrifying America: Social Meanings of a New Technology, 1880–1940*. Cambridge, MA: MIT Press, 1990.
Nye, David E. *Image Worlds: Corporate Identities at General Electric, 1890–1930*. Cambridge, MA: MIT Press, 1985.
Nye, David E. *The Invented Self: An Anti-Biography, from Documents of Thomas A. Edison*. Odense, DK: Odense UP, 1983.
Nye, David E. *When the Lights Went Out: A History of Blackouts in America*. Cambridge, MA: MIT Press, 2010.
Nye, Joseph and Robert Keohane, *Power and Interdependence: World Politics in Transition*. New York: Little Brown and Company, 1977.
Oakley, Ann. *Housewife*. New York and Harmondsworth: Penguin, 1985 (1974).
Oldenziel, Ruth. *Cold War Kitchen: Americanization, Technology, and European Users*. Boston, MA: MIT Press, 2009.
Oldenziel, Ruth. "Man the Maker, Woman the Consumer: The Consumption Junction Revisited." In *Feminism in Twentieth-Century Science, Technology, and Medicine*, edited by Angela N. H. Creager, Elizabeth Lunbeck, and Londa Schiebinger, 128–48. Chicago: Chicago UP, 2001.
Olsen, Tillie. *Tell Me a Riddle*. New York: Dell Publishing, 1976 (1961).
Olson, Laura Katz. "Whatever Happened to June Cleaver? The Fifties Mom Turns Eighty." *Race, Gender and Class* 10.1 (2003): 129–43.

O'Neil, Paul. "The Only Rebellion Around." *LIFE*. November 30, 1959. 114–30.

O'Neil, Tyler. "Your Dishwasher Takes Too Long and It's the Government's Fault. Here's the Solution." *PJ Media*. July 3, 2019.

Oppenheimer, Jess, Madelyn Pugh, and Bob Carroll, Jr. "Never Do Business With Friends." *I Love Lucy*. S02E31. June 29, 1953.

Oppenheimer, Jess, Madelyn Pugh, and Bob Carroll, Jr. "Sales Resistance." *I Love Lucy*. S02E17. January 26, 1953.

Oropesa, R. S. "Female Labor Force Participation and Time-Saving Household Technology: A Case Study of the Microwave from 1978 to 1989." *Journal of Consumer Research* 19.4 (March 1993): 567–79.

Ortíz, Ricardo L. "L.A. Women: Jim Morrison with John Rechy." In*The Queer Sixties*, edited by Patricia Juliana Smith, 164–86. London and New York: Routledge, 1999.

Osae-Brown, Anthony and Ruth Olurounbi. "Nigeria Runs on Generators and Nine Hours of Power a Day." *Bloomberg*. September 23, 2019.

Osteen, Mark. *American Magic and Dread: Don DeLillo's Dialogue with Culture*. Philadelphia: U of Pennsylvania Press, 2000.

Oster, Judith. *Crossing Cultures: Creating Identity in Chinese and Jewish American Literature*. Columbia, MO: U of Missouri Press, 2003.

Oz, Frank. *The Stepford Wives*. Los Angeles, CA: Paramount, 2004.

Padavic, Irene and Barbara F. Reskin, eds. *Women and Men at Work*. London: Pine Forge Press, 2002.

Page, Clarence. "Politicizing Nancy Pelosi's Ice Cream Is a Fridge Too Far." *Chicago Tribune*. April 24, 2020.

Palladino, Amy Sherman. *The Marvellous Mrs. Maisel*. Amazon Prime, 2017–.

Palmer, Christopher. *Philip K. Dick: Exhilaration and Terror of the Postmodern*. Liverpool: Liverpool UP, 2003.

Paradis, Kenneth. *Sex, Paranoia, and Modern Masculinity*. Albany: State U of New York Press, 2007.

Parr, Joy. *Domestic Goods: The Material, the Moral, and the Economic in the Post-war Years*. Toronto: U of Toronto Press, 1999.

Parr, Joy. "Modern Kitchen, Good Home, Strong Nation." *Technology and Culture* 43.4 (October 2002): 657–67.

Patterson, Andrea. "Germs and Jim Crow: The Impact of Microbiology on Public Health Policies in Progressive Era American South." *Journal of History of Biology* 3.42 (Fall 2009): 529–59.

Pattillo-McCoy, Mary. *Black Picket Fences: Privilege and Peril Among the Black Middle Class*. Chicago: University of Chicago Press, 1999.

Pellerin, Pierre-Antoine. "Jack Kerouac's Ecopoetics in *The Dharma Bums* and *Desolation Angels*: Domesticity, Wilderness and Masculine Fantasies of Animality." *Transatlantica* 2 (2011).

Penhall, Joe. *Mindhunter*. Netflix, 2017–2019.

Perec, Georges. *Life: A User's Manual*. Translated by David Bellos. London: Vintage, 2008 (1978).

Perec, Georges. *Things: A Story of the Sixties with A Man Asleep*. Translated by David Bellos. London: Vintage, 2011 (1965).

Philipson, Ilene. *Ethel Rosenberg: Beyond the Myths*. New Brunswick, NJ: Rutgers UP, 1993.

Phillips, Polly. "I'm Proud To Be a Tradwife and Don't Regret Being Paid a 'Wife Bonus' By My Husband." *The Daily Telegraph*. January 21, 2020.

Phillips, Sarah T. and Shane Hamilton. *The Kitchen Debate and Cold War Consumer Politics*. Boston, MA and New York: Bedford/St Martin's, 2014.

Piercy, Marge. "Barbie-Doll." *Off Our Backs* 1.19 (March 25, 1971): 7.

Piercy, Marge. *Braided Lives*. New York: Ballantine, 1997 (1982).

Piercy, Marge. "Breaking Out" (1984). In *My Mother's Body*. New York: Knopf, 1985. NP.

Piercy, Marge. *Going Down Fast*. New York: Fawcett Crest, 1969.

Piercy, Marge. *Parti-Colored Blocks for a Quilt*. Ann Arbor: U of Michigan Press, 2001 (1976).

Piercy, Marge. *Sleeping with Cats: A Memoir*. New York: HarperCollins, 2002.

Piercy, Marge. *Small Changes*. New York: Penguin, 1987 (1973).

Piercy, Marge. *Woman on the Edge of Time*. The Women's Press, 2000 (1976).

Piercy, Marge and Dawn Gifford. "Interview with Marge Piercy." *Off Our Backs* 24.6 (June 1994): 14–15.

Pink, Sarah. *Home Truths: Gender, Domestic Objects and Everyday Life*. Oxford: Berg, 2004.

Pitkin, Donald S. *The House that Giacomo Built: History of an Italian Family, 1898–1978*. Cambridge: Cambridge UP, 1985.

Plath, Sylvia. *The Bell Jar*. New York: Faber and Faber, 1963.

Platt, Harold L. *The Electric City: Energy and the Growth of the Chicago Area, 1880–1930*. Chicago: U of Chicago Press, 1991.

Postrel, Virginia. "How Job-Killing Technologies Liberated Women." *Bloomberg*. March 14, 2021.

Puckett, Jeffrey Lee. "GE Appliances Actually Applies for 'Big Boy' Trademark after 'SNL' Skit." *Courier Journal*. December 14, 2018.

Raphael, Tim. *The President Electric: Ronald Reagan and the Politics of Performance*. Ann Arbor: U of Michigan Press, 2009.

Raskin, Jonah. *American Scream: Allen Ginsberg's Howl and the Making of the Beat Generation*. Berkeley: U of California Press, 2004.

Rebeta-Burditt, Joyce. *The Cracker Factory*. Deadwood, OR: Wyatt-MacKenzie, 2010 (1977).

Reed, Kit. *Weird Women, Wired Women*. Hanover, NH: Wesleyan UP, 1998.

Reed, Peyton. *Down with Love*. 20th Century Fox, 2003.

Rees, Jonathan. "Ice Boxes Vs. Refrigerators." *The Historical Society: A Blog Devoted to History for the Academy & Beyond*. December 12, 2013.

Rees, Jonathan. *Refrigeration Nation: A History of Ice, Appliances, and Enterprise in America*. Baltimore, MD: Johns Hopkins UP, 2013.

Reilly, Maura. "Taking the Measure of Sexism: Facts, Figures, and Fixes." *ArtNEWS*. May 26, 2015.

Reynolds, Malvina. "Little Boxes" (1962). Track#3 on *Malvina Reynolds Sings the Truth*. Columbia, 1967.

Rickett, Oscar. "We Were Already Knee-Deep in Nostalgia: Coronavirus Has Just Made It Worse." *The Guardian*. April 20, 2020.

Riismandel, Kyle. *Neighborhood of Fear: The Suburban Crisis in American Culture, 1975–2001*. Baltimore, MD: Johns Hopkins UP, 2021.
Roberts, Adam. *The History of Science Fiction*. New York: Palgrave Macmillan, 2016.
Robinson, Cedric J. *Black Marxism: The Making of the Black Radical Tradition*. Chapel Hill: U of North Carolina Press, 2000 (1983).
Rochefort, Christiane. *Les Pétits Enfants du Siécle*. Paris: Éditions Bernard Grasset, 1961.
Rodden, John and Marge Piercy. "A Harsh Day's Light: An Interview with Marge Piercy." *The Kenyon Review New Series* 20.2 (Spring 1998): 132–43.
Roiphe, Ann Richardson. *Up the Sandbox!* Greenwich, CN: Fawcett Crest, 1972 (1970).
Romansky, Evan and Ryan Murphy, *Ratched*. Netflix, 2020.
Romero, Mary. *Maid in the USA*. London: Routledge, 2002 (1992).
Rose, Mark H. *Cities of Light and Heat: Domesticating Gas and Electricity in Urban America*. University Park: Pennsylvania State UP, 1995.
Rosenthal, Bob. *Cleaning Up New York*. New York: The Little Bookroom, 2016 (1976).
Rosler, Martha. *House Beautiful: Bringing War Home*. 1967–1972. Martharosler.net.
Ross, Gary. *Pleasantville*. New Line Cinema, 1998.
Roth, Philip. *Goodbye Columbus*. New York: Bantam, 1982 (1959).
Rottenberg, Catherine and Shani Orgad. "Why the Rise of the Domestic 'Tradwife' Tells Us More about Modern Work Culture than Feminism." *Prospect*. February 10, 2020.
Rozhon, Tracie. "Turf; Now, the Six-Figure Rent. (Yes, Rent)." *New York Times*. January 8, 1998. NP.
Rubell, Jennifer. *Ivanka Vacuuming*. Installation. Flashpoint Gallery. Washington, DC. February 1–17, 2019.
Russ, Joanna. "Science Fiction and Technology as Mystification." *Science Fiction Studies* 5.3 (November 16, 1978): 250–60.
Russ, Joanna. *The Female Man*. London: Orion/Gollancz, 2010 (1975).
Russ, Joanna. *The Two of Them*. Middletown, CT: Wesleyan UP, 2005 (1978).
Rutherford, Janice. *Selling Mrs. Consumer: Christine Fredrick and the Rise of Household Efficiency*. Athens: U of Georgia Press, 2003.
Samuel, Lawrence R. *Brought to You By: Postwar Television Advertising and the American Dream*. Austin: U of Texas Press, 2001.
Sanders, Joe Sutliff. "'Blatantly Coming Back': The Arbitrary Line between Here and There, Child and Adult, Fantasy and Real, London and UnLondon." In *China Miéville: Critical Essays*, edited by Caroline Edwards and Tony Venezia, 119–38. London: Gylphi Limited, 2015.
Saner, Emine. "Recipe for Disaster: What's Behind the Rise of 50s-style Domesticity?" *The Guardian*. July 2, 2018.
Savage, Stephanie. *The Astronaut Wives Club*. Disney/ABC, 2015.
Savvas, Theophilus. *American Postmodernist Fiction and the Past*. New York: Palgrave Macmillan, 2012.
Scarborough, Mark. "Red Scares." In *Beat Culture: Lifestyles, Icons, and Impact*, edited by William Lawlor, 295–6. Santa Barbara, CA: ABC CLIO, 2005.

Schapiro, Miriam and Melissa Meyer. *Heresies: Women's Traditional Arts: The Politics of Aesthetics*. Winter, 1978. 66–9.
Schatz, Ronald W. *The Electrical Workers: A History of Labor at General Electric and Westinghouse, 1923–1960*. Chicago: U of Illinois Press, 1987.
Schlafly, Phyllis. "What's Wrong with 'Equal Rights' for Women?" *The Phyllis Schlafly Report* 5.7 (February 1972): 1–4.
Schleifer, Ronald. *Modernism and Popular Music*. Cambridge: Cambridge UP, 2011.
Schmidt, Christopher. *The Poetics of Waste: Queer Excess in Stein, Ashbery, Schuyler, and Goldsmith*. New York: Palgrave Macmillan, 2014.
Schnepf, J. D. "Domestic Aerial Photography in the Era of Drone Warfare." *Modern Fiction Studies* (Summer 2017): 270–87.
Schulman, Sarah. *The Gentrification of the Mind: Witness to a Lost Imagination*. Berkeley: University of California Press, 2012.
Schuster, Marc. *Don DeLillo, Jean Baudrillard, and the Consumer Conundrum*. Amherst, NY: Cambria Press, 2008.
Schwartz, Amy. "At Home with Marge Piercy." *Moment Magazine*. June 3, 2019.
Scott, Jonathan. *Socialist Joy in the Writing of Langston Hughes*. Columbia: U of Missouri Press, 2006.
Scott, Lynn Orilla. "Revising the Incest Story: Toni Morrison's *The Bluest Eye* and James Baldwin's *Just above My Head*." In *James Baldwin and Toni Morrison: Comparative and Critical Perspectives*, edited by Lovalerie King and L. Orilla Scott, 83–102. New York: Palgrave Macmillan, 2006.
Shapiro, Laura. *Something from the Oven: Reinventing Dinner in 1950s America*. London: Penguin, 2004.
Simmons, Todd. *Science and Technology in Nineteenth-century America*. Westport, CN: Greenwood Press, 2005.
Simone, Gail. Women in Refrigerators. https://www.lby3.com/wir/.
Sirk, Douglas. *Imitation of Life*. Universal Pictures, 1959.
Slesin, Suzanne. "Design Bookshelf; Some Attractive New Volumes Look Forward, Others Back." *The New York Times*. December 13, 1984. C10.
Smith, Andrew. *Eating History: 30 Turning Points in the Making of American Culture*. New York: Columbia UP, 2009.
Smith, Andrew, ed. *The Oxford Encyclopedia of Food and Drink in America*, Vol. 2. Oxford and New York: Oxford UP, 2013.
Smith, Chris. "Poster Boy." *New York Magazine*. April 27, 1992. 20.
Smith, Jessie Carney. *Encyclopedia of African American Business: A-J*. Santa Barbara, CA: Greenwood Press, 2006.
Smith, Robert Paul, R. L. Mott, Bill Gammie et al. "The Vacuum Cleaner." The Chevy Showroom Starring Andy Williams S01E04. July 24, 1958.
Snediker, Michael D. *The Apartment of Tragic Appliances*. Brooklyn, NY: Peanut Books, 2013.
Snitow, Ann, Christine Stansell, and Sharon Thompson, eds. *Powers of Desire: The Politics of Sexuality*. New York: Monthly Review Press, 1983.
Snyder, David. *Cold War Hothouses: Inventing Postwar Culture, from Cockpit to Playboy*. Princeton, NJ: Princeton UP, 2003.
Solomon, William. *Slapstick Modernism: Chaplin to Kerouac to Iggy Pop*. Chicago: U of Illinois Press, 2016.

Spangler, John. "We're on a Road to Nowhere: Steinbeck, Kerouac, and the Legacy of the Great Depression." *Studies in the Novel* 40.3 (Fall 2008): 308–27.
Spigel, Lynn. *Make Room for TV: Television and the Family Ideal in Post War America*. Chicago: U of Chicago Press, 1992.
Spigel, Lynn and Denise Mann, eds. *Private Screenings: Television and the Female Consumer*. Minneapolis: Minnesota UP, 1992.
Sprengler, Christine. *Screening Nostalgia: Populuxe Props and Technicolor Aesthetics in Contemporary American Film*. New York and Oxford: Berghahn Books, 2009.
St. Clair, Margaret. "New Ritual" (1953). In *The Best from Fantasy and Science Fiction*. Third Series, edited by Anthony Boucher and K. Francis McComas. New York: Doubleday, 1954.
Stage, Sarah and Virginia B. Vincenti, eds. *Rethinking Home Economics: Women and the History of a Profession*. Ithaca, NY: Cornell University Press, 1997.
Stahl, John M. *Imitation of Life*. Universal Pictures, 1934.
Steward, Samuel M., ed. *Dear Sammy: Letters from Gertrude Stein and Alice B. Toklas*. Boston, MA: Houghton Mifflin, 1977.
Stimson, Thomas E. "A House to Make Life Easy." *Popular Mechanics* 97.6 (June 1952): 65–9; 228–30.
Stone, Oliver. *JFK*. Warner Bros, 1991.
Stone, Oliver. *The Doors*. Tri-Star, 1991.
Strand, Ginger. *The Brothers Vonnegut: Science and Fiction in the House of Magic*. New York: Farrar, Strauss, Giroux, 2016.
Strasser, Susan. *Never Done: A History of American Housework*. New York: Henry Holt, 2000 (1982).
Strasser, Susan. *Waste and Want: A Social History of Trash*. New York: Metropolitan Books, 1999.
Swinth, Kirsen. *Feminism's Forgotten Fight: The Unfinished Struggle for Work and Family*. Cambridge, MA: Harvard UP, 2018.
Tabuchi, Hiroko. "Inside Conservative Groups' Efforts to 'Make Dishwashers Great Again.'" *New York Times*. September 17, 2019.
Talbot, Margaret. "Money, Time, and the Surrender of American Taste: Les Trés Riches Heures de Martha Stewart." *New Republic*. May 13, 1996. NP.
Tan, Samuel J. "Top 5 Best Retro Fridge Freezers." *Colour My Living*. ND.
Taylor, D. J. "Ducks, Newburyport by Lucy Elmann review." *The Times*. September 20, 2019.
The Darling Academy. "Cleaning Up the Mess." *Instagram*. January 25, 2020.
Theoharis, Jeanne. *A More Beautiful and Terrible History: The Uses and Misuses of Civil Rights*. Boston, MA: Beacon Press, 2018.
Thomas, Betty. *The Brady Bunch Movie*. Paramount, 1995.
Thomas, Craig and Carter Bays. *How I Met Your Mother*. CBS, 2005–2014.
Tiptree Jr., James. *10,000 Light Years from Home*. New York: Ace Books, 1978.
Tobey, Ronald C. *Technology as Freedom: The New Deal and the Electrical Modernization of the American Home*. Berkeley: U of California Press, 1996.

Todd, Richard. "The Masks of Kurt Vonnegut" (1969). In *Conversations with Kurt Vonnegut*, edited by William Rodney Allen, 30–40. Jackson: UP of Mississippi, 1999 (1988).

Truman, Harry. "Message to the Congress on the State of the Union and on the Budget for 1947." Released January 21, 1946. Dated January 14, 1946. Public Papers, Henry Truman, 1945–1953.

Updike, John. *Rabbit, Run*. New York: Penguin, 2006 (1960).

Valente, Catherynne M. *The Refrigerator Monologues*. New York: Simon & Schuster, 2018.

Veblen, Thorstein. *Theory of the Leisure Class*. Oxford: Oxford UP, 2007 (1899).

Vettel-Becker, Patricia. "Clarence Holbrook Carter's *War Bride* and the Machine/Woman Fantasy." *Genders* 37 (2003): 1–1.

Viney, Will. *Waste: A Philosophy of Things*. London: Bloomsbury, 2013.

Vlagopoulos, Penny. "Rewriting America: Kerouac's Nation of 'Underground Monsters." In *On the Road: The Original Scroll*, edited by Jack Kerouac, 53–68. London: Penguin, 2007.

Vonnegut, Kurt. *Bluebeard*. New York: Bantam Doubleday Dell, 1998 (1987).

Vonnegut, Kurt. *Breakfast of Champions*. London: Vintage, 2000 (1973).

Vonnegut, Kurt. *Cat's Cradle*. London: Viking Penguin, 1986 (1963).

Vonnegut, Kurt. *Deadeye Dick*. New York: Random House, 1999 (1982).

Vonnegut, Kurt. *Galápagos*. London: Flamingo, 1994 (1985).

Vonnegut, Kurt. *God Bless You, Mr. Rosewater*. London: Vintage, 1992 (1965).

Vonnegut, Kurt. *Hocus Pocus*. London: Vintage, 2000 (1990).

Vonnegut, Kurt. "Science Fiction." *The New York Review of Books*. September 2, 1965. 2.

Vonnegut, Kurt. *Slaughterhouse-Five*. London: Vintage, 2000 (1969).

Vonnegut, Kurt. *While Mortals Sleep: Unpublished Stories*. London: Vintage, 2011. 3–24.

Wade, Laura. *Home, I'm Darling*. London: Oberon Books, 2019 (2018).

Waldeland, Lynne and Warren G. French. *John Cheever*. New York: Twayne, 1979.

Walker, Alice. *The Third Life of Grange Copeland*. New York: Phoenix/Orion, 2004 (1970).

Walker, Harriet. "It's Like *The Handmaid's Tale*." *The Times*. April 20, 2020.

Wallace, Molly. "'Venerated Emblems': DeLillo's *Underworld* and the History-Commodity." *Critique: Studies in Contemporary Fiction* 42.4 (2001): 367–83.

Waller, Davhi. *Mrs. America*. FX on Hulu. April 15 to May 27, 2020.

Ward, Jesmyn. *Salvage the Bones*. London: Bloomsbury, 2011.

Warner, John. "'Ducks, Newburyport' by Lucy Elmman…" *Chicago Tribune*. September 3, 2019.

Washington, Mary Helen. *The Other Blacklist: The African American Literary and Cultural Left of the 1950s*. New York: Columbia UP, 2014.

Waters, John. *Hairspray*. New Line Cinema, 1988.

Watts, Steven. *The Magic Kingdom: Walt Disney and the American Way of Life*. Columbia, MO: U of Missouri Press, 1997.

Weems, Robert E. *De-Segregating the Dollar: African American Consumerism in the Twentieth Century*. New York: NYU Press, 1998.

Weiner, Matthew. *Mad Men*. AMC, 2017–2012.
Weir, Peter. *The Truman Show*. Los Angeles, CA: Paramount, 1998.
Weldon, Fay. *The Life and Loves of a She Devil*. London: Sceptre, 1988 (1983).
Welsh, Tom. "The 'Make Dishwashers Great Again' Movement Isn't as Crazy as It Sounds." *Daily Telegraph*. February 2, 2020.
Wething, Hilary. "Job Growth in the Great Recession Has Not Been Equal between Men and Women." Economic Policy Institute Blog. August 26, 2014.
Wetzsteon, Russ. *Republic of Dreams: Greenwich Village: The American Bohemia, 1910–1960*. New York: Simon & Schuster, 2002.
Whelehan, Imelda. *The Feminist Bestseller: From Sex and the Single Girl to Sex and the City*. New York: Palgrave Macmillan, 2005.
White, John H. *The Great Yellow Fleet: A History of American Railroad Refrigerator Cars*. San Marino, CA: Golden West Books, 1986.
White, Winston. *Beyond Conformity*. Glencoe, IL: Free Press of Glencoe, 1961.
Whitman, Walt. *Leaves of Grass, and Selected Prose*. New York: Holt, Rinehart, and Winston, 1949.
Whitman, Walt. *Poetry and Prose*, edited by Justin Kaplan. New York: Library of America, 1996.
Whittaker, Wayne. "The Story of Popular Mechanics." *Popular Mechanics Golden Anniversary Issue* 97.1 (January 1952): 127–32; 366–82.
Whyte, William H. *The Organization Man*. New York: Simon and Schuster, 1956.
Wightman Fox, Richard and T. J. Jackson Lears, eds. *The Culture of Consumption: Critical Essays in American History, 1880–1980*. New York: Patheon Books, 1983.
Wilentz, Sean, ed. *Fred W. McDarrah: New York Scenes*. New York: Abrams, 2018.
Williams, William Carlos. "Introduction." In *Howl and Other Poems*, edited by Allen Ginsberg, 7–8. San Francisco: City Lights, 1965 (1956).
Williams, William Carlos. *The Collected Poems of William Carlos Williams Volume 1: 1909–1939*, edited by A. Walton Litz and Christopher MacGowan. New York: New Directions, 1991.
Williamson, Kevin. *Dawson's Creek*. The WB, 1998–2005.
Wills, Garry. *Reagan's America: Innocents at Home*. New York: Penguin, 1985.
Wilson, Hugh. *Blast from the Past*. New Line Cinema, 1999.
Wilson, Sloan. *The Man in the Gray Flannel Suit*. New York: Avalon, 1955.
Wise, George. *Willis R. Whitney, General Electric, and the Origins of U.S. Industrial Research*. New York: Columbia UP, 1985.
Wojnarowicz, David. *Close to the Knives: A Memoir of Disintegration*. Canongate, 2016 (1991).
Wolcott, Victoria W. *Remaking Respectability: African American Women in Interwar Detroit*. Chapel Hill: U of North Carolina Press, 2001.
Wolfe, Andrea Powell. *Black Mothers and the National Body Politic: The Narrative of Positioning of the Black Maternal Body from the Civil War Period through the Present*. New York: Lexington Books, 2021.
Wuebben, Daniel L. *Power-Lined: Electricity, Landscape, and the American Mind*. Lincoln, NE: U of Nebraska Press, 2019.

Yarrow, Andrew L. *Measuring America: How Economic Growth Came to Define American Greatness in the Late Twentieth Century*. Amherst: U of Massachusetts Press, 2010.

Yaszek, Lisa. *Galactic Suburbia: Recovering Women's Science Fiction*. Columbus, OH: Ohio State UP, 2008.

Yates, Richard. *Disturbing the Peace*. London: Vintage, 2008 (1975).

Yates, Richard. *Easter Parade*. London: Vintage, 2008 (1976).

Yates, Richard. *Revolutionary Road*. London: Vintage, 2010 (1961).

Yates, Richard. *The Collected Stories of Richard Yates*. London: Vintage, 2008 (1996).

Yates, Richard. *Young Hearts Crying*. London: Vintage, 2008.

Yu, Renqiu. *To Save China, To Save Ourselves; The Chinese Hand Laundry Alliance of New York*. Philadelphia, PA: Temple UP, 1992.

Zappa, Frank. *Chunga's Revenge*. Bizarre/Reprise, 1970.

Zarlengo, Kristina. "Civilian Threat, the Suburban Citadel, and Atomic Age American Women." *Signs 24. 4, Institutions, Regulation, and Social Control*. Summer 1999. 925–58.

Zemeckis, Robert. *Back to the Future*. Universal, 1985.

Zemeckis, Robert. *Forrest Gump*. Paramount, 1994.

Zhang, Jenny G. "Quarantine Baking in Times of Crisis." *Eater*. March 13, 2020.

Zhang, Yunhui et al. "Blood Lead Levels among Chinese Children: The Shifting Influence of Industry, Traffic, and E-Waste Over Three Decades." *Environment International* 135. February 2020.

Zimring, Carl A. *Clean and White: A History of Environmental Racism in the United States*. New York: NYU Press, 2015.

INDEX

CPSIA information can be obtained
at www.ICGtesting.com
Printed in the USA
LVHW080913240322
714282LV00002B/46